Praise for
FOUR MILES WEST OF NOWHERE

Stranger in a strange land is my favorite kind of read, because the writer notices things we overlook or just take for granted. Since there is no stranger writer than John Phillips or a place stranger than America, this book makes for an excellent ride.
—Jay Leno, former host of *The Tonight Show*

The leap John Phillips took at retirement, from the urban Midwest to Montana, was not for the faint of heart. But Four Miles *attests to the great rewards available to late-in-life risk takers. Phillips' observations are the work of either a likeable man or a devious agent, but I'm sure his neighbors are glad to have him. His Montana town is filled with interesting souls and the usual irate locals. Phillips observes with affection and comic detachment.* Four Miles *is both a romantic idyll and reluctant account of a changing West. As a guide to starting a new life in a small town—not easy—this is how to do it.***—Tom McGuane**

So you want to get away from it all? Better check what your "it" is. Better realize that the farther away you get, the more "all" you encounter. Better read Four Miles West of Nowhere. *John Phillips has found bliss in the far, far away. But it's a funny kind of bliss. That is, John is hilarious about his tussles with Mother Nature. And Mother Nature does hilarious things to John. You'll love his book. But would you love being "four miles west of nowhere?"*
—P.J. O'Rourke

Car and Driver *readers have known for years that John Phillips is a National Treasure. The immense wit and vigorous powers of observation that made him such a popular magazine writer are on full display in his retirement odyssey. This book reminds that, if one is attuned to it, nature can supplant the self. As it should.*
—Eddie Alterman, former Editor In Chief of *Car and Driver*

You will be reminded of Mark Twain—think A Connecticut Yankee in King Arthur's Court*—with a dash of curmudgeonly Mencken thrown in. City man, plus saintly wife, moves to remote Montana wilderness. Encounters all manner of strange fauna, including neighbors, mountain lions, and wily trout. Lives to tell about it in charming turn of good humor and self-awareness. A lovely memoir.*
—**David Abrahamson**, Professor Emeritus, The Medill School of Journalism, Northwestern

Four Miles *is a hoot, a sideways* Tilbury Town *of Montana's prickly and particular, the ungoverned and ungovernable, the misanthropes and...well, it's mostly misanthropes, but John's writing makes you love them anyway. That's how good he is.*
—**Dan Neil**, Pulitzer Prize winner, *The Wall Street Journal.*

If he wasn't a friend of mine, I probably wouldn't be as envious of John as I am because of his scythe-like wit, his wicked sense of humor, ability to entertain, and flat-out smarts. But he is, so I am.
—**Steve March Tormé,** recording artist (and son of Mel)

John Phillips can find trouble in any situation. So when he moved to the wilderness, mayhem was sure to follow, which John relates with his usual twisted hilarity. You will laugh out loud.
—**Csaba Csere,** former Editor of *Car and Driver*

If Phillips hopes to discourage fellow adventurers from following his trail, he fails joyfully. Colorful characters artfully rendered against a small town in Montana make it much too appealing.
—**Doug Mepham,** President of McDonald Public Relations, Toronto.

What happens when a brilliant guy with a wacky world view, a warped sense of humor and the comedic writing chops to rival George Carlin, has the courage to live out his life of adventure? In Four Miles, city boy Phillips travels way outside his comfort zone, taking us for one hilarious ride. I dare you not to laugh out loud.
—**Diane Magnum,** two-time Emmy Award-winning broadcast journalist for ABC and CBS.

In Four Miles West of Nowhere, *John Phillips delivers a Pythonesque travelog of his retirement journey from Ann Arbor, Michigan, to remote Darby, Montana, (population 475, no Starbucks, no traffic light). There, along the Continental Divide, Mother Nature sets out gasp-inducing scenery and also her best birds, bears, and brook trout. To this fauna-rich utopia Phillips adds broken snow plows, a reclusive ex-smuggler, threatening winters, electricity famines, and heartfelt ruminations about fly fishing, guns, survival, Darby's dress code (pre-owned grubby), forest fires, irritating neighbors, helpful neighbors, a voluptuous barber, Republicans (he found one good one), septic tanks, alcohol, and pre-existing conditions. He occasionally claims to dislike his fellow persons, but then delights everyone with eyes and a sense of humor by presenting writing that entertains, informs, and confronts. His wicked wit addresses both human frailties and environmental missteps, but through it all Phillips is wildly funny. He could make you laugh at your own bankruptcy. He made me laugh out loud at his falls into the icy Bitterroot while learning to fly-fish. Also at his descriptions of hospitalizations, truck wrecks, tire chains, and acquiring his first Carhartt bib overalls. Phillips has crafted a swift, seamless diary of life at the Double-J Cat Ranch, the mountaintop home he shares with wife Julie—a willing co-conspirator. The diary's eighty-some episodes recounting John and Julie's first year as "feeders" (Darbrarians who do not hunt) never make you feel voyeuristic. Not once. Hell, to invade their privacy you'd have to stop laughing.*

—**William Jeanes,** former Publisher of *Road & Track*
and author of *The Road to Pickletown*

FOUR MILES WEST OF NOWHERE

A City Boy's First Year in the Montana Wilderness

JOHN PHILLIPS

ISBN# 978-1-941052-54-9 Trade Paper
ISBN# 978-1-941052-04-4 eBook
ISBN# 978-1-941052-55-6 Hardcover

Library of Congress Control Number:
2021942456

Cover Design: Antelope Design
Cover Photo: Ravi Miro Fry

Poem by Blanca Varela (1926-2009)
from *Rough Song*, a collection of poetry published by The Song Cave,
translated from the Spanish by Carlos Lara

Interior photographs by
Julie Renee Gothrup and Ravi Miro Fry
Mountain Lion photo by Steve Morris

This is a memoir.
Not everyone remembers events in the same way.
These recollections are exclusively those of the author.

PRONG HORN PRESS
PronghornPress.Org

For Julie. For Angie.

The dear animal
whose bones are a remembrance
a signal in the air
never having shadow nor place
from the head of a pin
I thought
he was a slight glint
the grain of the earth upon the grain
of the earth
the self-eclipse
the dear animal
whose passing is endless
it leaves me spinning.

—Blanca Varela

Table of Contents

August

September

October

April

INTRODUCTION

In the waning years of my working life, I felt as if I were standing in the surf, rocked not so gently by some inner tide, about to be blindsided by an amorphous wave that would drive me skull first into the seabed, lights out. A vague but nagging unease, a *dis*-ease. I needed to surmount some nameless impediment: write a bestseller, love my wife more openly, own a Rolex, become a veterinarian. Who knew? But I was dissatisfied with what my life amounted to. Writer Jim Harrison told me that when a man reaches 60, he'd better murder his ego because his accomplishments in the workplace will be emotionlessly outpaced and coldly dismissed by a younger crew who never seemed to work as hard or know any history or offer respect or even faux sincerity to outgoing elders (this, of course, described me as a young man). My reaction was to flee the sticky wicket of swarming empire—"it's not the heat, it's the *humanity*"—abandoning the illusions and diversions that so often landed me in conflict, perhaps in the process doing nothing to subdue my ego. Maybe just smother it with 12 hours per day of natural Montanan splendor.

It worked for naturalist John Muir.

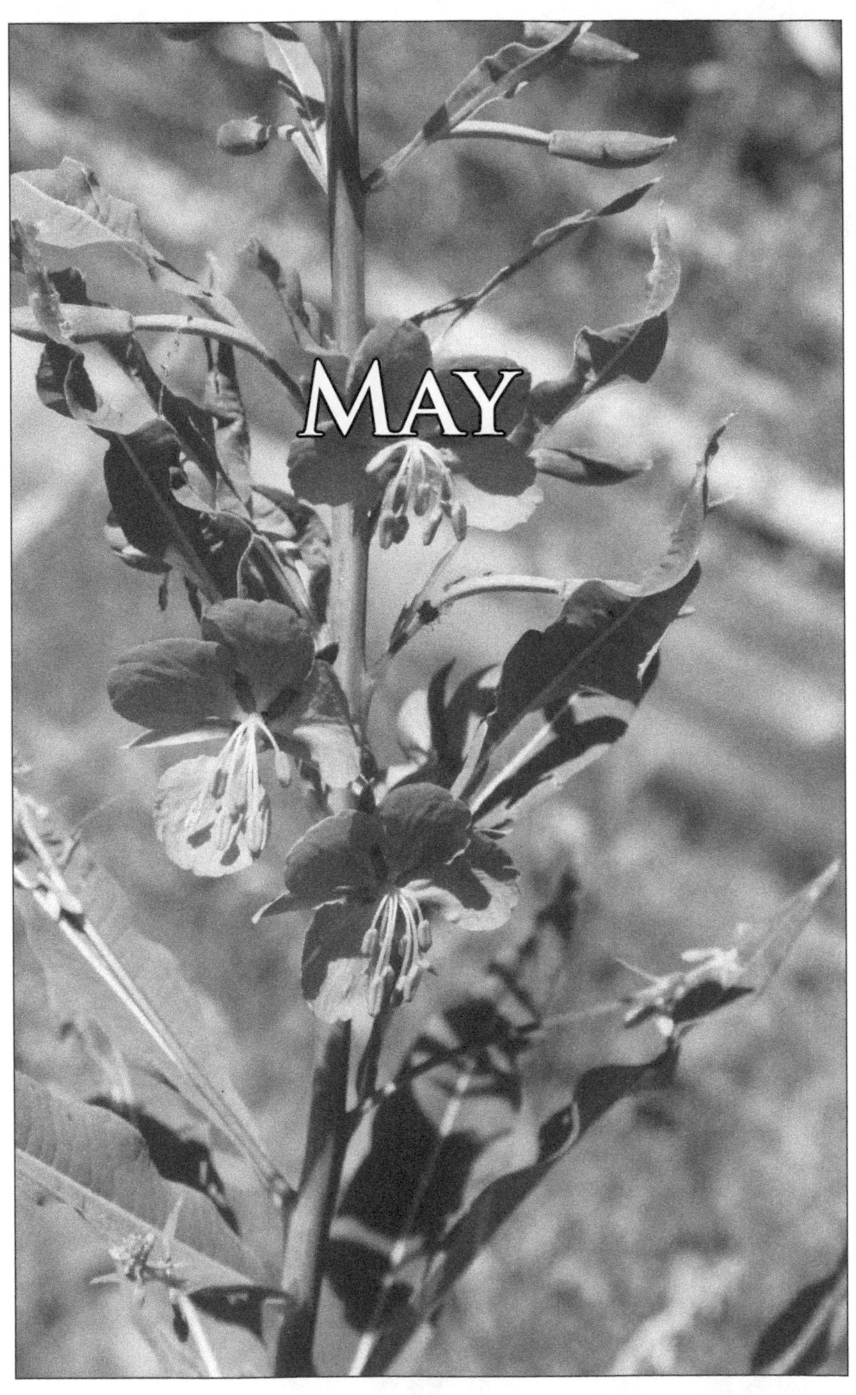
MAY

Muir's Cure

I was in the water, inverted. So, no further views of the mist rising off the lake in twisted nets, with the shoreline pines—in some places so bent they wore the shape of the wind—dripping slush in glutinous rivulets. It was the foul face of appalling, to be honest, such that death by aquatic misadventure, right then, was unfolding as I'd always imagined: a Poe panorama in which every cubic inch of my high-cholesterol corpus was resisting. I felt like a manatee hit by a Nigerian freighter.

Here's all I recollect: Fishing from my kayak, a wobbly enterprise at best, I had just latched onto a grayling, a species on every fly-fisherman's platinum-plated pail. While retrieving this one-pound, one-12th-scale sailfish in flat water in the center of Montana's Miner Lake, the two of us traded places.

The mechanics of this juxtaposition are hazy, a veil of watery astonishment. I had somersaulted into 39-degree meltwater, immediately ascertaining there were no finger holds on the kayak's brittle plastic hull. So I slithered off and aspirated a second mouthful of lake. Breathing ceased, gasping began. My esophagus became a pressurized irrigation ditch. My head jutted to-and-fro involuntarily, like a dog preparing to vomit, which is what I did but in a snorkeling sort of way. Expelling liquid from lungs apparently exhausts every mortal muscle, because my arms ceased paddling and floated up around my neck, seemingly deboned and numb as crowbars.

"He's passed out," I heard my wife, Julie, say. She had been fishing 50 yards distant in her own kayak. I hoped she knew I hadn't, because it felt shameful to nap through my final self-produced drama. If I were transitioning to a comical planetary exodus, I'd have arranged fireworks launched from a barge.

That's when a handsome fisherperson—a veterinarian, as it turned out—seized the front of my shirt, which was expensively embroidered with leaping trout. I was grateful because his interference tilted my head forward, permitting less violent retching, a kindness not offered since college. Then another wonderment: I was blind. I could not recall blindness as a symptom of near-fatal submergence.

I felt my wife hook an arm under my left armpit and the veterinarian my right, both maneuvering me until I was Dagwood in a kayak sandwich. They towed me ashore, with my head pinballing between hulls. That took two days—well, maybe ten minutes. Somewhere along that route, my right eye pinged open, slot-machine style, and I noticed that the sky had turned hunter green and the water as dark as Faust's bible.

Even as I expected to survive this mortifying ordeal, my legs from mid-hips downward succumbed to hypothermia. Not a bad feeling, really, because there's no feeling. I'm not proud of this, but here's what cycled through my sputtering consciousness as I belly-crawled to shore through a thicket of dead water lilies anchored in mud smelling like fishy doughnuts:

1. I'll bet my wallet is AWOL, along with $300 therein.
2. I'll bet my $800 Orvis rod and reel have pulled a full Captain Nemo.
3. I'll bet my month-old $250 Yeti cooler now serves as a trout condo.
4. I'll bet my fishing vest containing $200 worth of dry flies is anything but dry. Plus, I'm pretty sure Miner Lake had swallowed my Montana fishing license.

Kayak mismanagement had cost me $1550. Then I hacked up what looked like melted Jell-O with black-eyed peas.

I didn't die. The graying did.

Me at the wheel right then would have comprised felony endangerment, so Julie drove us home as I squished in my seat and dug at blocked ear canals.

As we neared the bottom of our driveway, she parked, then said, "Cocktails will be delayed."

I asked why. She simply gestured toward our long, lumpy two-track driveway whose jarring corrugations were becoming geological cleavages worthy of someone's doctoral dissertation. The path was clogged with nutty-brown torsos, vanilla arses, and velvet-covered antlers: our Tin Cup herd of elk, 99 by actual count, who apparently called for a Phillips-property caucus whose purpose they then forgot. They all looked pregnant. But it was just this year's lush forest grass that had morphed them into great, reclining soporific Henry Moores, sunning themselves and reciting elk poetry.

On the other hand, they might all be pregnant. All I know about elk is that my grandpa frequented the Elks Lodge, and here before me slept another.

We descended from the truck and walked. Another day in paradise found—no other humans, no neighbors' lights, no noise save an occasional squeaky elk bugle and the pacifying whoosh and whisper of the hula-swaying ponderosas. Plus a near drowning.

Did you know that in Latin "noise" means "nausea"?

Double-J Cat Ranch

Yesterday, I read in an esteemed science magazine that the earth hums as it rotates. Physicists claim the humming emanates from the bottom of oceans. I'm pretty sure it emanates from my backyard.

Here's why: For decades I've dreamed of "intentional grounding," as I called it, in which I would retire to the yet wild Bitterroot Mountains. Montana is sometimes described as "the last best place," which, of course, is an invitation to unchecked influx and decline, although it hasn't happened yet.

In return for half of my retirement savings, I'm now at least close enough to my dream to see its face. If you glance at a map, you'll notice that Montana's southwestern border resembles the silhouette of a human face, tilted slightly downward as if examining something disgusting on the sidewalk. The benign tumor in the road that is Darby is where the silhouette's nostril should be. If Montana picks its nose, it now gets me.

Back in 1882, the village of Darby was known by the Salish as "the place where they would lift something." I love the nonspecificity of "something." A wet dog? Sacagawea's skirt?

And who was doing the lifting? When white people settled here, they named the town Doolittle, which I suspect was not so much a surname as a candid descriptor. As the residents became inclined to do a little more—starting with a general store, saloon, livery, and whorehouse—Doolittle remained something of a civic sinus infection, so it was renamed Harrison. Harrison promptly burned to the ground, as towns so gleefully did back then. That's when the local postmaster, James Darby, imposed his imprimatur on the place, asking no one for prior permission. I am told Mr. Darby was an aficionado of calamity, a template for loose cannons. His kind have been settling here ever since, earnestly bamboozling but rarely prospering. Nowadays, at least a dozen Darbrarians have dogs named Darby. It's a good name for a dog.

The joke in my adopted village of 400 souls is that the village-limit signs share the same post. If you're old enough, visualize Andy Griffith's Mayberry, although Mayberry had a stoplight, as I recall, and Darby does not. Also, our lone town constable—Marshal Larry, as he is known to all—is less like Andy than, say, Dick Cheney hunting lawyers.

Julie and I purchased a petite Darby house with 12 years of use on its clock. It clutches perilously to the foothills of 10,157-foot Trapper Peak, which to my eyes recollects a spire of Chartres Cathedral.

The peak is geologically a new mountain, poking into rarefied air, with whippets of snow bolting off its crests, spurs, and ridges. Our house holds fast to the incline, as an owl grasps a vole, which is a daily spectacle here. Our property is four miles southwest of town and 440 feet above it. The front door opens 30 feet from the neatly defined border of U.S. Forest Service land. It's not clear how far the Bitterroot National Forest stretches behind my kitchen, but a Darbrarian claims it extends for 22 miles, all of it free of human molestation, apart from a logging road abandoned in the 1940s.

That's my backyard, a Coney Island of coniferosity. Whose woods these are I think I know. Mine, I guess, by geographic happenstance. That such swaths of largely semi-virgin forest still exist strikes me as a miracle given Americans' thirst to convert landscape to their own convenience. Which, of course, is what I'm doing.

We named the place the Double-J Cat Ranch, in honor of our previously stray shelter cats, one weighing 23 pounds, big as a bobcat.

From our deck, which faces north, Julie and I observe a woodsy hogback ridge a half mile distant, behind which glisten the towering Three Sisters, a trifecta of rocky slabs scowling down on lavender Lake Como, named for its resemblance to the Italian alpine original. Our panorama eastward encompasses the Bitterroot River and the Sapphire Mountains, which folks call the "Rye Creek Hills." They are carpeted in rye grass, almost to their 7,600-foot summits—some of it sun-dried unto hard wire—and annually cycle through hues of caramel, honey, toast, and bourbon. Our property is a maze of 200-year-old ponderosa pines and Douglas firs, throwing monster shadows. I keep expecting to see Rod Serling loitering back there, smoking one of his unfiltered Chesterfields and summoning us to enter.

Some nearby forest parcels are "the first edition." In recorded history most civilizations have built on top of themselves. Not here. What you see is what emerged 12,000 years ago, upon the glaciers' retreat. It is what Missoula developers call "unimproved wilderness," those bestowers of strip malls somehow believing they can create yet more wilderness or, better yet, improve that which already exists by depositing in its splendor a Taco Bell.

My home is not on top of the mountain, but I can see the peak from here. It is snow-covered eight months of the year. If you drink one too many gin and tonics on my deck, you could fall and roll and flail about a quarter mile, until a pine snagged you, likely crushing your chest into soggy mashed beets. It's never happened to any of my guests, but a man can dream.

When a FedEx or UPS deliveryman arrives, he'll say, "I've never been real comfortable up here." *Up*. Peering across the valley from my porch is like flying a final approach to a Nepalese runway. In early October, the deliverymen warn, "See you next year." They refuse to navigate our potholed, strut-twisting drive beyond Halloween. After that, packages are deposited in town at Mr. T's Mercantile, where you simply sift through boxes strewn on the floor, scooping any that bear your name. No receipt, no signature required.

The mute clerk rarely shows himself. In fact, when I did eventually encounter a salesman, I told him I was new to the Bitterroot Valley.

"Oh, really?" he asked. "You stick out like a finger on a foot."

He made it clear that living in the Bitterroots meant ceding overall management to Mother Nature, who rules the outcome of every hour—not the Dow, not a Mercedes filled with venture capitalists, not a network of so-called influencers.

IMMEDIATELY DO NOTHING

When it comes to loitering in wilderness, I'm not wholly inexperienced. I've written for magazines all my life, and for one assignment I attended a forest-survival course, then trekked solo in northern Ontario's woods for five days with nothing but a space blanket, a compass, and a hand-drawn topo map. I ate raw crayfish and the underwater stalks of cattails, which taste like raw potatoes.

Decades later I endured 10 weeks of survival training taught by a Colorado woodsman named Tom Collins and a former British SAS sapper/sergeant, both of whom, in previous lives, must have thrown lightning bolts and been in charge of punishment for Marines. Their task was to harden me for a different rough-country assignment—a month in the rotting jungles of Sabah, Malaysia, avoiding miniature rhinos and camp-robbing orangutans.

In sodden Sabah, I ate a few kumbangs, which are beetles the size of your thumb. I became serene in the company of leeches. When I woke every morning, the first word I uttered was *"fuck."*

So, it may surprise you, and it surely shames me, that when I initially explored a sliver of the vast tract behind my new Montana home, I carried no compass, no knife, no coat, not a single accoutrement of survival whose value had been so fiercely imprinted by professionals. Further, wife Julie was performing errands, and I'd left no note. I carried two items only: a canister of bear spray and a liter of iced tea. I departed the house at 3:30 p.m., not planning to be gone long, a laughable cliché that is to veteran outdoorsmen what alternative facts are to research librarians.

The trees on my Montana acreage are mostly lodgepole pines and ponderosas with orange bark and surprisingly small root balls. Some are 250 years old. They would have held dominion over this woodland even as Lewis and Clark hiked its length in 1805. My forest's density waxes and wanes, an arbitrary arboretum. There are unexpected natural clearings, everything dead and flat and rotting, the effect of perpetual shade thrown by the colossal ponderosas. When the wind isn't heaving, these open oases offer a sharp, minty aroma of decomposing pine needles. It smells like dress shirts just back from the dry cleaner's, a vaguely chemical tang.

There are also parcels chockablock with randomly strewn boulders that are the size of pickup trucks. "Erratics," a geologist friend told me, adding, "some sedimentary, some metamorphic, some igneous—I see incompetent rock and inequigranular fabric." It was a perfect trifecta of geological dross dumped by pulsating glaciers, as if shucking hobos off a train. Scattered more sparsely are lone rock towers, some resembling skinny smokestacks, formed from yellowish volcanic rock called rhyolite.

This forest so swarms with creatures—white-tailed deer, foxes, wolves, elk, moose, bears, ermine, owls, turkeys, wolverines, and mountain lions—that some of the game trails resemble freeway cloverleafs, so wide and worn you'd swear the Forest Service fashioned them with heavy equipment. A few were trodden by Native Americans, who morphed them into avenues for white settlers, and they are littered with scat and cast-off clumps of fur, sometimes ending so abruptly I can't imagine where the animals went. An about-face? If so, why at this boilerplate denouement are there no footprints in reverse? These are questions to which the animals owe us answers. In truth, we owe *them*.

Four Miles West of Nowhere

At first, I felt lucky to locate a broad promenade of a game trail, following it for a mile or so southwest of my house. I clomped into a clearing of glacial till, one sharp-edged slab of which seemed to sport a brown nose. It was a nose but didn't belong to the boulder. It belonged to a yearling bull moose with a respectable starter rack, a moose we later named Walter Sobchak after John Goodman's character in *The Big Lebowski.* Like Goodman, Walter is bulky and imperfect but endearing and comical. His chocolate coat is riven by a teak racing stripe that traces his spine. The pelt surrounding his butt seems perpetually moth-eaten, with paintbrush-size tufts ready to blow. His antlers are vertical rods with orbs at the tips—like Martian antennae—and a chunk of one antler is missing. Walter's soft, flexible nose folds and squats and rotates on the forest floor like one of those robot vacuum cleaners.

Right then at our new homestead, we were being overrun by locusts: green and yellow missiles with titanium-hard shells and Olympic leaping skills. When spooked, they'd strike my legs and face. It felt like being shot by a BB gun. If I'm not mistaken—and I often am in my current phase of ossification—Walter was making sport of the grasshoppers when we met. They'd vault into his legs and he'd lunge awkwardly, startled over and over, although I think for Walter it was a kind of reindeer game minus the reindeer.

Walter was 60 feet away, maybe less. He'd certainly seen me, yet was surprisingly indifferent. His rubbery nose just kept vacuuming forest grasses. Sometimes he'd back up to inspect a particularly juicy hopper. Then he'd abandon that patch and relocate.

Because he never bolted, he was easy to follow, and because my eyes were more or less locked on Walter's muscled arse, I wasn't absorbing directional changes as we penetrated one clump of dusky woods after another. I was a pinball following whatever trajectory Walter flipped me. We traversed a thicket as dark as a closet. I felt certain Walter was pulling a fast fade, but, no, on the far side he reappeared, no longer tormenting insects but now scratching an itchy flank on bark.

How long this lasted I cannot recall. I had no wristwatch,

having removed it forever on settling in Montana, thereby setting a modern-day record for outdoor unpreparedness.

And so we ambled as an odd couple in a woodsy polka, Walter and I, surveying the forest primeval without any particular destination, until we reached a mountain stream—more like a groundwater seep—where, as I refilled my drink bottle, Walter evidently recalled personal business that did not include my creepy stalking. He jogged hard right, then galloped like Secretariat down the middle of the creek, throwing up mud and rocks and a roostertail of cold water. Again, a wilderness mammal artfully pulling a two-second skyhook. It's like snapping a photo of your wife and discovering later she's nowhere in the frame.

I was abruptly solo, with basic situational awareness revealing, first, that I was no longer on a game trail; did not know which direction might provide one; and could determine only coarse east-west coordinates against a sun right then seeking cover behind the mountain.

All this information fell as if from a cliff, startling me as surely as a stranger grabbing my shoulder from behind. I remembered the SAS sergeant saying, "If you get lost, immediately do nothing." Or, as I've since heard it expressed, "Don't just do something, *stand* there." So, I hummed a Warren Zevon song, but doing nothing seemed like picking scabs, so I again refilled my bottle with spring water, then peed on a tree.

I had no food, not even cattails. Right about then, my wife would be questioning my whereabouts. The temperature was dropping and, to avoid fixating on that, I studied a black, scudding cloud, wondering if it might portend mere inconvenience or hypothermia.

I walked in a direction I estimated was northeast, but you can't walk a straight line in the forest even when you're sober. For one thing, I kept colliding with wall after wall of what Montanans call "piss fir"—the low, leafy fishnet entanglement of greenery that clogs swaths of the forest floor. There came a moment when I considered digging a coffin-size hole in the pine needles to make a bed, as my Canadian survival trainers had instructed, because bumbling around in the dark would only earn me a concussion. Or an introduction to a mountain lion, one of which I would eventually catch on camera eviscerating a white-tailed deer I'd named Ronda. From nose to tail, that lion measured seven feet. From nose to tail, I measure less than six.

I eventually knelt on all fours trying to slip under three interwoven larches that comprised an opaque scrim, and that's when I succumbed to the acid reflux of self-inflicted disaster. Plus, now my pants were wet. I stood, resumed stumbling, and—this would have been funny if someone had videotaped it—exploded out of a tangle of vines and thorns, butt-skiing down a four-foot embankment into another clearing that was long in length but not in width. That's because—as I slowly grasped from my position on my ass—it was the 1940s logging road.

I'll withhold further details of this mortifying drama except to recollect later shuffling through my new front door, having survived my own chunk of dumb, about as exhausted and filthy as a human can become without some body part falling off.

My wife asked, "You were in the woods?"

"A hike," I corrected.

"Nice collection of scratches on your arms and face. Your hair is, well...you look a little crazy."

"I'm okay with that," I said.

"See anything wonderful?"

"Nope," I lied. "Just a walk."

It was tempting to think this had been Montana's way of introducing herself. I don't think she wants me here.

John Phillips

ONE WORLD AT A TIME

I fled to southwestern Montana to retire, in theory, arriving in the fashion of the Beverly Hillbillies, employing a 35-foot-long U-Haul truck towing a 17-foot tandem-axle trailer, with Julie driving her Toyota in my weak wake. For the most part, I could maintain 55 to 60 mph on I-90, but it induced the sort of stomach knots that I recall the night before taking the SAT.

The distance from Ann Arbor, Michigan, to Darby, Montana, is 2,020 miles—four days of never-let-go clinched steering, accompanied by minor intestinal cramping, with me in putative command of a rented 2005 GMC TopKick C5500. I fixated on restricting the transmission to fourth rather than third, third being the brute's preference for powering through difficult impediments such as insects. Anything beyond 60 mph choked fuel economy to five miles per gallon and induced a racket that obviated the use of the one-speaker radio. In fact, I'd already donned earplugs.

The truck additionally elicited from the 100,000-mile V-8 the alarming sound of lag bolts in a wood chipper. In fairness, the truck never broke. A steady friend. But I talked to it a lot, congratulating it at each day's conclusion, using the tone you'd employ to soothe a sick pet.

Throughout the trip, I remained flabbergasted that any American with sufficient cash in his trousers would be permitted to rent—apparently, with the consent of this country's enthusiastic litigators—a 12,600-pound truck towing 7,400 pounds of magazines and La-Z-Boys and, further, to attach to that already thundering payload of road-borne missiles a 1,920-pound trailer stuffed with a bonus 2,480 pounds of cat-mauled Broyhill sofas. At what point in my career did I qualify to shepherd 12-plus tons of potentially lethal furniture through Chicago at rush hour?

A decal on the truck's dash said, "Anticipate Your Braking." It should have said, "Anticipate Your Crashing." Maybe worse than crashing was every 57-gallon fuel stop, by which I mean the demonstrably real and positively toe-curling likelihood of having to back up the whole shitter-jigger rig. My wife helped direct, but she was of limited use. For one thing, I couldn't see more than ten square inches of the trailer until it pretzeled into a cockeyed L-shape attempting to snap safety chains that would, no doubt, perforate some child's eye.

So I bought two C-clamps at a Shell station and attached blue Dixie cups to the fenders as locator beacons. One was torn off by a chain-link fence that someone apparently erected while I occupied the men's room in Billings. That left me so unnerved that I backed into a fire plug. Well, I don't know what it was. I didn't look. I just drove away. Julie told me later. An alarmed witness shouted a vulgarity that Julie hadn't heard before. I missed that, too.

As I dropped off the rig in Hamilton, Montana—25 miles north of my new home—my wife wandered across North First Street to Jerry Wessel's tire shop, where she was studying a set of 22-inch mud-and-snow tires that might have been developed for the Siberian Road of Bones. This was May 12. It was snowing.

Before moving to Montana, I reread some of my H.D. Thoreau, thinking it would offer somnolent guidance. It did.

When Henry was on his deathbed, friend Parker Pillsbury asked what death right then was looking like. Thoreau answered, "One world at a time, please."

For purposes of settling in Montana, that became my credo, too.

MR. BIDEN RECOMMENDED IT

As I write this, I am 65 years old. I spent all of those years writing for a living, a terrifying prospect, now that I think of it. I can't imagine what else I could have done. I would have failed as a game-show host.

My first job was in Canada in 1975 at an auto-racing tabloid called *Car Weekly*, which we secretly spelled "Weakly." I was paid 50 bucks for each race I covered, so, that first year, I attended 30. I was absent so much that my Swedish girlfriend started dating our pharmacist. She might have married him. All I know is I came home from a race to find the pharmacist's wristwatch on my nightstand and no enjoyable sedating prescriptions by way of apology.

My most lucrative tenure, by far, was at *Car and Driver,* where I wrote features for 32 years. I've interviewed Charles Kuralt (still have his mittens), one of the Pythons, G. Gordon Liddy, Pink Floyd's Nick Mason, J. Geils, 12,000 intellectually torpid race-car drivers, and two vice presidents—Joe Biden and Dan Quayle.

The Quayle interview was scheduled for an hour but lasted 20 minutes because he answered every question with a concise sentence, then stopped dead, ready for question number two. It was like talking to a vending machine. As opposed to Biden, who had me emitting wet pig snorts as he recounted so many off-the-record ribald recollections of boyhood mayhem that I had to call back to ascertain which were publishable.

Biden invited me to the U.S. Naval Observatory to perform burnouts in his brother's Cadillac CTS-V. He told me that retiring to Montana was a good idea. By the way, if you phone someone even vaguely upper echelon at the White House, there will be multiple recordings of it, a fact they'll firmly establish beforehand as decree.

I asked Biden's handler, "You want my passport number or anything?" and she said, "Already got that, John."

By the time I retired to Montana, I'd resolved to write no more. Not even a check. Not even my signature for FedEx. Now, if I write at all, it's freelance at my convenience. According to the Authors Guild, the median income for American freelancers is $6,080, or $16.65 per day. Fiscally speaking, I'd be better off covering races.

You know what Robert Benchley said about this? "The freelance writer is a man who is paid per piece or per word or perhaps."

THE BIG LENTICULAR

I moved from Ann Arbor, planetary headquarters for *Car and Driver,* to Darby, planetary headquarters for Logger Days, featuring a V-8–powered chain saw that backfires blue flames, causing dogs to take cover behind the Cenex station.

Darby reposes in the southwest corner of the state. Drive farther and humanity dematerializes for the next 75 miles. Half of Darby is tucked hard against the Bitterroot Mountains to the west, featuring granitic spires and slab-faced precipices. The other half squats in the Bitterroot Valley, bisected by the icy Bitterroot River, famous for blue-ribbon trout, though any I've caught have been ribbonless. The scene from my deck recollects a Charlie Russell painting, if his paint had been supplied by Lamborghini.

The 400-some quiet and reclusive residents are known as Darbrarians, and many have built their homes on fearsome grades, like auks nesting on cliffs. For a while, we had no internet, no TV, no phone—three Bitterroot Valley drawbacks the locals claimed they could cure "but not in an immediate time frame."

My pine-packed property borders 1,000 feet of U.S. Forest Service land, home to roving gangs of whistling elk and a few castoff rusting iron implements designed to fell trees in the '30s. Where I live, I perceive no one else's lights at night. Where I live, there's one paved, maintained road—Highway 93—that is confined to the bottom of the valley's "V."

I can hear neither cars nor trucks, just the occasional Forest Service helicopter tracking animals with radio collars or assisting with forest-thinning operations. I introduced myself to one of the pilots, a Vietnam vet, who—thinking I wanted a ride—said, "There are eight cracks in this helicopter's airframe." Later that fall in Idaho, he crashed and died.

My homemade mailbox wobbles a couple of miles from my front door. A sign on our access road warns, *"Chains and 4Wheel Drive May Be Necessary."* I delight in the Montanan understatement of that—*"may."*

Darby's post office has but one delivery Jeep Wrangler, which appears to have rolled through a gravel pit where it was T-boned by a dairy tanker. In Darby, that's possible.

Not that it matters to me now, but Montana ranks third in the nation for shortest commute to work: 18 minutes. Only the Dakotas do better, and I'm pretty sure being beaten at anything by the Dakotas does not mandate celebration. What's more, I have never seen a swimming pool in Montana. Not one. The telephone book for the entire Bitterroot Valley is the size of an airport romance novel, which I don't think anyone publishes anymore, with all names in extra-large type, concluding with Rhoda Zylstra. Another great name for a dog.

The state's population hovers at one million, with most residents having settled here from elsewhere, as did I. Per square mile, that works out to 7.1 people—"I already know six of them," goes the joke—a population density lower only in Alaska and Wyoming.

Montana has but one congressman, Greg Gianforte, who, as I write this, has been charged with assault but refused to pose for his requisite mug shot, claiming political privilege. He is off to a flying start, having set some sort of early-bird record for aggressive mendacity, felony duplicitousness, and possession of untruths for the purpose of distribution, all this before he even found his congressional seat, which I hope is preloaded with a whoopee cushion that inflicts explosive injury to his testicular bundle. (In 2021, he became our governor, at which point he was worth $315 million.)

We also have one area code for the whole state—406, a common bumper sticker for insiders—yet Montana is as big as Japan, if not quite as elongated and with no satisfactory beaches. If you zoomed along Interstate 90, you'd experience 554 miles of Big Sky, all of it moderately stunning and characterized by lenticular clouds that humble and ruthlessly miniaturize all creatures brave enough to afford upward glances. Said author Larry McMurtry: "Montana skies seem deeper than the skies of Texas or Nebraska. Their depth and blueness robbed even the sun of its harsh force. Always, somewhere to the north, there was a swath of blueness, with white clouds floating in it like petals in a pond."

If you are a light-aircraft pilot, lenticular clouds represent spar-dashing winds and imminent loss of colon control.

Generally speaking, the eastern half of the state is as flat as a trailer park, the western half atrociously lumpy. Montana is so large that its 545-mile border with Canada touches three provinces. There are barns in Montana bigger than Westminster Abbey. A Montana ranch called the "LF" was recently listed for sale. It comprises 42,400 acres and is crisscrossed by 31 miles of private creeks and tributaries. Price: $52.5 million. (I know a real-estate agent who can steal it for fifty, even. Let me know.)

Early Spanish explorers dubbed this region *Montañas del Norte*, only to have two U.S. Congressmen say the name "had no meaning." They'd apparently heard that the state comprised badlands and prairie only. Armed with falsehoods, they wandered to their own empurpled conclusions and launched a D.C. tradition that chugs along to this day. Other names suggested: "Mountainia," which a resident said was "feminine for mountain." Also "Montano," the masculine singular, which for a time was the postmark on letters from Virginia City, Helena, and Bannack, the latter now a preserved ghost town not far from my home.

By the by, the state capital hereabouts is pronounced "HELL-nur." Two syllables. Usually uttered without lips moving.

John Phillips

Julie and I wed ourselves to Big Sky on May 12, amid a snowstorm whose flakes were so large they folded in half. Julie had lived every previous day of her life in Michigan, and as we unpacked boxes, I fretted about dragging her to the cliff face of uninhabited alpine highlands. It's one thing for friends to be remote but quite another to encounter none at all. The most common road sign in Montana reads, "Pavement Ends." I wondered if it applied to my marriage.

I am a baby boomer with every trait implied: I celebrate happy hour not long after my morning poached eggs and prunes. I comb my eyebrows or they resemble alder bushes. My beard suggests an amateur hobby in forestry. All my life I've heard fellow boomers talk about retiring to sylvan wilderness. "Get back to basics," they'd intone. "Get back to nature."

Not one of them made the move. I did. But, of course, with no clear notion of how or if it might fulfill me, never mind my wife, who I began to view as the bystander most likely to pay for collateral psychological scratch-and-dentery.

MRS. THOR'S CLEAVAGE

Julie and I became mesmerically entranced by rocky southwestern Montana 18 years ago. It was during a vacation in which we rented a cabin on a sprawling ranch that now belongs to Charles Scripps, he of Scripps colleges and Scripps TV and Scripps wire services and oceanographic institutes and a dozen other S-branded endeavors. He is portly and resembles the town banker from a Frank Capra movie. Also like a banker, Charles—or Charlie to us—drives a red Bentley, which makes sense because he has indulged a lifelong affair with fire engines and hosts firefighters whenever there's a conflagration near his ranch. Which is every summer. When I say "hosts," what I mean is he stakes out an area allowing 400 Forest Service firefighters to erect individual tents in his backyard. It is a sight to behold, with his wife serving cookies and brownies.

Overnight, a tent city appears, complete with mucky alleys and low-hanging haze from 400 cooking fires. Then Charlie rolls past silently in his Bentley, which, in this locale, is about as useful as a Roman chariot. On the other hand, it *looks* like a Roman chariot, and Charlie spends his winters on a yacht in Florida, perhaps communing with Spartacus, so the analogy is complete. Charlie owns a couple of eight-wheel-drive fire engines. I am not sure what he does with them.

All those years ago, when Julie and I awoke that first morning in the Scripps cabin, we peered down a valley that included Painted Rocks Lake and the West Fork of the Bitterroot River, which at that elevated locale is no wider than a sidewalk. The rock formations there—cathedrals, really—are Eocene granite, 55 million years old. As vistas go, it taunted the Alps and was at least equal to the assembly line in Ferrari's Maranello plant.

The hair on my arms stood erect. Not really. That's never happened to me. But, truly, there before me towered a buffet of jagged stacks striped in green moss and ecru lichen, attempting to crush a hunter-green valley that looked like Mrs. Thor's cleavage. There were columns of sunlight filtering through the pine canopy, poking down like chrome cannons, like the light that creeps through an open door. Then, at a distance of 50 feet, a bighorn sheep strolled past, Ma Nature's Super Bowl commercial. I'm being honest when I say I right then chose to effect a nearby retirement. Right as I stood there.

Here's something else about that moment, as if it weren't already numinously grand. A filthy little terrier trotted up to us, emanating from the Scripps kitchen, which holds grandstand seating for TV audiences because Charlie previously expected his network to film a cooking show there.

The dog led us on a walk to the river, where he stored a cache of cattle, elk, and deer bones. Then he herded us through pastures and along the edge of an orange and green granite escarpment. The dog presented three or four places to ford the river without soaking our shoes, glancing back to confirm we were following. Our own Montana tour guide, free for the asking, as long as we'd *ooh* and *aah* over his collection of gnawed ribs and femurs.

We named him Western Jake. He had balls of mud hanging from his balls. He made it clear he did not care. Then, poof, he disappeared like a muddy wraith, a pooka, and we never saw him again, even though we searched.

We thereafter returned to the Bitterroot Valley yearly, staying two or three weeks at a shot, renting a log cabin on the West Fork of the Bitterroot River. As the years passed, we examined homes and bare plots of land that were for sale. But there weren't many.

We'd already invested four years of searching when—*voilà!*—our real-estate agent, Sherry Wildey, trotted out a detailed map of the valley. Her fingers traced the rare little white islands on the map, and she said, "That's private land you could conceivably buy." Then she pointed to everything else—a vast ocean of green and blue tracts—and explained, "All of that belongs to the Forest Service or the state or the feds. Not available at any price." Turns out, 74 percent of Ravalli County, where I now live, is public land.

Sherry revealed another fundament: Montanans aren't fond of zoning regulations. You can build a crematorium and a Dairy Queen between two trailer parks alongside a $3 million log home with a combo tanning/hair salon in its foyer. The overarching Montanan philosophy is that no government can tell you what to do on your own property. That works dandy, of course, until a uranium strip mine opens adjacent to Baby Sue's Day Care Center. Then there's some friction.

With that in mind, we located a 40-acre parcel of bare land atop a mountain looming 350 feet over Painted Rocks Lake—the rocks are, indeed, all available primary colors—and it was affordable.

We contacted an excavator who said, "Uh, first, you'll need a driveway." When I inquired about cost, he silently counted on his fingers as we sat in a sandy clearing at the site's summit. "Well, I'll have to shoot [blast with dynamite] a bunch of hairpin turns, but it won't be too bad. I'd say around $80,000." For the driveway *alone*. "Course," he added, "you won't be able to use it in the winter unless you own a snow machine." Julie and I stumbled down the mountain and climbed into our rented Toyota 4Runner.

This set us up for Flood House.

Sketching Giraffe Anatomy

Before discovering our petite house in petite Darby, we'd been drawn to a two-story dwelling so far in the wilderness that the bears required passports. I'm not sure you could situate a home farther from civilization without help from NASA. Further, there was slim evidence of anyone ever maintaining the access road, where pine limbs extended over and inward, creating a verdant tunnel that brushed dust off my truck but also grooved the paint. Living in that secluded homestead, we'd have been babes secreted within dark copses, coverts, and coppices, with forest clawing at the bedroom panes and a 78-mile round trip to buy a loaf of bread. Still, it seemed doable, at least after two hours at Darby's Sawmill Saloon.

The house had been built in the '80s by a reclusive clan of White Russians, whom the locals yet revile for being "stuck up" and consorting only with other White Russians, of which there were six. The house was in fair condition apart from one distraction. The previous owner had disappeared to Texas but had failed to turn off the water beforehand. Montana winter descended, the plumbing ruptured, and so did some wallets. Hence the name Flood House.

This wasn't overtly unfixable, and the owner collected an insurance settlement when she returned the following spring. In the fall, she departed for Texas again and—you must trust me when I tell you this—forgot to turn off the water. Wanton forgetfulness often feels sustainable and fun.

The second flood skirted boundaries biblical. Water washed away the master bedroom and bath, then pooled to a depth of five feet in the basement, which wasn't completely awful because it drowned the resident pack rats. The main-floor bedroom alone was a $25,000 project, yet the house was otherwise sound, sort of, as long as no one hosted a square dance.

The owner returned from Texas and, for the second year, walked bravely into her insurance agent's office and said, "You're gonna laugh when you hear what happened." He did not laugh. Neither did he reimburse her. She happened to share our Hamilton lawyer—Montana real-estate bylaws have apparently been written by confidence men from Estonia—and that's how we learned that she'd asked him, "Would you like to help me sue my insurance company?" The lawyer said, "No. Never. Would never be good for you?" and began doodling a pencil sketch of giraffe genitalia on his oak desk. (That last part might not be right.)

Our lawyer told her, "Roses are red, violets are blue, you're clearly a moron, no way you can sue." Then he showed her the door, one that wasn't floating.

That's when two competing banks foreclosed, hoicking the house into a complicated, animated, contested short sale. Fiscal wrestling. This was maybe good for us. We had budgeted $300,000 to buy Flood House and $100,000 to repair it. Our plan was to live on the second floor—which was wholly dry and unmolested except by the aforementioned pack rats who had shat the carpeting to death. We could live up top while overseeing repairs below. A date was set to auction the house on the steps of the Ravalli County courthouse. Our lawyer promised, "You'll get it for $289,000, trust me."

The complexity of this financial Hail Mary had me pounding Pepcid. Apparently, money can buy happiness but only if the banks allow it. What's more, I could not reconcile the concept of purchasing a house at auction. Why not at a pawnbroker's or a Holy Rollers' tent?

"It's a breeze," our lawyer counseled, reminding me to bring wads of certified checks in all denominations, because the banks demand payment on the spot. I crammed into my Levi's $300,000 worth of certified paper—I had a hilarious speech prepared for any curious TSA inspector—then purchased airfare to Missoula, having packed my most cowboyish shirt. That's when the lawyer called to say the auction was off. "New shit has come to light," I believe were his words.

Here was the new shit: The owner of Flood House—in a fit of pique aimed at the banks and insurance companies—had paid a contractor to enter her soggy domicile and tear out the upstairs bath, that being a room untouched by flooding. The tub would not fit through the existing door, so the contractor had to knock down a wall adjoining a bedroom. Then, per the owner's vivid directive, he toted the tub to a rent-a-shed in Darby, where the Texas lady could admire the item at her leisure. Just so you know, the tub, when new, was worth about $299 at Lowe's.

Now, of course, the upstairs of Flood House was likewise uninhabitable, leaving only the pack rats to ascend in the quality of their difficult lives. In fact, the last time I parked in front of Flood House, a sleek and devious rat climbed into my truck's engine bay and endured a 20-mile ride to a pasture by the river. As Julie and I ate lumpy turkey-and-mayo sandwiches at a picnic table, we watched him lower himself from the radiator shroud. He dangled his rear feet to within inches of the ground, then wiggled them to-and-fro like paddles, hoping to latch onto something that wasn't made by Toyota. A rodent clog dance. Eventually, he just flung himself to earth, where he solemnly surveyed what was, for him, a new planet. He stopped dancing.

Whatever level of water you are seeking, you are better off with your head above it. So that marked the conclusion of Flood House. But maybe all was not lost. The odd Texan owner informed that she also owned 20 acres adjacent to her waterlogged structure, bare land. Were we interested? Julie and I flew to Missoula to investigate, mid-October.

As we strolled among Douglas firs and pink-barked ponderosas on Ms. Forgetful's property, a senior couple beckoned from the gravel frontage road, inquiring after our purpose. I explained we were keen to buy land from the Texas lady. The couple both shook their heads as their lips curled into perfect Os of astonishment.

The wife remarked: "Oh, that's funny, because *we* own this land."

Stuff like this happens in Montana. A lot, said our lawyer. A lot, said our real-estate agent. A lot, said the rightful property owners. The male half of that duo said of the Texas lady, "She's a person who'd be stumped by alphabet soup."

I wrote that down.

"Don't be cruel," his wife intoned. "It's just that she has to sit down to think." Then the couple invited us to their log home, a half-mile distant, where we shared non-alphabet soup and hot tea to ward off the icy drizzle. They were the kindest folks on this side of the Continental Divide, and now I can't remember their names. In Montana nowadays, the former Flood House owner is about as welcome as turds at Tiffany's.

Having terminated that whole spastic exercise in deep-woods futility, Julie and I motored back to our rental cabin and emptied the liquor cabinet of previous guests' unfinished dregs. That's how I came to know the tangy squalor of Sour Apple Amoretti—kerosene, ear wax, and curdled vinegar, I believe—but I was operating on the principle that if I were going to be in more pain, I'd inflict it myself.

I later phoned the agent who'd listed Flood House. She suffered what I'd honestly estimate was a nervous breakdown mid-conversation, complete with gasping sobs and periods of audible chest heaves and snot snuffling.

We later related the Flood House story to one of our first guests in Montana, who asked to view the place. We were halfway up the drive when a bearded pirate in a black Ford F-150 came roaring down, chock-full of homicide. I leapt out of my car, hand outstretched in peace, which was refused.

"Hi, my name is…"

"You were trespassing," said Mr. I.M. daWalrus, whose face was crimson and contorted.

"Yes, I was, and I apologize," I said, explaining we'd come merely to view the house, which we believed was yet for sale. He interrupted with, "Excuse me!" while holding up both palms to ward off my approach and any further utterances from my person.

"You do not wanna get crosswise with me," he informed, as if my goal were to ignite his pre-inflamed psychopathy. I'm sure he had a gun. "Just...," he said, as his palms flew up again, followed by some stuttering and contorted facial expressions, and then, "Trust me. You need to leave."

Trust *him*? Half of his mouth wadded up while the other half hissed compressed air and foamy saliva.

Somewhere there's a moral here about dealing with insane people and hoping at each successive contact that the madness might lift as gently as San Francisco fog.

It won't.

SPAGHETTIOS AS BURGLAR ALARM

We searched for six years, with the aid of our be-sainted real-estate agent, before happening on a house with the perfect view and a Remoteness Quotient of 8.2. People ask, "Why so remote?" and I tell them, "Because there are two kinds of people in this world, and I dislike both."

A facile response but mostly so. Poet Robinson Jeffers described the human race as "a civil war on two legs." My wife and I prefer any woodland creature over any Homo sapiens, and that includes scaly pangolins, Karelian bear dogs, and a small rattlesnake we aroused on a hike up to Baker Lake.

The jostling power skirmishes of the office, in particular, had inflamed that part of my brain I'd come to call the Hypocorpus conflictus. As had 20th- and 21st-century life in general: Everything we see, hear, read, and internalize focuses on our puny affairs—the relentless pettiness of politics, our own histories sculpted and carved and reshaped to please us, the daily worship of our own machines' grand specifications.

I mean, what has mankind accomplished, apart from despoiling the thin surface of the planet, to deserve this 24-hour bacchanalia of self-worship? What about the history of hawks? The politics of penguins? The overarching governance of germs? Why does even our goddamn prophet so precisely resemble the Santa Claus of costly material bling? Why is one of our mistakes—the leaning tower of Pisa, let's say—somehow more worthy of praise than the orange lichen attached to rocks in my backyard? Great art and music? Oh, yeah, *we* think it's great. But ask a chihuahua what he thinks of Chopin, or a mole what he thinks of Monet.

Anyway, I was apparently looking for ataraxia, or tranquility, and expected to find it not within but behind our two-level house, which cost $400,000, our entire pot and the saucer, too. The house comprises 1,300 square feet on the main floor and 800 on the walkout lower level. Think of a nice double-wide stacked atop a concrete patio.

Like a bucktooth, the house protrudes from an incline so steep that a tumble means a plunge long enough to floss your teeth. In places, the 100-foot surrounding pines block much of the sunlight. We're basically on the side of Trapper Peak and attached tenuously to 10,000 feet of rocky slab, certainly the craggiest protuberance in the Bitterroot Range. It resembles the Matterhorn and even in the summer doldrums wears a snowy fedora. There is a trail to the summit, marked by rock cairns. The entire trek, 16 miles to and from, is above the tree line, so you must carry lunch, a gallon of water, multiple windbreakers, and maybe a ball of opium to forestall spiritual sag.

Built in 2000, our house has stained pine siding, a green metal roof, and a high-ceiling "great room" that comprises the kitchen, the living room, a wall-mounted bookcase holding 1,000 books, and a view of mountains to the north, which apparently have no names until we decided on "Hannibal" and "Clarice." The house is a spacious rabbit hutch. The dining room table is 48 inches from the front door. Guests who barrel through the entrance might plop face-first into a bowl of SpaghettiOs, a built-in burglar alarm that relies on scalding entrées. Of course, we don't lock our doors. Any evildoer who ascends half a mountain deserves a bowling trophy.

It is quiet here, quieter than any place I've experienced except the Contemplation Room in McGowan's Funeral Home. *Hymns to the Silence,* as Van Morrison sings. The only vehicles we hear are those delivering propane or UPS packages, inching slowly far below. One jet overflies each afternoon at 3:00 p.m., bound from Missoula to Salt Lake City, announcing itself by lacy contrails alone.

It is so quiet that the absence of noise can startle. I've been vaulted to wakefulness by a tree falling 100 yards away. Also by owls. Also by forest creatures leaping from our deck's handrail onto its surface—foxes, ground squirrels, skunks, a raccoon the size of a black lab, and eventually a dozen black bears. I've been awakened into raw-nerve consciousness, heart pounding, by half-pound pine cones bouncing off our metal roof. The wind sometimes rattles the garage door as if a sasquatch were testing it for strength. I once investigated a midnight racket to discover Rennie and Silver Streak, our resident foxes, dragging tasty crusts from a Glad trash bag whose discarded cans comprised the alarm.

My annual two-and-a-half-day drive back to Ann Arbor reminds me of the obscene cacophony that civilization so blithely imposes: clatter, jangle, clank, hum, echo, swish, thud, crunch. It's relentless. Listen some time to the cataclysm that is a lone 18-wheeler humping along. A single night in a city, listening to police sirens and garbage trucks beeping in reverse, would now kindle insanity. Know why birds fly upside down in New York City? Because there's nothing worth shitting on. (A joke of the West, not my own.)

Know what we also do not have? Smells. No wafting diesel stench, no whiff of sulfuric industry, no reek of refuse. In 1700, health reformer Thomas Tyrone called such odors "gross stinking fogs, relics of putrefaction running through the streets, multitudes of people living in rooms uncleanly kept." Not in my forest.

In our first week in the house, I was prepping for bed, wearing only a T-shirt and Jockey briefs, when I heard a snuffling *oom-pah* out front, a noise my wife rarely makes. I ventured onto the patio and, in the gloaming, nearly collided with a bull elk devouring our decorative crabapple. He bore the kind of antlers you see in Cabela's and was plucking leaves ten feet above the porch's surface. (Really. I measured the next day.) He was the size of a Blue Grass quarter horse and turned to study me in my Scotch-plaid Y-fronts. He stared for five seconds, then resumed grazing. It was like walking into your bedroom and finding farm animals gamboling atop the quilt.

In the morning, the crabapple had endured a hideous haircut, was smaller by a third, and the petunias below were pulped unto colorful little piles of French tricolor goo. Naturalist Craig Childs observed, "Deer are pieces of crystalware; elk are galvanized-steel lunch boxes."

The rule hereabouts is that you can dissuade the Bitterroot forest's critters but only via a ten-foot-tall electrified fence buttressed by cables interwoven through the chain link. Of course, *something there is that doesn't love a wall,* chimed Mr. Frost, so no fences for us.

Our nearest neighbor, Kemp Conn, recalled a fruit tree he was nurturing, protected by a new electric fence. Yet on the day he and wife Patty were to harvest plums, they met a yearling black bear who'd already completed the job. He was still tree-bound, belching and farting and bawling, belly distended, with a half dozen branches snapped off. Patty yelled, *"Bad bear!"*

But the bear wasn't bad, didn't care if he was or if he was dishonest or conniving or guilty of theft, because those weren't precepts he'd ever require. Unlike me, he wasn't chasing after meaning, which so often distracts from living. And his life wasn't a story, because a story is always gored by reality. Which I'm pretty sure comprised two of the misperceptions right then bubbling at the root of my dissatisfaction.

HE SHOULD HAVE HOSTED *THE TONIGHT SHOW*

When Julie and I retired here, our realtor showed us how to escape a forest fire if the wood bridge over Tin Cup Creek was ablaze, it being our lone tenuous link to civilization. She explained we'd have to open an imposing metal gate 100 yards from the stream, then undertake some minor off-roading for a mile or so, then use a stranger's driveway for another mile, stomp out a rain dance, smoke four cigarettes, and—presumably low on gas by then—we'd intersect Highway 93, the only north-south road bisecting Darby and the entire valley.

"But I don't have a key to the gate," I complained.

"Yes, you do," she insisted.

"No, I *don't,*" I replied, adding emphasis. She pointed to the front bumper of my truck and said, "*That's* your key."

Life in Montana includes a lot of mundane fixes that are self-evident. Montana is not complicated. Which felt soothing. Certainly, I had previously worked slavishly to fashion a life as complicated as possible, because—as in the case of Swiss watches and political campaigns—complexity seemed to animate my existence, suggesting a retail life more valuable.

The Bitterroot Valley extends south from Missoula to the Idaho border, 120 miles of Mother Nature's most ornate handiwork. Our valley is bordered—imprisoned, really—by two mountain ranges: the Bitterroots and the Sapphires. The Bitterroot River flows in the vee, meaning we live on the side of a profound trough. Yet back in the Cretaceous period, 70 to 90 million years ago, those two ranges comprised a single fat spine. For reasons unknown—irreconcilable differences, I guess—the Sapphires sheared off, then scuttled northeast, scraping across 1.7-billion-year-old Precambrian bedrock.

It's of interest to me that this valley, from its Cretaceous period, is famous for at least one archaeological amazement: the oldest known fossilized ants. You'd think someone would have set traps and saved a hundred-million subsequent picnics. I'm sorry. Just put the book down for a few minutes. (An hour, tops.)

Some 15,000 years ago, glacial runoff flooded the Bitterroot Valley until a natural dam burst and a titanic wall of muddy water bulled its way into what is now Washington State, creating the Scablands. ("You say you live in the Scablands? You're not picking at it, are you?")

The flood's source was so-called Lake Missoula, which filled and emptied as many as 40 times—so geologists say, but few of them were here at the time—and once reached a depth of 4,300 feet not far from where I draw my evening baths. Somewhere between 9,000 and 14,000 years ago, when the ground was less soggy, the valley welcomed its first nomadic people, part of the Plateau Culture. I don't know whether that's important or not. I've never met any Plateauers, but I imagine their affect is flat.

When Julie and I arrived, we spent the first three months unpacking boxes. Hundreds. I bought a dozen six-foot-tall metal shelving units in Missoula, 70 miles north of us. They took three days to assemble while I sang Ry Cooder songs and learned much about Judge Judy. Still, most of our books were yet in the garage, which was, as the TV advertisers say, "water-resistant but not waterproof." The dampness had already warped a first-edition James Thurber, a signed *Dalva* from Jim Harrison, and a dozen signed by three-decade workmate P.J. O'Rourke.

The ugly unpacking was made bearable by a raven we named Ed; his other two family members were Al(ice) and Poe. Ed was, and still is, larger than either of our cats and easily boasts a wingspan of four feet. He is perversely curious about our labors and performs a daily low-altitude flyby at 4:00 p.m., cruising always from east to west.

He was punctual. I marveled at how he'd tilt his head to peer into our living room, a voyeuristic corvid. Whenever I viewed his aerobatics, I'd wave and shout his name. He was so close that I could see him blink. One day, he failed to fly past at 4:00 p.m. but did an hour later, on the dot. I mentioned his tardiness to Julie, who replied, "Well, we set our clocks ahead last night." Leave it to a raven to know the correct time and possibly the lyrics to "*Bohemian Rhapsody*." I read in a book that the "comical commerce of corvids"—a fine piece of alliteration—demands only two hours per day for food gathering. The rest of the day is spent, and I quote, "screwing around"—talking to one another, flying upside down, dive-bombing smaller birds, reburying bits of food, and writing bad checks.

Ed even taunts the deer, who charge him whenever he sets talons to terra firma. He escapes by flying 20 feet, alighting, then flapping off for another 20 feet, hopping around as if attending a rave and inciting deer angst until they tire of the sport or Ed realizes it's time for his daily flyby. As he passes, I remind him to trim his ailerons, adjust his flaps, and exercise his elevators.

Here is another Ed skill: On a day when the temp never rose above zero, I tossed some fried-chicken remnants over the deck. Ed arrived two hours later. He located a yet meaty bone about five inches long, examined it as if it might be counterfeit, then tucked it under his right wing so that it was lodged in his armpit, if ravens have armpits.

He hopped vertically atop the snow and examined other meaty curios for five or six minutes. Then he withdrew the original bone from his black armpit and devoured the scraps therefrom. Had Ed been thawing the meat for easier consumption? Behaviorists would likely equivocate, but I later tossed four Ritz crackers to Ed, who stacked them neatly like poker chips, later covering them with leaves so they'd be dry for lunch the next day. I've had high-school teachers who weren't that smart.

What's more, Ed proved to be an accomplished mimic. He'd perch in our tallest ponderosa and riff through his repertoire of forest chirps, squawks, awks, cries, and rodent squeaks—he could impersonate any creature apart from wolves and was notably adept at mocking the Steller's jays. He further developed what Julie called "a monkey shriek." I daresay there are no simians in Montana, apart from our congressional representative, so Ed's mimicry in this instance remains a mystery. I'd shout, "Ed, do the monkey!" and he'd cease cawing for a moment, regard me with one sphinxlike eye, then resume his monologue, snubbing me as if I were a drunk heckler.

Ed sometimes flubbed his recital—performing his jingles in the wrong order, or just miscalculating his Steller's screech—then would chastise himself in frustration, letting rip with a couple standard raven yawks. Then he'd start over. Ed later performed his stand-up act for a guest on our porch. The guest said to me, "You've got a tape player in the trees, don't you?"

When I read more about ravens, I learned they possess a strong sense of self, of memory, of past and future. They hold wakes for departed colleagues. They form gangs to attack owls. They actually co-wrote a lot of Poe's material when the man was in his cups.

When Ed is cawing in the trees, I'll call his name and he'll go mute, then he'll fly closer to stare and talk back. As long as I repeat his name, he'll pay attention to me. If he begins to fly away and I shout, "Ed, come back," he will. Ravens have been known to mimic radio static, the flushing of urinals, the revving of motorcycles, and explosions intended to set off avalanches. Ed could have hosted *The Tonight Show*. Birds must be the grandest facts of nature.

I noticed a gray jay land on our deck, a species first

formally identified by Lewis and Clark. Ed then settled on the adjacent railing and vented bird abuse on Mister Jay until the poor thing flew off mortified and a little deaf. Ed had mocked him with "quorks," a "rap-rap" sound, a guttural "ahh-*AHH*," and a sound like two wooden bats knocking together.

Julie and I once conducted our routine picnic trek behind the house, scouting for elk antlers, which in these parts are called "shed"—a noun, not a verb. To our surprise, Ed hovered above us the entire four miles, repeatedly strafing our noggins from an altitude of ten feet. He'd caw and cackle as if worried we were lost. It's likely we were inferring our own interpretations of dusky Ed's enigmatic motives, but when I later mentioned this experience to a Forest Service ranger, he was unsurprised. We'd either wandered from Ed's protected territory into the domain of a competing raven, he suggested, or Ed may have considered us apex predators, meaning we might kill something and leave a tasty gut pile. Ravens follow wolves for the same reason.

Not that it matters, but the ranger's name was Ed.

Despite our resident raven's oratory, strain attached itself to setting up the house—what to do about the electric hookup, the propane, the cable TV, the mailbox, the garbage, the village of mice in the garage, the hair growing out of my ears. It led to a fierce argument, the source of which was murky. I slept downstairs a night or two to cool off, and Julie drank merlot and couldn't say anything optimistic for a few days. I hurled a can of spray paint at the garage wall, where it created an image of the Virgin Mary, although Darby possesses no record of her visit and I am not one of the wise men.

I'd encountered this brand of emotional meltdown before. In the course of writing for magazines, I'd moved from my Columbus, Ohio, birthplace to England, Toronto, Detroit, Newport Beach, Costa Mesa, Dexter (Michigan), Ann Arbor, Pinckney (Michigan), and now Montana. Sometimes I think my arriving has all along been for the sake of departing. In total, I've lived in 20 dwellings, which has to have damaged my sense of place. In each case, there have been similar paroxysms a month after arrival, fueled in part, I'm guessing, by the stress of making new friends.

After the tears dried, a kind of lingering animus hung like black mold for a week, then we shared a venison dinner with our real-estate agent, after which, for some reason, life normalized marginally. Which was lucky, because in Sherry's gravel driveway we almost ran over a rubber boa—a real-life constrictor, as in snake. The thing resembled half snake and half newt. A "snewt."

"They won't hurt you," Sherry reassured, knowing this because she was born in Darby. Then she added, "Actually, I don't know what they do." Julie and I find snakes more polite than telemarketers, so she nudged the boa into a soft pit of pine needles. Rubber boas move at the speed of tree rings. They cannot sneak up on you. Don't want to, either.

We later met a reptile less cordial—a bull snake, six feet long, beige with fetching lateral stripes, who was sunning himself on Rye Creek Road. I locked up the truck's wheels to avoid creating a bully tortilla. As I prodded him to the berm, he tightened into a coil, then lunged while making the hiss of an 18-wheeler bleeding off its brakes. I was wearing shorts, and the curmudgeon nearly nailed me on the inner left thigh.

My Idaho-born friend Ravi Fry said, "Bull snakes are always in a bad mood. They inflict an agonizing bite, but they're not poisonous." Sort of like office colleagues.

I related this story in the Sawmill Saloon, and a stranger inexplicably claimed that rattlesnakes in the valley are called "buzzworms." I've since asked 20 folks if they've heard that term. Not one had.

Then, another mountain-aerie aggravation, namely, a mailbox, which we did not have. Mail was being delivered to the distant Darby post office, which was a hassle and a half, especially when weather stymied the trip. So I drove two miles to the ratty row of mailboxes at the end of our dirt road, carrying a post-hole digger and various metal straps and hinges and support beams and two-by-fours and three beers and some bear spray.

I fiddled around for two hours, ever fretting that none of our neighbors' mailboxes had been erected in sequential array, instead popping up as each man arrived. How the mailman decoded this muddle was unknown, although he one day left a handwritten note in my box declaring it a "nuisance." Turns out he wanted it 40 inches tall, and there were six metal screws jabbing him from within. I covered them with wine corks. He left a note declaring it "wonderful!" See? Another Montana crisis easily dispatched to the dustbin of memory.

The mailbox was vital. Because of my freelancing, I still subscribe to 27 monthlies and three weeklies. Reading would be my baseline entertainment in Montana, apart from the 24-hour PBS Nature series unfolding daily for free outside our windows. In truth, my subscription list is out of control, which I noticed after receiving a copy of *Fixed Ops Journal*. Fixed or loose, I don't know what an op is. Also *Leisure Living in Leather.* Well, not really, although it's a magazine Montanans might like.

Another hitch: Montana mailboxes require relentless maintenance. The snowplow crushes them, or at least knocks them drunkenly askew. The roads' granitic dust freezes the pop-up flag at half-mast. Packages are occasionally suspended from the lid's handle, yanking the box to fierce angles. Ice builds up, deforming the lid and forcing out nails. The snow collects until it touches the bottom of the boxes—yes, even in May—so that they appear to be levitating atop a white table.

I agree with the letter carrier; it *is* a nuisance. You can see why the postmistress and her dog, Gidget (who is as active as anyone else in that establishment), prefer PO boxes accessed in a heated room. On the other hand, more secret assignations and assassinations have been plotted in our post office's foyer than in all the hallways of the United Nations. I wonder how many marriages and careers were dashed in that confined space, which always smells like wet wool and burnt Sanka.

Our post office sometimes closes for lunch yet was once open on a Sunday during the Xmas holidays. It's like Hope's Cutting Corral, my barbershop, whose hours are known only to Hope and a psychic in Rangoon. I once accidentally met her at the hardware store where I complained about her recent absences.

"Let's go, buddy," she said. "I'm driving you to the shop right now." She was willing to chauffeur me in her white F-150 with the license "HOPIE." That's never happened to me in 60-some years of haircutting, and one of my barbers was my own Uncle Jack.

One more thing about Darby's post office: I was in the Sawmill Saloon last week—merely inspecting—whereupon conversation fixed on the post office's notoriously clunky door. It had been repaired. Celebration ensued, plus some backslapping, as if the Darby Tigers had scored a title-winning touchdown. Then we all broke off into discussion groups to ponder the meaning of a new PO sign, affixed above the wastebasket. It says: "Do NOT go through the trash." I accused midget Gidget the dog, who once stared at the bin as if ready to paw through debris all afternoon.

Then another vexation: At first, I was simply bundling our rubbish into Glad bags and wedging them beneath an inverted steel wheelbarrow weighing 40 pounds. The pile deepened, situated directly below our bedroom window. One morning, I found the trash strewn as if by Hurricane Andrew and noticed that the tin lid of a discarded mayonnaise jar had not been unscrewed but torn off. More worrisome, the heavy wheelbarrow had been relocated 50 feet into the woods, where it sat upright, as if appropriated overnight for a construction project.

Julie sifted through the debris to discover a tuft of black fur that would have made a nice start for a Gallic toupee. For the remainder of the month, we piled our garbage in the locked garage, and neither of us said a word about the trenchant pong. Eventually, we won a kind of garbage lottery, inheriting a third of a small dumpster near the paved road. That is, we share it with two other households. Spent differently, the rental fee would lease a 7-series BMW.

At every turn, we made mistakes. Darbrarians called us the "come heres," pronounced "COM-ears." When I asked what span of residency would render us Montanans, neighbor Kemp Conn replied, "Twenty-five years." Of course, such claims emanate from folks who've retired here as we had, and few had yet lingered a quarter century. So we're all greenhorns, like it or not. And native Montanans don't.

You know, as California's Jerry Brown was retiring to his family's ranch, he said: "I have to understand the animals and the archaeology and the geology, the trees, the insects, the rattlesnakes, and the wild boar and the elk and the fauna and the flora. There's a lot to govern up there. A lot of complexity, and I'm going to work on that."

My assignment, too.

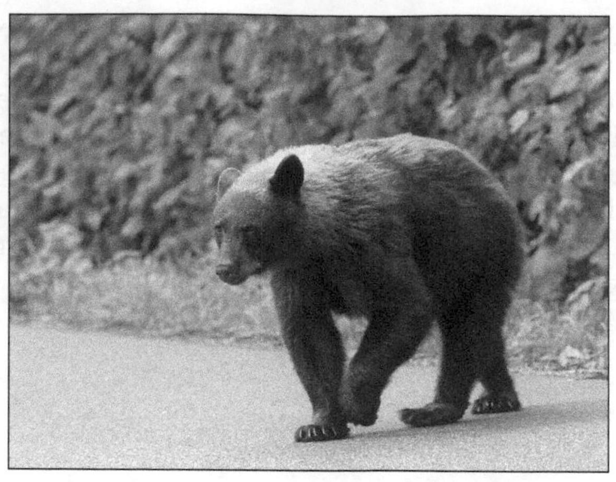

Coyote (Peter) Introduces Bear (Terry)

"B-day" at our house wasn't a birthday but a bear invasion. Our guest at the time, Terrie Howe, Julie's girlhood friend from Lansing, was reading a book on our deck. She shouted, *"Bear!"* Screamed it. I was downstairs at my desk and thought a bear had pulled some sort of B&E in pursuit of that morning's pancakes. So I rolled up a magazine as a weapon. (Okay, laugh, but it was *Scientific American*, which at least the bear would respect.) Alas, our ursine visitor was merely ambling below the deck, flattening an arrangement of dandelion stems, which he was also munching. He then made a bed between two dead trees, 20 yards from our own bed. There he slept until we forgot about him and, presumably, he about us.

He returned at dusk, peering through a downstairs bay window as we were watching Ken Burns's documentary *The West*, with narrator Peter Coyote extolling Lewis and Clark's exploits in the Bitterroot Valley—that is to say, our backyard, which right that moment was swathed in electric pink and purple sunset hues and a dusty miasma of yellow pine pollen. The only image missing in Burns's documentary was the

Bitterroot bear right then gawking through our window, at us, watching his Bitterroot homeland on TV. Time and history turned inside out.

It's a cliché, but our jaws dropped, in my case expelling some steamed asparagus. But it was also a free tutorial. One of those two views was contrived and the other was Francis Bacon's "contemplation of things as they are," and it was up to me to choose which might fulfill and which might cough up counterfeit expectations rendered in a thousand pixels per square inch, yet another lifelong displeasure I should never have so blithely appropriated from the '60s. My parents hadn't.

After the bear noticed what a pig I was, he was startled back to his bed between the tree trunks. More napping. Maybe you've noticed how bears waddle. They are pigeon-toed and possess flabby butts and seem averse to straight trajectories. They walk like farmers at the Ohio State Fair. One more thing: When bears eat too much, they'll sometimes dig a trench in the dirt to accommodate a ballooning gut. I do the same but with quilts.

We continued watching our TV documentary, then the bear returned to our sliding-glass doors on our walkout level to examine three 40-pound bags of deer feed—yes, our rookie mistake—whereupon he punched his substantial left forearm effortlessly through the cloth-reinforced plastic, creating a hole the diameter of his snout, which was absent fur and looked like a brown PVC pipe. He flung himself on his stomach, fully relaxed, and jammed his face into the bag to chew about 12 pounds of Rocky Mountain Sweet Mix. This took place on the far side of the glass, two inches away. We guessed he weighed 200 pounds, with a splendid coat as black and glossy as a wet inner tube. He ate with purpose. It allowed us time to count his scars: five in total, each appearing barbed-wire related. Then he lolled back to his 'tween-pine bed with custom-dug belly trench, content with our accidental and stupid generosity.

We named him Terry in honor of Terrie, who first spotted him, but also in respect for his/her gender, which was unknown. The bear's gender, not our guest's. Terrie and my wife had climbed naked into the Kiphart's hot tub the previous weekend, so I can confirm that she is a she. Terrie, that is. My wife, too, by the looks of it.

Julie and I policed the grounds. Before discovering the Sweet Mix, Terry the bear had dismantled our Weber grill and tossed its lid into the decorative evergreens. He also devoured five or six charcoal briquettes, perhaps to sweeten his breath, then de-lidded one of our 55-gallon steel barrels that contained sand and salt for the driveway. That particular barrel was topped by a steel lid, a one-inch-thick plywood "cork," and a 20-pound chunk of granite stacked on top for security. Terry had tossed these impediments into the shrubbery and jammed his blocky black head deep within. When he came up for air, I'm pretty sure he said, "These fuckers eat a lot of salt." Terry would go on to flip the lid five times. I replaced it five times, then realized we were locked into some sort of Pavlovian call-and-response routine and retired.

Julie worried that Terry would return, pester the neighbors, and "get into trouble," which hereabouts is the euphemism for a 30.06 ballistic invitation to dear departedness. In fact, Terry *did* find trouble but escaped. Neighbor Laurie was in her backyard, bordering Tin Cup Creek, whereupon Terry charged. "Hah," I told her, "I didn't even know he had a credit card." It was a bluff, although Laurie continued screaming "like an insane woman," as she put it. Terry fled as if evading an outstanding warrant, never glancing astern.

"He really wanted me to stop screaming," Laurie reported.

Julie suggested she should have shouted *"shush,"* that being the Navajo word for bear. Of course, it would have been like someone yelling "person" in order to scare off a mugger, a confusing command at best. In any event, I came to regard bears as comical characters. Ricky Gervais came to mind, an image that wouldn't last.

You know who wasn't even slightly afraid of Terry the bear? Our cat Megatronics. As Terry chomped Sweet Mix on the porch, Megs flattened her nose against the glass and threw eyeball daggers, quivering-lip feints, and a smorgasbord of growls—everything from a tenor hoot to a wolflike grumble.

She is a Montana Humane Society cat, thus equipped to cripple a grizzly, perhaps in attitude, perhaps in deed.

When Julie opened the door to shoo off Terry, Megs slipped between her legs and flattened into a determined stalk. She later huffed herself into similar aggression when she smelled the mountain lion who ate my "tame" deer Ronda, a hundred yards from our front door. But in the end, nothing almost didn't happen, then didn't happen anyway.

Montana breeds bravery. Though not yet in me.

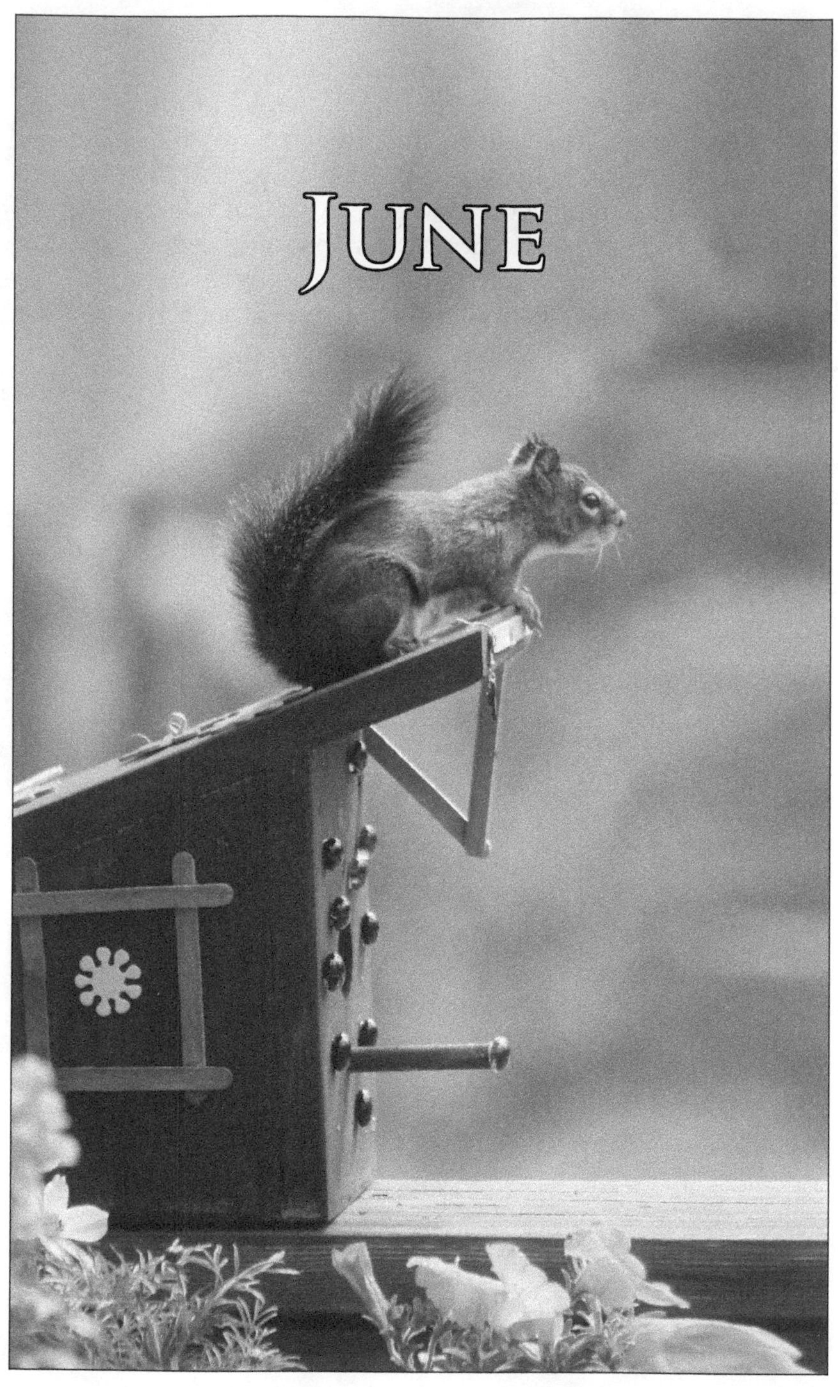
JUNE

BURNS AND ALLEN AS BRUINS

The real invasion, not of Dunkirk but Darby, didn't fully manifest until two yearling bears ambled into our sphere. My sister named them Dugan and Dolly, after ill-behaving high-schoolers in her Ohio French class.

Dolly was a pale cinnamon hue, was wont to nap beneath the deck, and her sudden arousal scared the tar out of Julie watering the plants. Dolly's face was masked, like a raccoon's, with fur in shades of milk chocolate and bronze. I feared folks would conclude she was a grizzly, with grizzled results.

Her all-black brother, Dugan, fancied himself some sort of junior alpinist, scaling our deck's support columns night after night. He'd ascend 15 feet, tumble over the railing and onto the deck with a resounding *kah-LUMP*, then examine all furniture purchased at considerable expense by yours truly.

By "examine" I mean knock over. Upturned were two chairs, one glass coffee table, one birdbath, two end tables, one love seat, four cactus plants in terracotta pots, two throw rugs, and three plastic hummingbird feeders (some parts of which Dugan ate).

This exterior undecorating was undertaken repeatedly between 2:00 a.m. and 4:00 a.m. It sounded like the Marx Brothers bowling. I caught Dugan mid-riot but couldn't see him, everything being as black as Dickens's blotter. From his perch above Julie's prize Christmas cactus, he readied himself like a boxer in his corner, then shimmied down the post, leaving claw marks as a kind of Pink Panther memento. A furry Cato.

I returned to bed only to awake in an hour for Round Two. And so forth. Dugan drank all of the birds' water, then swatted at the hanging petunias, shattering their plastic pots into poker chips and sending the flowers flying 35 feet down the mountain. Bear volleyball. We considered repotting, but the deer had already eaten the petunias for breakfast.

This noisy performance was repeated until Julie, sleep-curtailed, stomped right into Dugan's grill and screamed, *"For fuck's sake, that's enough,"* at a volume that would have knocked birds out of the sky. Plus, she was pounding on the sliding door's glass, whose replacement cost I began to calculate.

Dugan listened attentively to this character assault, then did nothing. He sat and contemplated us through eyes as black and lustrous as eight balls, and I felt as if I'd somehow landed in a John Irving novel. Then he shimmied down the support column to take a shot at any remaining Sweet Mix in the sealed metal bin, with me absolutely positive he could not pry off its "bear resistant" lid. Which he did, of course, yanking out an entire 40-pound bag.

With sister Dolly as co-conspirator, the siblings dragged this hefty loot down the hill to the trunk of a sawed-off pine, cleverly steadying it in the tree's crotch and adding it to their growing collection of decapitated suet cages. Each bear then ate approximately 15 pounds of stolen goods. I felt as if I should offer a tray of Pepcid.

The next night, Dugan wandered to our basement's sliding doors and stood up, peering inside while steadying himself with a right-front paw on the glass, as if pondering a burglary while smoking a cigarette. He left a massive five-toed print on the glass, which I left as forensic residue to frighten my mother-in-law.

The yearlings became our own Burns and Allen act who later sat and pontificated in our driveway, blocking the path for neighbor Dana as she attempted to deliver our weekly dozen eggs. The bears wouldn't budge until Dana beeped her ATV's horn, causing them to amble off slowly but apparently in jovial spirits, siblings enchantingly dependent on each other's company and encouragement. As she departed, Dolly batted at a red snow-depth marker, then ripped the lid off our septic tank, apparently for entertainment. Like a kid. I wondered what I'd do if she fell in.

Our house was their den for a month, as they ate dandelions and licked salt and foisted sleeplessness on the residents. One morning when I opened the garage, there both sat, side by side, staring as if I were the clerk who'd lead them to Aisle Nine for Froot Loops and fudge. Dolly yawned, which allowed a view of her dentition. Although whiter than piano keys, her teeth in no way suggested murderous potential: incisors no larger than my last dog's.

Dolly's grizzly-hued fur marked her for conflict in the Bitterroots, although residents here claim to know the difference: Grizzlies display a hump just aft of their necks. Grizzlies develop a slightly concave nose, whereas black bears present a classically Roman nose that is almost tubular. Grizzlies' toes squeeze closer together and their claws are longer—five-inch daggers, really—although those distinctions cannot be ascertained until the bear has left you pondering your duration in rehab.

One common trait of grizzlies and black bears both: They hate to be surprised. That's why bicyclists, quick and silent, are so often dismounted by a massive swiping paw. You may not know this, but when a grizzly hosts a surprise birthday party, two or three bears will be hospitalized.

You might also wish to note that the latest instructions for bear confrontations have been revised. Now it's, *"Don't* climb a tree." Black bears can scale a 100-foot tree in less than 30 seconds, quicker than a lumberjack and without spiked boots. Grizzlies are less keen about climbing but can pull down the whole goddamn tree. On this general topic, Montanan Tom McGuane said, "The closer you get to Canada, the more things'll eat your horse."

Here is another bear-related datum to which I was

not previously privy: Bears are attracted to formaldehyde. Who cares? The entire Bitterroot Valley cares. Formaldehyde smells like formic acid that ants produce, and bears adore ants. Turns out that countless plastics include formaldehyde: hot-tub covers, bicycle and snowmobile seats, refrigerators, and insulated vinyl siding in all its forms, including Yeti picnic coolers. Hot-tub covers are scattered all over the Bitterroot Forest. Plus, of course, funeral directors pump formaldehyde, so keep an eye peeled during Aunt Betty's interment.

I can't help wanting all of "my" bears to hang out nearby, a terrible impulse. There are reportedly 13,307 black bears in Montana, which seems like a thicket, although North Carolina boasts 20,000. Of the Montanan bears that have become acclimated to doughnuts and pizza, 177 are killed per year, on average. They become an official nuisance, inflicting damage on homes and landscaping but never because they were threatening schoolchildren. In fact, more humans were killed by dogs in just three years than have been killed by black bears in all of recorded history. Or so says the *Living with Bears Handbook,* which I was quick to reference after fleecy Terry leaned on my basement office window as if awaiting a probing tax audit.

America's first environmentalist and all-around hero, John Muir, adored bears. He wrote a sentence that makes me cry every time I read it: "Bears are made of the same dust as we and breathe the same winds and drink the same waters, his life not long, not short, knows no beginning, no ending, to him life unstinted, unplanned, is above the accident of time, and his years, markless, boundless, equal eternity."

Oh, great. Now I'm crying again.

THE OSSIFICATION OF ANTELOPE CHARLEY

Before moving to Darby, I knew trifling little about Montana's history. To wit:

1. On Montana's state flag you will find the Spanish legend *Oro y Plata.* It means "gold and silver" or "the bison were missing before I arrived."

2. In 1870, a fellow named Truman Everts, 54, found himself lost for 37 days in Montana's upper Yellowstone Valley. He was treed by a mountain lion. He ate little but thistle roots, which blocked his bowels. His feet became frostbitten. He sought warmth by sleeping between two hot springs—enveloped in a perpetual steam bath—until he broke through the crust and scalded his thigh. Frozen feet, burned leg.

Then a runaway campfire "crisped the nails of my fingers," as he put it. The conflagration also removed his hair, consumed his lean-to, and pretty much set the entire damn forest ablaze. Mr. Everts weighed 80 pounds when rescued by two recluses who earned a $600 reward. Everts afterward said of Montana's natural wonders, "They had lost all charm for me."

3. In 1894, a cadre of workers in Butte gathered to protest the fed's lack of make-work projects. "Hogan's Army," as it was called, planned to carry their protest to Washington, D.C. To that end, they appropriated a Northern Pacific locomotive, one boxcar, and six coal cars to carry 450 indignant dissenters. They reached Billings, where authorities asked that they kindly return the train to its annoyed owner.

Accidental gunfire ensued, killing a Billings tinsmith standing guiltlessly on the station's platform. When the train was searched, three guns were found. The first was inoperable; the second was a modest squirrel-hunting .22; and the third was made in the 1860s, meaning no cartridges for it existed. That is to say, the defense for all 450 angry men comprised a trio of metal sticks.

Hogan's Army's eventual punishment, as adjudicated by Montana judges, was not to do it again.

4. In 1899, a man named Tom Dunbar was poking the banks of the Missouri River when he discovered a "petrified man" who weighed 365 pounds, his heft owing to being solid rock and all. Extracting this item from the sand required ropes, and, as Dunbar put it, "That's when the left ankle and the great toe got broken off."

Dunbar toured with his "Remarkable Petrified Man" at statewide fairs, befriending a character named "Liver Eating" Johnston. "Liver Eating" claimed the petrified man was in fact his former colleague, Antelope Charley. If true, A.C. had somehow ossified in the span of 25 to 30 years, which is an archaeological/geological record unbroken to this day.

Dunbar eventually lost interest in his faux fossil, storing it in a warehouse in Livingston, after which the calcified gent's whereabouts became a mystery between a rock and a hard face.

5. In 1910, the mining town of Butte overflowed with 275 saloons, which fairly begged prohibition crusader Carry Nation to descend. Armed with an iron rod, an assortment of rocks, and a four-foot cane, Ms. Nation stormed the town's taverns, referring to her action as the "hachetation of Butte."

Approaching the ABC Dance Hall, she faced 1,000 unruly townsfolk defending their chilled evening cocktails.

The bartender raised a towel and shouted, "For God's sake, woman, get out of here."

"I will not," Carry Nation hooted. "It is precisely for God's sake that I came." At which point the ABC's band belted out a song they called *"What the Hell Do We Care?"*

Carry headed for the Windsor Saloon. The owner there, May Malloy, wrestled Ms. Nation into the street, tore her hat from her head, wrenched her arm, then let fly with a powerful kick. Defeated, Carry Nation fled the saloon, the city, the state. *The Livingston Enterprise* noted: "She is welcome to come back and try again. For there is room for improvement here."

6. Prior to World War I, patriotic hysteria swept Montana, fixing suspicion on Judge Charles Crum, who alleged that America was bankrolling duplicitous allies. Montanans then formed the Third Degree Committee to pass judgment on citizens who didn't buy Liberty Bonds, didn't kiss the American flag (as in, actually smooch it), and didn't recite the Pledge of Allegiance multiple times daily. The committee renamed sauerkraut "liberty cabbage" and spelled "German" with a lowercase "g."

Judge Crum was impeached for "high crimes and malfeasance in office," although there was never any evidence of crimes or even sauerkraut.

7. Montana was the last state in the union to be colonized by *Rattus norvegicus*, the Norway rat or common brown rat. That was in 1938. Apparently, a Missoula lab discarded seemingly deceased rats in the dump, whereupon feisty survivors founded a colony noted for immense belt buckles and one-tenth-gallon hats.

That's all I knew about Montana. Well, except for thinking it was awfully pretty.

John Phillips

Honey, This Here's Montana

Darby is a John Ford–style berg that could have hosted Hollywood westerns, complete with a log-built marshal's jail. Yellowstone tourists—both those from the national park and those seeking a glimpse of Kevin Costner in Paramount Network's *Yellowstone*—stop all summer to snap photos and sip draft beer.

One block of Darby has a candy store that also sells antiques, coffee, and faux Turkish lamps. The berg offers two gas stations, one grocery, a general mercantile, a dwarf gym, a yoga studio, a senior center, a tannery / taxidermist, an electronic poker casino the size of a bass boat, and signs forbidding loitering and skateboarding and any contemplation of sin.

There's Hope's Cutting Corral, known for "NASCAR haircuts as quick as a pit stop." Well, less than four minutes, and if there's no chitchat about weather or taxidermy, three. Price: $5 to $12, depending on Hope's mood and whether she judges your hair senior-discount worthy. Hope is a wellspring of domestic reportage, referring to one prickly Darby union as "a marriage made in the ER."

Darby is moreover blessed with two saloons directly

across from each other, serving a tsunami of beer, alcoholism squared. One is called the Sawmill, the other Dotson's, recently renamed the Big Cat, then the Valley Bar, then the 406. As you read this, it will have a new name.

A decade ago, I sat in Dotson's and inquired about the closing time. The bartender—hair piled skyward and resembling Miss Kitty from *Gunsmoke* (no exaggeration), said: "Honey, this here's Montana. Closing time *is* when closing time *is*." She aimed a finger at the stash of liquor behind the bar in a kind of chain-link cage. When the regulars become too insentient to exit bipedally—it happened to Sam Peckinpah—she locks the cage and allows the self-handicapped to bed down in situ.

"Sometimes they're still asleep when I show up the next day," she explained. "So I gotta mop the floors." I hadn't the courage to ask why.

The Sawmill Saloon, incredibly, is open 365 days a year. Who'd want to inhabit a bar on Thanksgiving? Okay, probably I would, so that's a poor example. How about Christmas? Still a bad example. It reminds me of Larry McMurtry's fictional town, where the café never closes, not even on Christmas, and serves as the village's self-managed psychiatry clinic, open for vinous medication and emotional counsel, a perpetual-motion machine.

The Sawmill's bartender once said to me: "Son, find fulfillment in the warmth of life itself—those who promise happiness need you to suffer."

If you drink enough beer at the Sawmill, you'll earn little wooden dollars that can be exchanged for more beer. The "coins" are filthy from potato-chip fingers, spilled suds, and, well, random biological fluids, is my guess. I noticed four tokens on the floor and bequeathed them to a cadaverous fellow smoking butts on the saloon's porch, wondering if more free beer would finish him off. I never saw him again.

The Sawmill's 12 barstools are upholstered in black vinyl. All are ripped. Duct tape has been applied liberally, pieces of which occasionally exit the establishment attached to a patron's ass, earning a round of applause. Behind the bar is a doorway hacked out of the wall, allowing access to the adjacent

Little Blue Joint Café. You can thus savor beer on one side and garlicky pizza on the other. Food can be delivered by the bartender or by patrons who happen to be returning from the men's room. The Sawmill smells like sawdust, mold, stale beer, urinal-cake disinfectant, sweat, hair oil, and gum disease. As western bars go, it is the genuine article. I adore the place and schedule it for all guests.

Dragging Darby at least into the 20th century is our Dollar Store at the north edge of town, directly adjacent to the south edge of town, ha-ha. It is by a span of decades the town's newest structure. At its grand opening, there materialized a semi-spontaneous celebration in the cramped parking lot, motivating neighbor Dennis Bush to string up ropes to keep Dollaristas from cutting across his rent-a-garage property.

You will accuse me of farfetchedness here, but locals turned out as if it were the christening of the Guggenheim. I treated Julie's mom and Aunt Irene to this soirée, whereupon Irene tumbled while U-turning at the end of an aisle. Just-hired Dollar Store clerks swarmed, maybe or maybe not affecting concern. Irene suffered a bloody elbow, so we drove home to drink white wine from a box.

Thereafter, I noticed half the town wearing Dollar Store sweatpants / sweatshirt ensembles that *Vogue* has yet to endorse. I'm not being judgmental. Buying basic clothing previously required a 50-mile Kmart to-and-fro. Well, Mr. T's Mercantile sells a few shirts, though coated in a quarter inch of cracked-corn dust.

After bandaging Aunt Irene's elbow, we happened across another crowd in town, this time hovering before our volunteer fire department. The spectacle? A new scarlet pickup truck with a hose and pump in its bed, the kind of equipment you'd dispatch to a barbecue fire in Palm Springs. But it bore on its doors "Darby Volunteer F.D." in faux gold leaf, and it was as shiny and rubicund as a twice-cooked lobster.

The onlookers clapped as the truck idled down the ramp, still entombed in a plastic condom to protect the chrome. Spectators began shoving, in a fun way, to see who'd rip off the most plastic, all of this to the sound of encouraging hoots and whistles. Have taxpayers in any big city ever celebrated minor fire apparatus? Darby's citizens were elated. I was, too. Not for the truck but for those it had so genuinely delighted. More psychological progress for yours truly.

Julie and I dropped her mom and aunt at the candy store, where it was their custom to lollygag, finger merchandise, and pester the clerk for repeated chocolate lattes. On this occasion, I had delivered them in a gray BMW belonging to *Car and Driver.* After the ladies had caffeinated themselves unto tetchiness, they sauntered outside to climb into a gray SUV parked by the curb. There they sat contentedly until the clerk ventured to inquire why the ladies were occupying her car.

"Waiting to be driven home," said mom-in-law Agnes.

"But I didn't drive you here," said the clerk.

"We know," added Irene. "Our driver is in the gym. He is not reliable."

The clerk walked back inside, allowing them to remain in her car, then explained where I could find them when I returned to the candy store.

In the Bitterroot Valley, Darby is where the rail tracks cease, the southern terminus. The lumber mill closed in 1998, putting 98 people out of work, and the tracks haven't been used since. As such, Darby has devolved into a societal end of the line. Drive south and you'll encounter only woods and mountains and bighorn sheep cooling their gummy hooves in the river.

Wild, unmolested country continues like that for 75 miles, by which time you will enter Salmon, Idaho, which is Sacagawea's birthplace and home of the Fighting Sacs. Darby is your last chance for a Bud Light or a four-minute haircut. Over and out. It is a fact of geography, migration, and misanthropic excommunication that I find irresistible. I reside on the slippery lip of worldly occupation, where the Marlboro Man dispatches rustlers and rattlers with a Colt .45 in one hand and a tube of *Just for Men* hair dye in the other.

Reckless Bidding On Septic Suction

Julie and I attended two ritzy fundraisers in support of our architecturally attractive library. Well, ritzy insofar as the locals were wearing clean boot-cut jeans, four-inch-wide leather belts with ornate silver buckles made in Taos, and custom Stetsons worn three times per year. By the way, those hats, when removed, are supposed to be placed crown *down* by strict cowboy decree but usually are not. Bad luck reportedly pours wraithlike into the hat. Have you seen Bob Dylan wearing his cowboy hat? If so, you'll smirk at such headwear for a lifetime.

In return for the price of a ticket—all proceeds for books—attendees are afforded unlimited access to wines that range from zesty to grape Tang.

"Trace of tarmac," I said to Julie, who was one of the volunteer bartenders. "Hint of burned ant traps; vivid base note of Prestone."

There's also a silent auction, in which one item being sold was a free suction from Patrick's Septic Service. As it happens, I had already employed Irish Patrick, who charges $265 per dredge. So I bid $300, being generous in the name of a ship-shape tank and the library possibly purchasing books unadorned by Batman illustrations. But I was outbid. So I raised the stakes to $350, whereupon someone who possibly owned a septic tank the size of an Olympic pool offered $400. I jammed my checkbook into my hip pocket and was a little huffy until I returned for more Napa Valley Kool-Aid from Julie's station.

As is true of most small towns, Darby thrives on a daily ration of gossip, venom, venality, metaphorical dog bites, actual dog bites, dog whistles, and a salty disdain for anyone who doesn't live in a 30-mile radius.

The residents are often dangerously related in personal, legal, and illegal entanglements. Heidi, my gym trainer, is married to Scott, who refurbished our kitchen, whose best friend, Dave, is my Orvis fishing guide (who also built our knotty-cherry cupboards,) who lives with Corinne, our most outspoken liberal who builds expensive pedibikes used as taxis in equatorial cities and has a tattoo of Hunter Thompson on her back.

I find all of that marvelous. Bedding someone's spouse in Darby is as perilous as buying shrimp from the Texaco station. Any tryst is public knowledge in 24 hours, and if you are carnally guilty, there's no way you could risk a Hope haircut because she would slice off your ears with garden shears and stick them in a toaster.

Something else you should know about Hope: Her body dimensions are Rubenesque, nay, may I say, Dolly Parton–esque. As Hope cuts your hair, she must perforce reach around your cranium, an action that directs one ample bosom into full mashed contact with the customer's shoulder, ear, and jaw. It's like being massaged by a goose-down duvet. Hope doesn't know or care, and I always offer a five-dollar tip. In Darby, such largesse is remembered but also ostentatious.

Here's another local wonderment: The entire town is situated on the west bank of the Bitterroot River. All of it. A single-lane steel bridge from the '30s leads to the eastern side, but the structure is closed to the public because there's not one shred of human occupation on the far side—just a ridiculously steep hillside, sage, rye grass, and an impressive herd of bison owned by Craig Barrett, who seasonally must replace fences the bison relentlessly trample. If you fish in the river and face east only, it's perfectly appropriate to pretend you're Lewis or

Clark eyeing dinner for the Corps of Discovery, because that's certainly what they observed while treading on land mere feet beyond your nose. How wonderful is that? History faithfully popping up in 3-D.

In 1900, a U.S. Forest Service supervisor said of Darby, "It was conceived in iniquity and born in crime." But there's little crime now. I think the inhabitants don't have the energy.

Putative peace is maintained by our law officer, Larry Rose. "Marshal Larry," as he is known to all, became the village's entire police force in 1984 and has held the post since, apparently unchallenged. He displays six gold stars above his breast pocket, signifying some sort of constabulary status that the rest of us do not comprehend. During a town-council meeting, Larry once punched Darby's judge, David Lowery, then handcuffed him.

Since my arrival, Larry has hired a deputy named John Ringer, who evidently was or was not needed but was undeniably controversial. "Not needed" seems to be the consensus, a judgment perhaps applying to Larry as well. Our marshal perceives vast legal encroachments throughout his tours of duty, interspersed with sanguine coffee breaks at the Montana Café. Every pink cell in Larry's face implies he's an enraged Texan longhorn, which cannot be true. He has never treated me badly.

His age is in dispute. Larry is either 69 or 122 years old. He is a wiry terrier, with blondish-gray hair, ever evincing a grimace as if he's just returned from a crime scene that had splattered his gold stars. He can frown not only from ear to ear but from chin to hairline to knees. The man is all tendons and gristle, as if held intact by rubber bands. Larry's cruiser is a white Chevy Traverse SUV with shiny cop paraphernalia, about as intimidating as a Mazda Miata.

The first time I met Larry, he was parked outside Darby's one-room liquor store and was operating a radar speed trap. Julie and I exited the store carrying two clanking cartons of wine, which I mention because Marshal Larry is professionally On the Wagon, having earlier in life allegedly associated himself somewhat earnestly with spirits, applying both dedication and authority to the job.

I lowered my box of wine, leaned through the prowler's passenger window, and said, "Marshal Rose, I'm John Phillips, and I've just moved to Darby. I live way up the mountain—I imagine we'll see you patrolling."

Marshal Larry stared in silence far longer than was polite, then said, "I don't never go up there. Never." And when Larry repeats a word, that marks a conversational denouement, as I would soon learn.

Marshal Larry once stopped David Letterman for speeding through our happy hamlet. Letterman was incensed and referred to the matter during one of his TV monologues. Turns out, Letterman had been scouting the Bitterroots as a retirement destination, but after encountering Larry, he wrote off all of southwestern Montana in favor of Choteau, east of Glacier National Park, whose chief attraction was 200 miles of separation from Darby.

Whereupon, if you'll bear with me for a minute, drama ensued. Namely, a bear broke into Letterman's kitchen. How big was the bear? "It was the biggest bear I've ever seen in my kitchen," Letterman reported to any Montanan who would listen, which was all of us. The animal loitered for five hours, eventually falling asleep in a guest bedroom. Letterman tossed firecrackers, which affected the bear not so much as the carpet. After his siesta, the bear ambled casually through an open door, onto the deck, and toward Glacier.

The trauma to the kitchen "was on the border of inestimable," Letterman reported. For one thing, the bear had pulled out drawers, then twisted them to ensure future uselessness. Julie was principally tickled that the bear had eaten a bowl of peaches, then "spat the pits into the dog's dish," or so claimed Dave. Here's what humorist Jack Handey had to say about the matter: "If you get attacked by a bear and survive, see if you can't get attacked by another bear, because then maybe you could get the nickname 'Two Bears.' "

Two bears? I'm already pals with seven.

Come Back With a Warrant

Marshal Larry has long posited a metaphorical burr under Darby's Sergio Leone–themed saddle. For one thing, his age and cowboy boots suggest that any youthful perp might successfully flee with one leg jammed into a stolen sack of potatoes. Larry is a man of few words. Possibly 20 or so. He has already embroiled himself in some sort of caustic domestic dispute, with the perp shot dead. He then dunked the town into a festering pool of rage after installing 16 video cameras along Darby's main drag. I am ambivalent about this surveillance and wonder if Darbrarians grasp cameras' ubiquity in the outside world. In any case, a few citizens wouldn't mind introducing Larry to a Grape-Nuts enema, in part because we already enjoy safeguard from the Ravalli County Sheriff and state Highway Patrol, although I'll admit they appear more on a seasonal basis than Larry.

Darby is infamous state-wide as a speed trap, so Letterman was a bozo to test Larry's omnipotence, which was underscored when one of his secret video cameras solved a crime. To wit: The owners of our local gym, called the Right to Bare Arms, arrived at their establishment one morn to discover an immense front window blown to shards. They summoned Larry, who applied forensic cunning in the fashion of Lieutenant

Columbo, observing that the gym's gravel driveway had been disrupted by a fishtailing car. Larry theorized that the perp had spun his car 360 degrees in the dead of night, pitching stones like fastballs, perhaps never intending to inflict damage.

Larry promised to "study the tapes," and that's how he deduced that the criminal in question was—oh, yes—a young relative. The boy self-reported to the gym, crying in great heaving bursts, sobbing so earnestly that Heidi, the gym owner / manager, hugged him in shared grief, and they worked out a payment plan on the spot, all thanks to a few inches of 3M videotape.

So maybe Larry has latched onto something clever here, but I am alone in that supposition. In fact, he went on to install a secret camera in a flower barrel in front of the jail. Kids on the sidewalk jammed pebbles into the peephole. "But I catch 'em," Larry noted in a newspaper interview, which gives you an idea of the cunning criminality with which the town must deal.

Otherwise, Darby doesn't offer much chance to erect crime-scene tape. Stroll into the gym, for instance, and you'll observe on the front desk members' phones, car keys, wallets, wristwatches, necklaces, ID cards, and, in one case, a money clip containing a sheaf of presidents. You will also find fresh eggs. Just open an Igloo cooler, withdraw a dozen, and insert two dollars on the honor system. On a subzero day, the gym owner asked if I'd be so gentlemanly as to warm up her truck. "Of course," I said. "Hand me the keys." She replied, "They're in the ignition." (In four other cars', too.)

In Hamilton, 25 miles north, there's a hardware store housed in two buildings. The store that sells the lag bolts and hacksaws is separated from the store that sells the downspouts and rattraps. So, you sometimes walk with your purchases from Building #1—without paying—to Building #2, where the final sale is effected. The owner trusts you, with arms full of C-clamps and half-inch sockets, even as you stroll past your own automobile.

I asked how many customers had driven off. "A couple, I guess," said the clerk. "An old woman did once, but she swore she'd just forgotten, so we let it go."

How charming is that?

If there's a misdemeanor in Darby, the perp is "hard gossiped," as it's locally described, then is interrogated, shown incriminating tapes, introduced to creationism, and threatened with incarceration in a jail the size of a dog crate.

Suspicious activity is closely monitored, including an organized annual mass "hike" through town, in which 30 or so residents traipse in a knot along byways and alleys, provoking dogs into a group howl. The hikers resemble urban gangsters with only mud for club colors.

All of this raised Marshal Larry's internal threat level to Fifth Column Extreme. Red-faced and deeply unhappy, he commenced hovering, a tactic probably not taught in the police academy. If it was his idea to arrest someone, Julie was out of the question, because she can run.

Historically speaking, Darby once had the suggestion of crime. One resident, who reportedly provokes the constabulary at every turn, installed a professionally penned plaque on his door. It said, "Come back with a warrant."

What's more, in 1945, there existed an infamous recluse in the nearby foothills, whom locals called the "Ridgerunner." Mr. RR was a rough and stinky piece of work. To stay alive, he broke into unoccupied cabins and devoured canned leftovers, leaving the place looking as if bears had thrown a kegger for Smokey. This continued until the locals grew weary of restocking baked beans. The RR was thus captured, tried, and sentenced to 90 days. On his release, he immediately invaded another cabin and fogged the place with flatulence.

His real name was Bill Moreland—a wild man living alone in a wild country for 24 years, a professional seeker of loneliness. Moreland's story reminded me of the oft-gored bullfighter Antonio Barrera, who said of dedication to lost causes, "You've got to put all your meat on the grill."

It was in June that *Car and Driver* shipped out a $100,000 Range Rover for me to write about and for them to photograph in my backyard. Also dispatched: a video crew, a photographer plus assistant, a spare driver, and two hangers-on whose purpose was apparently alcoholic in nature.

When this unwieldy group flocked to refuel at our local Cenex station—directly across from the jail—Marshal Larry materialized at the nearest pump, hovering instead of pumping. So I explained our purpose, which he accepted as if I were reciting the finer points of Gravitational Crapularity in correlation to the Sierpinski Triangle Theory.

I then persuaded Larry to pretend to arrest me at the wheel of the costly Range Rover, his cop car parked directly behind, red-and-blue takedown lights strobing. Larry was surprisingly agreeable. It is the magazine's custom to thank civilians who assist our photo shoots, so gofer "Bobcat" Beard proffered a *C/D* baseball cap.

Larry studied the hat as if it were a June bug in his Jell-O, then said, "I don't wear no hat."

Bobcat replied, "Well, that's okay. I'll give you a couple you can hand to kids."

Larry replied, "I don't wear no hat."

I jumped to Bobcat's assistance.

"These are the real deal, Marshal, $30 apiece," I informed. "Silk stitching, the works."

Third time: "I don't wear no hat."

We all drove away.

God On Double Kettledrums

Russ Wildey, the husband of our real-estate agent, was raised in Darby in the 1940s, when few of the town's streets were paved. Russ is a true mountain man but the antithesis of Grizzly Adams: he is skinny, zero body fat, with fine but thinning black hair. He grew up in a cabin on the south side of town—no electricity, no plumbing, tons of wood to be chopped, no TV, only the Bible to read, little fun. For entertainment on weekends, Russ and a pal would tow an upside-down automobile hood behind a dissolute Ford. They'd tear down Darby's main drag, one man driving while the other rode the inverted hood as if surfing. "You shoulda seen the sparks," Russ told me. No one discouraged this pastime.

Today Russ says little and is rail thin, although Montana rails usually aren't, and his spine has been kinked, coiled, and twirled by years of jostling on the steel seat of a bouncing excavator. Russ knows everything about the Bitterroot Valley. For instance, as a kid he watched Yellowstone elk being unloaded from railroad boxcars at the north end of town. "I couldn't understand why they were here," he said. When I later told a couple hunters that the elk they were exterminating were imported, they howled and slapped their thighs and began talking about me in the third person.

In his teens, Russ endured a couple winters that nearly extinguished him, so the climate in the Bitterroot Valley is for him not exactly Montana's "Banana Belt," as it is known statewide. That nickname, in any event, is a misnomer because there's minimal humidity here. Darby lingers in the Bitterroot Mountains' rain shadow, so dry that Julie and I perform a lubricating eyedrop routine every morn. We both contracted conjunctivitis in our first month in Montana, our eyes raw and as crosshatched as road maps.

Here the first snow of the season tends to remain until a succeeding season, not necessarily spring. Our snow doesn't morph into that cheerless cement that typifies the Midwest's miserably monochromatic winters, although if you were to look carefully at snow—I did, for the first time—you'd notice it's generally a reflective wash of the sky: gray, pink in the evenings, but often as not a sullied shade of blue.

In 1868, a Bitterrooter named John Owen wrote in his journal: "The first days in January govern the remainder of the winter—well, if so, we will have a mild, open winter, for the past three days have been quite soft and mild." A week passed, and Mr. Owen's next entry read: "Jan. 10. So cold in fact that grown chickens tumble over frozen stiff in daytime."

The "bright lights" of diffident Hamilton are but 25 miles distant, yet July is the only month in which the town has never recorded a frost. Which is no big deal if you happen to live in Loma, Montana, population 92, where the temperature in 1972 bolted from 54 degrees below zero to 49 above in 24 hours. It was the most extreme variation ever recorded in the U.S., a meteorological Wall Street collapse and rebound, and Lomans are proud of it—well, those yet with ears.

In the Bitterroot Valley, June in its entirety is yet spring and presents its own cold weather phenomenon: an otherworldly frosty mist that descends and thickens until you want to swipe at it with a broom. There's still plenty of sunlight, and sunglasses are mandatory, but the sunlight diffuses into a visual equilibrium in which nothing casts a shadow. Locals call it "gray light," and I've encountered it before, during an assignment at the Eureka Weather Station on frozen Ellesmere

Island. The Bitterroot gray light undercuts three-dimensional clues. Items on the ground that formerly possessed width and depth become nominally two-dimensional or, more precisely, not dimensional at all. Ruts and depressions appear identical to mounds and inclines. Tire tracks recede, and you navigate via the estimated distance to mailboxes on the left and barbed wire on the right. One mile from my house, while driving at two mph, I had to exit the truck to locate anything approximating a thoroughfare.

Days later, at that same point, I encountered Julie driving the opposite direction. We parked side by side to talk, at which moment her truck began inching laterally toward mine, both vehicles squirming on ice hidden beneath an inch of slush. It was like being caught in an undertow, and there was nothing to do but accelerate away from each other or suffer a door-to-door collision. Anyone watching would have assumed we'd had a nasty argument.

As warmer weather rolled in, Julie and I attended the Darby Rodeo—yes, it was my first rodeo—where the highlight didn't involve bull riding so much as a lightning strike on the metal grandstands. It sent one cowboy and two spectators to the ER with smoking tailbones.

Darbrarians adore their rodeos, but the afflicted folk in the grandstands cleared out as if set upon by Honduran bees. The thunder echoed for about 20 minutes, I'd say. Julie said not. Thunder becomes trapped in our valley between the two parallel mountain ranges—the Bitterroots and the Sapphires—creating a unique paradiddle *boom-zzzzxxxik-POW*, God on double kettledrums. One local described it as "imperative groin thunder," and it makes you want to seek a bunker.

All summer the valley lightning continued in blue-white SS zigzags. In one instance, 45 cattle on a Darby ranch were dispatched by a single empyrean bolt, followed by thunder that surely bent flatware.

At first, I doubted the news reports. I mean, 45 animals in one forked wallop? Then Julie bought a copy of our local *Ravalli Republic*, and there it was. I assumed the cattle concluded their sedentary lives as tasty ribeyes, but, no, the luckless beasts were all bulldozed into a pit. Apparently, death by lightning causes cattle to excrete something—and I'm pretty sure I would, too—that imbues the meat with an astringent taste that even puckers the lips of Met flugelhornists.

The lightning wasn't finished with us. South of Darby, on the berm of Highway 93, stands an ancient ponderosa that the Salish revered in Lewis and Clark days. The trunk of this particular pine had scooped up, then grown around, the skull of a bighorn ram, curlicue horns and all. The Salish thus deemed it magic, a Medicine Tree, and used it as an unlicensed pharmacy. They'd strip the bark to eat the vanilla-scented cambium, which perhaps explains why the forest behind my house occasionally smells of sugary confection.

It couldn't have been particularly healthy for the Medicine Tree, yet it survived two centuries near the riverbank until it was likewise felled by lightning, more or less upon my arrival in Montana. Thirty feet of the limbless trunk yet stands, with odd consecrations attached: ribbons around its girth, bottles and coins at its base, and spray-painted verses for "Sally 69." Whether the now lifeless tree yet stimulates some sort of spiritual comportment I could not say, but it reportedly helped the Salish learn to seek wisdom without looking within themselves. I thus stood with my spine against the tree one day, rubbing my shoulder blades across its splintery base, hoping for osmosis or even one original thought.

You know what else semiregularly flings itself from the firmament here? Airplanes. Yesterday, a Beechcraft Bonanza plowed a dandy trench through a field not far from where it briefly achieved 1,000 feet of flight. A different aircraft executed an emergency landing on Highway 93 just north of Darby, causing a traffic snarl involving as many as three cars. A Glasair crashed on the nearby West Fork Road, busting all four legs of the occupants.

Then there was a crash just south of our house, on the apron of Trapper Peak and across from the Forest Service's game-check station. In that accident, two men demolished a rickety chrome-yellow Aeronca Champ while attempting to land in a hayfield during a storm. There was, unfortunately, an unseen ditch to overcome, plus they landed in the manner of an anvil auguring through the bottom of a canoe. Both wings collapsed, wingtips scratching at the ground in a forlorn frown. The two passengers were likewise forlorn and spurting blood, occasioning an airlift to Denver. I must say if it had been me right then, I'd have declined a second flight. One of the flyboys lived on the West Fork, a few miles from here, and we never heard from him again.

We drove out to view the wreckage and encountered Marshal Larry contentedly parked alongside, and I could tell he wished he possessed a bullhorn and crime-scene tape the same color as the ruined Aeronca.

He said, "Git on, nothing to see."

I responded, "Sweet baby Jesus, Larry, there's a *lot* to see, so just give me a minute." He did. I keep hoping to get mad at Larry, then he responds with courteous decency.

Have you ever noticed that, after an airplane crash, there's inevitably someone who says, "I was supposed to be on that flight"? In this case, it was our neighbor Carol Batcher, an intended ride-along sightseer. Like Sky King, she has since ceased inspecting our mountain majesties from on high, at least in aircraft made from masking tape and Elmer's glue.

And then Darbrarians John and Cherril Longhurst, along with dog Darby, were killed in the crash of their Cessna 182 Skylane. The craft apparently stalled on takeoff. John was a fellow fly-fisherman who lived up Tin Cup Creek—which, by the way, is hereabouts pronounced "crick." Always.

In any event, we felt consoled that additional dogs named Darby yet survive in Darby and their owners are not pilots. I am right now studying textbooks to pass the FAA exam for private pilots, mostly for the intellectual challenge, I think. But I am told that flying between two parallel mountain ranges presents a piñata of meteorological deceptions, hoaxes, and tragic traps that will snuff my life if I so much as sneeze at the rudders.

Right about then, Darbrarians further delighted in a car chase. It involved a confused young fellow, freshly released from "psychological maintenance," who pilfered an ambulance in front of the Hamilton hospital. He made a run for Idaho, expecting sanctuary and baked potatoes, arrowing through Darby at a speed that interested Marshal Larry, who may or may not have joined the pursuit—stories vary—although he would have been chasing a diesel-powered, 7,000-pound meat wagon and I think the capture probably rang hollow.

It occurred to me that the perp might have registered only two or three degrees beyond me—or below me?—on the international scale of mental bustification. The insanity that I'd expressed during a career of subtle intraoffice and anti-girlfriend aggression was societally okey-dokey. But if I'd swiped an ambulance, no, sir. Isn't that a little odd? I'd trampled feelings and wrought damage. Whereas the perp hadn't even damaged the ambulance.

I love everyone in Darby. Almost everyone.

Half of them.

Kevin Costner Eats Pop Tarts

Years before relocating to Montana, I came across an unofficial and ill-informed website touting the Bitterroot Valley. Since taken down, the site claimed that the median household income was $25,000 to $27,000 and that 24 percent of the population sustained life below the poverty line. Our real estate agent told me that, on graduation from high school, most Bitterroot Valley kids flee like crabs evading a tidal bore. "As in *all* of them," she added, "because you can't be a lumberjack anymore."

It reminded me of writer Ian Frazier (*Great Plains,* and also a not-too-distant neighbor), who said: "What's hard about small towns is that, if you grow up in one, you have to leave when the growing up is through. You will never know another place as well, just the way you'll never get another language fixed as intricately in your heart. But for some reason you feel invisible if you keep on living in the town."

The amateurish website touted other oddments: 91 percent of Darby's occupants were said to be white. Zero percent black. Zero percent gay. Zero percent lesbian. Zero percent transgender. Zero percent Native American. Which, according to my math, left nine percent unlabeled.

Julie said, "Well, two percent alcoholics, two percent meth cooks, four percent itinerant fly-fishermen, and one percent fugitives."

As a matter of fact, out on the East Fork Road, there's an entire ragtag gulag of cabins and trailers called "Felony Flats." Also missing from the census were our so-called leather tramps (nomads who walk) and rubber tramps (nomads who hitchhike). I haven't heard anyone use the term "tramp" in 40 years, but I learned that the rubber versions refer to themselves as "Rainbow People." They glide meekly through the valley in the summer—through "Trampton"—hoping for free "Trampagne" or lite beer. No one knows where they're headed. They are much reviled because they affect hippie-ishness, loiter at Mr. T's for the air conditioning, and use various small businesses' toilets. Worse, their hair often appears to have mopped up a petroleum spill. But I've never heard of a Rainbow Person doing Darby the slightest mischief. They arrive. They stand inert. Like mayflies, they disappear overnight.

Paradoxically, anti-hippie Darby has performed a hippie-ish deed. A fire ravaged a small business on Main Street—before my arrival, so don't look at me—leaving a missing tooth in our west-side storefront lineup. If you saunter through what once was the entrance, you'll now find yourself in a "pocket park," as I'm told it's called. Pocket, indeed, maybe twice the size of my garage and similar, inasmuch as it's all concrete—left wall, right wall, floor. Nothing to lighten the "architecture" but a few worrisome cracks. It resembles a place where you'd exercise prisoners.

Because Sacajawea tromped through what is now Darby—twice, with Lewis and Clark peppering her with rhetorical questions—our prison of a park's centerpiece is a $10,000 bronze statue of "the Sac," as we call her, carrying infant son Jean Baptiste Charbonneau, nicknamed "Pompy" by the Corps of Discovery. Our Bandit Brewery contributed to the purchase, thanks to Mayor McDowell. It was a princely gesture that only locals will appreciate and even know about. I said something similar when Walt Disney began building his second amusement park.

For some reason, I'd like to sit in the park and sip a pint

of Pendleton wrapped in a wrinkled paper bag, purchased from Robin at the liquor store 40 feet distant. Of course, as rebellious gestures go, functional alcoholism emerges low on Sacajawea's totem pole, and I say that because I recently learned that pretty much the entirety of Rye Creek Gulch—just over the top of the mountains to the east—has been so enthusiastically cultivating marijuana that Willie Nelson has turned his bus in our direction. Marshal Larry, if you are reading this, just look away. Not your jurisdiction.

Darby is so fetching that the 1989 film *Disorganized Crime*—starring Fred Gwynne, Lou Diamond Phillips, and Hoyt Axton—was filmed here. Yes, indeedy, my friends. You will see our damnably cute bridge and our insanely scenic riverfront. Hoyt Axton so attached himself to Darby that he bought a nearby ranch and growled around the premises for the remainder of his days. I think that's actually true, but I heard it in the barbershop, so you might take a personal stab at the facts. The movie made a dashing beeline to the darkest corner of nowhere, with Siskel and Ebert awarding it not just twin thumbs down but a rare "thumbs amputated," referring to it as "slapstick and cornball barnyard humor." I recommended it to Netflix, a request that went straight to their "Probably Never" bin.

Darby shares another Hollywood connection. As I write this, Kevin Costner and Paramount's film crew—throngs and multitudes of them, running hither and yon carrying tons of unidentifiable lights and tripods—have rolled into Darby, 700 yards as a motivated crow might fly from our house and 440 feet below, in what is called Chief Joseph Ranch. They're filming a TV series called *Yellowstone* even though the actual park is 100 miles away and plays no role, typical Hollywood bloviated misdirection.

There's an old ranch house subbing as the Dutton homestead, with Costner portraying the rapaciously amoral patriarch. The house is a state historical site, in fact, although owned privately by a couple who have fled to a condo in Missoula. The ranch includes a monster barn with a copper roof that sparkles and refracts like one of those biblical illustrations of God casting healing sun rays. Then somebody tore off the roof.

The man who previously owned this ranch also owned the land on which my home rests today. But when Julie and I ambled down to investigate Mr. Costner's wardrobe trailer, we were blocked at the gate by a sour Paramount security guard tucked beneath a blue tent where he was vetting credentials and eating Doritos. I wanted to show him my credentials, namely, the four square feet of my roof visible on the mountainside above scenes being shot right then, with 50 or so of our chirping elk posing as unpaid walk-ons. But he was celebrating newfound authority, always a reason for citizens to back off until his ego collided with on-the-job tedium and minimum-wage dining.

There were smallish forest fires that day, and the mountains were occluded by rust-colored plumes. I wondered whether Costner would fly home (via private jets departing daily from Hamilton to Burbank) denying that southwest Montana was a festival of rugged terrain and icy peaks, but then I realized that if he wished to view craggy prominences, Paramount's set builders would construct them out of papier-mâché and Popsicle sticks. Those workers were already hanging klieg lights to the tip of a crane and illuminating the June night as if a theme park were aborning, keeping my gym instructor awake.

The movie moguls further wished to film the façade of Hope's barber shop for a scene. But when they refused to reimburse Hope for ten missed haircuts, she told them to assume an anatomically unlikely yoga position rarely taught in gyms. Paramount then erected a 30-foot-tall, back-illuminated scrim to brighten the entrance to our feed store so that TV viewers would not have to endure a cloudy day that was, for those of us living here, a meteorological reality. But who wants reality? If Paramount had produced the trailer for Melville's greatest work, they'd have described it thus: "Sailors chase Dick all over the world."

The casting director advertised for extras, and Julie applied. The tryouts were at nine a.m. in Hamilton, 25 miles north, at the only decent motel within a largish radius of everywhere. I think Paramount scheduled the early interview to weed out hangover victims, slackers, and churchgoers.

When Julie arrived, she was the 97th person already in line. Eventually, there would be a thousand standing in a restless queue that snaked around the parking lot. She was handed a tag that read, "#97." I asked if they had affixed it to her ear.

She waited alongside her friend Carin Kiphart, who'd brought her résumé. My understanding was that the chosen *Yellowstone* walk-ons would be judged only by their ability to stride in a straight line while never under any circumstances or conditions, even in the event of an earthquake or tragic fire, to so much as *glance* at Mr. Costner. For this skill, walk-ons would be paid $101 per day. Why not an even $100? No one knows.

When Carin handed the talent scout her résumé, he said, "What's this?" then added, "Well, just hold onto that."

Eventually, Costner proved amiable. Our neighbor cornered him in the Conner crafts store, where he stood patiently for selfies. Ditto the ladies in our Montana Café. Jesse, who manages People's Market, observed Costner four times as he shopped for cherry licorice whips and Pop-Tarts, viewing the actor with indifference until sufficient interest was expressed that Jesse offered up the store's security tapes.

Then the locals learned that Costner couldn't reserve a bed at Triple Creek Ranch, even for rolling-rich screen supernovas. Speculation suggested that "K.C.," as we started calling him, was stashed either in Hamilton's Stock Farm (a gated community, like Heaven), or in one of the 50 rolling RVs that the film crew had parked in Darby's little Logger Days park. We were barred from door-to-dooring in our own park, of course.

What's more, the speed limit, extending 1.5 miles south of Darby, was reduced from 70 mph to 35—here again, Tinsel Town's influence surpassing any municipal government's. I sought Marshal Larry for an explanation but found only Dave of Bitterroot Glass replacing a windshield. So I contented myself by gossiping with Dave, knowing full well that windshield services are so frequently mandatory that it is wise to bestow the boy with rodeo tickets and candy-store gift cards, while leaving new speed limits to professional producers and directors who know what they're doing.

In fact, I have bumped man fists with Hollywood before. For a writing assignment, I observed a film crew shoot a TV commercial for GMC pickup trucks on land they'd rented along Big Sur. Their budget was a million dollars per day. The shoot required a dozen 18-wheel trucks, 120 employees, 12 identical GMC pickups (in case one attracted dust, I guess), a rolling cafeteria, and a trained dog who was to sit in front of a truck and look endearing. You will doubt me, but I am telling you with hand on heart that this film crew had also hired a stunt-double dog in case Dog #1 became irritable or suffered from spontaneous mange, in which case Dog #2 was tanned and Alpo-refreshed.

I asked if I could photograph the canine stars. "Not with a flash," warned the trainer. "Can I pet him?" I asked. "No," came the reply. "He's resting."

I mention the Big Sur commercial because Hollywood productions require the kind of waiting around known only to hungry Soviet-era peasants queuing for hardtack. The loitering to film-action ratio is easily 100:1. I warned Julie. "I'll take a book," she declared. After her investment in Project Walk-On, she was not selected, and we still cannot stroll over to Costner's RV to ask for a cup of sugar or cocaine. But the rumor is that he holds fondness for Darby and has secured a three-year lease on the Chief Joseph Ranch. There were even rumors he was house hunting, but Hope the barber proclaimed this to be the most odiferous of bovine pasture pies.

Darby devolved into a beer-fueled shindig when the *Yellowstone* crew closed Main Street one day. They were filming inside Bill's liquor store, with Bill sitting not behind his own counter but in the Sawmill Saloon, observing the action from a suds-smeared table by the window.

An actor played the part of Bill, which struck me as unnecessary because Bill is hugely experienced as the clerk in Bill's liquor store. But Paramount must not have desired a trace of reality, because they also removed Bill's street-side sign to erect another proclaiming, "Big Belt Liquors."

"After they leave, I'm gonna check the whole bourbon inventory," Bill told me. "You bet your ass."

I shall indulge no more Costner tattling save this: The man himself strolled into Darby's antique store, accompanied by two handlers whose job was to keep the touchy-feelies at bay. Costner became fixated on a cut-glass doorknob but was skeptical of its $200 price. He asked our neighbor, Jody Smith, to explain. "Well, it's handmade," Jody said, "and 150 years old."

"Well, I really like it," replied K.C.

"Are you kidding?" asked Handler #1.

"Have you lost your freakin' mind?" said Handler #2.

Costner looked like a spanked puppy and returned the doorknob to its shelf. Let me ask you: Would *Bull Durham's* Crash Davis have shown a backbone so feeble and flimsy? Hell, this is Darby, son, where big plums and big doorknobs are as obligatory as pearl-handled pistols and secret video cameras mounted in flower pots.

Now Darbrarians say, "Oh, I don't give a shit about movieland," and that includes Jessie at the grocery, the clerk at Mr. T's (who took in $4000 on a single day from the Paramount best boys), a Blue Joint waitress, Gene at the junkyard, the other Gene at the candy store, and, of course, my beloved Hope.

I am proud of them. Where else can you watch, first, an Oscar winner eating red licorice, and, second, cops ticketing famous talk-show hosts while small planes fall out of the sky?

WEE PURPLE DANGLERS

Montanans should seek counseling for huckleberry addiction. What we're talking about is a berry closely related to the blueberry but sweeter in a nutty way and, as they say here, "More gushier." In almost any Bitterroot store, you'll find huckleberry jam, syrup, soap, macaroons, honey, muffins, cobbler, pies, ice cream, and, for all I know, huckleberry hydraulic fluid. What you won't find is fresh hucks, because the little bastards are so fragile and opposed to being touched that they clump into a morass of violet gloppola if left to their own devices. Here's another reason you rarely find them in a virginal state: They fetch at least $15 per pound. I once tried to buy a dime bag.

Huckleberries are their own snipe hunt, confounding to locate, although the foothills are reportedly lousy with them. They'll grow only in sunny glades between 3,500 and 7,200 feet. They prefer nesting in avalanche chutes, old clear-cuts, and burned pastures, although they are slow to do any of that, requiring 15 to 20 years to establish themselves as responsible adults.

Huckleberries adore verticality, which has the benefit of dissuading bears and maiming most humans. They are masters of camouflage, growing only six to twelve inches in height.

Veteran Montana pickers claim to hunt hucks by smell. That sounds apocryphal, but, of course, it's how the bears find them, too. Huckleberry hounds warn that bear spray is as vital to this endeavor as a plastic bucket, and if a bear approaches, you offer His Blackness the sum total of that day's pickings and a mumbled, *"Bon appétit,"* then trot elsewhere. Do not run or the bear will consider you a shoplifter.

Not long ago, a woman employed by U.S. Fish and Wildlife was attacked not far from here, and she was a bear expert, performing a genetic study. As the bear pummeled her head, using all manner of illegal Fight Club tactics, the woman reached for her spray and—here we go again—blasted her own eyeballs. Every canister I've examined is fitted with a nozzle that, for ergonomic reasons inexplicable, closely resembles its handle. You know, if EMTs were shocked 50 percent of the time they applied defibrillation anodes, they'd request a redesign. It's impossible to consult bear-spray directions as Big Black lumbers toward you like a runaway Lincoln limo.

Anyway, Julie and I were impatient to locate our own hucks but didn't know how, inasmuch as locals never divulge berry locations, not even to family members with terminal dementia. So we sweet-talked Heidi Kaminski, my gym trainer, into confessing, "Just the general area where a person might look, if he or she were persons similar to us," and Heidi coughed up some vague coordinates.

We drove as far west as Tin Cup Road would allow, turned left toward a trail head, and parked at the foot of a mountain. Across the valley, we could see the roof of our own house, an angled green glint. It appeared to be the size of a garden shed. Then we hiked a half mile until the steepness made me cry, and that's when I spotted the devious little pixies—maybe 75 on a bush five feet tall, which was a miracle because it meant I'd not be kneeling on arthritic knees.

Julie and I ransacked the bush. Besieged it. Berry-free in two minutes. We stuffed the bounty into plastic jugs attached to our belts and also into our faces, creating Tammy Faye's lipstick look. We walked higher until we acquired a second bush that was bent with the weight of the wee purple danglers. The mother lode. And it was another stand-up routine, thanks very much, a miracle on the order of squeezable cheese.

Our hands, I guessed, were permanently stained with berry blood, although in Montana that would be a stain of honor. My bluejeans, for sure, were splotched a far deeper shade, courtesy of *Vaccinium membranaceum*, which must be the least appetizing name for a berry so appetizing. We noticed that the top of a nearby bush had been curiously lopped as if by a wood chipper, and Julie said, "I think a bear did that." I thought so, too, so we moved on.

I later read in a book called *Bear Attacks* that grizzlies, during peak feeding, can consume 200,000 berries per day. This stat was calculated by an actual living person who followed the bear and dutifully counted seeds every time the beast defecated, which was often and also a job for which the statistician should have earned more than minimum wage.

But who cares about bears when you're rollicking in huckleberry heaven? At that altitude, the air was cool. No sweating. By four p.m., we'd amassed eight quarts of berries. It was unheard of. Two rookie pickers, maybe three hours' work, and a two-gallon harvest? We were ecstatic and a little sick. It was more evidence of our putative Montanan-ness. If we were stopped by cops on the way home, the fix was simple:

Me: "Sorry for the speed, Officer, but I'm packing hucks. An hour old."

Officer Bladdergutz: "Hand over a quart and none of this ever happened."

Back home, we spent two hours cleaning our haul. Berries directly from the field are a carnival of extraneous leaves and dried-up ants and the occasional rock, which can spoil your huckleberry experience to some extent. We separated them into eight Ziploc bags—not the correct method of preserving them, by the way—and stuffed four in the freezer.

As a reward for Heidi's directions, we presented her with one quart. She was puzzled, which I construed as grateful astonishment. She sprinkled berries onto the gym's reception desk and tentatively popped one in her mouth. "Nice," she said, "but did you find any huckleberries?"

"*What?*" I said, because I am quick with droll rejoinders.

"What you've collected here are serviceberries," Heidi explained. "Or Juneberries. Sometimes called shadberries. Saskatoon berries, if you're Canadian."

I wanted to slap her. We'd already eaten a pint of the goddamn things. They could have been castor-oil beans, for all we knew, and we would have been dead or, at a minimum, sitting for hours on the toilet. So we were thrust back to rookie status in a matter of seconds. It was mortifying until we contented ourselves with a serviceberry pie, Juneberry jam, shadberry cobbler, and Saskatoon smoothies. All superb. Your basic serviceberry in Montana is viewed with disdain, the huckleberry's feckless cousin with parole officer in tow. But it was the tastiest berry I've ever picked.

I pleaded with Heidi not to reveal our harvesting naïveté to gymsters, who would wet their pants on the stair stepper. She told everyone. Many weightlifters wore fat leather belts to contain their hysterics. Next year, I may cough up sixty dollars and covertly buy a gallon of the little hucking sonsofbitches and imply we picked them. Save time. Failing that, I'll spray-paint serviceberries until they're the correct color and disallow Heidi any sort of taste test. Tell her I'd have delivered more but we were robbed at bearpoint.

I doubt I'll do any of that.

A SCRATCHING POST FOR BOBCATS

As the last of the snow was melting, six men hunting wolves drove their Chevrolet Suburban off the two-track that leads to our favorite campground, called Paradise, which right then wasn't. Their truck flipped after colliding with a mini avalanche—that's what the tire tracks indicated—then splashed into the Selway River, which was running at about nine feet of flabbergasting flood stage. Four of the six men were swept like worms over Rainbow Falls. Only a boot was found. The river was whooshing along so alarmingly that the would-be rescuers couldn't retrieve the Suburban for two days, even though it sat six feet from shore. It took the sheriff seven hours merely to arrive at the scene; the site is but 20 miles west of my home, yet to drive there is usually a two-and-a-half-hour jaunt, except when there's snow, which there was. Nor could rescuers cross the river to search the far side for corpses. So two helicopters were summoned, as were cadaver dogs and at least a dozen rescue specialists.

Their search meant standing on the riverbank, kicking dirt, and wondering how many miles the bodies had already traveled. The sheriff mentioned that the missing men would have to decompose until their chest cavities filled with gas, then they'd float and maybe summertime rafters would find a quartet of grisly carcasses that spoiled their vacations but supplied a vivid tale for a lifetime. But the sheriff doubted even that would happen. He reckoned the bodies were permanently trapped underwater against logjams—"postage-stamped" is the term used here—and that there'd never be anything of substance to ship home for burial. Forgive me if this is indelicate, but brown trout are carnivorous. Brown trout eat other brown trout. Also mice. Also anything that wiggles, including fish being retrieved by an Orvis rod. Little freshwater sharks is what they are.

The search-and-rescue vets loitered at the scene for two days, then drove home. The New York relatives of two of the victims were indignant that officials had so blithely thrown in a wet towel.

The sheriff tried to explain that this wasn't a burbling stream meandering through Central Park, that it was "as remote as Siberia." The relatives nonetheless demanded that grappling hooks be thrown. The sheriff patiently informed that hooks might never even hit the bottom, given the hellish current, and might instead pull the thrower to his grave. One month later, a lone victim was found. He was 43 miles downstream.

Excuse me, but heavily armed men from New York came here to kill our wolves? Would it be indecorous to mention how intergalactically shabby that is? But I came to realize that Darbrarians accept outdoors mayhem with equanimity, and it induced me to drive 25 miles to Hamilton, our county seat, to talk to the Ravalli County Search & Rescue team.

Turns out that a gentleman had recently driven his vehicle off the curlicued Skalkaho Pass to descend—far from intentionally—600 feet to a rocky conclusion.

"When we arrived, the guy's car was pancaked," said Burleigh Curtis, president of Ravalli County Search & Rescue. "A lot of ropes, carabiners, clips, and rappelling was involved. When we winched down, the guy was like, 'Hey, glad to see you, dude. What took so long?' He wanted breakfast. I began laughing. It was a lesson about assuming a guy is dead. Then he isn't."

Burleigh is 69. He is compact, sturdy, wears wire-rim glasses, and chews on toothpicks. His military-cut brown-and-gray hair makes him look like your last phys-ed teacher. He's been rescuing inattentive valley adventurers for 22 years in the kind of wilderness that might forgive a mistake but usually portends a memorial.

"Our most dangerous rescues are in fast-moving water," he told me. "We look for an eddy to form upstream of the stranded car or boat. You can't do anything from below, because the vehicle is too likely to drift down on you. But an eddy in front, we can dive on that."

Every year, Burleigh rescues five or six motorists who've driven into our otherwise picturesque Bitterroot River. He never inquires as to their method of entry, which mystifies me. It's like not asking what Sean Penn ate during lunch with El Chapo.

Ravalli County Search & Rescue comprises 25 burly Burleighs, specialists in mountaineering, orienteering, swift-water recovery, scuba diving, helicopter basket lifts, scent-dog training, off-road driving, CPR, and interrogation. The latter comes into play because the initial 911 call is often vague.

"Ninety-nine percent of our calls are from friends or relatives, not the subject," Burleigh explained, steadfastly avoiding the term victim. "For instance, a wife will say, 'My husband left and never came back.' I have to question her, attaching a numerical estimate to her responses, then the resulting score tells me the urgency. Does the subject have a medical history? Does he have overnight gear? Has he come back late in the past? Does he know the territory? And then the first thing we do is scramble one of our Jeeps to the trail head to see if the subject's car is even parked there. We look for cigarette butts, tire tracks, litter. One time we found no car at all, because the guy was in Salt Lake City with his girlfriend."

To qualify as a rescuer, applicants must be county residents, CPR-validated, and guilty of no felonies. Or not too many. There's plenty of staff turnover.

"People think it'll be a romantic experience full of John Wayne heroics," Burleigh said. "But when you're standing wet and shivering on a river bank for nine hours, poking around for a bloated corpse, the fun wears right off." The S&R team also imposes a standardized chain of command, and direct orders are to be obeyed as if issued by Mad Dog Mattis. "A lot of people can't take orders. They get emotional about it."

Burleigh's motorized arsenal is reassuring: a Jeep Wrangler with Yeti-approved snow tires; a truck carrying an ice raft; a 4WD Knapheide ambulance that seats five rescuers plus a patient strapped onto a titanium litter so light it can easily be carried on a backpack; four Yamaha snowmobiles (one with a shielded sled for the victim); four Polaris ATVs, six Zodiac rafts, and a 4WD six-wheeled command center that looks like a Compton SWAT post. It cost $160,000 and carries a further $4,000 worth of radios attached to telescoping antennae. Inside are sofas flanking a table that accommodates any of a zillion topo maps stored in a wine rack with no corkscrew. The cadaver dogs reportedly love the RV's sofas.

"Despite all the vehicles," Burleigh told me, "I can tell you that the principal method of transportation is always…" and then he points at his legs. He has a blown-out knee to prove it. Each rescuer carries a backpack with 72 hours' worth of survival gear. They never know how many nights they'll be tramping. They work 30 to 40 rescues per year—plenty of blown-out knees.

At headquarters, there's a small interrogation room where friends and family huddle. They're kept isolated from what might be morbid radio transmissions. Burleigh never tells them he's calling off the search. Instead, he says, "We need more information." When confirmation of a subject's death arrives, the family is usually watching TV.

The sea change in S&R has been cell phones, although most don't work in the back country near my home. You may as well throw your phone in the river and hope Flipper finds it.

"We had a guy call on his cell, saying he was lost," Burleigh recalled. "We pinged his location—latitude and longitude—and talked him through orienting his compass. Then we just 'walked' him back. Our last instruction was, 'Uh, you should see your truck 'bout now,' and the guy goes, 'Oh, yeah, jeez, it's right in front of me.' "

Ravalli County S&R won't respond to folks who've drained their car's battery or drowned its electrics.

"We need some evidence you're in a life-threatening situation," Burleigh explained, "not just a matter of convenience to be extracted. We're not mechanics. If you have food and water, you may be stuck for a couple days."

Neither will they salvage your car or gear. They'll hoist you to safety, but your kayak becomes a scratching post for bobcats.

Burleigh recalled a hiker who panicked after noticing that a creek he crossed was rising with speed sufficient to block retreat. "The next day, we flew the helo in," Burleigh remembered, "winched down our rescue guy, and two of the campers said, 'Hey, we're fine, don't need no help.' But the third guy was freaked and cold. So we hoisted him to the helo and flew him to the trail head. That's when he complained we'd left behind his backpack." Burleigh says more and more campers equip themselves with GPS, emboldening them to deeper wilderness havoc. "And they always forget spare batteries," he added.

One of S&R's most difficult tasks is locating suicides. "They seem to be attracted to high country," Burleigh said. "And they may leave a suicide note at home but never directions where they're gonna perform the deed. We searched forever for one suicide who'd crawled into a culvert. What's more, they often change their minds. You might be searching for a guy in high country and meanwhile he's at the bar feelin' better about life."

Burleigh's most memorable rescue was on Darby's own stretch of the Bitterroot River, my favorite site for brown trout.

"A canoe slammed up against a log and got stuck," he recalled. "The guy scrambled to safety, but the woman was pinned, with her head barely above water. A diver tied a rope to her—a live-bait vest [so-called because it's a line with something squirming on the end]. Meanwhile, the diver had reached the canoe and was attempting to cut it in half with a chain saw. Yeah, I know, crazy. Suddenly, the girl was pulled under, so the diver dove after her. Grabbed her and held on underwater for 50 meters, on one breath. The rescuer earned a medal of valor for that. But, I swear, I'm surprised I didn't witness four drownings."

I interviewed Burleigh immediately after an early-June snowstorm at our house. I told him that Julie and I were momentarily embarking on a tour in *Car and Driver's* rear-wheel-drive, 365-hp Genesis G90 with summer tires. Our goal was to traverse Montana's Beartooth Highway, a road that achieves 11,000 feet. Burleigh stared at me, then said, "Wow. Okay. Guess I'll see you later."

I smiled. Burleigh did not.

URINATING FOR NINE MINUTES (WHICH BRINGS US TO PART II)

Julie and I did attempt Montana's Beartooth Highway. It's not far from here. As G. Gordon Liddy once mentioned to federal prosecutors, "There might have been a loose thread in the fabric of our planning."

First, some facts: The Beartooth Highway rises to 10,947 feet—similar to our own Trapper Peak and likewise a thousand feet beyond the tree line. The road is 68.7 miles long, makes visible 32 lakes from just one lay-by, and connects two destinations you've never planned to visit: Red Lodge, Montana, and Cooke City, Montana. Cooke City isn't a city. It's a raggedy-ass former mining village with a one-room schoolhouse and a block-long strip of '50s *Psycho* motels and desiccated bars, one with a 1972 Ford Maverick parked on its veranda, perhaps for safekeeping.

The Beartooth Highway was a Depression-era project, completed in 1936, legislated into reality by Hoover—and not the Hoover who wore skirts. On average, 150 laborers, called gippos, worked on the road daily. One name proposed was the Dorris Stalker Highway, which should have been adopted. The gents who oversaw its construction had the surnames Siegfriedt, Shelley, McNutt, and Pyle. Pardon me, but that is *the* single greatest-ever name for a law firm, especially since the partners were serenaded at work by Art Lumley's Melodians. (Not something you need to know.)

The road was originally gravel and was 14-feet wide. That's 84 inches per lane in which to maneuver your Buick Roadmaster. Original maximum projected speed was 20 mph, but until guardrails were erected, drivers were so terrified of the proximate drop-offs that they steered into the oncoming lane for emotional comfort. No end of body damage ensued, human and automotive alike.

Truth is, I have ached to drive the Beartooth since 1995, when I drove Charles Kuralt's CBS motorhome to its enshrinement in The Henry Ford Museum in Dearborn, Michigan. Kuralt had just departed Montana, where he had a secret second wife, a fun fact for everyone but the wives. Charles told me, "The Beartooth beats any drive in America, flat out. When it's open." It's the "open" part that is such an issue. In 1947, for instance, a weekend blizzard stranded 70 motorists, some in 15-foot drifts. Three required hospitalization and three park employees were buried in what turned out to be their tombs.

But, of course, no such entombment would happen to cautious me. Know why? Because I had waited until June 15. Summer. I was packing lemonade.

Julie and I drove from south to north on the highway, having departed Cooke City where it was 50 degrees. With each mile out of town, the thermometer lost a degree. "Not to worry," I told Julie, until the snow began falling in flakes the size of Post-it notes.

The car's tail squirmed and crossed the center line. Julie popped a pink Nauzene pill. I killed the radio as we passed a seven-foot-high wall of snow on which someone had spray-painted "Butte Butt Rats." The car's various traction warnings flashed, but what would be the point of acknowledging them?

Julie's face resembled Mark Zuckerberg's during a congressional hearing. I tried to lighten the moment, saying, "American beauty on the left, natural splendor on the right," but the view, in truth, was more like a clothesline of frozen bedsheets. Trees? Nope. Valley vistas? Nope. Just whiteness everlasting.

I fended off fear until I noticed the oncoming lane had disappeared under who knows how much snow, and who didn't know either. If anyone else were on the mountain, we'd be sharing the identical pair of indistinct tracks—yup, back to the old 84 inches of width in 1936—and any three-point turn would place the car in terror incognita, and that is not a typo.

Then descended the mother, father, and second cousin of all whiteouts. I had to open both side windows to view anything abeam, a tactic that soaked my left sleeve and Julie's hair, although it did reveal what was actually out there: a yellow snowplow the size of Nassau, a locale I was right then conjuring.

The driver dismounted and ran—*ran*, I say—to my window. *"Go back!"* he screamed over the roaring wind, waving an index finger south. "Just closed the highway. Got motorcycles and RVs in ditches. Go back. *God.*"

God, indeed. I figured God must be within 100 or so feet. Did I mention this was June 15?

Truth is, I was trying to turn around. The plow's driver didn't care. He climbed back into his truck. Still, I've never been so grateful to see a man since Larry Gartner tutored me for my SATs.

I backed down the mountain to gain speed, then performed a 180-degree hand-brake turn without a hand brake. Quite a maneuver, if I do say so. I wish someone had videoed it.

I thereafter followed in the plow's tracks, mere feet behind its bumper. Even so, the car's nose became its own plow, occasionally lifting the front tires. To this day, I haven't a clue how much of the Beartooth Highway we covered. If deep space were white instead of black, that's where we went.

We eventually slogged to the foot of the mountain at four or five mph, with the plow driver shepherding us through a monster steel gate, which he lowered and locked behind us. We were the last people off the Beartooth Highway.

I drove into Cooke City, where I urinated for maybe nine minutes. It was in Cooke City that a resident told me that June 15 didn't even remotely denote summer. He recalled that in 1953 an avalanche obliterated Montana's Going-to-the-Sun Road, also a Depression-era project pretty much replicating the Beartooth. It was a pip, annihilating two park employees, seriously injuring one, and burying another under seven feet of snow, from which he was dug up alive and well seven and a half hours later. Wet and annoyed, maybe, but breathing. A bloodhound named Joy had found him, later rewarded with a badge designating her an official park ranger but with no salary or benefits. In addition, one of the park's snow-removing machines, called a Snogo, was pushed 2,000 feet down the mountain, where it rested in not-so-useful condition. The road did not open to the public that year until June 24, and even then it was a slushy dodgem-car rink of ruination.

So, June 15. I'll only drive on that day if I've got chains and a cookie jar filled with fentanyl.

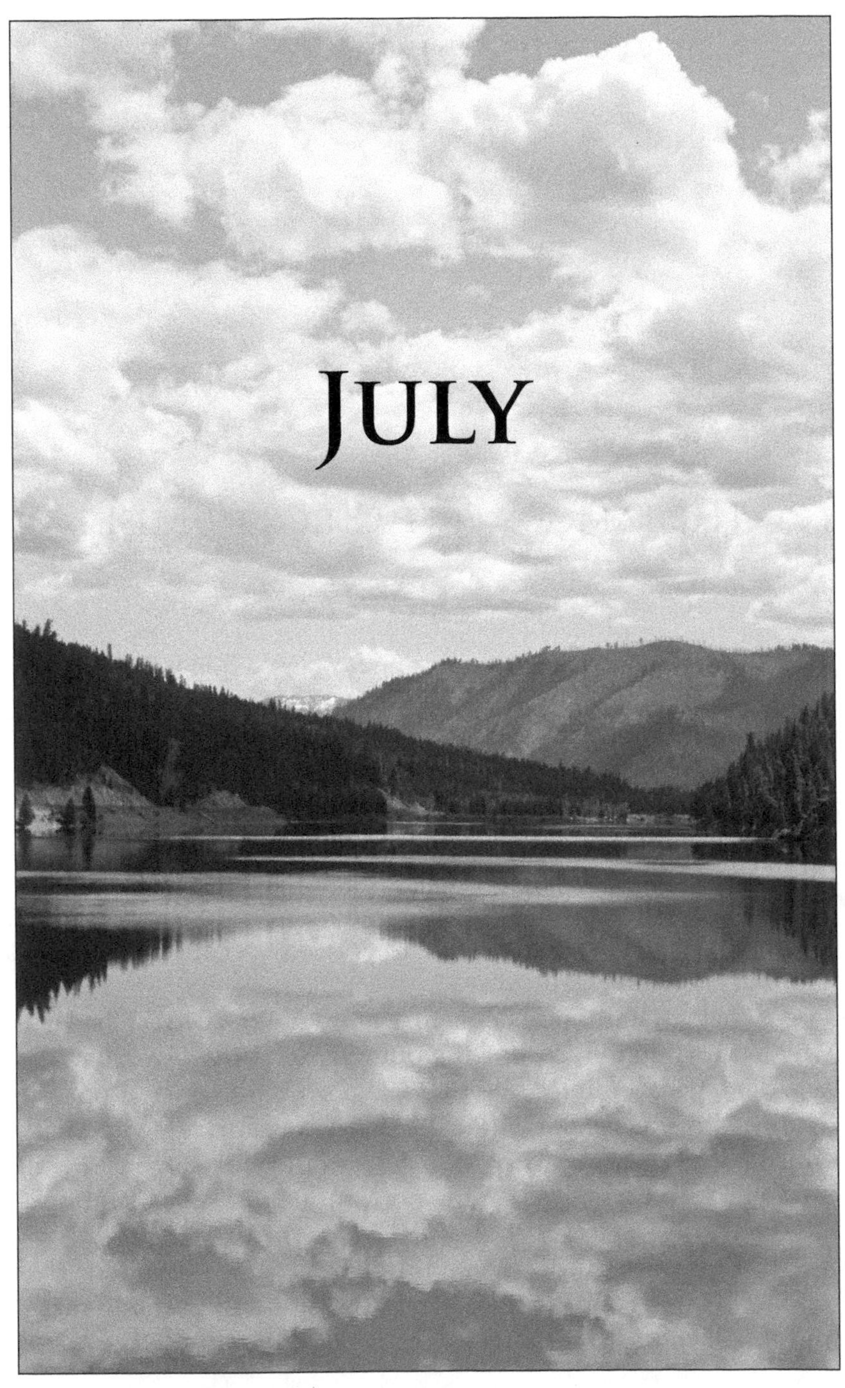
JULY

John Phillips

The Famous Free-Chicken Ruse

We were yet enjoying spring flowers when July's Logger Days was upon us. Logger Days is Darby's remembrance of the failed logging enterprise responsible for the town's existence. Also the Sawmill Saloon's. Logging hereabouts is now a kind of manicurist's endeavor. You file papers to petition the cutting of a species, then hire a helicopter to pull them out, one by one, like Gulliver's toothpicks. That prevents logging trucks from churning up muck that slides downhill and into the Bitterroot River, which, believe me, will be noticed, because fishermen stand in the water daily.

In fact, Julie and I booked a Saturday float trip on the West Fork, and when we reached the put-in, a semi-dissolved barrage of sediment had tainted the river, its oncoming wave of opaque maltiness in spectacular contrast to the clear, sapphire water with which it was merging. There had been a landslide somewhere up the Nez Perce River, back in the no man's land known simply as "the Selway," and it had choked the waterway overnight.

Our trout guide, Dread Pirate Dave, said, "I've seen this before. It's not good for the fish, but it isn't a man-made mess, and it will clear up tomorrow." He was right, although the fish we caught the next day all had an irritated look, as if someone had been potting petunias in their living room.

Julie and I support Logger Days, but it plays out in our five-acre civic park at the south edge of town, a park notable for having no trees in a valley famous for trees—hence the lumberjacks we were celebrating. So there's no shade, but the park does boast a facsimile of a 12-foot-long ax.

Logger Days is a cacophony of yapping two-stroke engines, whooshing hand saws, and clanking climbing spikes. Events include the double crosscut, the ax throw, the speed cut, the single crosscut, the choker race, the split and stack, the pole climb, the Jack-and-Jill crosscut, the springboard chop, and the hot saw. The latter entails a customized single-cylinder saw slicing a 20-inch larch log. Saws have been known to catch fire and spray molten internal parts, which greatly enthuses spectators, notably me.

Of course, if municipal conflagration is the eventual goal, onlookers need only await Darby's hallmark V-8–powered saw. It takes two to four men to lift, depending on beer intake. It shoots blue and orange flames. It would herniate both Paul Bunyan and his ox.

There is also the traditional log-rolling contest that is held in a makeshift puddle six inches deep. No chance of drowning but a good chance of concussion. The filthier your Carhartts, the more you are applauded.

Our favorite event is the "cookie stack," in which competitors cut one-inch-thick slices off the top of a log, then place those "cookies" atop one another on a nearby stump, using nothing but the chain saw's bar to complete the stack. A kind of gas-powered Chinese pickup sticks, with obligatory chess-master concentration. He who stacks the most in 90 seconds wins (I saw no prize for this), but it is common for the cutter to topple his stack accidentally at, say, the 80-second mark, and the crowd cries out as if someone's dog has been run over. Just holding one of those fat saws perpendicular to my body would sever ligaments, forget any sawing.

One year, a tanned, raven-haired woman entered this competition. She appeared to be in her early 30s, weighing maybe 115 pounds (referred to locally as a "quarter pounder"), and her chain saw said Mattel on the side. (Not true, but it makes for a better story at the Valley Bar.)

In a ballet of balanced bursts, with sawdust billowing, this supersonic Thin Woman chained her way to victory. Spectators corralled each other to ask who this ringer might be. Was she a secret pro, perhaps touring the log-cutting circuit, which I don't think exists? The crowd afforded her polite applause, much as you'd offer at the library's annual cowboy poetry contest, but you could tell the onlookers would have preferred a steroidal Bolo Billy scattering sawdust into the next county while chugging whiskey and cutting off a couple fingers.

I wanted to approach the Cookie Queen to offer praise, perhaps requesting one of her cookies as a keepsake. But she had raced to the beer shack, where someone was treating her to twin pints that she downed in audible gulps, foam escaping the corners of her mouth.

Logger Days is one of those civic events in which each successive act is staged with increasing delay, such that epochs pass with no performers on stage. Onlookers fidget, enhance their melanomas, and assign their offspring to fetch alcohol, which is maybe the point.

"They need some kind of producer/director to speed things up," I told Julie, who suggested I volunteer as the event's official Speeder Upper Executive (SUE). She hatches clever ideas like that, forgetting what a pleasure it is to gratuitously malign the voluntary endeavors of strangers while doing nothing personally to rectify the problem.

I mention wasted time for a reason: Logger Days officials have devised a system wherein cash is useless behind the grandstands, even though that is where you must wander to purchase barbecue chicken and sign up for NRA membership (arrive early to qualify for a large automatic weapon). To make such purchases, you instead obtain tickets in denominations of one to five dollars. If you're smart—a little gullible, too—you'll stand in line to buy tickets only once, acquiring enough to produce a softball-size bulge in your pants. Which means that, at the conclusion of Logger Days, every attendee walks home with orphan tickets wadded in his pockets, hoping to remember to retrieve them next year, which he won't. And that's how the organizers fund clandestine trips to the Caymans, where they stage a rodeo of their own involving ladies dressed in just the cutest Nurse Nancy outfits who tend not to patients but to offshore accounts in anonymous PO boxes in George Town. That's not true. Also unfair. "They're dressed in standard nurse uniforms," Julie corrected.

This voucher scheme constitutes a cold-rolled steel dagger of marketing virtuosity, in which you sell an item to a buyer who then, hours later, abandons ever using it and demands no refund. And yet, as brilliant schemes go, the Bitterroot Valley can top even Logger Days: Come spring, our farm-supply store sells chicken feed of the variety guaranteed to turn your fryers into knee bucklers and incite your laying hens to discharge 40 bullets daily.

Now, pay attention here, because the subtle brilliance of this will leave you speechless. Each time you purchase a 50-pound bag of magic chicken feed, you are offered two free chicks from the incubator in the middle of the store's main aisle, which you must circumnavigate to gain access to any other aisles not devoted to poultry husbandry. Take your pick of chicks. No sane person can resist. First, the chicks are as cute as the June Taylor Dancers covered in cedar shavings. Second, they are free, which I may have mentioned.

So you carry your adorable chirpers home, but now your enlarged brood demolishes the bag of feed somewhat sooner than expected, so you return to the mercantile for a replacement bag, whereupon, of course, you grab two more free chicks. The silken, lustrous perfection of this closed-loop system induces goose bumps. Chicken bumps. Let Wall Street financiers invent credit default swaps and triple-bogy eyebrow-popping go-to-prison derivatives. But they'll never come up with anything that tops the two-free-chicks ruse. No one has.

When the aliens finally contact us, this is what I will trot out to demonstrate our advanced thinking, and they will shout, "Holy Pluto on a plate of planked plantains, that is *brilliant,"* and they will contemplate the stratagem in a dark-matter alley. But unfortunately for the aliens, they will unwittingly carry off two free chicks into the gravity-free cosmos, so they'll be back in two weeks for more feed.

In this fashion, we will master the universe.

ON WEARING PANTS BENEATH CHAPS

Armed with leather gloves, a farm jack, two 50-foot strings of barbed wire, a sledgehammer, nails, a wire cutter, an ax, and a six-pack of Corona, I undertook a maintenance tour of the National Forest fence that abuts 1,000 feet of my property. I was told the fence's upkeep was in some manner my obligation, which felt unfair because, as a taxpayer, hadn't I already paid for it? But I am quick to welcome guilt, so I chugged forth with Julie as co-counsel.

Pumping away at the farm jack, we enthusiastically uprooted rotten fence posts, replacing them with not-much-sturdier versions that Mother Nature had scattered generously across the forest's floor. We cut the posts to size, then banged them into a wobbly facsimile of verticality, handling the wire gingerly, although I twice gouged my leg as I transformed a pair of Levis into a colander.

Here we were, my wife and I, "riding the rails," a patently Montanan chore. Sure, I was deploying a Toyota Tundra instead of Old Rusty, but I was otherwise involved in cowboy responsibilities, or so I told myself.

The Forest Service's fence has three strands of barbed wire. Along 200 feet of its length, nearest our kitchen, the top wire had come unglued, if cowboys use glue, after having been trampled by our Tin Cup herd of elk hoping to eat the slim perimeter of grass surrounding my house. Sometimes the calves refused to jump the two lower strands. Left behind, they evinced heavy elk angst that had them mewling and bawling, thereby breaking our hearts. So I left the top wire where it had fallen in rust-encrusted strips probably bristling with tetanus. I'm possibly guilty of Destruction of Government Property, with my home in danger of seizure, but I want to be fair and point out, in my own defense, that it was Julie's idea.

When we finished, I had one question: What do you do with 200 feet of corroded barbed wire? I'll tell you what. You cut it into pieces about four feet long, then bundle the thorny tangles into individual nests, then affix plastic twist ties to bind them. After that, you carry one bundle per week to the dumpster for the next 12 weeks, hoping no other users notice or complain.

While bundling, by the way, I discovered the value of safety glasses, having punctured one eyebrow, and learned to imbibe Corona after, not before. When was my last tetanus shot? As a kid, I was terrified of developing lockjaw because it would prevent me from telling my mother I had developed lockjaw, and she'd euthanize me as she did our beagle Happy, an event that introduced me to the concept of irony.

No Stetson for me, but what I am going to buy—already have—are Carhartt bib overalls. They count as my first item of fashion, since I was eight, featuring permanently attached suspenders. I'd already been heckled for wearing suspenders and a belt, which to Montanans denotes "not from here" as well as criminal effeminacy. My new Carhartts offer no belt loops at all. Just a loop for a hammer or a "help me I've fallen" transmitter. They are orangish-brown, from a palette Mother Nature does not possess, but the only other hue was black, surely a summer sauna.

My overalls were purchased at a farm and feed outlet that also sells pearl-button cowboy shirts one aisle removed from varnished plaques citing Bible verses. One entire aisle is devoted to work gloves. Julie and I take guests to this store, one of whom tried on 12 pairs of gloves (purchasing six) and a hat shaped like a cow's head. One of Julie's girlfriends bought cowboy boots inked in a Grateful Dead hallucinogenic motif, which isn't a certified western tableau. They were expensive.

In just months of Montana residence, I had befriended Maureen, one of the feed-store clerks, and when I approached her checkout register, Carhartts in hand, size 36/34, I was unfortunately wearing a starched button-down shirt, penny loafers, and khaki pants with a military crease.

"I'm guessing these are your first Carhartts," Maureen mumbled as she tore off various tags and stickers. "A big day in a man's life," she added. "Where were you when you bought your first Carhartts?"

I assured her this wasn't an event I'd celebrate annually, but I didn't know that for sure. I later bought Carhartts for Julie as well—a Christmas gift—because I am a caring husband. She wears size 30/30, the smallest offered. There were maybe 20 pairs in that size as yet untouched. As opposed to the men's half of the rack, where the selection *began* with Large, and that is no joke. One of the waist sizes was 56 inches. I'm hoping they were intended for livestock, but a quick purview of patrons revealed numerous proportions rivaling Bossie's.

At home, I modeled my overalls for Julie, who noted they looked "incredible," as in not credible, because they weren't dirty. But a fix was imminent. My next homestead chore was to thin the pine saplings surrounding my house. They had skyrocketed to a height of eight or nine feet, and I was assured by friend Ridlon Kiphart that they would "positively cause your house to burn to the ground come fire season."

The wonderful thing about neglect is that you don't have to work at it to achieve an impeccably high standard. So I purchased a pair of immense stainless-steel loppers, which I named Cindy, and tuned up my twin Husqvarna chain saws, whose diminutive size was already a source of cabaret-quality entertainment for Kemp Conn, our nearest neighbor.

My goal was to topple ten pines daily, each the size of a Christmas tree that my Midwest parents would have purchased for $35. Then I began stacking the "slash"—that is, the limbs—into the Toyota's bed, hauling load after sap-bleeding load to a portion of my property featuring a steep drop-off, where you'd expect Wile E. Coyote to perform hilarious defenestration capers. Over the cliff I pushed the bushy limbs, hoping that if they later caught fire the conflagration would be contained by the face of the cliff. It might work, although the counsel of Forest Service experts was solicited in none of this. The goal was to eliminate any low-lying combustible hazard within a 75-yard radius of my living room, as Ridlon had instructed from his temporary abode in Florida, where, right then, he was nailing plywood over windows in preparation for a killer hurricane. A rich vein of irony there. Eliminating trees seemed a sustainable task if I were to adhere to my schedule of ten topplings per day. Simple.

Not really. In some places on the steep hillside there stood a confounding welter of trunks that ranged from one inch to nine inches in diameter, some wrapped around others in boa-constrictor snarls. The chain saw responded with a kind of stutter somewhere between a seizure and a *Riverdance* stomp. Then it entwined itself in the twisted one-inchers and stalled, so it was simpler to lop those by hand. If I could hack those knotted clusters manually, the Husqvarna could eat the tree-size soldiers, although some of those had to be rolled by a peavey.

At the time, I thought a peavey was a rock-and-roll amplifier, although I'd read in Montana about one being swung to fatally gore a barroom assailant. The peavey cost $129. It is little more than an aluminum bar with a lethal-looking red hook at its base, a combination that leverages tree trunks into positions to make dismemberment simpler. I don't own a gun, but I might hide my peavey under the bed. If you stand downhill of a peavey-rolled log, your ankles and toes will fracture into pieces of bone china. It says so right in the inch-square instruction manual.

I eventually trotted out a metal footstool that I moved from thicket to thicket, sitting thereupon as if shining shoes. Some days I'd just fell trees. Some days I'd just load limbs into the truck, which I occasionally parked at an angle so steep that adding another 100 pounds up high would surely elicit a rollover, which weighed heavily on Julie's mind.

What did happen was that I lowered the truck's tailgate, forgot about it, then backed into a Douglas fir sufficiently rotund that it would have been here during the Civil War. The initial impact made no noise. The truck just stopped. So I added throttle, then more throttle, until an explosive puff of pine needles descended on the hood and roof, followed by a sedimentary layer of dust as an exclamation point.

When I examined the tailgate, it was bent to a depth of, oh, about nine inches, and the interior structure was also wrenched, which I learned only later from J&D Auto Body, which unbolted it and carried it away for three weeks of spa treatments. In the meantime, I lashed an aluminum stepladder sideways to act as a proxy tailgate—at least it kept the larger articles safely in the bed—although it fell out on Rushing's Hill, and I didn't notice until the following day when Jim Rushing asked, "You want your ladder back?"

I later mentioned my forest-thinning project to the clerk at the feed store, and she thrust upon me items I'd surely need beyond the deadly peavey. Wedges, for example, which are used for felling trees whose waist exceeds my own, and an $18 maul.

"After the trees are down, you'll have to go to the maul," explained Maureen, which made both of us smile. In Hamilton, we enjoy the Bitterroot Mall, and here's what's inside: a UPS drop-off and a Chinese takeout. That is all. Our mall is thus useful only to dispatch sweet-and-sour chicken to Toledo. Here's one last thing about the maul: I have never used it. It serves as a paperweight in the garage, where there is no paper.

In any event, I toiled at my pine-pruning project for the entire month. I'd delay this forestry until 3:00 p.m., then 4:00 p.m., on the theory it would be cooler, but in truth I didn't want to harvest trees at all. For one thing, pine trees have developed, via extravagant Darwinian evolution, splinter-like needles that are astonishingly adept at poking holes in human eyeballs, the needles having learned, against all odds, to bend around sunglasses and then straighten in time to inflict seeping retinal wounds. Mother Nature coughs up stark permutations that leer at our evolutionary failings.

Dressing for my daily deforestation was an event, too. For starters, I am 65 years old, and my joints snap, crack, and pop like the *Santa Maria* in an Atlantic gale. So each day I'd affix Velcro knee braces, a Velcro back brace, two plastic knee pads, steel-toed boots, a handkerchief for sweat, safety glasses, and a squirty bottle upon which I'd tape three Tylenols. I'd work until the water and Tylenols were consumed.

A neighbor also lent a pair of official lumberjack chaps—leggings that intentionally catch in a chain saw's chain, causing the machine to stall instead of severing a femur. The neighbor told me, "You'll want to wear pants under the chaps. You know that, right?" I'd wear an athletic cup if it helped.

It will not surprise you that my orange Carhartt coveralls now appear to have dry-mopped an abattoir. And my work resulted in a veritable Himalayan range of slash at the bottom of my little cliff, which I suspect is now far and away the most combustible hazard in the valley, another irony given my goal of forestalling all nearby ignition. All that slash is out of sight, out of mind, and maybe already on fire. Upcoming headline in the *Ravalli Republic*: *"ENTIRE VALLEY BURNS TO A CRISP. OUTSIDER GUY CHARGED WITH DUMBFUCKERY."*

Following the pine-sapling extermination, which I think went relatively well, I bought a pickax and attacked the six-inch corrugations that the truck's tires had churned up while climbing our gravel driveway. The corrugations were slightly smaller than waves off Maui. The FedEx and UPS guys had complained, and those men must be made content or one's existence in the Bitterroots, already a blind trip to the undertaker's parlor, morphs into a forced march sans granola bars. Leveling the driveway was work worthy of a chain gang, and I began uttering quotes from *Cool Hand Luke*: "Gotta take a break here, boss," and "Caught short here, boss." But the only boss was Ed the raven, who cawed imploringly above, hoping for microwaved pizza crusts. He did seem intrigued when I pissed on the largest gravel corrugation.

Using the pickax first, then a hoe, then a shovel, then a rake, I managed to flatten the worst of the hillocks, enough that visitors' complaints ceased. A month later, every mound reappeared, resembling starter kits for a ski slope.

I thus summoned Brad and his King Kong commercial grader. He said he'd think about it. Brad parks his six-wheel Caterpillar at the south end of town in an abandoned carwash. A whiff of $50s will be involved, because Brad swore to Julie he'd never again expose himself to our driveway's precipices and lethal overhangs. But I believe Brad is a man who forgives and forgets, and I will have to rely on the "forgets" half of that equation.

No Flies On Frank

Julie and I learned of a Frank Lloyd Wright house on the northwestern edge of Darby. This seemed as unlikely as the brewery's banjo player composing a cantata, but it's true.

In 1909, there were plans to build a resort city in the valley called Bitter Root—with the "Bitter" half of that appellation again a cautionary—to be fashioned by Frank his own self. In those days, the valley was little more than a roughshod assembly of dusty sawmills, sugar-beet plantations, orchards, hay farms, hay rakes, and hayseeds. Some of the original orchards remain, producing apples so old they have glaucoma.

Anyway, as a sort of warm-up for his bold endeavor, Mr. Wright schemed a Darby resort called University Heights. There was no university, of course, but at least the "heights" were real, odd again because this was all to be in his trademark Prairie Style, not on a prairie but on a mountainside, which you'd think Frank would have noticed.

University Heights was to comprise 60 log cabins in a circle, served centrally by a clubhouse and manager's office. None of the cabins had hallways, which Wright thoroughly loathed throughout his career. He went on to ensure that customers loathed them, too, by designing passageways so narrow that, for people to pass, they had to vaccinate each other. Also, none of the cabins had kitchens, because, well, kitchens were smoky, stinky grease traps that were cramped and represented drudgery in a locale free of electricity, as it was on outlying hillsides back then.

Mr. Wright, in his authoritarian, nay, even *fascist* style, demanded that all vacationers dine in a central mess so they could commune and, one imagines, eat whatever Mrs. Wright felt was fare appropriate to the prairie that wasn't a prairie.

Wright issued a warning: "If you want level floors and a nonleaking roof, I'm not your man," which was as true here as in the Johnson Wax building.

In Darby, alas, only 12 University Heights cabins were ever erected, and as time passed, they tended to burn or rot or leak or be sold wholesale for shipment to anywhere but Darby. Somewhere in eastern Idaho, a fellow is unknowingly parking his Rambler Ambassador in a Frank Lloyd Wright garage. In any event, only one cabin remains. But it's a true F.L. Wrighter, right here in the funky honkiness of Darby.

Julie and I and our friend Jeff Dworin, an architectural buff, went searching for the FLW cabin. You wouldn't think this would be tricky in a berg of 400 souls and about six roads, but we spent two maddening hours roaming dirt paths northwest of town, eventually nosing down a dead-end track that led directly into a rudimentary covered garage belonging to an angry homeowner who right then, coincidentally, was following in his Jeep Wrangler.

That put me in the awkward position of having to ask a fully fuming resident, into whose premises I had just trespassed, to rearrange his Jeep so I could turn around. I nonetheless inquired where the FLW cabin might be located, and he proffered the Marshal Larry stare, so, once again, I just drove away, studying the rearview mirror for colorful shotgun blasts.

Our friend Jeff reminded us of Wright's utterance: "Early in life, I had to choose between honest arrogance and hypocritical humility. I chose the former and see no reason to change."

Hypocritical? When Wright occupied New York's Plaza Hotel, he decorated his room—this, in the face of his "pure function, organic" philosophy—with velvet curtains and gold wallpaper. I wish he'd tried that in Darby.

We did eventually locate the cabin and judged its architecture disappointing in the manner that characterizes, say, the sketchings Monet drew when he was in ninth-grade study hall and a teacher was smacking him on the back of his head.

GOATS HOG THE ELLIPTICAL MACHINE

As is true in many small towns, Darby's political scene is, at once, contentious, passionate, confused, seething, and as all over the place as nine ferrets in a carpet mill. Election outcomes seem accidental. I am qualified to say this, because I once ran for Sewage Commissioner in my former home in Pinckney, Michigan, not much larger than Darby. I had three campaign signs: (1) "Vote for John, he's got his shit together." (2) "No stools in your pools." (3) "If it floats, John's got his eye on it." I lost that election not in a landslide but a tragic avalanche: six votes for my opponent, Mrs. Colone (really), and two for me, one of which was my own, cast merely to maintain a shred of self-esteem. I immediately asked for a recount. Mayor Tom Reid loved me after that.

I was thus forearmed with what today is called "pattern recognition" as it pertains to basement politics, so I waded on tippy toes when it appeared as if Julie and I might be dragged into Darby's political drowning pool. The village was pondering whether to buy our local gym, the Right to Bare Arms, thereby saving it from ignoble uselessness.

We adore the local gym. For starters, when you're sweating on the stair stepper, you're facing a wall of windows through which you'll observe a forest where turkeys, pileated peckers, and white-tailed deer frolic and frequently approach with looks of wonder on their stinking-cute faces. Plus, I had just proposed that the gym consider a new slogan: "If shoulder blades were really blades, you'd bleed to death during jumping jacks." (Rejected.)

Here, gym-wise, was our dilemma: The town promised to buy the operation, but, after retaining a cadre of lawyers and financiers and CPAs, didn't. What's crucial here is that the town was purchasing only the exercise equipment; the building itself was leased. The sale price was something like $15,000, which, as Julie and I kept pointing out, wouldn't even buy a nice used truck or a golf-ball-size chunk of meth.

Our beloved mayor, J.C. McDowell—who owns the Bandit Brewery, which partly explains his belovedness—was 100 percent pro purchase, especially after a nearby health provider promised to open a "wellness center" within the restored gym, dispensing wellness to the well and unwell alike. How could we lose? Well, we couldn't, but it was difficult explaining that to the Darby councilmen, who wore camo baseball caps during Town Council meetings, making them difficult to see. Meanwhile, volunteers had lined up, including Julie, to staff the gym if it were municipally owned, working pro bono until the arrival of someone versed in the matter of retail exercise. But, as is so often the case in small-town politics, the council's credo was "Try to be just, and if you can't be just, be arbitrary."

In their arbitrariness, a kind of showdown transpired, perfectly appropriate to High Noon Darby. Our minuscule Town Hall, attached to a jail even smaller, overflowed with vocal and bellicose pro-gymmers, including us. Maybe 100 folks amassed, which I'm told was the largest valley turnout since the Salish hand-painted the medicine tree.

During the public comment period, the hall devolved into a metaphorical carjacking. There was shouting, unfriendly gesturing, nervous squirming, gratuitous flailing of arms, false charges, huffy walkouts, some spitting, one insult using the term "shit sucker," and a baseball cap that was tipped off a gentleman's head, which I thought was over the line. Could there be fisticuffs? I hoped so.

Darby's Marshal Larry was nowhere to be seen, but his wife was taking notes, perhaps recording names of citizens who would later suffer felony jaywalking citations. At one point, when a councilman said, "There are actually a lot of folks who oppose buying the gym," I leapt to my feet and shouted—really, I shouted—"So where the fuck are they?" In fact, I'm sure there were dissenters in attendance, but they said nothing, not even to Mrs. Marshal Larry, because who wants a broken hip?

I was later ashamed of myself. I felt like one of those construction workers who wolf-howl at passing women. I sat silently in my small pile of shame, watching the other participants barking at one another and circling like vultures over a gut pile. Darby's politics is a Punch and Judy show in which the sole plot is Punch punching Judy. Mrs. Marshal Larry never spoke a word.

I will spare you further anarchic details except to mention that when the irate citizenry fled Town Hall, certain of victory and resembling the LAPD after administering one of their finest beatings, the Town Council went ahead and did what it wanted to do in the first place, which was nothing.

Then Mayor McDowell lost the election, yielding to a conservative named Buck Titus, which to us sounded like an itchy disease. ("After camping, I got bucktitus between my toes.") But the rumor from Hope the barber was that Buck didn't want the job and ran merely to be elected, at which point he would cede mayoral duties to one of the camo-hatted councilmen. How a plan so Machiavellian could play out in straight-shootin' Darby is beyond me, but I do love sitting on a municipal bench and spewing ill-informed opinions, the longest and grandest of American traditions.

It must be noted that, just before the big mayoral vote, a debate was scheduled between McDowell and wannabe Buck, who, on the only occasion I encountered him, was wearing work clothes that appeared to have been retrieved from a feedlot drainage ditch. In advance of the debate, substantially more unwarranted disdain had been leveled by Buck's side than the mayor's. A crowd amassed for the debate, everyone waving hats and uttering complaints about what federal governments have done dating back to Caesar's decision to turn off the baths. I'd hoped there'd be a moderator who'd announce the two candidates as if preparing for a World Federation Wrestling match, but no. With all that tension brewing over the debate, ready to boil over into actionable indictments that Marshal Larry could seize upon, here's what happened: Buck failed to show. It was perfect. Is there a word beyond "perfect"? If so, let's use that. It turned into a one-man debate, and because many of us think of Darby as a one-horse town, the symmetrical equivalence was God's own gravy train.

Peace again descended on our attractive village when a pro weight-lifting couple from Denver purchased the gym. The female half is Dana, and since living in Darby, she has doubled her deltoids, glorified her gluteus, made a Vesuvius of her vastors, propagated her pronator, and topped off her trapezius. She sports muscles in her eyebrows. If the woman isn't as solid as a Jersey barrier, she at least could lift one. Plus, she brings to the gym a massive bulldog named Odin—who would have tickled George Patton—as well as two miniature goats named Billy and Chrissie. Odin herds the goats. You don't often see that in a gym.

I suggested to a camo councilman on a stair stepper that Darby's chamber of commerce motto should be something Latin, such as "*novum,*" or "new thing."

Julie disagreed. "Should be '*No novum,*' " she insisted, "except that sounds like a birth-control drug."

Harmony in Darby was but a fleeting spark. No sooner did we solve the gym dilemma than Marshal Larry, new deputy John Ringer, and the former town clerk sued the mayor for creating "an unbearably hostile work environment," for a "deliberate and public campaign" to fire city workers, and for having "demeaned and harassed them in public settings."

No one knew what it meant. We couldn't find anyone who had witnessed any harassing or demeaning, apart from me once blurting the F-bomb, for which I'd already apologized.

Eventually, a Montana superior court laughed the case into the nearest Tractor Supply men's room, suggesting that all parties meet at three p.m. at the bike racks and duke it out, perhaps later retiring to the Sawmill for frosty tall boys and an alehouse tan of fissured facial veins. It recalled that old saw about early western towns relentlessly telegraphing Washington with the same request: "Send lawyers, guns, and money." I believe it was made into a song.

I'm trying not to align with one side or another, which is untrue, but Mayor McDowell was not only an eloquent Darby advocate but also a sudsy savant in the matter of pale ales, and his microscopic Bandit Brewery—housed in a former heavy-equipment garage in an alley excruciatingly difficult to find—welcomes humans and canines alike. Or did. Recently, a doggie insurrection erupted, with the submissive loser relieving himself near one of the stainless-steel brewing vats. The patrons hooted and howled as if someone had dropped a tray in the school cafeteria. Sadly, Mayor McDowell thereafter banned pets on grounds of bad behavior and not paying for their beer. I tell you, the place hasn't been the same.

To add some humanity, J.C. bolted half of a rusty wrecked car over the entranceway. You might wonder if it is hazardous, appearing so unsupported, but if there are building regulations in the Bitterroot Valley, they are unknown to any local contractors. Fact is, Montana ranks third in the U.S. for number of craft breweries, with Darby's its tiniest, and I think that's the reason we also have a state lullaby, which is true. It further tickled me that our favorite moose, Walter, trotted onto the brewery's front porch, standing contentedly under the rusty wrecked car that is still attached but leaning in a direction favoring the engine. Photos were taken.

One more note about Darby's political leg traps. During our Logger Days parade down Main Street, one "float" consisted of an outhouse on a flatbed truck carrying a hand-lettered sign reading, "Obama's Presidential Library." I puffed up into a purple rage, in part because so many locals refused to pay a cent for our own library. Whose address, I might add, is

101 1/2 Marshall Street, next to the Marshal's office, meaning that the library's version of that street is misspelled, and it might be the only U.S. library ever awarded half an address.

Still mildly irked, ex-mayor McDowell and I drank a couple of growlers, and when I drove home I noticed horse turds on Main Street, dropped in an arrow indicating the defecator's direction. It reminded me of a quote from the original tree hugger, John Muir: "There could be no news of importance about a town."

Except my town.

NOT A DUMP, PER SE

Darby occasionally orbits itself in compactness, and our only current option for dinner is the Little Blue Joint Café on Main Street. It seats 28 and is a '50s-style eatery that Edward Hopper would have painted. The menu comprises tacos, pizza, burgers, pizza, and pizza pie.

The owners, Monica and Mike Campbell, are expanding to seat 78, which would represent something approaching one fifth of all Darby's inhabitants, possibly a recipe for civil unrest. Mike claims he wants "a real restaurant that serves butter-soaked scallops," which I guess must be the apogee of haute cuisine. No matter the menu, the refurbished café has the townsfolk swarming, herding, and droving. It's obvious they approve because the only way to draw patrons out is to tempt them with alfalfa.

The Campbells are moreover refurbishing a B&B above the Sawmill Saloon, whose rafters are elaborately adorned with a dozen decorative chain saws of the commercial-logger type, some potentially operable and occasionally dripping oil. If oil splats on a patron, it is considered good luck.

The saloon shares a wall with the Little Blue Joint Café and was originally a bank in the early 1900s. Everyone knows the date because a canceled check hangs behind the bar. Just for useless reference, that was only 11 years after an earthquake altered the course of the Bitterroot River overnight, which would have come as a surprise if your house had faced a fishing hole that by breakfast was a gravel pit.

The Sawmill Saloon yet employs two walk-in vaults. One is refrigerated and holds kegs of beer, the other dry goods. Back in 1933, the upper half of the building served as a hotel employing working ladies, and conscientious whoring was then the town's most profitable enterprise, save logging. The new B&B now occupies the top floor, haunted by ghosts suffering specterish syphilis.

When the Sawmill's bartender strides into the vault to retrieve a replacement keg, he kicks and rolls the thing, creating the clamor of a 20-bike collision in the Tour de France. Last time it happened, I was sipping beer alongside a patron who screamed, "Jesus Christ, the *noise*," and from the bowels of the vault Gus blasted back, "Go fuck yerself!"

One further observation: In July, I found myself exiting the barbershop on Main Street, having enjoyed a three-minute cut and a salty chinwag at Hope's Cutting Corral. Her shop is roughly eight feet wide and 20 feet deep—one chair, of course—and is always humid, slightly tropical. Anyway, a car of tourists rolled to a stop curbside, and the driver/father leaned his crimson noggin out the window, just as a kid in the back seat screamed, *"Get your fuckin' hands off me."* The father ignored that outburst to ask, "You got a Dairy Queen in town?"

"Nope," I said.

"How 'bout a Burger King, Wendy's, sumpin' like that?"

"Nope," I repeated.

As he rolled up his window, he mumbled, "Boy, what a dump."

FOUR HOLES IN GENE'S BRAIN

Speaking of dumps, seven miles from my house molders a junkyard with nearly as many wrecked cars as my town has wrecked inhabitants. A jubilee of junk, is what it is. Exploring "salvage" yards—another implacable euphemism—is, for me, soothing. Know why? Every single abandoned car, stray hubcap, and pot-iron Cadillac badge is something I can afford. At what other retail store does that ever happen?

So I spent a blissful afternoon scrutinizing this gala of discards, recording in my official reporter's notebook two-dozen autos of interest. To me, at least. Everything from a turd-brown 1966 Mercedes 250SE to a shipshape 1990 Subaru Justy to a collectible beige 1960 Willys station wagon with a bumper sticker exclaiming, "No Zoning! No Setbacks!" (Montana politics in a nutshell.)

Farther on I examined a pair of 1970 Datsun 240Zs abutting a 2002 Pontiac Aztek, pristine apart from a traumatized windshield, a Walter White Special. Nearby was a 1960 Cadillac Sedan de Ville, on whose windshield someone had scrawled "SAVE!" Then a 1985 Pontiac Fiero whose right-front tire I kicked because it was a car of mortifyingly shameful shittiness, ossifying alongside a 1983 AMC Eagle with factory carrot orange paint highlighted by tan accents the color of seasickness, like something floating in a ditch. There was even a not-yet-crumpled 1994 Mitsubishi Montero that I could morph into a dedicated off-roader, a simple DIY project inasmuch as a fishing rod was already resting against its fender.

Junkyards, moreover, invariably contain "mystery cases." I stumbled across an otherwise sanguine 2002 Chevy Cavalier, for instance, whose door, trunk, and hood had been sealed with stickers warning, "Evidence, do not touch." There are always a few "death cars," too, whose airbags and upholstery are blood-bespattered, plus a few involved in deer / elk / moose collisions—notably a 2016 Dodge Ram with a tuft of fur still clinging to its twisted radiator. Nearby was the carcass that precipitated both deaths—deer and Ram alike.

Why a deceased deer in a junkyard? Because it's Darby, that's why. I even climbed atop a monster machine that squashes cars into compact trapezoids, with its iron teeth seized on the front third of a 1980 VW Rabbit immobilized by square wheels, a tableau recollecting an anaconda eating, well, a rabbit. If you anthropomorphize cars, as I do, a junkyard is a thousand wakes at once.

The man who owns this little slice of salvageable rapture is Gene Honey, 64. Gene is a bear of a guy, coarse gray hair but bald on top, hands like calloused catcher mitts, eyebrows drooping like a kindly uncle's. He is a peaceable soul, born and raised in Darby, now perpetually followed by faithful Socks, his junkyard dog who won't protect even one rusted bumper but will bite if you touch Gene. Even to shake hands. After administering the first biting surprise, Socks untied my shoelaces. A dog with skills.

On a spooky night, Gene and I gabbed like magpies in his catalog-clogged office, with Socks refereeing from a bench seat unbolted from a minivan.

"My blood came to this valley as gold prospectors in the 1870s, and they worked way out on Hughes Creek," Gene told me. "They trapped martens, also killed mountain sheep for stew meat, then channeled fresh water to the town from on top of the mountains. The Tin Cup Water Company, they called it. It's where you live now," he pointed out.

As a teen, Gene toiled briefly in the local sawmills—

"Fantastic pay," he remembers, "ten bucks an hour with benefits. Dangerous as hell, of course, but try to find starting pay like that now." He was a logger as well, specializing in "landing and chasing chokers," while working for the U.S. Forest Service. "I loved being outside, but then came the environmentalists and the spotted owl, then the Canadians' lumber undercut ours. I mean, hell, in 1969, there were four sawmills in Darby."

Gene's life and skull were drastically reconfigured when he was in the eighth grade. That's when his brother, Dave, shot him. In the head.

"It was a .22 rifle he was cleaning, an accident, nailed me right here on the left side," Gene said as he fingered a lumpy portion of cranium. "Doctors said I was dead, no chance. But they cut out parts of my brain, then drilled three holes"—he points to those as well—"bringing the total to four. I was in a coma for 28 days. When I left the hospital, my speech was like a chipmunk's. My mom taught first grade in Darby, so she was equipped to teach me to read again. When I went back to school, I had an awful time, my big fat head all swole up and a brother feeling guilty as hell. They called me Fathead."

Today Gene's speech is perfect, and I'd never have noticed his ballistic damage unless he'd been so eager to present it.

After graduating from Darby High in a class of 30 kids, Gene sought to dissipate brother Dave's angst by hiring him at his newly founded towing service. That was in 1986, and the brothers quickly prospered.

"Dave was the mechanic, a genius at it," Gene recalls. "We were crushing cars, too, $100 apiece until the price of steel went to shit. But throughout that time there was always something bothering Dave. You know, mentally. Then he married a Filipino woman, real sexy. They had a bad argument. The next morning, when Dave didn't show up for work, I walked to his house. Turns out he'd shot himself ear to ear with a .357 Magnum. Terrible to find him like that. Took all the wind out of me. First Dave shoots me, then Dave shoots Dave. My life has kind of deflated since, the business, too."

The whole town grieved. Brother Dave now reposes in Darby's cemetery, across from the junkyard.

Because so much of my life has been controlled by iron-fisted fact checkers, I opted voluntarily to obtain Dave's death certificate. Sure enough, "Self-inflicted gunshot wound of the head." But here's a happier fact: Dave's widow declared her name to be "Queenee B." So she was Queenee B. Honey. Her legal name. Only small towns produce material like this. Assign blame, but know it by this name: a fine, fine line between the sacred and profane.

Gene nowadays relies financially on towing. "A lot of tourists abandon rental cars, especially Californians," he reports. "And I can't tell you how many cars I've pulled out of the river. Not long ago, I was called to the Rocky Knob [a local roadhouse] for a car that hit black ice and spun into the ditch. By the time I arrived, three more had joined him, and by the time I hooked up the first guy, there were eight. I thought, jeez, I oughta go into the Knob, drink a beer, wait for an even dozen."

Today, though, Gene is dutifully sober. "I'm sometimes on call 24 hours," he explains, "and it's bad form to show up at the crash of a drunk driver drunk."

On the day we talked, Gene was preoccupied not with junkers but 2,100 pounds of wood pellets, his only method of warming the shop.

Pellets stockpiled, Gene cocked his NAPA hat aslant, then directed me to a 1937 Chevy coupe, unrestored but trendy in its flaky-blue patina. "My first car," he noted. "Bought it when I was 13 and drove it to school. Too young? Who cares, it's Montana."

Over the years, other cars filtered through his meaty hands, but Gene collects only the "rare Yanks": a 1966 Chevrolet Impala SS two-door, a '55 Willys wagon with desert rat motif, a 1939 Chevrolet Carryall Suburban, and a 1965 Ford Ranchero. He's not big on modern machinery. "When I arrive at a crash, those new cars, God, there's just plastic pieces all over creation."

Gene never married. "Didn't get around to it," he says. "Then I cut my face with a chain saw and didn't look like a guy you'd want to marry anyway. If it happens, amen. If it don't, amen. I like working."

Gene and I chatted until darkness spawned shadow monsters across the hulk-riddled yard. Preparing to depart, I reached again to shake Gene's hand and Socks shot Scud-like from the filthy floor, biting my hand and knocking my arm into a Pepsi machine bearing a huge "OUT OF ORDER" sign. As if to apologize, the dog moments later stuck his tongue in my ear, then peed on a truck tire.

I found myself alone in the dark with Socks.

Me: "What do you think of being stereotyped as a junkyard dog?"

Socks: "Well, it's like anything else, you know. Theatric tonalism subintegrating spiritual transcendence."

Me: "Do you enjoy working with Gene?"

Socks: "One struggles to disengage from the Buddhist samsara of perceived slights, of course. My white feet, for instance, which have appropriated an appellation of lower-extremity footwear that I, myself, will never require."

Me: "What's up with the biting?"

Socks: "What biting?"

As I climbed into my truck, Socks stretched his front legs on Marshal Larry's SUV, parked in front of the garage awaiting a tuneup. He inflicted claw marks a foot long. I promised to post his bail.

A few paragraphs ago, I mentioned the Rocky Knob, a decrepit roadhouse south of Darby on Highway 93. Neither its floors nor ceilings are level, nor many of its patrons. I mentioned Gene's story about the Knob to a man drinking across from me in our little Bandit Brewery, and here's what he said:

"My grandma used to work at the Rocky Knob. It was a bordello, you know. She was their best whore."

Darby, Montana. Greatest place on earth.

A Basket of Evil Evel Knievels

In July I was assigned to interview Evel Knievel's son, Robbie, in Butte, just one valley east of us. The occasion was Butte's 13th or 14th "Evel Knievel Days"—no one was sure—in celebration of a dead man who had dedicated his life to swindling, philandering, fairy tales, and occupying jail space. Plus a few ten-second bursts of televised anatomical ruination. So I called Alicia Knievel Vincent, Evel's daughter, to arrange the meeting. This was prior to Robbie's proposed motorcycle jump over a 120-foot-wide Butte building. Moments before I set out, Alicia emailed: "Robbie has no license…LOL!" Okay, so forget overflying the building. Robbie would now jump over 26 cars parked on private property, no driver's license required.

Unfortunately, Robbie chalked up another DUI in a longish string of motoring disorders, and no insurance company would cover his leap into Montana airspace.

"I don't think it's gonna happen," warned Alicia. "He's too upset to talk." I asked her to have Robbie call me. "Don't know where he is," she replied but promised a posse to investigate. So I checked into the Butte Holiday Inn, right then charging $214 per night. "That's evil," I told the desk clerk.

"Yep, 'cause of Evel," she replied.

Butte's festival of all things Evel included Pig Snout (a band), a wake-board contest in a pool you might assemble in your foyer, and the Thrillbillies Mega Ramp Show. I missed all that, having discovered the products available at the Evel Beer Garden.

No call from Robbie.

I viewed a larger-than-life statue of Evel pulling a motorcycle wheelie, then missed the Red Line Motorcycle Safety Experience, the bike parade, and Blistered Earth (another band). Again, the Evel Beer Garden.

No call from Robbie.

The next day I pretty much missed everything, having driven to Mountain View Cemetery to view Evel's tombstone. Two grave diggers led me to the six-foot-tall monument, which had been initially erected at the Snake River Canyon in 1974 but was "commandeered by Evel and his family," explained one of the diggers.

"Like stolen?" I asked. He wouldn't commit, instead offering, "You know what they say about Robbie in this town? He's what Evel deserved." Then he pointed a few hundred yards south to Butte's airport, "where Evel kept his jet," then a few hundred yards to the east, "where Evel's house fronted the golf course—living high right there," he said, sweeping his hand to the southeast, "and living low right here," pointing at the grave.

Surrounding the headstone were random shot glasses, cigarettes, coins, and half-smoked joints. More appropriate would have been a stack of bounced checks.

"I know where Robbie is," announced grave digger number two. "He's parked in his friend's driveway, in his camper. Wanna go see?"

What I wanted to see was the Beer Garden again but instead drove to Evel's former house, upon which the bank foreclosed before the man died and also the site of an 11-year-old Robbie posting a sign out front that said, "See Evel Jr. jump —25 cents."

I drove home Saturday night, in time to catch my phone's final ring as it switched to recording. All I heard was a voice say, "Robbie Knievel." That was two weeks ago. I've yet to play back the message. I'm pretty sure I never will.

Do Not Call the Man "Bison Bill"

Extremely busy not interviewing various Knievels, I found time to sample two Butte delicacies beloved statewide. First, a fried pork-chop sandwich, which tastes exactly as marvelous as you'd expect, though wholly dependent on bun. Second, a pasty, which is a mobile pot pie rolled into a shape that miners could grip in low light and low crawlways, Butte being home to one of the largest underground excavations in human history. Pasties comprise onions, turnips, potatoes, and meat. The flavor is improved when accompanied by a "Montana Mary"—Wild Turkey, vodka, tomato juice, and beer, with portions dictated by the thickness of one's stomach cladding.

I was wondering whether Montana might be famous for any food in particular. "Beer," posited Dread Pirate Dave. So I quizzed the chef at our own Broad Axe Lodge, noted locally for prime rib but more for its homemade horseradish, which customers carry home in doggie bags instead of the beef.

Here's all I can report: Elk and bison are Montana touchstones, both notable for leanness, such that rendering them even marginally beyond medium-rare turns them into drywall. In Montana, by the way, it's always "buffalo" instead of "bison," the species' name in error.

When I asked why, friend Theo at the bar said, "Because no one would ever call the man 'Bison Bill Cody.' " So, Darby wins that debate.

It's rare to find elk or bison steaks. The meat is usually ground, then deployed in burgers, chili, and meatballs. I once overcooked a bison meatloaf and later used it to repair my deck. Elk/bison burgers taste like hamburgers but with no grease. A lot of folks miss the grease. (Me.)

Huckleberries are also a famed Montana ingredient although not an entrée. I nonetheless fell in love with huck-glazed pork, huck pie, and huck breakfast buns that shame anything produced by Cinnabon. Darby's very own Wildflower Confections prepares pink-frosted huckleberry pastries they could sell to Escoffier. Price? Three bucks per. I'd guess they weigh a pound apiece.

Lapins and Rainier cherries from near Flathead Lake are celebrated statewide as individual flavor firecrackers. But what's most revered from that lake is invasive lake trout, caught by the Confederated Salish tribes who have official dispensation to fish commercially. The idea is to encourage flagging populations of native Westslope and bull trout. The Salish filets are often as big as 20 ounces and are so savory pan-fried that any condiment spurted thereon can earn the cook five years in Riker's and a papal beating. Julie and I once bought 14 monster filets from a Missoula organic-foods store, annihilating their stock and our cash. We ate them in a month.

I kept looking for any other quintessentially Montanan dish, something the world should know about. Then I heard on the radio about a festival in which plugs of Montana-grown Big Hole beef were being jammed onto the tines of a pitchfork and plunged into boiling oil. That's when I stopped looking.

John Phillips

Tangled Up in Piss Fir

In the Bitterroots, the fiery debate over forest fires is itself flammable. Right up there with wolves, gun laws, inner-fender F-150 rust, and whether Smokey Bear could possibly be 76 and taking Celebrex for his arthritic paws.

Darby was originally a minor hub for logging, and that wasn't too long ago, as in the '70s and early '80s, when billowing mustaches and bell-bottom jeans were also fire hazards. There are more fires now than then. In fact, the Department of the Interior cites 71,499 wildfires in 2017, burning 10 million acres. Feel free to insert a square-mile comparison with Rhode Island.

In Darby, one group of citizens wishes to return to the 1930s, allowing loggers to clear-cut everything their chain saws can chew. They believe that lumber jobs trump environmental outcomes. A second camp lobbies for selective thinning and clearing of the forest floor, an expensive venture that often relies on helicopters, and if it can't be undertaken from the air, then roads must be carved into pristine wilderness. A third camp advocates that every human being on the planet keep his filthy mitts off every limb, stump, hanging branch, and stinging nettle—back off, you prancing baboons. And a fourth camp promotes dousing man-made fires pronto—by 10:00 the following morning—but allowing lightning-initiated fires to burn, per Mother Nature's mandate.

Of course, here again we nominate ourselves as Mother Nature's hall monitor because, well, sometimes she is a sloppy slut. Unfortunately, we often don't know what triggered a fire. Maybe this latest bolt of lightning wouldn't have struck if humankind hadn't heated up the planet, causing more thunderstorms. Maybe the fire wouldn't have spread if consumers hadn't demanded so much air-conditioning juice from PG&E, exploding its transformers.

"Ecosystems are not only more complex than we think," said ecologist Frank Egler, "they're more complex than we *can* think." That is such a perfect quote that I've memorized it. The point it illustrates, among many, is that our own role mystifies us. We're like a football coach who doesn't know the score, doesn't know the names of his players, and doesn't know the team he's playing. Yet he confidently sends in Hail Mary stratagems and occasionally punts on first down.

Among the first to question fire suppression was a Montanan named Elers Koch, a legendary woodsman and horseman who reportedly hiked 20 miles to establish an appetite before dinner, an urban myth of the finest bullshit. In the summer of 1910, Koch helped battle the infamous "Big Burn," a blaze that killed 87 people as it annihilated three million acres of western Montana and neighboring Idaho.

Said Koch of firefighters: "Has all this effort and expenditure of millions of dollars added anything to human good?" Whether or not humankind profited is, to me, irrelevant. But Koch won me over for his insistence that certain wilderness plots remain untouched. Said he, "Roads are such final and irretrievable facts."

Since moving to the Bitterroots, I've noticed it's mostly conservatives who are fleetest to abandon their contempt for government spending when it protects the homes they knowingly built in the "wildland-urban interface." Here's a stat new to me: Fighting forest fires—not to save the trees but to save homes—accounts for 95 percent of all suppression costs. It made me feel guilty. I put out extra corn for the deer.

John Phillips

During my first summer in Montana, there were 28 helicopters and 18 fixed-wing aircraft overflying woodland infernos in my corner of the state. At least two of the blazes devolved into so-called project fires, in which firefighters abandoned hope of snuffing them, settling instead on shepherding the flames to exact the least human mayhem.

Nevertheless, more than a million Montana acres were morphed into swaths of opaque dust bunnies. Four thousand firefighters were run to exhaustion, with two killed by falling trees. It cost Montana $75 million—the Lolo Peak fire 70 miles north of my home cost $48 million alone—then an additional $240 million when tourists canceled their vacations, afraid of inhaling smoke and of blistering cinders burning holes in their Patagonia vests. Cowards.

Of course, after fires erupt, a bumper crop of morel mushrooms reliably propagates. Morels, it turns out, resemble huckleberries in their predilection for singed ground, though they won't grow at all where the fire has been so fierce as to sterilize the soil. They're known as "chicken of the woods" here. We had morels back in Michigan, so I'll say no more about the addled 'shroom hunters, with their filthy pillowcases and roadside stands that occasionally poison customers. I have ethics but no morels.

Did you know Native Americans regularly set fires intentionally? They understood that the aftermath supplied an abundance of nuts, berries, seeds, fatter elk, and systemic gout. Indeed, if you read your L&C diaries carefully, you'll notice that Indians also set forests alight as a means of telegraphing danger. Such as, "Two white guys inbound. Anyone have an antidote for measles and the clap?"

Because I am from the Midwest, I still feel guilty about everything from corrupt Ohio presidents to the Lindbergh kidnapping, and here before me is another reason to cringe. When California started burning to the ground, I read a lot about the wildland-urban interface, in which humans—me, for one—erect homes on the margins of, and sometimes *in*, unspoiled forests.

Here's a whopper of a stat from *In These Times:* "Since

1990, wildlands have been converted into WUI at an average rate of three acres a minute." That doesn't seem possible, yet I'll wager that somewhere a Sierra Club member studying a U.S. map has stuck a red pin into the site of my Montana residence and is right now saying, "Look at this crypto-Nazi in the woods. Let's gas his cats."

Of course, the WUI stats also mislead. I mean, every time a Native American or white Pilgrim, from Day One, built any structure at all—a tipi, a trench latrine, a stable—it was smack-dab in America's WUI. If there were no humans at all, we wouldn't be having this problem, which is true of virtually all the natural world's vexations, including my difficulty with math. When Lakota chief Red Cloud ceased fighting, he mentioned to a white delegation: "We didn't need all this land. Neither did you."

It used to be that the "piss fir"—the tangled low-lying scrub that tripped loggers and what hikers call "dog hair"—would weld itself to the ground so tenaciously that it held snow and moisture, thus becoming moderately fire-resistant. No more. That tangle has now dried and is eager to ignite. In fact, it's where the Lolo Peak fire began, just up the road, and accounts for the loss of 16 houses in our Roaring Lion fire.

Fire expert Richard Manning said, "Wilderness has a better grasp of global warming than we do…the difference between the human and the wild's grasp of the matter is the denial. Wilderness has no reasoning, no wishes, no preferences. Instead, it deploys death and fire to prepare the way for whatever is to come."

Our extinction is "whatever is to come."

In a small combustible pile on my desk I corral confounding statistics, and I will trot them out now because I can and also because I'll be glad to be rid of the pile. So here goes: Eighty-four percent of wildfires in America are ignited by humans. The length of the season for human-caused fires is now 154 days—ten weeks longer than in 1972. The most common day for fires is July 4, no surprise, but here is a corker: From what can be established via modern record-keeping, we humans have burned 44 percent of all the acreage in the continental United States. I daresay the only way to achieve that would be to re-create the incendiary bombing of Tokyo.

It's both horrifying and reassuring, because it sure doesn't appear today as if we've torched half our homeland. Mother Nature is more forgiving than Mother Teresa. She's still a little sluttish, though.

A WHIFF OF FIREPOWER AND FLOMAX

Julie and I were invited to the neighborhood's July 4 party. Not knowing more than two attendees, I tried to align myself equally with each of the four forest-fire constituencies, but nothing forestalls the arguments.

"You must be from California" is what one neighbor offered, knowing full well I'm a Midwesterner who catalogs the precise moment when corn will tassel. As he flipped burgers the size of cow pies, he referred to liberals as having "poisoned Ravalli County and the University of Montana."

His hooded, steady gaze made it clear I was among the poisoners. So I steered the conversation toward the other subject that reliably inflames, namely, the elk population nearest us, the so-called Tin Cup herd with 99 members. They grind grass daily behind my home, but my neighbor claims their numbers have been hideously decimated by wolves, who are nothing but teeth on the trot, fashioned by Al Gore.

He then rammed his steel spatula into something impregnable in the back of the grill and shouted: "Montana Fish and Game are *liars*! They *hate* hunters."

Why he should loathe the folks presiding over a bumper crop of elk is a mystery, but he is not alone. We were joined on his porch by a man who earned riches pirating email data.

The grill master said to Computer Cal, "*This* guy"—pointing the spatula at me as if waving a pistol—"doesn't get it. He just does *not*..." But he was too worked up to complete the sentence, so he hissed a light obscenity that emerged with a spray of saliva. I made note of which burger was baking in his bacterial shower, then laid down some government elk-census numbers.

He replied, "You know, there's always a flip side to the flip side," which I felt was a way of saying I'd won the argument.

The only thing that Montanans hate more than Montana Fish, Wildlife & Parks is the U.S. Forest Service and advice proffered by anyone who knows the difference between a conservative and a conservationist. In Montana, *Canis lupus* is Al-Qaeda but with sleeker winter wear. Montana's hunters claim wolves have killed every mammal between Darby and Mount Fuji and were complicit in the murder of Nicole Brown Simpson.

Funny thing is, when the wardens began monitoring elk corpses, they discovered that wolves were far down the list of assassins, well behind bears and disease and "human interaction," which includes rifle activity, arrows, Wayne LaPierre, and the chrome grilles of Chevy Suburbans cruising Highway 93. But you dare not mention it here, because it makes a government agency appear to be doing its job—maybe doing it well—which is simply impossible.

Carl Sandburg said, "If the law is on your side, pound on the law. If the facts are on your side, pound on the facts. If neither is on your side, pound on the table." But I'm afraid to, because it might negate future invitations to neighborhood parties offering free alcohol.

Now that I've located more free alcohol, here are the stats expensively generated by Montana Fish, Wildlife & Parks: In the 1990s, there were 65,000 elk in Montana. Now there are 115,000, their numbers yet rising. I'm not sure why hunters are in such a steaming swivet over this, but my experience in life is that hunters, as a group, complain a lot. To counter their specious assertions about "depleted herds," I sometimes tentatively mention that one tactic to expand their number would be to stop shooting them. Just for a month or two. Such affrontery around here invites a septum deviated, detached, discarded. South of town reposes a roadside game-inspection station, where a billboard cites accumulated kills: elk, white-tailed deer, bear, moose, mule deer, bighorn sheep. I expected to see wolves at the bottom of the list, but, instead, someone had written in "Ex Wives."

Here's another characteristic of Bitterroot riflemen: They are overwhelmingly age 60 and beyond. I wonder if their complaints have more to do with their arthritic knees carrying them into the forest little farther than peeing distance, a zone the animals already know to be lousy with firepower and Flomax. If you're about to keel over from a pound of cholesterol in your coronary arteries, a vigorous pursuit of an eight-point buck is off the table and onto the operating table. But I'm just speculating.

To my Montana critics, I am "pro-animal/anti-human," as if there's a difference, and they condemn my theories by asking, "Have you ever hunted before?" The answer is no, but I'm not sure what that teaches us. I ask in return, "Have you ever spent a summer *not* hunting, or have you ever shot photos instead of bullets?" Such comebacks emit wet snorts of outright derision. Next comes what hunters believe is the ultimate put-down: "Have you ever butchered an animal so you know where your food comes from?" My reply: "Have you ever operated a 50-ton stamping press so that you know where your Ford comes from?" There was a factoid in *Harper's* that encapsulated my biases: "Year in which bison were last observed in Germany before a sighting in September: 1755. Estimated hours after the sighting that the bison was killed by a local hunter: *five*."

Not much later, the senescent grill master fled our rustic wilds, noting, "I'm sick of fighting the elements," one of the elements being me. We refer to those folks—him now, especially—as the "flatlanders," because, unlike us, they are not embedded on the side of a mountain and thus lead lives of indolent leisure. They are to be pitied. Their lives are shit.

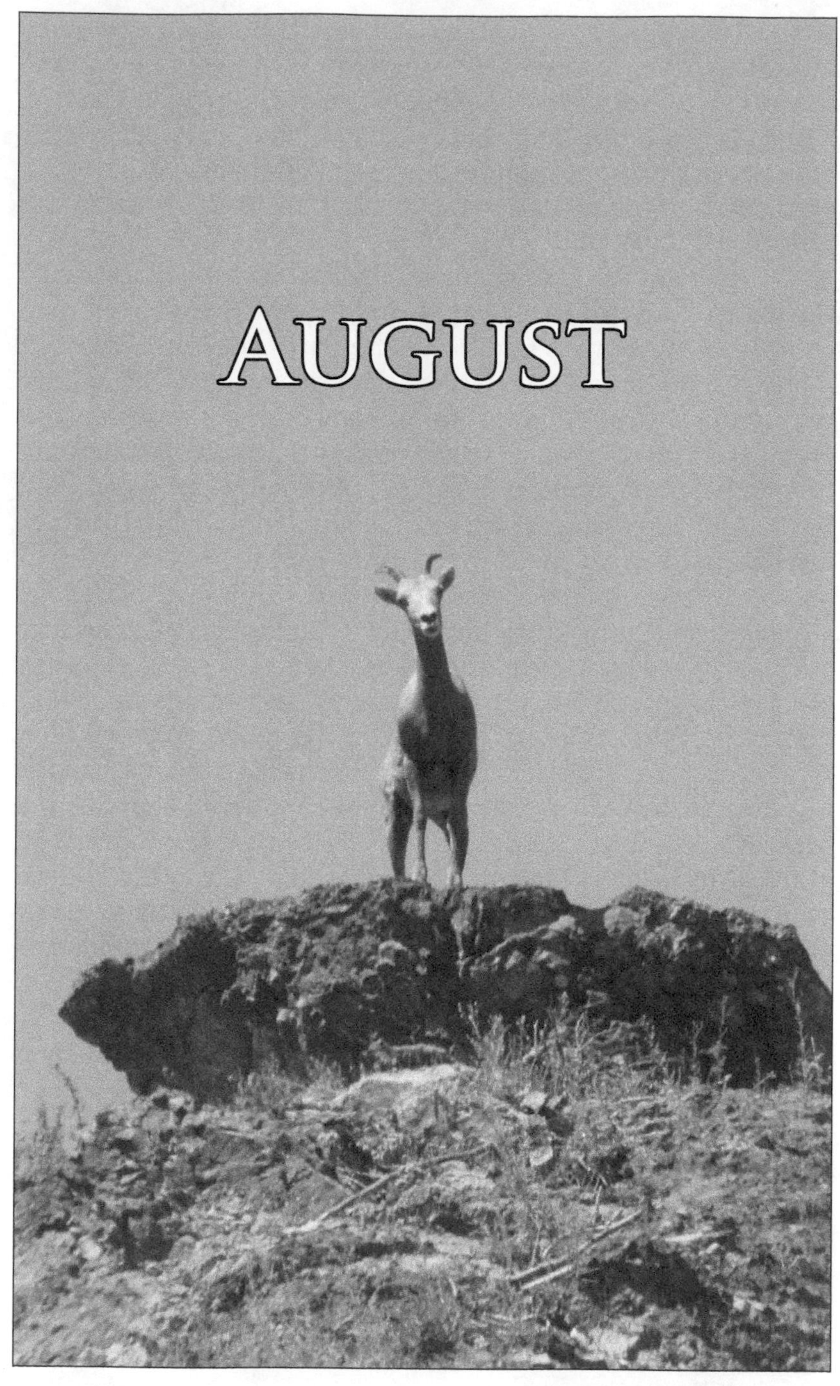
AUGUST

A CIA Officer in Rubber Pants

I had been examining myself for mental carbuncles and piratical tumors of the psyche. So far, the wilderness's foremost revelation was silence. I had right then ceased talking to humans, there being few hereabout to talk to anyway, and my silence felt as soothing as a sugar pill. Given all that spare time not yakking, I set about listening—to a single Steller's jay, to begin with. She eyed me as I plopped stale bread on the porch. In ten seconds, she emitted a low, resonant whoop, summoning three family members who flitted to branches behind her. She turned to stare at her relatives, then at the bread—she was showing them the target—whereupon all four flapped to my supplied country buffet. I wasn't surprised that animals worked in league to their communal benefit. But I *was* surprised I'd been quiet long enough to observe them do it. I felt some contentment in that. Like warm grape jelly stuck to your wrist.

It had me listening to the Bitterroot River, too, among Mother Nature's sparkliest gems, a 50-mile-long showcase of swirling Swarovski eddies and whirlpools. It is among the top trout streams in America, with three varieties on tap: cutthroat, rainbow, and brown, plus the occasional Rocky Mountain whitefish swimming along as a scorned minority.

John Phillips

Trout are said to slurp, sip, or suck hand-tied dry flies, but they are goddamned cagey about it. They examine flies as if each might explode. Tom McGuane called them "uncompromising creatures in whose spirit the angler attempts to read his own fortune." Not really. When Lewis and Clark came upon the Bitterroot River in September 1805, Lewis wrote: "The banks are low and its bed entirely gravel. The stream appears navigable, but from the circumstance of there being no salmon in it, I believe that there must be a considerable fall in it below."

Lewis's remarkable rivercraft warned him of a sizable waterfall, blocking salmon migration. More important to him, of course, was that waterfalls represented a pain in the shoulders for men portaging 300-pound canoes. Of course, by then they'd already stashed the watercraft—hidden them from the Indians, in fact.

By the time they reached my valley, the Corps of Discovery had been disabused of the notion of a navigable route from St. Louis to the Pacific Ocean, which must have been an emotional damp squib. I always wondered why they didn't quit right then. Thomas Jefferson had granted prior permission to do so. Certainly, Jefferson would not have recommended they engage in rookie mountaineering, which is precisely what they next did. Mind you, Jefferson had his own whimsies: Having seen woolly mammoth fossils, he had instructed L&C to bring back a *living* example, on the theory it would impress European ladies. Bring a live mammoth back in what? A three-foot-wide canoe? A shopping bag?

In any event, with a river like the Bitterroot in my backyard, it had become my ambition to acquire the rudiments of fly-fishing, having never previously lifted a fly rod. Compared with L&C's travails, it would be easy, I thought. Simply remit to Orvis $800 for the rod and $200 for the reel and $600 for various accessories that veterans patiently explain are vital to the experience.

Then I hired a $50-per-hour Orvis guide. His name is Bruce Hemmings, a retired CIA officer who speaks Arabic, taught Middle Eastern history, and lived there for years monitoring the comings and goings of weaponry, in service of the "Company," as he yet calls it. I imagined it was all pretty shadowy and cryptic but Bruce said not. On assignment, he taught one of the Saudi princes to fly-fish, which brought to mind trout flopping across fine white dunes.

Bruce looks quintessentially Irish: red cheeks, burst blood vessels, heavy nose, expansive forehead, and a head as big as a pumpkin. Think of Ed McMahon in waders. He is a bachelor in the sense that his behavior leaves him no choice—Bruce's description, not mine—and his daily dinner is a Hungry-Man frozen concoction that's about 59-percent salt and as heavy as plumbing equipment. Throughout his microwaved meals he smokes cigarettes. He later taught a six-week adult-ed class on the Arab Spring, which I attended and enjoyed.

During my first fly-casting lesson, Bruce insisted the process was so simple it could not be screwed up. "It's on the order of a defective screwdriver," he claimed. That was a lie.

My first rod turned out to be the Countrywide Financial equivalent of fly-fishing rigs. "What you gonna do, *spear* the trout?" Bruce asked.

So I whipped out our fly shop's Bible-thick catalog to purchase a nine-foot, five-weight carbon-fiber rod with superfast action and quick damping of tip vibrations, mated to a heavily ported, mid-arbor, self-lubricating reel with a sealed dual-action drag body loaded with hybrid ceramic bearings with an oversize drag knob and a CNC-machined spool of 6061-T6 aluminum alloy. At least I think that's what I have. It may still be a spear.

Then I purchased a similar setup for Julie. "It's still less expensive than golfing," she encouraged, but I have my doubts. "Give a man a fish, he eats for a day. Teach a man to fish, the fish laugh for a lifetime."

Bruce knows my connection to cars and told me that my latest dry-fly outfit represents the difference between a Ford and a Ferrari. But I've driven a lot of Ferraris, and I can tell you that no Testarossa ever wound itself around my ankles and toppled me into a black pool of 39-degree water.

"Calm down," Bruce instructed over and over. "You're scaring the fish. And me."

Eventually, my four new fishing magazines arrived. In one, there was a debate about fly lines: helium microspheres versus carbon nanotube spray-on coatings versus self-healing plastic polymers. It was like reading the ingredients of a bottle of tamoxifen. In another, an editor wrote, "The drag cylinder itself is available in contrasting tone…kind of like those flashy bright-red Porsche brakes." Apparently priced by Porsche, too.

Whenever I'd seek guidance through this maze of piscatorial vernacular, I'd utter awful inadvertent blunders, and Bruce would cringe, then look away, then light another cigarette as he fished in three feet of fast-moving water. I once asked if I could wade without my Simms boots. "Let me ask you this," Bruce replied. "How do you feel about a broken hip?"

Really, this sport is not welcoming. Dry flies, wet flies, nymphs, or streamers? "Match the hatch" comes the age-old reply, but the available flies are as numerous and befuddling as tax forms. You've got your Royal Red Humpys and Mystery Meat Skwalas and Chubby Chernobyls. In the Big Hole watershed, the favored dry fly is called Cat Vomit, which you'll want to alternate with a Turd & Worm. Now, when another angler asks what fly I'm throwing, I shout, "Pale Morning Dun" or "Purple Haze," those being the only two I can identify in a box that appears to have contained a bird explosion. If the trout spit those, I'll club them with my $135 Brodin net's teak handle, which might have been lifted from the dash of Charles Scripps's Bentley.

One of dozens of gratuitous complexities is simply withdrawing a new tapered leader from its package. The leaders are nine feet long and are shipped in an intertwined circular loop. One third of the leader is as thin as a vole whisker, meaning I can't see it unless I place it up to my nose, causing my eyes to cross. I usually tangle the leader into knots 30 seconds into the removal sequence, creating a $4 nest of uselessness. Not just Gordian knots but an entire knots Berry Farm.

For their own fishing adventures, Lewis and Clark

were more modest, purchasing 70 large hooks, as well as "drum lines," "India lines," and eight "stave reels," whatever those are. Total cost: $25.37. I spend that much on lost flies on every outing. It made me laugh to see what Lewis and Clark had hidden among their fishing-supplies invoice forwarded to the federal government: "One Sportsman flask, $1.50." I bought one, too, but mine cost 20 times as much and so did the contents.

I was beginning to feel like a fisherman in the way Napoleon thought of himself as a bed-wetter. That's when Julie and I drove to Livingston, Montana, to tour the mecca of fly-fishing worldwide, Dan Bailey's, whose storefront is adorned with three metal trout the size of Great Whites. When I entered, it was like my first visit to the Louvre, except the pilgrims were softly whispering about Griffin rotating hackle pliers. One guy referred to his rod as his "stick," his "rifle," his "cannon." I imagine he calls his car a Beemer.

I wrote checks for a pair of wading boots with felt soles and another with rubber soles embedded with cleats that make them look like lumberjack spikes. I bought a Filson 12.5-ounce Tin Cloth hat and flip-down magnifying glasses so I can locate the microscopic goddamn flies—sizes two through twenty-two, a numbering system that was explained to me by the CIA agent and instantly forgotten. Without fail the hooks sink their syringe-sharp barbs into my fingers, although I now own three stainless surgeon's forceps to effect the bloody extractions, and all three were recently necessary to withdraw a Purple Haze from the headliner of my truck. I once embedded a hook so far into my right index finger that I had to enlist Julie to remove it. I almost fainted. I almost puked. But it was far and away my heftiest catch of the day.

I later learned from a Big Horn River guide how to retract hooks: Loop two strands of tippet around the hook's eye, then use a stick to push against the hooked finger in the direction opposite the barb. Then you entreat your fishing buddy to yank upward suddenly and mercilessly with no "one, two, three" as prologue. I underwent the procedure twice. It left a divot that gushed blood—"just drag your hand in the water a while," the guide replied to my moaning—and I must say the process was relatively painless, in the sense that appendicitis doesn't really hurt that much at first.

I parked beside the East Fork of the Bitterroot River last week and spent 20 minutes strapping on all my gear. I took breaks to avoid hyperventilating and to mop sweat. It was like preparing for a spacewalk. If I fell into 12 inches of water, I'd be hard pressed to save myself, wearing so much rubber. I remember strolling to a fresh fishing spot and on my first cast snagging the hood of my sweatshirt, which slammed shut over my face.

"Cold?" Bruce asked. He never seemed amused by my blunders, but I wasn't positive, because I've never seen him smile, even when he hooks a 19-inch rainbow, after which he smokes a cigarette.

Here's what fly-fishermen don't tell you: Yes, you will hook a fish, but, no, you will not land it. Not in the first three months, anyway. Either you'll pump enough adrenaline that you'll jerk the line so hard the fish sails right over the boat and lands in an adjacent river, where it will spit the hook, which by gentlemen's agreement in this valley must be barbless. Or you will be patient and "play" the fish, which is what it is for the fish, too. And then he'll spit the barbless hook.

I told Bruce that my best bet was to detain a fish. No boast is more lame than "I almost had him." It's like saying, "I could have made love to that girl if I'd taped a Popsicle stick to my dick." In Montana, Smokey's admonishment, "Only *you* can prevent forest fires," has been transmuted to, "Only *you* can invent fishing lies."

Here's what John Steinbeck said about fishing: "Any man who pits his intelligence against a fish and loses has it coming." I had it coming but didn't know it. At the end of another trout-free day, the CIA agent said, "If you don't learn to fish, John, you're gonna be one of those guys making lists of overflying birds." At least I can *see* the birds.

Here's another top-secret fisherism: You will fall into

the water. Not just a couple times. A couple dozen times. Not simply because you'll slip on snotty moss-covered rocks in a strong current, which you definitely will, but because you'll fall right off the goddamn boat. I don't know why I keep dunking myself. Despite Bruce's prediction I'd become a birder, I'm really more a swimmer. Understand, the water in the Bitterroot River was snow about 20 minutes earlier, and if enough of it flows down the inside of your rubber waders, "Jim and the twins" will withdraw for weeks and you will develop negative buoyancy, which is a euphemism for drowning.

The first time I inadvertently plunged, it was because Dave Chenkovich—my second Orvis guide, known to me as Dread Pirate Dave—instructed me to "jump over the boat's bow when we near the pullout ramp, then tie us up."

Unfortunately, the wind was blowing, and the only part of that sentence I heard was, "Jump over the bow," which I obediently did into about five feet of water threatening to turn into a hockey rink. I can't remember how I made it to shore. I do remember pointlessly hanging on to the side of the boat for a spell, looking up at Dave's face for help. He didn't help. What he did was phone his girlfriend, Corinne, to whom he said about four times, "Yeah, really."

Dave and I then drove to the Darby liquor store, where manager Robin pointed a finger and said: "*You*, come inside," this to Dave. "*You*, wait outside," this to me, as I stood dripping a substantial portion of the river and wearing cleated boots that would have dented Robin's pine flooring. I leaked on the sidewalk like a wet hunting dog and shouted my order through the cracked door. Dave and I later sat in the truck and drank some Pendleton. More than some, actually.

The next time I fell off the boat, it was at dawn at Seeley Lake, 100 or so miles northeast of Darby, which to Montanans is merely "a hop, a skip, and a third-gear press." It happened as I tentatively stepped into the vessel—ten minutes earlier I'd been snoring and dreaming in the back of the truck. That's when Scott Kaminski's dog, Zoey, selected the same real estate to alight.

I don't know why I didn't win this ridiculous battle with a 50-pound retriever, but I didn't. I fell over the starboard side like a sack of axles, if axles could flail and howl while sinking. The instant I struck the first molecule of water, I knew it was an event that Orvis guides would be rehashing for months. What's worse, I couldn't stand up. I had to be physically hoisted by my belt, thereafter wrinkling like a prune until noon or so, when the sun's warmth permitted me to strip down to my Jockeys, which were lime green that day.

Dave later told me I was "flailing like a Mississippi paddle wheeler" and he promised to remember it forever. I topped off the day by catching zero fish, my established quota. You know that phrase "It's not about catching fish but enjoying a day on the water"? That's bullshit. A big stinking lie.

I fell in four other times, too, if slightly less spectacularly. It taught me two things: First, do not immediately attempt to stand. Just sit in the water for a spell, until you regain your bearings and colleagues can make you an object of derision. When you make a huge splash in water supposedly housing trout, the trout notice. So do nearby fishermen, who retrieve little index cards from which they'll read prepared remarks. When you fall, moreover, do not ever use your fishing rod for stream-bottom leverage, unless you find entertainment in writing $800 checks.

Some of my disgraces were forgiven, because I did eventually catch a 20-inch brown trout that, like a kid, I wanted to name and take home as a pet. "Can I keep him, Mom?" Brown trout and whitefish are the only species fishermen can remove from the Bitterroot River because they're not indigenous. Like me.

Anyway, my brownie was as colorful as a banana split and more healthful. Unfortunately, Dave knocked it on the head and tossed it in the cooler, his entrée for that night. I said nothing because the etiquette on the river is that the guide keeps whatever his appetite recommends.

Back home with Julie, I said, "Fucking Dave took my fish." But I had secretly stashed a Rocky Mountain whitefish in my backpack, a fish that had, for reasons unknown to me, expired in my net. Whitefish are castigated bottom feeders filled with needlelike bones, but Julie and I rated our dinner three stars with an equal number of inner-cheek punctures.

As a matter of fact, I went on to catch plenty of fish, both on the Bitterroot and on the Henry's Fork at a resort called Three Rivers Ranch. It was colossally beyond my budget but felt justifiable to demonstrate competence to the CIA agent, who still regarded me as some sort of Aldrich Ames type. And, indeed, I caught 20 trout on my first Henry's Fork outing. Julie caught ten.

For each fish I landed, I could have shelled out a $100 bill and chucked it into the freezing water, given what I was spending. Fly-fishing is so detrimental to good judgment that I fished right through a snowstorm, twin ropes of snot streaming off my chin. I might add that the resort is where Julie and I celebrated our wedding anniversary, and she evinced enthusiasm, although I wondered if she secretly viewed it as the equivalent of a gift-wrapped Hoover.

Behind our cabin ran a small but fetching stream overhung by larch trees right then a hue buttery gold, where anglers practiced casting before the big float. I nudged Julie to produce her new rod, price tag yet affixed. She cast weakly, flipping a tan caddis about five feet from the bank. Whereupon, against all odds, she hooked a portly brownie she had to drag ashore; we'd brought no net because we expected no fish.

I whooped and danced like three of the Village People. It was the first trout Julie had ever caught. Right after I unhooked the creature, the top eight inches of Julie's Orvis rod tumbled down the leader and plopped into the water. An $800 rod. First use. Still smelling of lacquer. In pieces. It encapsulated the fly-fishing experience: Unexpected delight followed by a fiesta of humiliation with a largish outlay of cash as dessert. It's like buying a new car, driving it home in a euphoric haze, only to meet a repo agent in your driveway.

There's a vodka called Dry Fly. Drinking it corrupts my intentions, but so does casting flies. So far, it's the only fishing product that has welcomed me. You read so much about fishing as a Zen-like mental salve. Hah. You want to engorge your ego with lead-acid angst? Spend eight hours on the water—in front of other men and your wife—exhausting every bodily corpuscle without catching a fish. You'll want to cripple some Girl Scouts.

A GUN AIMED AT HAM LOAF

There are six or so "highlander" households in my far flung and forested neighborhood. We cannot view one another, but we all talk briefly car-to-car on the gravel road that leads to the paved road that leads to our wrecked mailboxes. What did the Bitterroots do to you today? Two of our neighbors' houses are one-room affairs. The nearest was originally erected as a hunting cabin, but adjoining neighbors became exasperated when the owner took to blasting critters from the comfort of his own porch. Now a married couple lives there, and I can't imagine being so tightly spammed. Murder is surely a fixture in their matrimony. They even work together, operating a tiny drive-through coffee stand on Highway 93. I wonder nightly what weapons they possess and whether I should attempt confiscation before the inevitable *"Here's Johnny"* scene.

Next to their cabin—well, 40 or so forest acres away—reposes a mansion that might be worth $3 million. It belongs to the former CEO of Daltile in Dallas, an ever smiling gentleman named John LoMonaco. He married a woman 30 years his junior, a model for Karl Lagerfeld. "Karl was creepy," she claims. John came here because he is a big-game hunter. That is, he's big and so is the game. John appears on the covers of hunting magazines, and even at age 89 regularly dashes off to Siberia, Turkey, Romania, Pakistan, and various Whateverstans, where the locals would like to murder him but also where the mountains hide sheep with curlicue horns that extend five feet from their handsome skulls.

I know that sounds preposterous, but if you look up "Bukharan markhor from the Afghan/Tajikistan border," you'll see it's true. If you can't find one, it's because our man LoMonaco owns all the world's examples, displayed in a hangar-size log building he erected next to his manse, strictly to accommodate his vast and varied taxidermy. It resembles a church and includes stepmother living quarters, which makes me wonder if she's next.

One Russian bear in his collection cost $12,000 to stuff. There are so many marble-eyed mammals in John's trophy house that an 18-wheeler was required to deliver them. They were offloaded and briefly stored in a rented building alongside Sober Automotive—that's 440 feet below us in town—then ferried up the mountain in small 4WD box vans. The trophy house alone took 18 months to build.

I must say, we've eked out voluminous enjoyment from the LoMonacos, sitting at their dining-room table capable of revolving 360 degrees via electric motor so guests can glimpse the nearby forest critters eating and copulating and pecking holes in the chinking. If I owned a circulating dinner table, I'd wait until disagreeable guests were seated before their steaming entrées, then I'd crank the merry-go-round to about 2500 rpm so that a big cleanup ensued. The LoMonacos own a second amazing machine; it makes Italian gelato that would have put Mussolini into diabetic shock even as he hung upside down.

A half mile from our friends the LoMonacos is a single-room home that's off the grid. No electricity, no TV, no plumbing, one happy occupant: our beloved guitarist/ex-hippie Mike Phillips, no relation. His home is invisible from the dirt road, swallowed by the "piss fir." Mike has lived there as a solitary bachelor for 30-some years.

A half mile from Mike is a peculiar house that resembles a '70s-era motel, yet only two people call it home. The owner suffered a septic backup one day and referred to it as a "poonami." I wondered how one couple could create such a mess, then willed myself to wonder elsewhere.

On the first leg of the drive that leads to our home, one of our crimson-necked neighbors erected a sign depicting a stylized handgun with the legend: "There's nothing here worth dying for." The sign was so close to the road that I accidentally struck it with the Tundra's bull bar maybe 47 times in the space of three days, but it wouldn't fall.

The sign was offensive on its face but also self-canceling. That is, if there's nothing of value in the house, why shoot the intruder in the first place? Why even lock the doors? We don't. Why not urge the thief simply to steal the expensive stuff, namely, the sign and the owner's handgun? But these questions, like so many others in the West, have never been answered because they've never been asked.

Our closest neighbors are Kemp and Patty Conn. Kemp toiled for the Bureau of Land Management and is a vital source of forest lore.

"Are these wolf tracks?" I asked, to which he replied, "Only if you think a golden retriever is a wolf." We hiked another mile and Kemp pointed at the mud. "Now *those* are wolf tracks," he declared. Each print was the size of a tea saucer.

A week later, Julie heard the pack in a sing-along at 10 p.m. She ran to awaken me. Call me Jack London, but I must report that wolves possess mellifluous howling voices and occasionally collude in three-part harmony like Crosby, Stills & Canis lupus. There are ten of them, members of the Hughes Creek pack, which should have placed them 30 miles from our front door. We couldn't see their faces because they were arrayed below a grassy hummock. I wondered if they wore crisp barbershop-quartet aprons, with one wolf conscientiously flipping sheet music. Kemp later found their tracks, then pointed to bear tracks even larger. The trail behind our home is covered in more tracks than Paddington Station.

Our wolf saga continued. We had driven to the Big Hole Battlefield, where Chief Joseph met more military-inflicted misery, and upon our return espied a black figure a quarter mile ahead, crossing the road.

I reckoned it was a juvenile bear, and Julie declared it a toddler moose. Neither. It was a lone wolf, black as anthracite and weighing, we estimated, at least 100 pounds. We rolled up on him fast, like cops, and the wolf halted, perplike, to scrutinize us cautiously from a distance of 25 feet. For a few beats, we studied each other's motives and enigmatic worlds.

As it happens, I've locked eyes on wolves before. I encountered three in Alaska while writing about the Iditarod, then strolled among a dozen in Indiana while on assignment at the Wolf Park, where their behavior is studied as part of a Purdue mandate. I was shown into their spacious enclosures, where a 130-pound alpha male leapt up, draped his paws over my shoulders, and lasered me with an intellectual stare. His eyes were tangerine. Then he dispensed a kiss, full tongue, not unlike my first girlfriend but with worse breath. Monty Sloan, the Wolf Park's staff photographer, explained that tasting saliva is how wolves identify each other for a lifetime. They never forget spit. But I wanted to, inasmuch as this languid creature had moments earlier been chewing a moldering and maggoty deer carcass.

Back to neighbors Kemp and Patty: Both are devout Mormons who do not swear or drink caffeine or alcohol, although Patty is keen on NFL gambling and has launched a women's poker club that convenes monthly, from which Julie returns cashless. Via all-terrain vehicle, Kemp led us miles into the forest behind our house, with a hand cannon strapped to an equipment rack. We eventually reached a clearing created by loggers decades earlier. The three of us sat on stumps and ate tuna-salad sandwiches.

Kemp said: "I once brought a dozen Boy Scouts here on a camping trip. At exactly this point, one of them asked me for a Snickers bar. I told him I didn't have a Snickers bar. So he asked for a Coke. I told him I didn't have a Coke. When I said, 'Okay, boys, let's move out,' the complainer stood up and announced, 'Mr. Conn, we've been talking about it, and, well, sir, we've decided not to go any farther.'"

Kemp swiveled to face me. "Can you believe it?" he steamed. "The little fuckers *mutinied* on me." His face immediately turned red from having said such a thing, but Julie was already peeing her pants and I was expelling snot on nearby stumps. We've treasured Kemp ever since.

Another unconventional neighbor, Vara McGarrell, is an adulator of all four-legged beasts and a fierce critic of those importuning her on two. She fed a feral cat for 20 years until the raggedy feline climbed onto Vara's deck and huffed her final breath, as if she knew Vara would compassionately tend to the disposal of her lean corpse. Which Vara did, paying to have the cat cremated and memorialized.

Then Vara involved herself in another animal escapade, exhibiting all the earmarks of a 1960s Disney movie. Here are the basics: There had been a light-plane crash in the mountains near us, yet another in an endless string of Bitterroot Valley aviation disasters. The plane collided with treetops, which tore off both wings, then the fuselage inverted, coming to rest not too many miles from Highway 93 but obscured by dense cover. The seriously injured pilot and female passenger were eventually dragged out on sleds pulled by ATVs, but their German shepherd Valkyrie had fled the scene and who can blame him?

Vara tape-recorded the pilot in hospital, calling the dog's name. Then she replayed the recording at the crash scene for *ten* consecutive days, until the dog came bounding out of the thickets to greet what he thought was his owner but was, of course, Vara with a leash. Vienna sausages and a tennis ball were involved.

You couldn't make that up. It was reported in the newspaper, plus Vara recounted the story as we stood in the tiny post office vestibule where all Darby feuds begin.

Our few highlander households meet for get-togethers: New Year's Day, Thanksgiving, Fourth of July, the Super Bowl, and a late-summer pig roast. Yep, an entire swine simmering for 12 or 24 hours in a pit piled with rocks hauled from Tin Cup Creek. Whatever the cooking duration, it's a whale of a spell, yet from the pit the pig emerged this year wanting more convection, although the skin was crispy.

Julie and I launched a furtive hunt for a microwave in our host's kitchen, then were busted and ate the pork as delivered. We doused it with Stubb's barbecue sauce, which we had brought along because we are survivalists. The experience reminded me of writer and friend Jim Harrison who said, "For mental and physical well-being, I recommend eating the head of a calf." Jim wound up with a lot of medical issues.

These neighborhood soirées are collegial, but with so many kith and kin marshaled in containment, there's always the smell of burning ozone and Judge Doom, and I fully expect to glimpse Christopher Lloyd wander in with his hair exploding. In fact, Mr. *Back to the Future* lived in Darby for several years—having been lured to the valley by singer Huey Lewis—before deciding it was too weird even for him. If you think about it, my neighbors would naturally tend to have social-adjustment issues, same as mine, because you don't wind up here by accident.

Our first neighborhood party was hosted by a couple who own so much woodland property that they've carved out an eight-hole golf course—all of it what you'd call the "extreme rough"—that wends through lodgepole pines and includes a water hazard, home to geese and stocked trout. Also home to a lot of incoming golf balls, which the geese hugely resent and feel obliged to tell you about.

One fixture of the summer social is a fellow who catches brook trout in the Big Hole River, about 35 miles distant, then cooks them to perfection on a mobile flattop. I instantly latched onto the man, who handed me an eight-inch brookie cooked in butter and peanut oil and smothered in pine nuts. It was a piquant flavor explosion—fresh-caught, head, tailfin, and eyeballs yet attached, crisp skin, fall-away flesh.

I devoured it in 60 seconds and solicited an encore. The cook obliged. In ten minutes, I'd gulped five trout on the theory that I'd never again sample anything better, ignoring onlookers whispering, "Wow, check out the gut monger." Still chewing, I said to the cook, "I heard on the Missoula NPR station that the brookies are really thick this year."

He said, "Well, I don't listen to NPR because all the fucksicles up there"—and here he pointed north to Missoula—"are PC libtards and ass-fur turdbirds." That's more or less what he said. Or something close. I may have juxtaposed "fucksicles" and "turdbirds" because I was without my reporter's notebook, and further confusion set in when he called me "Señor Wankhandle."

I said, "You mean the students and professors at the University of Montana, that citadel of higher learning and also the home of the Fighting Rapists?" At the time, the U of M football team was crotch deep in a succession of rapes and felony gropings, later chronicled in a Jon Krakauer book that earned Krakauer and all his relatives a lifetime ban from Montana or until Mars crashes into the Lincoln Memorial.

The fisherman/cook glared, unhappy and hot. He said, "A bunch o' goat-diddling Dem-shits," a conjoined pejorative not directed at the Fighting Rapists. So I ate another brook trout and, hoping to calm him, said, "Did you know I discovered the Higgs boson in Tin Cup Creek?" No effect. "Did you know that Custer wore Arrow shirts?" Nothing. Then the geese started honking. I blurted, "*Do geese see God?* It's a palindrome. Spell it backward."

He did not. Would not. Perhaps could not. In fact, his face became empurpled, a word I now overuse, and then our conversation ceased as if I'd become an erg of antimatter. Rudeness is the defensive man's imitation of strength, and one of us had been rude. Maybe two of us.

That's why Julie and I were deleted as future summer-social attendees. Banned. Just like Krakauer. Although there was never an official stamp on our excommunication, Patty Conn tried to blunt the affront, explaining, "They just had too many guests." I was the one who qualified as too many.

At succeeding neighborhood soirées, I spoke as often as Tonto and consumed one entrée only. But it was difficult. As Julie and I sat at a neighbor's table, eating molasses-encrusted ham loaf, a man plopped down beside me and withdrew a handgun that would have intimidated the Red Brigade. He proceeded to "sight in" his laser scope, assisted in this fussy operation by our host. Much waving and aiming ensued, once or twice at Julie's head and once at my crotch, which I felt was intentional. Julie contorted her mouth into guppy lips, scowling.

I pushed pork around my plate, then said, "Hey, man, is that thing loaded?"

"An unloaded gun is a useless pound of metal," he replied, clearly pleased with such droll repartee. Julie and I vacated both the table and the premises.

"The hell was *that*?" Julie asked as we walked to my truck.

"Maybe looking for an elementary school?" I wondered. It was an indecorous thing to say, but pointing a gun at ham loaf was, too.

DON'T DISS SISTER PHISTER

I drove downstream to a particularly fetching, tree-enshrouded, bridge-covered stretch of the Bitterroot River called the Wally. I parked beside a scruffy man with raccoon eyes—in his 30s, I'd say—who was about to depart in an oxidizing Ford Ranger so rusty that, from some angles, I could see through it. He was so skinny that he needed buttons sewn into his shirt's armpits. Also, he was slamming things around in his truck's bed.

When he saw me, he said, "The river's closed. Fucking environmentalists."

I looked to see if water was still flowing. Affirmative. "Closed?" I asked.

"Can't fish from 3:00 p.m. to 6:00 p.m. 'cause the water's too warm. Stresses the trout, they say. Global warming, my ass. Fucking environmentalists."

On his truck's backlight he'd affixed a decal I'd seen often in Montana. It was the outline of that insouciant and ubiquitous Dennis the Menace character who is eternally urinating on some political football for reasons unclear. This time, Dennis was hosing down the word "Environmentalists." On the far side of the truck's window was an identical decal, except in that depiction Dennis was micturating on "U.S. Forest Service," official logo and all.

I was nervous, because I knew that a slice of this man's animus was aimed in my direction. I was one of the alien flatlanders who'd invaded his state and immediately offered advice and instruction. It would annoy me, too. But Mr. Pisscopalian right then was posed before one of the most elegant rivers in our contiguous union, hoping to catch that most delicate of crafty adversaries, a fish displaying colors of the rainbow. If an environmentalist comes along and says, "Hey, you're gonna ruin this amazing experience if you're not careful," well, how much fury can you really muster? Plenty, apparently.

It reminded me of singer Sheryl Crow, who suggested Americans use less toilet paper. The country came close to deporting her to Iowa, where, as everyone knows, there's no toilet paper. It is unseemly to launch insults at someone who's merely offering positive advice, even if the advice seems immaterial. I considered relating Ms. Crow's story to the aggrieved fisherman but didn't. I wish him well but from a distance that a .38 slug cannot travel.

Speaking of closed rivers, you may have read that Montana's portion of the Yellowstone River was closed to fishing during the summer of 2016. There had been a startling die-off of Rocky Mountain whitefish, exterminated by an indigenous parasite that created a "supersite," so to speak, triggered by water that had turned to room-temperature soup. So the Bitterroot River is not alone in this dilemma.

You will have heard of Norman Maclean's *A River Runs through It.* That book, and the subsequent movie starring Brad Pitt, directed by Robert Redford, did for Montana what *All the President's Men* did for investigative journalism. Folks in 50 countries ached to see that river, wade in it, bathe in it, drink it, take communion in its sanctified waters, and become obliquely philosophical about its greater meaning to humankind and reality TV.

In case you didn't know, the waterway in question is Montana's Blackfoot River, and it is indeed a singular gem.

Or was. See, beginning in roughly 1991 (the movie came out in 1992), mining and logging companies had dumped so much poisonous pudding into the Blackfoot that, well, the water first turned 50 shades of gray, then a disquieting orange. I'm not making this up. That's when the native Westslope cutthroat, among the most prized catch of fly-fishermen worldwide, made a choking sound as they attempted to make a life for themselves in adjoining tributaries. That went poorly.

It wasn't until 2014 that the rust-colored mountain of toxicity from various commercial operations was finally being scooped up: some 845,000 cubic yards of zinc, lead, arsenic, and cadmium. It all had to be trucked somewhere where it could poison other creatures but not the cutthroat. It is perhaps telling that workers at the site wore rubber gloves and plastic blue booties, neither of which were sourced from Orvis nor worn by Mr. Pitt in the movie. The workers feared their feet turning black, this on the Blackfoot River—ha-ha. Not so hilarious now, is it? Even the Romans knew what was floating in their most famous river.

I was an inch or two beyond dumbfounded by this. It's like a guy who owns a Renoir, then tires of it so he slops on more reds and blues and offers it to Goodwill. Do you mean to tell me the single most famous geographic feature in Big Sky was trashed while its residents were building back-to-back Starbucks in Missoula? Yes, indeed. Right you are, sir. It's phantasmagorical. Please report to Roy Blount, who said, "Americans have the Midas touch. Everything we touch turns to mufflers."

Even as I was talking to my feckless fishing insurgent, the U.S. Forest Service—on which he wished urine to cascade—was right then digging through 65 feet of cancerous, noxious awfulness in order to enliven his fishing and ensure his family didn't contract cancer of the elbows. When I related this story of criminal pollution—tactfully, I thought—the skinny angler offered a reply I've heard 50 times when the subject of environmentalism is raised: "They should just leave it as it is," he said, quite sure of himself and Mother Nature's medicine cabinet of self-fix-it remedies.

I've heard the same "solution" applied to 90 acres of clear-cut forest not five miles from my home. "Just leave it." Yeah, that'll restore it, but not in our lifetimes. Does anyone have Mother Nature's cell number?

Naturalist John Muir wrote, "Any fool can destroy trees. They cannot run away; and if they could, they would still be destroyed—chased and hunted down as long as fun or a dollar could be got out of their bark hides, branching horns, or magnificent bole backbones." Poor Muir. Psychologists refer to his mutterings as an "escalation of commitment to a losing course of action." The guy seemed clinically depressed his entire life.

Miraculously, or so it seems to me, you will find a great grandmother named Marietta Phister who lives on the Blackfoot River. She noticed that when the fishermen disappeared because there were no fish, the "inner tubers" arrived in multitudes. No one knows the split between locals and tourists, but the tubers, who are not quite as intelligent as the tubers growing in your garden, screamed and swore and chased ducklings and sank their empty beer cans in the river. A beer may have made Milwaukee famous, but it's the Blackfoot River that made Montana famous.

Along with her husband and 80 other worthy citizens, Sister Phister extracted 1,000 aluminum cans from the river on her first try. Now she does it every year. God bless you, Ms. P., even though any real God would never allow such desecration of his most spectacular hydraulics.

But forget the Blackfoot, because the sylvan paradise known as the Bitterroot Valley has been under attack for ages. Note this account from the U.S. Geological Survey's Richard Goode, recorded in September 1898:

> *The most striking feature presented...is the large portion of it that has been burned over, nearly all of it having been visited at different times by fires, and at least one-third of the standing timber having been destroyed...a scene of which all Americans should be ashamed.*

> *The aborigines held this region for many ages as a sacred trust transmitted from generation to generation. They recognized its beauty and utility and did naught to impair the grandeur of the one or the permanence of the other.*
>
> *And what has the Anglo-Saxon done? As a community is visited by a devastating scourge, as a face is disfigured by some foul disease, so have the forests been visited and disfigured by him. Reaping where he has not sown and failing to restore where he has destroyed, a noble heritage is slipping away through carelessness and cupidity.*

And yet the place still looks pretty goddamn grand. Which includes my own little house, built from timber rudely hacked out of a swath not far from where I sit typing, leaving a nasty hole the elk will have noticed. We are, all of us, hypocrites, as soon as our puffy brains convert Mother Nature's bounty to our own pillow-top convenience. We daily broadcast our own conjured realities, with the internet as the perfect echo chamber.

The Shit Highway is paved with many fans, my friend. The screw of history is upon us. Remember this old saw: A man is rich in proportion to the number of things he can afford to let alone.

A topic I will now let alone. Maybe.

Bigfoot's Wedding Chapel

Not many miles from here, behind Trapper Peak, is a trail leading to Baker Lake. The lake itself is nestled near the mountain's pinnacle, about as accessible as predicate calculus. To locate the trail head, you drive while negotiating perhaps 25 perilous switchbacks on a gravel two-track—in some places more like parallel game trails—and you never stop ascending.

After that, it's bipedal wretchedness for two hours. The hike is supposedly 2.5 miles, but the locals reckon it's more like three, and if you ever attempt this ramble yourself, you will slink to your knees (where you'll possibly have been already) and swear it's half the Ho Chi Minh Trail. The lake resides at 7,000 feet, in the shadow of Trapper Peak's craggy teeth, impediments where alpinists assemble to complain.

Approaching Baker Lake, the trail mysteriously peters out, and plenty of hikers—me, the first time—wish to turn back. It's a mistake, because another 50 yards of bushwhacking—well, more like rock whacking—leads across sharp-lipped SUV-size boulders, then there in front of you is the most picturesque body of water in the known cosmos.

The first time I absorbed this vision, it was enhanced by a cherubic topless lady sitting on a rock sunning herself and reading a book beside her napping dog. She was "Rubenesque," which, as a kid, I believed meant "sandwich-like."

Baker Lake is a color that resides somewhere between navy blue and purple, but it can express a full Pantone variegated kaleidoscope, depending on the sky. From shore, you can view the lake's bottom as through a glass of Smirnoff, complete with fish darting in and out of rocks.

Baker Lake is ringed by evergreens that are ever green, and the place is at an altitude that discourages the kind of clouds I call scudders. Moreover, for 275 degrees, the panorama is of other snow-capped majesties, all capturing the lake in geography that is unseen by anyone but the heartiest locals, because the hike scares the shit out of tourists. It is a destination that Bigfoot would have chosen for his wedding, with all of his portraits out of focus.

On our second hike to the lake, we sat motionless on the shore for 30 minutes observing a bald eagle catching inch-long fish. He dove like a pelican, with his entire body disappearing, half in the splash and half in underwater pursuit. At Baker Lake, you expect to see angels and fairies fluttering in shafts of brilliant sunlight and silver motes in the shape of smiley faces. (I think I did.) No need to aim your camera. Depress the shutter randomly and you'll capture either your foot or a landscape few mortals could conjure even in their finest college-era hallucinations. Julie and I don't trust there's a heaven—perhaps something more like a Trader Vic's buffet of valium kebabs? But if there is nirvana, it's Baker Lake, even though this lake and heaven presumably share the same architect.

That day marked another moment when I just sat silently, humbled by my own paltry exploits. No need to remark on the beauty, or how tired my legs were, or that I'd witnessed a shade of blue unique to my near-sightedness. How had such perfection been rendered in otherwise humble rock and water? Why would my brain currently judge it so, and why would other brains instead conjure a Pizza Hut to monetize the place? I right then found it simple to discard such distractions, because

Baker Lake was, of itself, sufficient. Simply a fetching locale, nothing more, but for me another minor psychological advance.

The last time I marched up to the lake—wearing new Columbia boots and socks as thick as mattresses—I lugged along my fly rod. Unfortunately, no one could reveal beforehand what fly to cast because it's not clear what insects, if any, attend a lake that is a suburb of Cloud Ten. So I selected a fly at random—a Purple Haze, as it happens—and flung it upon the purple water, and caught a nice little rainbow. On the first cast.

I tell you, that has never happened to me or any fisherman in something approaching eternity plus eleven months. On my second cast, I caught a lodgepole pine behind me, and that's pretty much how the rest of the fishing unraveled. As in a lot of unraveling. But who cares? Standing before that lake—more like a big pond—was as soothing as watching pro golfers putt in their sleep. (I had a journalism teacher, Dr. Don Ranley, who right now would be scribbling in the margin, "WFM," for "what fuck mean?")

Descending the mountain, we nearly trod upon an immature rattlesnake relaxing on the trail. Our galumphing roused him, and he slithered under a rock. I said to Julie, "On the count of three, I'll lift the rock and you take a photo."

This now sounds like asking my wife to attach my genitals to a trebuchet, but it seemed halfway reasonable at the time. So I lifted the rock, and the snake distinctly said to me, "I'll kill you and everyone in your family." I remember it clearly because he had a Bronx accent. But we obtained a striking photo of a coiled reptile preparing to strike. Medical attention was about three hours distant, maybe four, assuming I could walk, and, if not, well, Baker Lake is a fetching place to die, as I may have mentioned.

Experiencing this Eden comes at a price. The trail is an uneven repertoire of rocky slabs, scree, and craggy pants-snatching, needle-limbed protrusions, such that you're always focusing on what's underfoot rather than upward vistas. At the conclusion of my first hike to Baker Lake, I was missing one toenail and suffered a blister on my ankle that became a small volcano of pus.

After my second hike, I vomited colorlessly out the Tundra's window on the way home—too much aspirin—and had so much trouble walking the next day that my gym workout was annulled. I didn't visit the gym for a week, and when I did show up, I twice uttered the phrase "Christ on a bendy bus," a curse acquired during college days in Blighty. I could tell you what it means but it's doesn't matter.

Baker Lake recollected my favorite verse from W.H. Auden, who guest-lectured at my university during what I believe was his last year of peripatetic meandering. Auden lent me hope, because he graduated in 1928 with what he described as a "third-class degree," which was as much as I was likely to achieve. Anyway, here it is:

All together elsewhere, vast
Herds of reindeer move across
Miles and miles of golden moss,
Silently and very fast.

I cannot recall why I was asked to memorize those lovely words, but I did, along with the firing order of a small-block Ford engine I was rebuilding at the time: 1-5-4-2-6-3-7-8.

John Phillips

Of Mice and Men and More Mice

My Toyota Tundra's driver's seat is covered in a snow-white Merino sheepskin that I bought years ago in New Zealand. I was mystified when I began finding it peppered with black seeds.

"These aren't mouse turds, are they?" I asked Julie, who studied a couple as if inspecting for lice.

"Not turds," she flatly confirmed, lifting my mood until the debris reappeared the next morn. I placed one of the offending specks on a napkin and carried it inside for further forensic servicing.

"What you've got there is a turd," Julie stated confidently, which made me want to question her previous finding, but I let it go.

Between the truck's intake manifold and firewall, I located a quilt of chewed foam insulation sufficiently luxurious to star in a Hilton ad. I returned from the hardware store carrying, thanks to Darla the clerk, JT Eaton Bait Blocks, Tomcat Bait Chunx, Ramik Green Nuggets, eight trays of d-CON, a Farnam Just One Bite II bar, and four old-fashioned Victor spring traps. Also a Victor Ultimate Flea Trap, in case the mice were flinging fleas on my truck's carpet, although it quickly occurred to me that it might *cure* their fleas, encouraging them to return for successive spa treatments. Anyway, my bag o' death cost $52.

Twenty-four hours later, the mice had eaten two bowls of d-CON and had carried various rodenticidal hors d'oeuvres to all four corners of the cockpit. Forty-eight hours later, the same. How could a mouse family eat four bowls of d-CON and still be contentedly turdifying my sheepskin? Yet they had and were. So I baited all four Victor spring traps with crunchy peanut butter and turkey bacon plus a dash of salt, because I believe if I can make my own mouth salivate, so will a mouse's.

Here's something I never knew: You can drive around town with four loaded spring traps in the footwells and never set one off. Really. I drove to the liquor store where Bill the clerk helped carry out an exhaustive array of Pendleton and pinot grigio.

"Don't mess around inside the footwells," I warned at the curb.

Bill studied a loaded trap. "Theft prevention?" he asked. "You should buy the kind where the horn honks."

The next morning, two sleek white-bellied mice had met Mickey their Maker in the copper jaws of Victor traps. The day after, two more, each resembling a Little Debbie cake oozing raspberry filling. I performed a modest dance, flinging mouse corpses between festive leaps.

And I felt okay about it, because the corpses were disposed of nightly, recycled in fact, by a fox who is black and white and not red all over. We've named him Rennie, short for Reynard, which, of course, is French for a fox who strolls the Left Bank and smokes Gauloises. Rennie adores bacon and will eat it in front of us as we watch TV in the basement. He doesn't watch TV because he is easily startled by the flickering images. With attention spans being what they are, *all* shows are now flickering images. If Rennie does watch TV, it would be Fox News, of course, the channel that so confidently confirms to Americans that the world's outrages are not of their own manufacture.

To play god, you have to have an acquaintance with the devil. I was thinking about that as I removed a mouse from a trap in the truck's right-rear footwell, and as I was carrying the corpse through the house to the lower porch to donate it to Rennie's recycling operation, I noticed some stale bread, destined for the birds, abandoned on the kitchen counter. So I placed the mouse between two pieces of whole wheat, then deposited it in Rennie's preferred dining site. A mouse sandwich. It seems possible that I'm the first person to create this entrée. The next morn, I noticed the sandwich was missing, but Rennie had left the crusts. Like a kid.

Neighbors John and Robin LoMonaco memorialized Rennie on a motion-activated video camera. The fox had come face to face with a feral cat, who, of course, was being fattened by my wife. When Rennie spied the cat, he fled as if his tail were ablaze. The cat stood firm.

"I've seen some unlikely shit in these woods," John noted.

Whenever I accidentally left the garage door open, all mice caught in the traps were reduced to heads and decimated rib cages. The stern-most halves of the corpses were nowhere to be found, because they'd been eaten by Silver Streak, a second fox who has a unique racing stripe down her back. We believe she is Rennie's mother.

Then Julie discovered one trap that had caught not a mouse but a quarter-pound toad. This amphibian's right-rear leg was beneath the guillotine but apparently undamaged. He had managed to uni-hop his way out of the garage, carrying the trap into Julie's garden, where he appealed for assistance. Julie transported him to the gym, where owner Dana maintains a terrarium that already housed a toad whose status was, at the time, female and single. So now they're a couple, evidently content in their man-made Toad Hall behind glass.

Last Thursday, I underwent two hours of dentistry, obtaining a crown that required an entire fracking crew. Afterward, I climbed into the truck and spied a pink-nosed mouse whose last memory on this planet was peanut butter, his neck snapped in a trap behind the driver's seat. My mouth hurt and I imagine his did, too. It was the first time I'd vacated the dentist's office to enter a murder scene.

Eventually, I was catching between four and six mice per day, depositing the corpses on a rocky knob 50 feet from the house. In this manner, our two foxes became not exactly corpulent but their fur was shiny enough to blind bats. It became a rodentry Siege of Troy, and the carnage grated on my conscience. I do not wish the mice harm as long as they conduct their enterprises where my vehicles are not.

I recently read about Alaskan Eskimos who search the tundra for smallish caches of a sweet root called mussu, which bears purple flowers. As it happens, Alaskan mice seasonally collect this mussu as a hedge against winter starvation, but the Eskimos usually steal it first. By way of compensation, they leave a carrot or a piece of potato or, I don't know, maybe five dollars. I've never seen the compensatory part of this act. But it makes me wonder if my mice would respond to bribery as well. I'd happily leave them a lifetime supply of Cap'n Crunch. See if their teeth fall out.

To be fair, the mice were here first. Author Robert Sullivan wrote, "We humans are always looking for a species to despise, especially since we can and do act so despicably ourselves. We shake our heads as [mice] overpopulate, fight over limited food supplies, then go to war until the population is killed down, but then we proceed to follow the same battle plan." Operation Victor Trap is my battle plan.

And on the topic of unwelcome invaders, there's this: If you reside in a forest larger than many island nations, as I do, you will trend toward a first-name basis with bugs. Some are familiar: wasps, hornets, horse flies, the aforementioned locusts, and carpenter ants carrying power tools.

We encountered so many wasps in August that every guest was stung at least once, and I was nailed on the chin and ankle. So I related my annoyance to Darla at the mercantile, the faithful clerk who speaks only seasonally. She persuaded me to assemble a homemade remedy.

"Fill a five-gallon bucket with six inches of water," she

instructed. "Then, using strings and sticks, suspend a piece of meat over the water. The wasps will eat the meat, develop the gout or something, fall into the water, and drown."

It was the most she'd said in months.

As I was collecting the requisite constituents, I found myself standing alone in Aisle 4, contemplating several balls of string, whereupon Darla peeked around the corner and said, "Onions." That's all.

I replied, "Well, Darla, I do enjoy a good red. Do you sell onions?"

"No," she said. A longish spell passed as we stared at each other in confusion. Finally: "Your wife called. For onions."

This happened to me at a hardware store.

Anyway, I am sufficiently naïve that I dutifully rigged up not one but two wasp-drowning buckets per Darla's detailed directive, with my wife inquiring why I was carrying a piece of New York strip steak outside. "For the wasps," I explained, which satisfied her.

My buckets killed maybe 50 wasps apiece. I calculated that the forest held 100 million wasps. A Radio Shack calculator informed that my investment to kill the forest's wasps would thus amount to $12 million. I could be wrong, because I had to factor in a lot of cow meat at varying prices per pound. The thing is, I do not hold $12 million worth of animus for wasps. The buckets went back on the shelves.

There are other insectival interlopers whose species are new to me. We have, for example, stink bugs. They are roughly the size of a triangular dime. Officially speaking, they are Asian brown marmorated stink bugs, not indigenous. They don't look Asian to me. Malaysian, maybe.

These bugs enter my home by means unseen and roam as if searching for lost continents or socks. Dozens will cling to our window-mounted A/C unit, which has become their Ellis Island. They invade most eagerly in the fall, seeking warmth without paying. They are the same color as frass, which I learned is insect feces.

That seems unfair, a shit stigma from day one, but it

was entomologist Peter Jentsch of Cornell who called these pests "the Hummer of insects." Said he: "Stink bugs, indoors, seem inordinately graceless and impossibly dumb. But, as we all now know, being graceless and dumb is no obstacle to being powerful and horrifying."

Stink bugs have only one known enemy, the samurai wasp, which unfortunately emigrated to these shores in numbers insufficient to effect genocide. We are now pulling for the wasps, of course, because stink bugs reportedly cost the U.S. $20 billion annually. How? Well, they apparently will eat anything except samurai wasps.

In my house, the stinkers are bewildered by small impediments and will remain motionless for half a day, fashioning strategies to surmount fallen Q-tips or balls of lint. They are big on reverse gear, blazing circular routes back to square one, where there's infinite pause as they accept defeat. As far as I can tell, that's all they do. They do not bite or sting, and they grudgingly accept being squashed by human feet, which is generous of them. When a threat looms, the bugs emit a scent resembling cilantro or one of those perfume sprays intended to knock down toilet odors. It shares its basic chemical structure with Chanel No. 5, and that is a true fact. It is for the bugs an intense, brief protective strike that doesn't so much frighten as cause bystanders to mutter, "Ah, did you have to?"

When possible, Julie and I fling the stinkers outside, unharmed. But they have little pieces of Samsonite, I believe, because they return the next day ready to search for dirty socks and diabolical Q-tip mountains.

Our neighbors the LoMonacos were hosting their son and a female acquaintance from California. On day one, instead of ignoring a small fleet of stink bugs, the girlfriend ran screaming from the house, demanding to be billeted in the LoMonacos' stepmother's quarters. The hosts agreed, whereupon the young woman repeated her hysterics and continued on that distraught path until acquiring airfare to Palm Springs.

It made me like the stink bugs a little more.

John Phillips

I'M ONLY HERE FOR THE PIES

Every man, child, and ex-con in the Bitterroot Valley eventually knows, loves, and worships all couriers of freight. At the base of many epically appalling driveways rests a 55-gallon steel barrel with a plywood lid marked "UPS/FedEx." That's our winter receptacle, deployed when driveways are impassable even for 4WD Chevy Tahoe delivery trucks. Purchasing unusual merchandise where I live—speakers for my computer, for instance—can be more complicated than union contracts. Stores possessing such items are 70 miles north, so Amazon is our default setting, used almost weekly. Which means our delivery person, if he makes it to our door, earns soft drinks, cookies, and 20 minutes of conversation: sports, intestinal worms, the likelihood of summer sweet corn, rogue grizzlies on the golf course.

Among the principal carriers, we had one, since disappeared, whom I named "Loiter Bubba" because he seemed unstressed by work and enjoyed discussing NBA mergers and deadly lunar patterns that had Fox News all aflutter. He once arrived midsummer at nine p.m., honest to polygraphy, and when we didn't answer the door, he knew to walk around to the basement where we watch TV. He slinked past the basement windows, scaring the cats, then tapped on the wall, scaring us. In he came, wielding that week's Amazon harvest, whereupon he shared a slice of pizza and a small quantity of Rolling Rock. I later pulled his Tahoe out of a ditch at the bottom of our hill, deepening his loyalty to us without engaging in too much discussion about three-legged snow leopards.

I'd like to talk to both FedEx and UPS about packaging, however. I ordered a 12-inch-long wiper blade for Julie's truck, and it arrived in a box three feet long and 14 inches wide. It could have served as a doghouse. I ordered six pairs of work gloves that were shipped amid 30 wadded balls of newspaper and four inches of bubble wrap. I'm not sure how you could break a pair of work gloves. And now the discarded boxes resemble Fort Pyle in my garage, so I must burn them during the precious few months that I won't also set the surrounding forest alight. Meaning, I tend cardboard fires in the rain. Thanks to Amazon, the cardboard industry must be birthing billionaires who, I hope, reside in cardboard houses and worry endlessly about warpage and sparks from my fires.

Few humans can locate our front door, except for a bicyclist who arrived while we were drinking cocktails on the patio. He was wearing full Tour de France regalia and arrived huffing and puffing as if suffering tuberculosis. His bike was shod with fatso spiked tires that made us laugh. The rider asked for directions, as if our reclusive aerie might be a state-line tourist center.

"You want a drink?" I asked, but he was yet gasping and wheezing. He eventually accepted a G&T, and we enjoyed an evening chat as if he were Uncle Ned dropping by for his usual tipple and confab. We never asked his name. When he left, Julie said, "Did that just happen?"

Not long later, two 60-ish ladies showed up—Florence and Laura, one with bluish hair, the other a henna failure faded to pink—who said they were eager to "share the miracles." I told them that, first, it was a miracle I wasn't hungover and, second, it was a double miracle they'd made it up my drive, praise Jesus and the baby Jesus.

I asked if they were familiar with the late academic Joseph Campbell, but the name rang no bell. So I recollected a Campbell axiom: "There are roughly 700 active religions on this planet. And you've come to me dead certain that *yours*, against all statistical probability, is the dogma of the lone true prophet?"

Without the slightest hesitation, Flo and Laura nodded heads. "But what if you're wrong?" I asked. "Let's say you almost nailed it but missed by one prophet, the next guy being the true prophet's prophet, whose name happens to be Lennie Shlenztsenheimer, who now is fist-pounding angry that you've so brusquely failed to aggrandize Him, causing Him to make a reservation for you in purgatory—almost certainly Hartsfield-Jackson Atlanta airport—as punishment for worshiping false prophets such as Dr. Phil or Jim Bakker or a man-eating vulture who shits on Grand Canyon tourists."

"We know we're right," replied Laura. Then Flo inquired whether I was a "fallen angel." Fallen, sure, never an angel.

I gave them credit for attaining my front door, inasmuch as it was raining ropes right then and a dandy inland sea of muck had accumulated on Moose Meadow Lane. They'd forged ahead relying on unprovable whimsies, in which the Born Again proffer the word "faith" when what's meant is "No questions, please, because I cannot possibly fashion plausible answers."

Christopher Hitchens said he'd happily attend his friends' bar mitzvahs and Gothic cathedrals, "and I will continue to do this without insisting on the polite reciprocal," he noted, "which is that they in turn leave me alone."

Florence sipped her Coke and fetched pamphlets.

I asked the ladies if they were a little defensive on the off chance they weren't right—that little tickling doubt in the solar plexus—and were hoping like hell, so to speak, to enlist supporters to make them feel braver about their miraculous notions and the purchase of more hair dye. I declined membership in their club. I have my own. It convenes daily in my backyard. Walter the moose is its CEO and is on a first-name basis with all chief officers.

Flo and Lo were eyeing the door at that point, but I burdened them with a further Hitchens-ism: "Violent, irrational, intolerant, allied to racism and tribalism and bigotry, invested in ignorance and hostile to free inquiry, contemptuous of women and coercive toward children—organized religion ought to have a great deal on its conscience."

I was depressed for a week when that man died.

When the ladies departed, they were far merrier about the topic than I, with all my speechifying in support of knockabout theories that I couldn't prove any more than they could theirs. I had imposed a load of condescension and a smarmy smirk. I didn't feel good about it. They'd served a purpose I didn't see coming, possibly one of their "miracles."

Not long after, a teacher-student combo arrived but not to proselytize. They were selling homemade pies to fund Darby High's Spanish students' imminent visit to General Franco's tomato garden or something. Julie and I support all school-related trips and thus purchased twin pumpkin pies, which were to be delivered later, no specifics. Weeks passed, then I was notified that my pies awaited at Darby High.

I'd never visited the school and wound up entering via the gym, far from intentionally and far from classrooms, then lost my way. I searched for an adult—mind you, this was two p.m. on a school day. No humans were on patrol, nor students. My meandering became a little manic, because I resembled an aging pervert whose excuse was "Pies. I'm here for the pies."

After 15 minutes of a self-led tour of dark Lysol-scented hallways—inducing high-school flashbacks of Eddie King vomiting on my locker—I discovered the principal's office, from which a gracious lady led me to the Spanish classroom where my pies theoretically awaited. The teacher first stood at the blackboard, then pulled me by the shoulder into a Spanish lesson right then falling on the deaf ears of maybe 15 kids, who had stopped listening because of my bizarre intrusion.

"The pies," I said.

The teacher replied, "Fine, but *sit*."

It wasn't exactly barked as an order but close. She deposited me at an unoccupied desk, into which I crammed my slack portliness, and time immediately spun backward until I found myself in Mrs. Wooton's Russian III class at age 17, wondering if she'd write me up for being tardy and impersonating a pervert.

The Spanish teacher then snapped at a male student: "Get in your car and bring back his pies," with "his" spoken as if I were a ceiling sprinkler that had just mysteriously let go. Where that lanky young man drove, I cannot report, but it took 20 minutes (and, I imagined, three cigarettes) and in that period the remaining students began an interrogation.

A couple of boys were *Car and Driver* subscribers and asked if I'd ever driven a Lamborghini. When I said I'd driven every Lamborghini and had been paid for the privilege, they alternately screamed, "Sweet!" and "You lie!" That set up preconditions for low-grade chaos—exaggerated gesturing, the awful screech of desks being dragged over tile, and the slap of textbooks hitting the floor. The teacher remained indifferent. She was marking papers at her desk.

I kept saying—almost shouting—"Really, I can come back later," but she wouldn't look at me. A minute before the bell, my pies arrived, still warm.

I imagine I am responsible for Darby's Spanish students' shameful ignorance of intransitive adjectival dangling future-tense co-modifiers or some such, and it was all for $12 worth of squash dessert.

BEATEN WITH OARS ABOARD MY BOAT

One-thousand feet of my property is contiguous with U.S. Forest Service land. I've yet to spy a soul back there, not even a hunter. I think they become lost and die. Really, it happens every year, and no one works himself into any emotional shipwreck about it, either. One guy driving a red pickup disappeared for a year. You'd think someone would have noticed a sizable red object abandoned under the pines, but no. He was later found in the Bitterroot River, wrapped around a fallen tree. It had me contemplating the inborn wisdom of animals versus the clumsy confusion of humans.

The river creates and catches corpses every year, 16 in the past decade. The tale is familiar: The fisherman's boat slams against a tree, the occupant plunges into the waterway, and both hold steady for a spell. Unable to move right or left, the fisherman attempts to swim under the soggy obstacle just as his arms have gone comfortably numb. Unseen beneath the tree are limbs protruding like daggers to the river bottom—resembling a deadly comb—which efficiently summons the Grim Reaper, who does this for a living and isn't all that grim.

It recently happened to a local fisherman who had enjoyed retirement from dentistry for about 40 days. I hope his last thought was upbeat, something like: "At least I'll never see another goddamn molar."

Similarly doomed, near the Conner cutoff five miles south of us, was a fellow drifting on the East Fork. As he cruised serenely on a cloudless day, a tree lost its footing and collapsed on his cranium. A tree equal in weight, I'd say, to the front half of a freeway bridge. How can the poor guy's last words not have been, "Are you shitting me?" His dog survived, but it ruined his day.

In late August, I fished with Dread Pirate Dave in his pale-blue inflatable NRS drift boat, which I later purchased, leaks and all. Dave has one maritime regulation: "No glass in the boat," although I thought he'd said, "No *grass* in the boat," perhaps meaning he was high on abstinence alone. In any event, when you fish from a moving watercraft, you concentrate on the arc described by your tippet as it whips through the pollution-free ether. This is not the true horizon. Dave, who rows the boat, observes the true horizon.

As a result, I leaned far to port to counteract a robust cast that would have impressed most major-leaguers, and the entire watercraft seemed to lift magically on the starboard side, at least in that vast region of my brain dedicated to creating illusions. I grossly overcompensated and was within inches of falling into four feet of frigid water roiling along at the speed of your average Preakness winner. So I dropped the rod from my right hand, began flailing my arms for balance, involuntarily lifted both feet, then somehow punched my forehead with my right elbow, which I believe is impossible.

In that same moment—it was a long moment—I was brutally and undeservedly clouted so hard in the left shoulder that I wondered if there'd been some sort of missile strike. My shoulder felt dislocated. It came as a shock, I tell you, like falling down the stairs and only reconstructing the event days later in the Kalamazoo ER.

My plunge into the Bitterroot River had been arrested by Dave, hitting me as hard as he could with the left oar.

"Pay attention, shitbird" is all he said, having already pulled me from the river multiple times. I told him I'd suffered a brief but crippling bout of williwaws and was stunned, but then regained wearisome normalcy. And that's when I caught a 17-inch cutthroat, inspiring us to mutual congratulations and our previous topic, which was our various beatings and canings as youths.

The next day, however, I felt the mayfly insignificance of my mortality as well as a damaged shoulder that looked in the mirror like a lump of raw meatloaf.

I never mentioned my near river plunge to Julie. Dave did. Four times.

John Phillips

Did You Just Peck Me?

I've laid out seven salt blocks and fling approximately five pounds of cracked corn on the porches daily, drawing all manner of action, including five white-tailed deer (Rodney, Ronda, the Lumpster, and the Twins), who jam their wet black noses into the windows fronting my writing desk. That's their way of alerting me that the cracked corn has reached dangerous depletion, and they look to me for relief. The Lumpster has two fawns, as cute as Shirley Temple if she were twins, eyebrows and all, and they'll sometimes suckle as mom hoovers up as much corn as possible without choking. The cracked corn adheres to her nose, looking like yellow sprinkles on a scoop of chocolate ice cream. (Feel free to work further on that analogy.)

Julie and I both anthropomorphize forest critters and are sensitive to Montanans' scorn as we recount each of our damnably cute stories. We are known as "feeders," and it is not a compliment. To us, animals are never an "it." Always he or she, just as you'd never refer to a human infant as "it," which is unfair because most of them are.

Anyway, Ed the raven performs tricks recollecting some of my own, and the Lumpster is often irked by her offspring, like every mother at about four in the afternoon.

That's my excuse for anthropomorphizing, but I will add that it's vital to impose specific names in order to stipulate, over dinner, precisely which raven or which deer was that day responsible for the behavior our brains suggest is so impossibly fetching. I briefly named a molting elk "Scrofulous," then thought better of it. I named a different elk "Lawrence Elk," and I am sticking with it. Not long ago I read that people who anthropomorphize objects tend to hoard. I'll wager you could waste a lifetime trying to connect the two.

In praise of the world's furry tenants, I will now quote my boyhood hero, James Thurber, of Columbus, Ohio: "They say that man is born to the belief that he is superior to the lower animals, and that critical intelligence comes when he realizes that he is more similar than dissimilar. Extending that theory, it has occurred to me that Man's arrogance and aggression arise from a false feeling of transcendency, and that we will not get anywhere until he realizes, in all humility, that he is just another of God's creatures, less kindly than Dog, possessed of less dignity than Swan, and incapable of becoming as magnificent an angel as Black Panther."

Mr. Thurber might have added wild turkeys to his list of angels, because a troupe of 20 amassed on my front porch, asking for corn. I had previously encountered turkeys in Michigan, but nothing like these.

Montana turkeys are the size of microwave ovens. One of the toms knocked over a ten-pound salt lick for reasons known only to him and probably not. The hens follow Too-Tall Tom, as we call him, in single file, as if on the elementary-school playground during a fire drill. Unfortunately, the hens become distracted and fall over and stumble into bushes and crash over shadows, which scares the crap out of them—seriously, a lot of crap is deposited. Then they trip over roots and sometimes inexplicably fall while digging with one leg for tasty pieces of gravel.

Whenever one tumbles, Too-Tall Tom—who could weigh 20 pounds—huffs himself into a medicine ball, displaying foot-long beige-and-brown feathers that would have made excellent pens for Ben Franklin. The girls in the harem are afraid of him—of Too-Tall, not any of our founding fathers. His eyes fidget like a serial killer's, and he struts as if possessing a concealed-carry permit. Too-Tall rarely eats. I don't know where he obtains the calories necessary for all his jukes and jibes.

Our friend Jeff Dworin walked up to a turkey hen in our driveway and said, "Listen, dear, you gotta do something about the wattles. Do you know a surgeon in the Hamptons?" The hen froze and stared coldly, apparently offended. She didn't return until the following spring. My wife was a witness and will testify in turkey court.

As I fling cracked corn, the turkeys stand in it, on top of it, milling and fussing and defecating in it, too, and randomly insulting one another with low-decibel yawks. But what they mostly do is peck each other in the head.

Each turkey is ritualistically pecked in the head, I'd say, two or three times per minute. On each occasion, the victim glances upward, shocked, as if the cruel hand of Pilgrims celebrating Thanksgiving had descended from an on-high celestial orb made of cornbread stuffing.

Turkey #7: What the fuck, dude, did you just peck me?

Turkey #4: Say what?

Turkey #7: Peck me. Did you just peck me? Don't lie, I can see it in your eyes.

Turkey #4: Excuse me, but I'm not keeping a daily log of my pecks. By the way, you have shit hanging on your feathers.

Turkey #7: I've got shit right in *front* of me. I'm lookin' at it.

Turkey #12: Do not fucking tell me you just pecked me. Did you?

Turkey #7: Fuck off. I'm trying to get to the bottom of a previous pecking. Why don't you hop over to the salt lick and peck #13? She certainly deserves it.

Turkey #4: Did I ever tell you about the time I was pecked in the head so hard I fainted?

Turkey #7: No. Jesus. That's awful. When did that happen?

Turkey #4: Oh, about two minutes ago.

Then Too-Tall trots over and gooses them back to their cracked corn, which has a tranquilizing effect that resets their disputes—forgotten until the hens reformulate devious new plans to peck each other in the head. They never eat all the corn. All the cranial attacks wear them out, I think.

This strange business recollected a friend named Gary Magwood, who offered cruises on the River Thames. He told me about medieval Brits employed at "swan upping." That is, they lifted every swan on the river in an annual census, and it was a personal hazard to man and enraged waterfowl alike.

This "upping" inspired my plan to open the sliding glass doors and lift one of the turkey toms. Just hold him for a minute. They apparently sport about six inches of pillowy feathers, so they must be as cuddly as terry-cloth bathrobes. And if I held one, I could also more credibly vouch for Too-Tall's weight. Work some science.

I'm embarrassed to admit how much time I spent lurking by our sliding doors, ready to pounce like a carjacker. When the fat tom mashed his hind quarters against the glass door—meaning he had little chance of noticing predators from astern—I made my move, which would have impressed the mothers of both Jim Fowler and Marlin Perkins.

I bent over to grab Too-Tall, but when my hands were fully extended, I couldn't feel anything like legs. The turkey let loose with a profound "awk" and wheeled back on me with such strength and speed that my arms crossed. By then I'd located a leg and thought I was winning until he leapt at my face, knocking my head back.

My world went black for a sec, but that was because he was in my face and is mostly black. Well, blackish brown. There was another powerful squawk, and I perceived nearby hens scattering in panic, the mad flapping of their wings raising little turd twisters everywhere. Then the tom strafed me with one wing, a right-to-left jab across my face. I began to fall, which prevented me from seeing Too-Tall make his escape. What I do know is that when I regained my balance and my mind, my home was a 100-percent turkey-free.

Ten minutes after this inadvisable gambit, I noticed the whole troupe shoulder to shoulder, as if bracing for another grabbing attack by me, the Sacred Supplier of Corn, formerly considered a nice guy. They had circled their wagons 50 yards downhill. I walked close enough that I didn't have to shout, then said, "What the fuck? Did you just peck me?" I felt a drop of blood from a divot in my nose. It took that wound a week to heal while seeping a disgusting fluid that I imagined might be turkey saliva.

The next morning at the gym, I related the turkey assault to friend Scott, the carpenter whose birthday is December 25, so he's Jesus.

Jesus said, "You know, I just shot a nice wild turkey yesterday." He pointed to his pickup's bed, where two or three birds slopped amid a pool of blood.

I had been reading Gary Snyder and came across this: "If we do eat meat, it is the life, the bounce, the swish, of a great alert being with keen ears and lovely eyes, with foursquare feet and a huge beating heart that we eat, let us not deceive ourselves. We too will be offerings—we are all edible. And if we are not devoured quickly, we are big enough (like the downed trees) to provide a long, slow meal to the smaller critters."

So I later apologized to Too-Tall.

One last thing about turkeys: They are wanting in the matter of intellect. I once threw cracked corn on the front porch and an equal portion on the back porch. There hasn't been confusion like that since the U.S. invaded Grenada.

LONGFELLOW'S UTOPIA, INVERTED

On a late-summer day with a crescent moon shaped like a sterling-silver fingernail, Julie and I lashed our kayaks into the truck and drove to Painted Rocks Lake. We crossed at its choppy midpoint, taking on a curler or two as unintended ballast, then paddled up a ten-foot-wide tributary fed by meltwater. It's called Blue Joint Creek, and we've often ridden our bikes there for picnics at the creek's mouth. Until we were aboard kayaks, however, there had been no way to attain all the miniature gravel islands, tongues, and chutes that the creek spawns as it floods each spring. There ought to be trout in those translucent channels. My theory, not theirs.

We paddled until the current began turning us any direction but upstream, then ate ham sandwiches on a flat gravel bar dotted with 20-foot-tall alders. They lent shade and protection from the wind and shrouded us as if we were in a nether world whose human population numbered two.

A white-tailed deer watched. We sat on a water-polished log beneath an osprey's nest occupied by mom and two mouth-gaping chicks. She cursed at us in her squeaky Mike Tyson yelps. All around, the mountains rose brusquely as if racing one another, and we were dive-bombed by yellow butterflies the size of soup spoons.

"Mountain and shattered cliff, and sunny vale…the distant lake, fountains, and mighty trees…in many a lazy syllable, repeating their old poetic legends to the wind." Longfellow's utopia is what I right then was conjuring.

Post lunch, I tossed a pale morning dun into Blue Joint Creek, right where the tumbling current had dug a sapphire-colored trench beneath two overhanging logs, the perfect hangout for fish leery of the hungry ospreys directly above.

On the first cast, a trout struck. Also on the third. On the fifth, I hooked the cautious little bastard, hoping that the incoherent knots I tied earlier would hold—in fact, my knots are so unreliable that I now dab each with Krazy Glue, a tactic not specified in any Orvis manual.

A dandy battle ensued, with the fish dancing on his tail, churning up a little foam, and bolting marlin-like into his hidey hole every time he caught a glimpse of me or the shore. I'd carried no net, thinking I'd catch no fish, so Julie deployed the scooping-hands technique, eventually clawing the squirmer onto a dry rock ledge. He measured 12 inches, brown speckles on top, with crimson running boards and a pearlescent-white undercarriage. In my hands he felt like a piece of truck tire, unbendable, 100-percent tensed and condensed muscle, a wild ball of vitality held barely in check by skin as taut as a drum head.

We later showed the photo to Dread Pirate Dave, who said: "What you caught there is a nice little Westslope cuttie."

I almost cried, and later, after another hook sank a half inch into my ring finger, did. Many fly-fishermen have tumbled into their graves and come back twice to stalk Westslope cutthroats. It is the fish that made the Blackfoot River famous before they were all poisoned in Montana's earnest struggle to resist tourism. I tell you, catching that fish was sublime, another notch in the embarrassing belt I wear to become a Montanan with pants not pooled around ankles.

As we boarded our kayaks to depart, Julie steered sideways into the current, which instantly dumped her and her unworn life jacket upside down into water the temperature of a daiquiri. I paddled panicky to her side, grabbed her by the collar, then poled my way like a gondolier into a thicket of reeds and floating underbrush. She dog-paddled to rest chest down on barely submerged vegetation. When I stepped out—fell, really—I was up to my waist in mud and roiling water smelling like twice-cooked turnips. It took ten minutes to bail her kayak until it was light enough to flip right side up, and a similar span to fetch her life jacket, which had been carried by the ardent current a quarter mile into the lake.

We thereafter donned preservers—embarrassed not to have been wearing them but also to quell the shivering—and we uttered not a word for an hour, crossing a portion of the lake 90 feet deep. When we bumped the shoreline on the far side, beside our waiting truck, I said, "I'm never kayaking again."

Two weeks later, kayaking again, I encountered an aquatic creature less glamorous than the Westslope cutthroat. I was skirting the shoreline of Lake Como, holding close to shore because the wind farther out was of an order sufficient to keel-haul Billy Budd. I nosed through some gloopy seaweedy stuff, and there, resting atop a particularly opalescent gobbet sat what must be the sumo wrestler of water bugs.

I grabbed him for inspection: two and a half inches long, sturdy wings, pincers with knitting-needle hooks almost like talons, and bulbous eyes that locked onto mine. He affixed himself to my middle finger, which stung a bit, so I attempted to fling him back into the lake. But he was attached as if riveted.

I flicked at him with the forefinger of my other hand, yet he clung like a rodeo roach. So I banged him against the side of the kayak—death to Smoochie—but instead of his guts exploding, he flew away. Uninjured. A bug with armor. He left behind two punctures in my finger, suspicious indentations bubbling a clear frothy liquid along with a little fizzy blood.

Back home, I discovered that my cling-on had been *Lethocerus americanus*, Montana's largest aquatic insect, a bug noted for "extreme voraciousness." He's a carnivore, it turns out, that ambushes other insects, small amphibians, minnows, and the occasional ignorant kayaker.

Allow me to quote from *Montana Outdoors*: "After capturing its prey, the giant water bug stabs its sharp beak into the body and injects a powerful toxin. The toxin first paralyzes the prey, then liquefies the internal parts, which the giant water bug sucks up like a protein milkshake."

Ernest Hemingway gaffed a tiger shark off Havana. Big deal. I grasped a giant water bug who ran a matador number on my finger. More research: "In 1923, a Montana man observed a giant water bug floating on the surface of a creek near Ovando, waving its leg. A trout grabbed the water bug by the leg… whereupon the bug raised up and sank its beak into the top of the fish's head. The trout began to swim excitedly in circles. It finally turned over on its back."

Montanans richly deserve their reputation as hearty heathens with Brillo-pad beards and stoic nonchalance, so it is appropriate that the swimmers in this state affectionately call this bug the "toe biter." I'd like to mate the thing with an Indian paintbrush, creating a species whose GI tract is capable of digesting fireproof shingles. I'm telling you, if this insect appeared in, say, Ohio's waterways, there'd be a run on Charmin and the governor would summon snipers from the National Guard.

SATAN'S CANNONBALLS

In Montana, if you cannot see the forest for the trees, it's because they're on fire. We knew that before immigrating. Our basement is equipped with a so-called fire room—essentially a walk-in concrete closet 14 inches thick with a steel door hanging on iron hinges. It's a bunker for documents, not us. If you're sheltering in the fire room while your home goes all Tiki torch, the oxygen will be sucked out "and you will die," or so explained our real-estate agent. Whenever a bear visited, my home's previous owner locked herself in the fire room; there's a heavy inner deadbolt that only she could have specified. She subsequently moved to Virginia and claims to be happier facing nothing more alarming than mass shootings.

To dissuade combustion, our house's roof is all steel. Not the fancy standing-seam type that you see on governors' mansions. My roof is known as "hog sheeting." The trees surrounding the house have been thinned by the U.S. Forest Service, bless their soot-clogged hearts, and the flammable debris on the forest floor has been extracted. Well, some of it.

We also have a cistern that holds either 1,000 or 10,000 gallons of firefighting water. The building inspector expressed the gallonage but I didn't write it down. All I remember is that the cistern is sufficiently spacious that an inspection can be completed while walking erect within. No one, however, has yet explained how I extract the water. Buckets? I bought the sturdiest garden hose I could find. It had a two-year warranty.

I visited the Darby Volunteer Fire Department, asking how quickly they could douse a blaze at my location.

"Really?" the firefighter responded, shaking a strangely diaphanous beard that was surely flammable. "You know that flat-car bridge over Tin Cup Creek? Well, our tanker ain't rolling over that. And even if we reached your driveway, doubtful if we could climb it. I'll tell you what we *would* do. We'd watch the fire till she went out."

He might have been joking, but I had a vision of the DFD loitering at the end of my driveway, hot dogs and Mountain Dew in hand, maybe a boombox blasting Barry White. So I'm on my own. I bought a second garden hose and four five-gallon buckets.

In this valley, every bolt of lightning starts a fire. Really. A ranger in the Sula fire district, population 37, assured it was true. It's merely a question of whether one tree burns or one million. Sometimes at night, when we're on the deck, we'll see small fires on distant mountainsides, orange orbs that swell and contract. There's a selfish satisfaction in knowing the fire is several miles away and that we are gripping vodka tonics.

"The poor bastards over there," we say, feigning concern. But in truth there are no bastards over there because those fires usually burn in unreachable clutches of scrub pine on the sides of absurdly steep mountains, where not even the smoke jumpers will parachute, lest they be impaled or become part of an avalanche in a bear-laden huckleberry patch. Valley residents pray these fires burn *up* the mountain—vertically, toward the lenticular clouds—and not down, because we, all of us, live in the metaphorical "down."

Driving toward Darby, with exactly no rain falling, I witnessed a bolt of lightning strike the side of the mountain that is most visible from our deck. I sat in the truck for a minute, watching a bluish plume rising. As I completed my errands, the column widened, darkened, thickened. So I called the Forest Service, who knew all about it and insisted, "It will burn itself out." I was pretty sure it wouldn't, not that I know enough about fires to propagate a good one in my Weber grill.

Sure enough, the blaze proved intransigent and was aflame or smoldering for two weeks. Using binoculars, we watched the incandescence zigzagging between treetops, yellow explosions, really, that must have leapt 50 feet from the canopy.

The locals were irked that the fire hadn't been quelled sooner. You won't believe this, but fires of this magnitude not only launch firebrands but also burning balls of—well, I'm not sure what, but it's an amalgam of oxygen and toxic gases released from the wood as it combusts incompletely. These literal balls of fire—like weather balloons that have gone full Hindenburg—can float a mile before landing and begetting further fires. Satan's cannonballs. They're mesmerizing to watch. Better than fireworks. None floated our way.

The blaze crept upward until reaching the tree line, then calmed to a simmer, fueled only by a couple hundred years' worth of pine needles wedged between rocks. The valley smelled like smoldering peat moss, and there scudded above us, at a height of 400 to 500 feet, a bluish vapor that lingered for two days. At home, we sometimes looked down on it and felt as if the house were floating. Our clothes smelled of campfires. Black cinders collected on our truck, as if we'd driven through a bout of volcanism.

That's when I interviewed the young ranger in the Sula fire-spotting tower. It takes 90 minutes to drive up there, and I did so in low-range 4WD, bumping and creeping along and trying to recall which of the hairpin turns led to the tower and not to death at the edge of Rushmore-worthy precipices.

To my surprise, Sula Sam the ranger drives up there for multiple weeks at a time, alone behind the wheel of a clunky Oldsmobile Delta 88 with discount tires and a Rand Paul sticker on the bumper. It's not clear how he manages this.

"Slowly" is how he explained it. He is 30-ish, with a

floppy mop of brown hair and the sparkling eyes of a child. He graciously offered a tour of his mountaintop penthouse, constructed of rickety steel beams and darkly stained siding vandalized by woodpeckers.

The mountaintop's knob has been clear-cut so that any fires he's watching don't become fires he's in. I'd estimate that his cabin on stilts measures 15-by-15 feet, with the rear wall covered in books. Against the left wall is his narrow bed, and against the right is a one-burner propane stove and a pantry chock-full of hot sauces to intensify the nightly mac 'n' cheese. No fridge, no microwave, no TV. Just a laptop computer loaded with "a whole bunch of sci-fi stuff," but even his fire-spotting tower, with lines of sight extending to Idaho, connects to no cell tower. Satellite phone only.

The cabin's centerpiece comprises a four-foot-square table with topographic maps detailing the nearby wilderness in a 360-degree swath. Suspended in the table's center is a spotting scope that mechanically pinpoints what the ranger is "glassing," as the hunters say.

Sam claimed to remain dimly alert 24 hours a day, catching catnaps as necessary but rarely an uninterrupted dream-state slumber. Thunder snaps him into hyper-alert wakefulness, even if he imagines it.

"For some reason, it usually happens in the middle of the night," he said. "Lightning strikes are so alarming that, afterward, I can't fall asleep."

He focused the scope on a single acre three miles distant, near the valley floor, and offered me a peek. In the middle of that parcel stood one immense tree, devoid of limbs but standing, as charred as hell's complaint department.

"Lightning, two nights ago," he explained. "I'll bet I watched that tree smolder for an hour. Didn't call it in, because it didn't set anything else on fire."

Sam claimed never to become lonely. He descends to Darby every second week to fetch groceries from People's Market. I asked whether, while in the valley, he also enjoyed a couple of boilermakers at Dotson's or the Sawmill.

"Maybe," he demurred, "but I shouldn't want to be encouraged to bring alcohol up here. You know, reporting a fire at three a.m. and saying, 'Hullo, this is your ol' pal in the sky, and…wait, hold on, goddammit…I've lost my drink.' "

I told him to consider a dog for company, but he mentioned that bears too often prowl below the tower's base. "A dog would escape," he added, "because I have to go down *there* pretty regular," pointing to the outhouse. Achieving the mountaintop one-holer meant hazarding four flights of steep steps. I asked if he occasionally drizzled the landscape from his aerial cabin's balcony, which coincidentally offered one of the most stunning vistas this side of the Tetons.

I further inquired whether the solitude had afforded him fresh avenues of ataraxia, or serenity—which, right then, I was likewise investigating. He seemed to blush. I warned, "I've already found that during any psychological inventory, it's best not to wear freshly laundered clothes." He liked that.

I eventually clomped down to his outhouse, located on a hogback ridge so sharp that making three-point turns in my truck felt like wing walking. Then, as I prepared to descend Sula Mountain, the ranger shouted, "Come back any time." I briefly thought of returning, say, at two in the morning and scaring him rigid, then realized the journey up there in darkness would first scare me rigid.

John Phillips

The Allure of Fireproof Underwear

Back in Darby, the fire nearest us was just a warm-up for a matchless August conflagration that darkened faces valley-wide. It ignited in a scenic canyon between my house and Hamilton—the Roaring Lion fire, named after the road leading thereto, previously a spacious lounge for cougars.

The Forest Service swarmed like fire ants, including a pack of eight who puffed cigarettes out on Highway 93, producing their own stately plume. Signs pointed to "Incident Command Posts." A dozen helicopters whumpped overhead, hour after hour. The first pilot on the scene reported the fire had required only 40 minutes to set alight 450 acres. That's more than ten acres per minute. The smoke formed a nuclear mushroom cloud that would have delighted Robert Oppenheimer. Our sunsets were tangerine with pulses of surging deep purple, a bizarre inverse of northern lights.

Our weekly paper informed us that a fire here in 2000 ripped its way down a hillside so fast it incinerated a firetruck parked in the middle of Highway 93. It didn't mention the fate of the driver, but I imagine he's still searching for insurance documents.

The Roaring Lion fire, or "our fire" as we began calling it, morphed into a perilous series of skirmishes, and there was no definable perimeter. A "feral fire," they called it. From above, it resembled an infernal amoeba or millipedal hydra that alternately reached skyward then flattened itself to swarm horizontally. It seemed alive, as if procreating, interspersed with temper tantrums including wind-driven hailstorms of ignited debris. Spotter planes often couldn't prioritize which portion to fight. Where *was* the edge?

The inside of our house smelled like a chimney sweep, and our clothes recollected a Dead Head reunion. When the fire concluded, 16 square miles of forest had been reduced to obsidian stumpage, bleak and barren.

Some of the larger ponderosa roots would continue to burn underground for a month—really, I'm assured this is true. They can suddenly erupt like mini lava burps, igniting more fires in a landscape stinking and smoldering and so superheated that a couple feet of topsoil had been sterilized. Firefighters who trod atop these burning roots suffer one boot crashing through to something like a miniature foundry. There were a gazillion morel mushrooms in that forest. I wondered how they smelled in those first minutes of roasting or if they merely carbonized in a two-millisecond poof.

I've tried to fireproof my house: weed-whacked dead grass, thinned nearby trees, collected deadfall. Then, once our location truly dawned on me—directly on the metaphorical rails carrying a freight train of tinder and instant ignition—I insured my home for one and a half times its original value. I'd already been assessed a surcharge for living within "proximate old-growth woodland sustaining behavior of incendiary constancy." I asked if that meant fires were possible.

"It's not funny," the agent said. I told him the description was, even as I looked up the phone number for his competitor. But here's the thing: I've now seen other burned home sites in the valley, where the surrounding trees are no more, meaning the landscape is a bleak, black scab. What's the point of rebuilding to contemplate that view every day?

Fires can conceive under the unlikeliest of circumstances. A bear, for example, who shinnied up a power pole, touched a line, and was electrocuted. The unlucky beast fell to earth, his coat yet smoldering, which set the forest floor ablaze. There are too many of us. Not enough of them.

Summer's fires made me wonder what could possibly inspire a firefighting career. Wearing Nomex underwear? If there's romance involved, it's the kind where litigants scald tongues and light the fuse of punitive damages. As far as I can tell, smoke-jumper training is 89 percent punishment and 11 percent sleep deprivation.

At Missoula's smoke-jumper campus, 200 folks apply annually but only ten make the cut. (I'd hold a wild party to fête failure.) Applicants must already possess ten years of firefighting service and be capable of 60 sit-ups, 35 push-ups, 10 pull-ups, and a mile and a half of jogging in nine-and-one-half minutes. Then vomiting is permitted. Stomachs empty, applicants run another three miles while carrying 110-pound packs, doing so in less than 55 minutes. These feats must be demonstrated annually to retain employment. By comparison, a career in bomb disposal resembles Seurat's *Sunday on La Grande Jatte.*

My wise Bitterroot cohort Russ Wildey recollected an argument as he and a volunteer army fought a mountainside fire in darkness. Russ urged the commander to extinguish the largest flaming knot pronto, but the Forest Service preferred awaiting sunrise so they weren't fighting blind. Throughout the verbal to-and-fro, the two men stood amid an insane scrum of confused shovel-carrying volunteers and clanking diesel bulldozers, everybody dodging, darting, thirsty, and filthy, even as the enemy—glowing and snapping a quarter mile over the nearest ridge—promised so many lethal feints, raids, and retreats that the average person would pluck out his eyeballs, which Russ said he considered. "I've never been in front-line combat," Russ told me, "but I imagine that's what it's like. Chaos, miscommunication, exhaustion." In the Bitterroot Valley, the fog of war isn't fog but pine smoke.

During the Roaring Lion fire, which eventually cost Montanans $11 million, a bighorn ram strolled down Darby's Main Street, affecting his own 1,000-yard stare. Months later, police charged three teens with igniting the blaze: two boys and a girl who abandoned their campfire to go walkabout. There was talk of braising their livers. Like happy swine in the muck, the human spirit wallows gaily in revenge, especially when it's served cold with a rye chaser at the Sawmill Saloon.

I looked for mistakes in my own teen years but, of course, found only perfection.

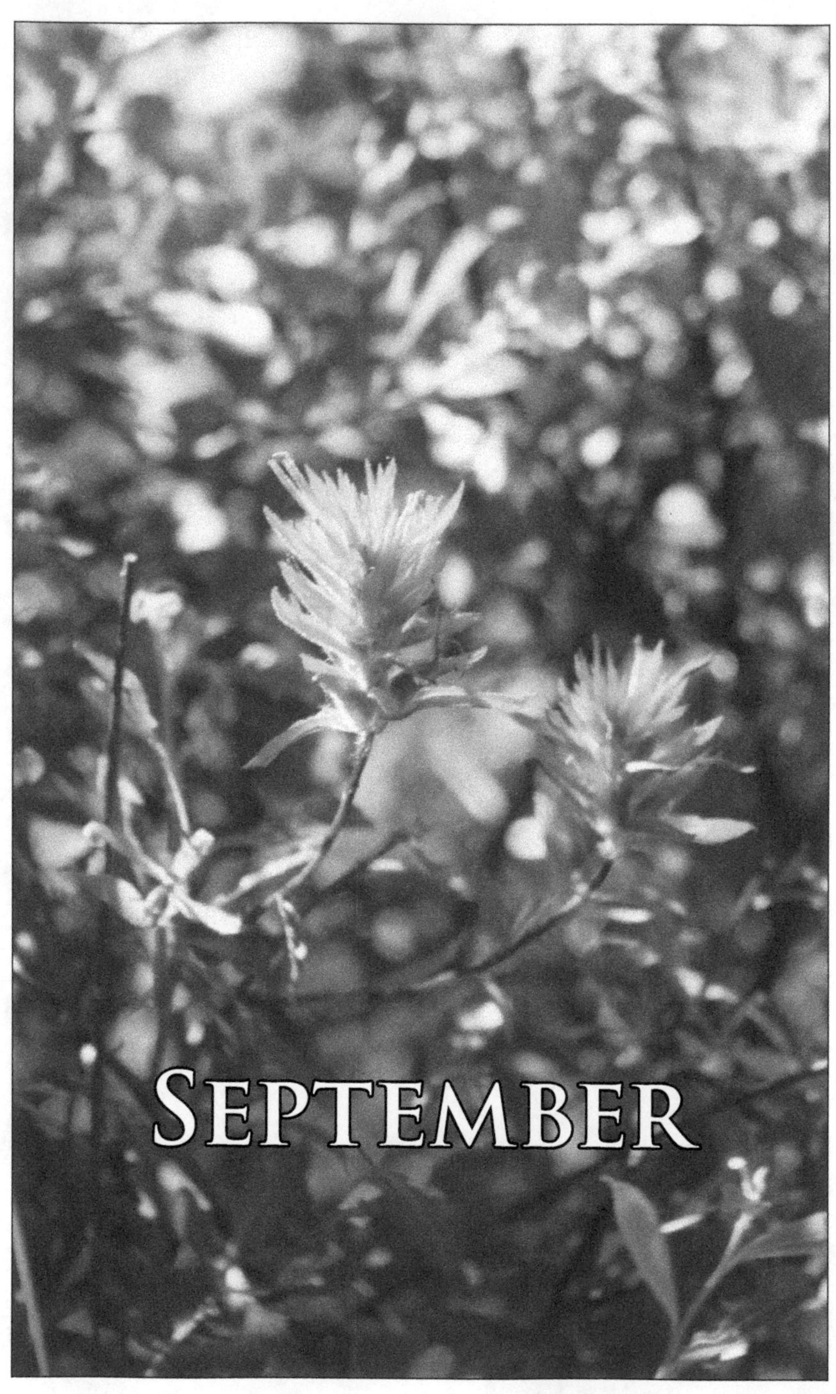
SEPTEMBER

DRIVE TO PINESDALE AND KILL YOURSELF

My Montana residency felt yet fresh when, on one dazzling day while fly-fishing in the Bitterroot River with CIA operative Bruce Hemmings, I did something in my pants that is not accepted in any country Bruce had ever spied on. There was no immediate way to attend to this unseemly matter, as you will know if you've ever donned a pair of waders clasped by suspenders, belts, clamps, rivets, and titanium welds. So I sat and pondered this unholy dilemma—it was something that had never happened to me before, which I know sounds defensive and maybe untrue. And that's when I noticed a stomach tsunami threatening to create Disgusting Mess #2.

Bruce, the CIA op, said, "You look awful. When's the autopsy?" He's like that. Encouraging. "If you catch a fish," he added, "it's gonna be posthumously." I drove home at 70 mph, vomited colorfully in the mud room, took a shower, threw up again, binned my Jockeys, fell into bed exhausted and moaning and without a fish.

John Phillips

Welcome to Montana, land of crystalline, crackling air and health so vigorous it makes you sick. Nobody mentioned I'd so soon be bedridden, punctuated by bursts of nausea. During my waking hours, my life's focus became flying phlegm.

At roughly the 30-day mark of grisly eructations, I located a general practitioner named Dr. Corky Shitzantinkle, possibly spelled and pronounced somewhat differently, who had evidently lost precious brain cells during the '60s. His framed degree was from a Wyoming college called the University of TB (Tuberculosis or Taco Bell?)

Anyway, this putative physician refused to touch me—I can't blame him—and said, "You have the flu." I asked if animal tranquilizers might be indicated. "Nope," he said. "It's a virus. Go to bed." I explained that I'd already explored all four corners of my bed for 40 days and 40 nights without locating my ass.

He stood mute as a hollow-headed sphinx, fingers intertwined as if praying, and I'll bet he *was* praying but it was for my corpus to become scarce. I felt like the first astronaut chimp—alone, queasy, in the dark.

So I waited until I'd truly gone viral, then presented my wheezing chest to the ER in Hamilton's Marcus Daly Hospital, Mr. Daly being honored as a rapacious land-grabbing robber baron. That's where I was greeted by a smiling gent named Patrick Grimm, which I swear is true, hand atop a stack of county-sanitarian citations.

The Grimmster prescribed a grocery bag of antibiotics and wouldn't allow me to depart until I was felt up by Dr. Calderwood, right then the chief of Ravalli County's Board of Health and the wife of our only ophthalmologist. She listened to my lungs' watery whooshing, which resembled a Lycoming engine with two warped cylinders.

Announced she: "Mr. Phillips, you have whooping cough. A number of the valley's elementary-school kids have it as well. It's sweeping the Bitterroot Valley because of the Mormons. They don't vaccinate."

I thought it was uncharitable to blame our valley's sect of Joseph Smith adulators—actually, they call themselves the Apostolic United Brethren, so no one's sure who or what they are. Forgive me, but it is illuminating to recall that Joseph Smith was charged with public disorderliness, banking fraud, counterfeiting, fornication, threatening a public official, conspiring to assassinate a public official, inciting riot, perjury, polygamy, treason against two states, depicting African Americans as Satans, having sex with a 14-year-old girl, and falsely declaring himself a lieutenant general. Who wouldn't pray to Joe?

Our valley's brethren reside in their own platted berg called Pinesdale, up Highway 93 a few clicks. They believe in vaccinating dogs but not their children, so it was left to the rest of us to suffer their inattention to detail, by which I mean plague. If you are 60 or older and contract whooping cough, you must report the matter to your county health official as a disease that was eradicated when the most sophisticated object on the planet was a B-17. And then your best bet is to drive to Pinesdale and kill yourself at the brethren's rec center. Make a gruesome mess of it. It's what they deserve.

Eventually, I achieved my own world record for whistling, rattling, gasping, expectorating, and blowing cork-size globules of snot. I was next referred to Dr. Woody Jones, a recent refugee from Alabama, whose partner is Dr. Smith. I commented, "Smith and Jones, you guys are laundering money, aren't you?"

Woody has favored me since, placing me on a month-long regimen of explosive antibiotics and tranquilizers that were originally intended to paralyze Percherons.

"You shouldn't really take this many antibiotics," he warned. "Might damage your organs, kiddo."

But it was fine with me. I wasn't using them anyway. I love that he calls me "kiddo," which is what my mother called me before delivering her patented "swift kick to the ass" or her switchblade fingernails traversing a supersonic path across my cheeks and nose. My mother could have choked out Jesse Ventura.

I was gratefully medicated into a crypto coma, at which point my sister arrived from Ohio to oversee my death and, gracious soul that she is, would have selected an expensive casket. But, miraculously, I was feeling slightly better. Better in the sense that the bullet passed through my spleen and not my aorta.

Speaking of spleen, I now walk around with gallons of bile coursing through my anatomical conduits, all of it directed at a small band of religious cultists who never look like they're having fun. I wish they all could spend six weeks in bed, preferably at the same time, watching Jerry Springer and sharing a defective toilet. It is shameful for me to hold such bias toward a group practicing their own festering sinkhole of nonsensical religion, but I do. They nearly killed me. Okay, great. Now I'm all worked up again.

For decades, the Bitterroot Valley represented Ground Zero for another antiquated killer: Rocky Mountain spotted fever. It started felling locals as early as 1873. But researchers in this very valley fashioned a vaccine, and it was administered to residents up until the '60s. Know what? It worked. It made me wonder if our neo-Mormons bypassed that medical nugget, too.

And while I'm simmering in a bowl of splenetic bile, I should point out that since retiring from Michigan, Julie and I were unable to acquire health insurance. Five years earlier, Julie suffered a breast tumor—so, a preexisting condition—and I was an overweight 60-something freelance writer with addictive tendencies, an exfoliating scalp, mild psoriasis, whooping cough, and on a psychological journey with an income placing me two degrees above homelessness in a wilderness that no insurance agent could locate on a map.

The health care reps were ecstatic about rejecting us: "Nope, no way, not a chance, not even for $1,500 a month, bye now, don't call back."

Julie and I had been faultless citizens for 125 years combined, had never accepted any handout or cheated on our taxes. And then came this Three Stooges slap in the face from a nation no longer interested in our contributions. It stung.

As health peeked its pink noggin around the corner, I returned to my regular diet of fried pork chops and bowls of vodka, which meant that Health was having a difficult time establishing residency. One night, after forgetting I'd swallowed one of Woody's Kentucky Derby sedatives, I served myself a Smirnoff-and-tonic Daisy Cutter that immediately whispered to my brain, "Big mistake, Bolo Bob."

My saliva dried up and I missed a couple steps on the stairs, almost crushing the larger of our two cats. I had trouble breathing, so I walked onto the deck and huffed those big inhalation/exhalation regimens that medics recommend for junkies, hoping that chilled air might shock my system back to merely miserable or, failing that, a peaceful hospice stay in a motorized wheelchair. But no.

I awakened Julie and said, "I might be having a heart attack." Except the sentence sounded more like, "Yei thin m'heave enannink fart tacky," but my wife has become fluent in that language and hustled me to the car. It was around one a.m. as Julie set out on the 30-minute drive to the nearest ER, which isn't near, where I'd hopefully meet the Grimmster again.

Just north of Darby, she dialed 911. The operator instructed her to park alongside Highway 93, inasmuch as an ambulance had already been dispatched to my little Lego village, even though the place was darker than a possum's ass. An ambulance serving whom, exactly? I feared it might have something to do with closing time at our two saloons, and I wasn't keen on viewing the after splatter.

Well, this was my first ambulance ride. I learned it includes a mandatory IV via a puncture inflicted by a javelin. A crater. My left cuff was soaked in blood, and it was my favorite Orvis fishing shirt. In the ER, a swarthy fellow named Dr. Moldenscum (again, the spelling may be slightly off) nerfed Julie aside to converse with her, even though I could still hear what they were hatching. I expected him to report my case was hopeless and that they must pull the plug, shave my back, and bury me with a pricey toupee.

Instead, the tanned sawbones from Crapper Academy pointed to me as you'd point to a homeless meth addict, and said: "Your husband is twice the legal limit"—uh, the limit of *what*, is what I immediately attempted to ask.

He then recorded in his official moleskin something like: "Sixty-something drunk, pale, blood-stained fishing shirt, can still name the presidents." In fact, I named 12 consecutively before he politely asked me to cease. For the sake of science, he asked what alcohol I imbibed. "Vodka and tonic," I told him. "The tonic has a soothing effect." He didn't laugh and looked far unhappier than I felt, which was reassuring. Then someone tested my liver, even though I could have told them I'd been testing it for 45 years. They declared it sound. So, there's a shining liver in every cloud.

Julie drove me home. Slumped in the back seat, still with half a swerve on, I stared at a cobalt moon. To her everlasting credit, my wife never again mentioned this midnight escapade. I can't tell you how much I admired her for that. But I thereafter dealt with an untreatable case of malignant mortification—like kerosene dripping slowly down my gullet—all the while scanning our weekly newspaper to see if I'd landed on the list of the ER's incoming deadbeats, who are known in the valley as "one of those guys who lives in the woods."

"A learning experience" as the Byzantines said after leaving an important gate unlocked.

Now I drink wine.

A BILLOWING BAG OF THUNDERCLAPPERS

The Bitterroot Valley, now my home, at first pampered Lewis and Clark, then nearly made cannibals of them. By September 1805, the two adventurers, en route to the Pacific, marched into the Bitterroot Valley, a 130-mile-long, north-south corridor extending from Salmon, Idaho, to present-day Missoula. Back then, the Shoshones called the valley the "Wars of the Red Osier Dogwood" or "a cool spot in summer." Meanwhile, the Salish called the Bitterroot River "Ootlashoot" or "Spitlem seukn." They were big on names, some that your average chamber of commerce would not have seconded.

When he first clapped eyes on the Bitterroot River, Meriwether Lewis wrote: "There is here a handsome stream about a hundred yards wide and affords a considerable quantity of very clean water." Then the natives led the curious white men to a pink-flowered plant with an edible root. From Lewis's diary (forgive his spelling): "[It] appeared to be fibrous; the parts were brittle, hard of the size of a small quill, cilindric and as white as snow throughout. [They] had a very bitter taste, which was naucious to my pallate, and transferred them to the Indians who had eat them heartily."

A bitter root, indeed, although the expedition's members had been without vegetables for months and were accustomed to eating nine pounds of bison daily—that's each man, nine pounds, an amount that would have had them banished from Old Country Buffet. The men thus devoured whole fields of what is now known as *Lewisia rediviva.* Diarrhea, indigestion, and "much wind ensued"—their words—and the men were later "so unwell that they were compelled to lie on the side of the road for some time." At least they hadn't contracted whooping cough.

More than two centuries have passed, as well as much wind, but the pink-flowered Bitterroot Valley would still be recognizable to the Corps of Discovery today, apart from a few million-dollar summer cottages, erected by tanned orthopedic surgeons from California. The valley yet leads to vast tracts of unmolested wilderness. My backyard, for instance. And even today, the Bitterroot Mountains, with their stiletto spires, block all commercial access headed due east or west. No roads. You just learn to deal with it. If there's a blizzard at the north and south ends of the valley—this happened last winter—then you're stuck. No way out. Time to huff a handbag of hucks.

That geographical arrangement annoyed Lewis: "We were entirely surrounded by those mountains," he wrote, "from which to one unacquainted with them it would have seemed impossible ever to have escaped."

Historian Daniel B. Thorp remarked that "Crossing the Bitterroots stands as the most difficult part of their 7,000-mile round trip." Expedition members later wrote of "very bad thickets" and "slopes nearly as steep as the roof of a house." The Flatheads positively warned the corps of these impediments. The white men did not listen.

My Bitterroot home is but a sparrow's flutter from where Lewis and Clark once sat calculating the size of their predicament, consoling themselves with 520 fish caught in one day, thanks to nets they fashioned from willow branches per the natives' clever instruction. Sitting idle, of course, the Corps was burning money. Well, at $40,000 for the whole multiyear expedition, not a lot of money.

I often sit on my deck and ponder their initial meeting with new tribes.

Lewis: "We have decided to call you the Flatheads."

Flathead chief: "That's funny, because we have decided to call you the Fuckheads."

As they lounged in the Bitterroot Valley, Lewis and Clark came to understand that there was, as Thomas Jefferson had assigned them to find, no "direct and practicable water communication across this continent." The Bitterroot Mountains put an end to that. All they could do was climb, eating a few ponies and dogs and sizing up one another in the process. But before that awful march, the corps enjoyed a few days of hard-won comfort in what is today's village of Lolo, at the north end of the valley. L&C called it Travelers' Rest, and they rested when they should have been beating feet to beat the snow. It was one of the few mistakes they made.

When Julie and I visited Travelers' Rest, a small team of archaeologists had commandeered a couple of college students wearing halter tops, whose task it was to excavate a pit that had been the Corps of Discovery's toilet. It turned out the adventurers' urine contained a lot of mercury. Both Lewis and Clark felt that a wallop of heavy metal could cure anything, including depression, sore throat, trench foot, piles, constipation, bad breath, and interest rates beyond five percent. The men were on a first-name basis with syphilis, which they thoughtlessly imposed upon the Indian womenfolk nationwide.

As Stephen E. Ambrose wrote: "It is possible that every man suffered from the disease. The treatment consisted of ingesting mercury in the form of a pill called calomel. The side effects could be dangerous; the phrase 'mad as a hatter' referred to hat makers who used mercury. Lewis administered it routinely." To be fair, the men at that point were out of whiskey.

For their entire cross-country adventure, Lewis and Clark had acquired $90.69 worth of drugs. Their pharmacy included "lancets, forceps, syringes, and other supplies, including 50 dozen Rush's Pills [known colloquially back then as "thunderclappers" for their laxative effect], along with

Peruvian bark, jalap, opium, Glauber's salts, niter [or saltpeter], and mercurial ointment."

Later in his life, Lewis began sampling the opium with an enthusiasm matched only later by John Belushi. He became enigmatically abnormal. In a guest house one night, he shot himself in the head and in the chest while simultaneously gouging his fleshy regions with a filleting knife. A slow-motion suicide that must have disturbed the guests.

The resident hotelier tried to intervene but failed. Lewis almost certainly suffered from depression, and I wish someone had asked him if surmounting the Bitterroot Mountains had anything to do with it.

WE AREN'T SAVAGES

When Darbrarians pass each other on the road, we wave. Not a wave, exactly, just one or two fingers raised vertically off the steering wheel. Anything more is mawkish and solicitous. To demonstrate deep friendship, you issue the soft double honk, two quick taps. My list of double-honkers grows daily, and on busy outings the tap-versus-wave agenda becomes convoluted. I double-honk at Pete Bonnell and Kemp Conn, wave at the Rushings, another honk at Scott the contractor who is Jesus, a double-honk at Robin and Bill who own the liquor store, a complex triple-finger lift-plus-wave for Hope the barber or Dread Pirate Dave, and a knowing nod for the apparently homeless man who pokes at the storm sewers as if he works for the town but doesn't. (Turns out he makes a living selling antlers.) Then, of course, twin angry middle digits for Jimmy Harrison, our bear poacher. There are no other angry salutations in Darby. Rudeness will get you "hard gossiped," affecting the quality of your haircuts, birthday acknowledgments, and probably the amount of foam on your beer.

Here's all I know about "Jimmy's Adventures with Felonies," as we came to call it. Mr. Harrison owns a Main Street store that manufactures cowboy hats: serious handmade lids, evidently superb, with many versions fetching north of $1000. "Jimmy the Hat Guy," a moniker he has painted on the side of his Chevy truck, was summarily smacked with five felony charges that included "unlawful possession of nine bears." When I read that, I imagined they were sitting at his kitchen table, adding honey to every entrée, making a mess. In court, Jimmy received a suspended ten-year term in the Montana State Prison, lost his hunting license until our sun explodes, and was forced to pay $1000 for each bear he caused to become deceased. Of course, he could cover the fine by selling a dozen hats. Moreover, in the matter of his license, Jimmy was hunting without papers to begin with, so it's not clear why this would upend his future plans for bruin massacres. Truth is, Jimmy had the gall to complain about the loss of hunting privileges. "I just don't think they should be taken away for the rest of my life," he moaned to a reporter. The bears might disagree.

Julie and I were gratified by the frothy outrage this induced. As loathsome crimes go, poaching is apparently up there with aggravated pederasty and inadequate postage. Jimmy evidently felt the heat and moved for half the year to the southwest, although he returns randomly to Darby to open his store's doors, perhaps by appointment. I cannot locate anyone who has purchased a Jimmy hat, although our nearest neighbor, Patty Conn, won one at a raffle in our civic park adjacent to Deb's Café ("Coffee strong enough to float a horseshoe"). Of course, when the Paramount moguls arrived in Darby to film *Yellowstone*, they scooped up Jimmy's four-figure hats as if in preparation for the Chisholm Trail, or so I'm told. Boy, howdy.

Anyway, I'll sometimes be futzing with the truck's radio and can't perform an adequate hand-waving salutation. If the passee were a pal, this snub must be rectified at the next contact by flashing a wave *and* a honk and maybe a bonus triple-finger lift. Also, you must coordinate with your spouse precisely who is or isn't currently on the wave- or honk-worthy list, which can change monthly, and it's not possible for a spouse to repair a snub for which you were responsible. There are rules. We aren't savages.

ALL ATE UP WITH CRAZY

We have a *"Garbage Czar."* It's his job to monitor what becomes of everyone's throughput, and it sure as hell better not wind up in a bin tagged with a neighbor's name, or the czar will treat you to a third nostril.

This was another Montana dilemma I did not initially grasp. If you've ever cast a baleful glance at someone's front yard covered in engine parts and cast-off refrigerators, it's not necessarily because the residents are pigs. It's usually a reflection of the money required to haul away the debris, and the pigs don't have it—money, that is, although it's possible they're still just pigs.

So we purchased what must surely be Rubbermaid's most stupendous offering, which requires two people to lift even empty, and then transported it to a yet larger dumpster we share with two other households. Trash day is an event for which a special trip in the truck is set aside, not least because the swallow-all container is 1.76 miles from our residence, on the far side of the bridge over Tin Cup Creek. It's over there because no contractor will drive a loaded garbage truck atop our flimsy flyover, and I don't blame them. The dumpsters are arrayed like soldiers on a narrow gravel pulloff, and it's a chore to open them because they're chained and padlocked. The locks thwart, first, the less well-off townies, previously referred to as pigs, who would appreciate a gratis dump. And, second, the bears. The bears can be pigs, too, but they don't mean to. Did I mention we can only fill the bin on the night before a pickup?

"Burnbrill is what you need," informed neighbor Chic Gerlach. I couldn't fathom what he'd uttered, so I asked again. "Burnbrill," he repeated. I asked twice more before embarrassment set in.

I deduced days later that he was saying "burn barrel," referring to a 55-gallon steel drum in which you incinerate paper and cardboard, about a ton of which we'd accumulated as we unpacked. But where do you buy a 55-gallon burnbrill? Turns out I had to drive 60 miles north to the Trader Brothers outlet, featuring a baffling collection of mismatched, pre-owned hardware and rusty guided-missile parts, interspersed with an array of guns sufficient to outfit the Ugandan Army. One Trader Brother led me to his barrel collection, which was outstanding. I studied them as if buying a first-issue Bordeaux, hoping to purchase one that hadn't previously seen use at Chernobyl. I found a sparkling black beauty for $15, so I bought two. Then Kemp Conn taught me how to cut air holes through the steel and fashion a rudimentary spark arrester—a ball of wadded-up chicken wire encasing a metal cruciform made from a steel mop handle, something never taught in Industrial Arts in Ohio.

I'd never burned trash outdoors and considered it a crime deserving flagellation. But in Montana I couldn't conjure an alternative. Recycling, you say? Hah. There is a recycling depot 35 miles north of us, open for about 45 minutes during trihedral cantilevered waning gibbous moons with Aquarius levitating. We drove there three times, only to face a cyclone fence festooned with locks and hand-scrawled signs warning how our personal police dossiers would burgeon should we cast cans / plastic / glass at the gate.

Facing so much trouble ridding the property of domestic detritus, I've started talking to myself in the grocery aisles: Why does a bar of soap come wrapped in cellophane, paper, and cardboard? It's soap. If it collects dirt during shipment, well, I'll run some water over it. Ditto toilet paper. Why the double cellophane wrapping with styrene inserts? Who'd reject a wad of TP if it were accidently wrinkled in transit? Yet everything comes boxed. At my house, all that cardboard is purged by fire. I've been told to save the ashes to help melt snow and ice. Have you noticed that animals don't create such clutter and disarray and rarely set the woods alight? Only humans create sewage. Only humans have to rear their offspring for 18 years, and only humans—so far as I know—have to be taught what to eat.

Anyway, the topic of garbage in Montana is perforce paired with bears, because one pursues the other. Our first bear visit was but a week into our residency. She mangled our Glad-bagged trash. Then, during a casual drive, we saw her with twin cubs, looking annoyed. Bears rarely attack, but the thing is, sometimes they do, especially if it's a sow and her offspring. As if to test this theory, a tourist stopped, exited his $85,000 Land Cruiser, then aggressively snapped close-ups wielding his phone. A smart phone in a dumb hand. Julie and I hoped ma bear might separate the photographer's face from his eyebrows. And maybe she did, but we drove off before the mauling, sparing momma added stress and ourselves the tedium of completing police reports.

Back home, I researched black bears, only to learn my fears were unfounded. From *Alaska Magazine*: "Across the entire North American continent, from Canada through Mexico, over centuries, there's not one documented case of a female black bear *(Ursus americanus)* killing or even seriously injuring a person in defense of her cubs."

Days ago, a different large female and cub knocked over four of our garbage bins so heavy that I believe hydraulic equipment was required. Only one bin spilled. Neighbor Pete Bonnell picked up every shred of aluminum foil and clawed Lean Cuisine cartons, bless his ruddy cheeks. Pete resembles George W. Bush but can't be because he can read.

I must admit that Julie and I enjoy the Schadenfreude

of "manimal" tragedies played out in state and federal parks. I particularly delight in parents who perch their infants atop bison for cutie-pie snaps. How intensely must park rangers loathe tourists?

Then came a cute yearling black bear loitering along Rushings' Hill, looking as innocent as Doris Day and frolicking across a pasture studded with dandelions, which he was munching. When we stared, he'd turn his head and act blasé, as if he'd lived here 20 years and was visiting relatives.

But our garbage czar—in his own personal race to shriveled mental capacity and senile fogeyism—was about to lap himself. He grabbed his rifle, then purloined an equally ignorant neighbor to act as spotter and chauffeur, because the czar's maximum walking distance is only as far as it takes to locate his Thorazine. In fact, he'd get winded in shag carpeting. The two set out in an ATV, tracked the yearling bear across the creek, then blasted its young brains all over the pristine forest. Yes, really.

As this played out, I was semi-hysterical on the phone, screaming at a ranger from Montana Fish, Wildlife & Parks. It was the first time—and last, I pray—that I uttered the words, "Shots fired as we speak." I continued to plead for assistance, but eventually the ranger said he'd "come out to have a look tomorrow," which felt to me like the first mate serving cocoa to the captain but forgetting to mention the icebergs.

No charges were filed, big surprise, and I was the bleeding-heart liberal ostracized for my failed attempt to shield a wild animal from human instincts so base and tribal—an undisciplined infliction of human influence where none was needed. It's also why we so often march our healthiest children off to wars.

I later discovered that one of the garbage bins had not been chained and was half full of watermelons, sweet corn, cantaloupes, and two loaves of bread. Someone had deposited bear dessert in the bin intentionally. Bear baiting. I took it personally. The bear, too, somewhat more grievously.

"They were here first," I later hissed at the czar during one of our neighborhood road-repair meetings. "Black lives matter." He grasped not a whiff of this, having never dipped a toe in life's amusing pond of irony.

We've had a handful of garbage-raiding bears since, but not many. I wonder if that single contact with the czar so demoralized them that they're now returning honey to hives. I guess I'm sad that I'm happy the bears are too scared to abide our viewing.

Because I tend to arrive late at our road-maintenance soirées, I often wind up sitting beside the garbage czar. No one else will. I always ask if anyone else has driven off Rushings' Hill. If you navigate over the precipice—it's on the way to our mailboxes—you'll experience a 70-foot drop to a property appropriately named Base Camp. Three neighbors have somehow performed the Big Dive, and one was the czar. He was unhurt, of course, in the manner of pliable drunks and children. The neighbors pretended they were worried he might have been injured but weren't.

One of them, Red Schields, reported that his first wife tipped over the cliff, perhaps in sympathy. She, too, escaped with nothing worse than the adrenaline shakes.

"I raced over to help," Red recalled, "and was amazed her car hadn't rolled. So I drove it home. Nothing wrong. Well, the antenna was missing."

Julie and I are determinedly nonreligious, although if you wanted us to pray to Mother Nature, we'd fall to our knees as spiritually starved supplicants. So I believe in heavenly places—like where we live and Baker Lake—but not the popular notion of a gated community floating on stratiform gauze. But if such a place exists, I hope Saint Pete assigns our murdered bear to guard the Pearly Gates until the garbage czar arrives, whereupon the bear will say, "Remember me? I'm the cutie you permitted one year to live, whereas you got 87." Then the bear tears and rips unspeakably at the czar's rheumy nether regions, followed by two hours of general mauling and chewing that celestial surgery cannot repair.

What's odd is that the czar *did* die not long after assassinating the bear. That man's reputation, in my mind, will forever be based on one deed. I think of him as spiritually hollow, unworthy of the transcendent environs in which he squandered his retirement. The czar's wife yet possesses his ashes in an urn—they might more appropriately have been stored in one of his beloved thermoplastic dumpsters—and when she walks past, she makes a rude hand gesture that is recognized internationally.

LITTLE SQUARE BURNT-UP MEN

Yet September, yet hot, but the cottonwoods had rainbowed into incandescent yellow flares, poking upward as if thanking the firmament. My mother-in-law, Agnes, was visiting, so I drove her to the confluence of the West and East Forks, where the Bitterroot River begins. It is a historic site, celebrated in fall by Darbrarians in a gathering that recollects an adult *Lord of the Flies* insurrection.

There's a gravel bar so flat and expansive that a light plane once landed on it, not the aircraft's destination. It is allegedly where Lewis and Clark spent a few of their happiest nights 200-some years ago. From Clark's diary, September 4, 1805:

> *Pursued our course down the creek to the forks, about five miles where we met a party of the Tushepau nation, of 33 lodges, about 80 men, 400 total, and at least 500 horses. Those people received us friendly, threw white robes over our shoulders and smoked in the pipes of peace. We encamped with them and found them friendly, but nothing but berries to eat, a part of*

which they gave us. Those Indians are well-dressed with skin shirts and robes. They are stout and light-complected, more so than common for Indians. The Chief harangued until late at night. Smoked in our pipe and appeared satisfied. I was the first white man who ever were on the waters of this river.

Now my river, Mr. Clark, or so I feel, paradise found and lost and found over two centuries. But to my mother-in-law, the Bitterroot Mountains represent one murderous slide to extinction. Drop-offs elicit shrieks and night sweats even during lunch, or so she says. If the all-fall-downy part of the mountain is on the right side of the truck, Agnes shuffles hard left and slams her eyes.

My favorite road of bones is the Skalkaho Pass (pronounced "SKULL-kah-ho"), a seasonal dirt road that extends 54 miles east-west between the Bitterroot Valley and the eastern edge of the Sapphire Mountains, thence to the village of Philipsburg in a valley paralleling ours. Agnes adores Philipsburg, which is an intact mining town cuted-up almost unto Disney-esque saccharin: three blocks of stores selling native sapphires, plus a mini brewery, a refurbished period hotel, as well as several saloons I enjoy because they smell like stale beer and urine. Minors who wander inside become miners.

From his 1962 classic, *Travels with Charley*, John Steinbeck later talked about these Montana dives: "Lots of small bars in the towns. I stopped in about six. Little square burnt-up men with little speech, all bent and warped with riding and sun and also cold, faces very red."

How's that for an attractive crowd? And did Charley the snooty poodle similarly occupy a stool? Steinbeck said of the Montana he'd just raced through: "What grandeur! It's like coming out into the north of England—huge and largely impractical...seems to me to be what a small boy would think Texas is like from hearing Texans." It would have required gallons of alcohol for Montana to resemble England.

In 50 hours, Steinbeck claimed to have driven 800 miles in and around Montana and Idaho while visiting six Big Sky bars. Quite a whirlwind toot, unless he muddled his facts. Montanans insist he did. What's more, the man was behind the wheel of a GMC pickup he named "Rocinante."

He said of Montana: "For the first time I heard a definite regional accent unaffected by TV-ese, a slow-paced warm speech...The towns were places to live in rather than nervous hives. People had time to pause in their occupations to understand the passing art of neighborliness."

Darby is no nervous hive, but Montanan neighborliness can lean toward tepid, especially if you're a writer who arrives unannounced with a prissy dog in a prissy truck with New York plates. Not that I am innocent in that department. One reason I named my own truck was so that I could remove its snow chains in spring and shout, *"Diego unchained!"*

When Steinbeck later crossed "the upraised thumb of Idaho"—just to our left—locals would have told him it wasn't a thumb but an upraised middle digit wagging at the U.S. government for long-festering grievances: establishing national parks, criminalizing polygamy, those goddamn black helicopters, the Trilateral Commission, Death Squads, and the Deep State, which I believe is actually in Mississippi. I have now met some North Idahoans—you must always say "north" and never "northern"—who seem permanently aggrieved that both U.S. coasts were ever allowed to fester.

Steinbeck fashioned what has become popular Montana doggerel appropriated into widespread refrain, often carved into wood that craft stores have distressed unto barn timber. He wrote: "I'm in love with Montana. For other states I have admiration, respect, and recognition, even some affection. But with Montana it is love. And it's difficult to analyze love when you're in it." Okay, Johnny boy, calm down.

Allow me to return to the Torments of Agnes along the Skalkaho Pass, which in 1924 was hacked out of the side of mountains just east of us. This gravel two-track is listed on a website titled "Dangerous Roads," and I guess it is. Trailers are forbidden because the switchbacks are too tangled. In the mountain fog, visibility dwindles to a few dozen feet, and head-ons are not uncommon at hairpins, although I believe they mostly occur at walking speeds. There are S-turns, U-turns, J-turns, T-intersections, why turns, interns, hairpins, and a G-string.

I've never traversed this pass without inflicting on my truck a pageant of dents, chips, and other flying-rock abuse. The road eventually reaches 7,260 feet, where it can snow at any moment and does, and it bifurcates a 23,000-acre wildlife refuge chockablock with dense spruce and subalpine fir. Bears aplenty, gathering perhaps to manufacture peanut butter for National Public Radio, and if you're lucky, you'll encounter a semi-reliable troupe of mountain goats that inhabit Dome Shaped Mountain—not a full dome, just dome-shaped. We once watched a moose on his front knees drinking water out of a pothole. After he slurped the contents, he moved to a second pothole, and so on. He'd turn to stare every few minutes, apparently fascinated by Toyota bumpers.

Along the way, Agnes's preferred landmark is Skalkaho Falls, where frigid water cascades some 70 feet, bracing both sides of the road and tumbling over the Precambrian Wallace formation, which makes you want to meet Wallace. The waterfall is barely contained. Most of the flow is funneled under the road, a thoroughfare already prone to peeling off the mountain, which it did again in 2017. What's more, one largish section was excised by a mudslide that closed the pass for most of the summer. Philipsburg's tourist income tanked. As I write this, the Skalkaho Pass yet awaits the arrival of the U.S. Army Corps of Engineers. Well, a platoon, anyway.

Toward the east end of the pass is a moldering sapphire-mining operation that has devolved into a gasbag commune. You buy a bucket of gravel from the proprietors, then wash it in the creek, then bend over while wearing reading glasses to search for sapphires the size of grains of rice. To me this sounds like a punishment devised by Homeland Security, and the gravel pickers are all grim-faced, every few minutes shouting, "Another bucket over here!" like John Cleese preparing to vomit.

If you really wanted to make money from this enterprise, you'd open a roadside stand selling Bag Balm, because the faux miners' hands and fingers are as beet-red, chapped, and lacerated as freezer-burned squid. It is painful to watch on several levels, and one of those levels is Tedium Squared.

Nevertheless, my two nieces purchased buckets of gravel, discovered six sapphire splinters, and declared the entire operation a stroke of mining genius, nearly equal in entertainment to tormenting Agnes.

OCTOBER

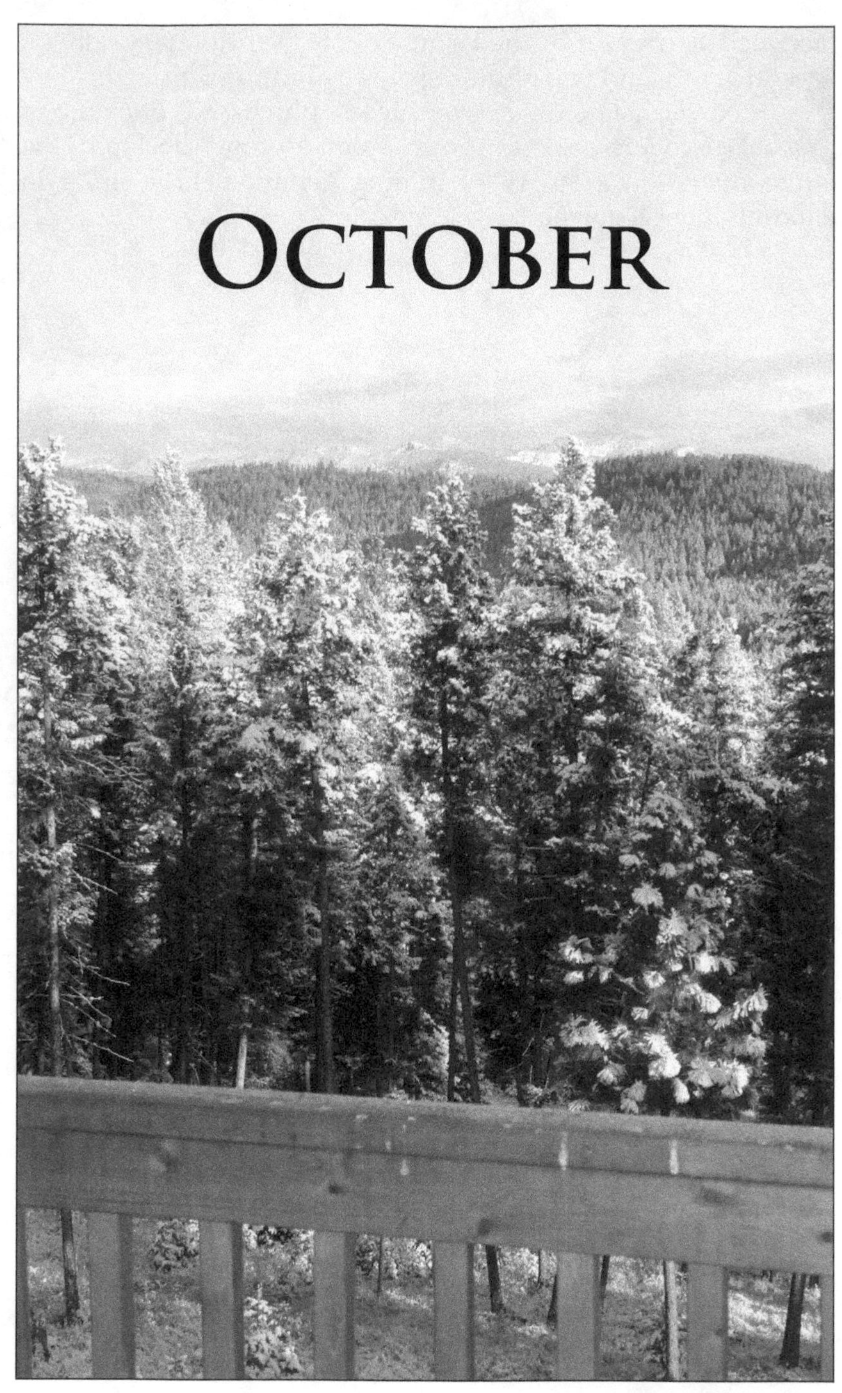

STETSON HAT, HERMÉS SCARF

Julie and I commandeered one of *Car and Driver's* long-term cars, a Honda Pilot, so we could fish on the famous Henry's Fork, not far from the Bitterroot Valley. The route led us through the Idaho National Laboratory, home of Experimental Breeder Reactor #1, not to mention Mud Lake and Atomic City. I am still glowing.

After I calculated the cost of the resort, food, wine, fishing guide, dry flies, and drugs, I figured I'd have been better off robbing Darby's Dollar Store. But catching a 20-inch brown trout induced a kind of fiscal amnesia. For our guide, it was the last day of the season—the third week in October—and he looked slightly deranged, as if he'd slept under a bar stool.

I said, "Do you ever wake up and say, 'I do *not* want to go fishing today'?"

He turned and said, "Yeah. Today."

The three of us right then were bent double in the boat, snow pelting down, with our six hands jammed against a propane heater on the boat's floor. I'd never experienced open flames in a boat. I kept measuring swimming distances in case our boat burned to the waterline. We actually *did* knock over the heater once. Nothing happened.

I should also mention that our long-suffering guide had been Dick Cheney's guide a couple weeks before. Floppy Dick was reportedly taciturn and quick to assign blame but otherwise uncommunicative. At day's end, Dick mumbled to the guide, "I'd like to hunt birds."

The guide conveyed this request to the resort owner, who declared, "We are not giving Dick Cheney a fucking gun." True story, with Julie as my witness. If you think I hold animus toward the former VP, let me merely say I'd like his right testicle, if he has one, to be stapled to his left knee, and his right knee to be sutured to a rhino with cholera. I would like him to suffer massive, crippling constipation for 18 months so he will be demonstrably full of what we knew was within him all along. Also, I would like Americans to deny that stuffed sack of smirking smugness any more body parts. If Dick Cheney inherits another organ, we should award him a little monkey wearing a velvet hat.

Okay, a smallish splash of bile, there. I'd apologize, but Dick never has.

Back to the Henry's Fork. When it began snowing in earnest—this coincided with a known aggressive bear climbing a tree four feet from our cabin—Julie and I opted to drive home. The Honda's nav system suggested Highway 20 north, then west on Fort Henry Historic Byway. The byway, marked as "scenic," would lead to the village of Spencer and the U.S. Sheep Experiment Station, both near I-15. I estimated the byway was 25 miles long. And who doesn't want to see experimental sheep?

It started out fine, paved and all, with perhaps three inches of snow and exactly no other humans. I knew when the pavement ceased because the Honda leapt skyward six inches while fording what I later realized was a small stream under ice. Maybe a tributary. After that, there was only mud, interrupted by gravel swales and potholes the size of kiddy pools, then mud. In some places, the snow erased the road altogether.

I can't remember exceeding ten mph. An ugly front rolled in, with purple clouds rear-ending each other on the Centennial Mountains a couple of miles to the north. The

Pilot's altimeter indicated I was never below 4,500 feet. The GPS introduced a little icon resembling a dung beetle spinning in circles on a blank brown field of, well, excrement, it seemed to me.

Occasionally, the road dissolved into the horizon, a mile or two of cold nothingness, which allowed me to fixate on the cessation of life as we know it. In places, there were not even abandoned barns or outbuildings or barbed-wire fences. No traffic signs, of course. My sense of critical distance collapsed. In theory, there should have been one village—Kilgore—but it apparently was a gassy aneurysm within some cartographer's stand-up routine. "Where's Kilroy?" came to mind. Also, hypothermia came to mind.

I had set out at noon. Now it was 2:30. A Dodge Ram duallie with snow chains came splashing in the opposite direction, our first human contact. "Does this road connect to I-15?" I asked the driver.

"Usually," he responded, his wife looking as if she'd only recently been let out of a box.

"Is the road passable?" I probed.

He thought about that for a ridiculous spell and said, "I suppose." Then he clanked away in a fog of diesel fumes. Idahoans think of tourists as wheezy chest wounds.

The Honda was by then coated in more primordial sludge than a swamp buggy. Not one piece of metal or glass was visible behind the B-pillars. The rear wiper skated over a hardening crust of opaque sediment. No one could see my brake lights, but there was no one to see them anyway. Sufficient crud had collected in the wheel spokes that a paint-shaker imbalance developed. The left rear door was sealed shut.

It became sufficiently dark that I switched on the high-beams. I think there were four warning lights glowing on the Pilot's instrument panel, and one of them said, "Did you notice the other warning lights?" I felt as lost as Robinson Crusoe's cat and contemplated how I'd fumbled into this monochromatic Twilight Zone.

We drove another 60 minutes—now three hours total—

with road and weather conditions morphing from merely awful to wretched. I crested a small hill and, sweet Jesus, there stood 250 inert cows blocking passage. We—them, me, all—expressed an identical look of wonderment. I slowly nudged the Honda through the pack, creating a parting of the black-and-white sea. I tell you, it is sobering to see an animal's head larger than a mailbox only two inches from your side-view mirror. Then I noticed a Marlboro man in Carhartts, leather chaps, crap-splattered Stetson, and what looked like an Hermès silk scarf, which my wife confirmed as imported and expensive and unlikely.

"Am I near I-15?" I pleaded, revealing a few sharp misalignments in my psyche.

"Cheesus, Choseph, and Mary," he drawled as he casually scanned the Pilot, which by then was a massive molten fondue of mud. "You drove the whole thing, didn't you?"

In fact, I was two miles from I-15.

Speaking of cows and boys, I've encountered plenty in Montana and have found my car locked within bovine aroma fests five or six times—cow jams, I mean—and must tell you this: The cowboy above was the only example adorned in full cowboy raiment, Texas lid and all. All the others wore jeans, baseball caps, and sneakers. Every single one.

Anyway, Julie and I survived this scenic trauma. I've encountered such black-hole vortexes before. I once flew to Ottawa, Ontario, for an assignment and rented a Dodge Charger mid-blizzard. Immediately disoriented, I wound up in Hull, Quebec—wrong side of the river, but close—where exactly no human beings were on display. So I dashed into a McDonald's, almost hugging the clerk, and asked, "Where's Ottawa?"

She froze unto granite and her face was blue, as if low on oxygen.

"Ottawa," I repeated, using more volume. "It's the capital of your country."

She turned and said something in French to the staff, who all locked eyes on me, fingers poised to tap out 911. She never spoke to me.

These pointed contemplations of nature were intended to improve me—well, my mind, at any rate. But here's all I learned: When you see "scenic" on a map, it doesn't mean you need to see it.

John Phillips

Teaching Trees to Run

The black-hatted villain of western Montana is not Jack Palance but the bark beetle. If you placed a bark beetle atop a nickel, he would be the size of the letters "LIB" in the word "liberty." He would also be the size of a mouse turd, a subject we've covered. These winged beetles, who are officially weevils, right now represent the largest forest-insect outbreak ever recorded. They have destroyed 46 million of this country's estimated 850 million acres of forests, and two million of those acres are in Montana. I resent it.

If you're a self-absorbed home owner, these beetles represent "viewshed contamination," a term I'd never heard until moving to Montana. It means that real estate devastated by beetles will disenchant subsequent buyers, because who wants a scene out of *Dr. Strangelove*?

I became so nervous about beetles that I asked native Bitterrooter, Russ Wildey, to examine my trees.

"You might be okay," Russ informed. "The beetles want lodgepole pines mostly, sometimes ponderosas."

I had plenty of the latter but few of the former. I was not calmed. For one thing, if you simply look at a tree, you cannot tell if it's infested. The bad news arrives only when the tree, come autumn, turns a shocking rusty-orange, a hue recollecting the Flint River. At which point the tree is as dead as disco and there's nothing left but to slice it into firewood, and even then you have to burn it in place.

I called about a prophylactic insect spray, which, at $1,000 per acre, would overpunish my purse, plus it has to be applied via helicopter.

Bark beetles have laid waste to the pines along a former logging road 30 miles from my house, the perilous road to Shoup, Idaho. We carried visitors up there to share the beauty, but now they inquire about various yields from nuclear blasts, that being what it recollects. On the other hand, the dead trees remain standing and, after a couple years, are valuable to loggers. No drying kilns are necessary, unless the whole place burns first, which it usually does.

In fact, Montana enjoys a cottage industry of so-called blue pine, the wood stained aqua by the beetles' unique fungi, which they inject into the trunks, little vandals that they are. My modest home has blue-pine molding throughout the lower level. The streaks are subtle, like veins in your hand. I thought they were pretty until I grasped this whole infestation business. These parasitic beetles, between 2000 and 2012, have killed trees that would otherwise cover the entire state of Colorado, which shouldn't be covered because it would preclude purchasing their marijuana.

Here's what's weird about bark beetles: If the temp plunges to minus ten or lower, just when the beetles are setting up household or packing to leave, they will freeze their tiny asses off and never awaken. Which explains why they are thriving, because true cold snaps have become so rare. Right now, our only solution, as one USFS ranger named Matt explained to me, "is to teach the trees to run."

I told him dogwoods would be the best runners. Matt said he'd already heard that one.

It was originally assumed that the beetles—who are indigenous, by the way—were assisted in their defacement by the forests' density, making it a fast-food highway as they fly mere feet from tree to tree. Too easy. So the Forest Service set aside a test parcel and planted trees generously spaced. Know what happened? The bark beetles killed every tree, screw the vast perimeters, a 100-percent massacre, dead as if drowned in Agent Orange. Didn't see that coming, did you, Matt?

When Julie and I first arrived here, we'd take all-day drives on the Magruder Corridor and collect chunks of wood, later unloading this shoplifted loot onto our pile for late-night wiener roasts. When Russ said, "That's a fast way to bring bark beetles home," I burned every scrap in a fire that might have been visible from County Cork.

Despite how much Montanans detest carpetbaggers like me, they do love their forests. Or say they do when the topic is excised from political bombast.

Here is a quote from *In These Times:*

> *One good way to understand Montana's political complexity is through the issue of public lands, which reflects class interests more than party loyalty. Despite a libertarian tendency to distrust the federal government, Montanans overwhelmingly support federal public lands. These lands...comprise more than 27 million acres in Montana, 29 percent of the state's land base. And almost all of them are free to access, camp on, hunt, and fish. Public land is one of the last egalitarian institutions in Montana—land where people of modest means can live as free as rich people and fill their freezers for the price of a $20 elk tag and some bullets.*

In fact, my friend Scott Kaminski, who is Jesus, does exactly that. He annually shoots one elk cow, one pronghorn, one white-tailed deer, and a couple pheasants he flushes north of Billings. He does not purchase meat. Ever. He is healthier than almost everyone I know.

The quote about geopolitical complexity in Montana sounds principled, unswerving, and idealistic. It might even be true. On the other hand, if U.S. politicians had 24 hours in which to save the world, they'd call for a three-day recess. That's a joke I wrote for a colleague delivering a speech to car dealers in New York. He never paid me. That's why I'm using it here. I hate waste.

John Phillips

Hitched To Everything in the Universe

I beckon you now to the world of *Puma concolor*, "cat of one color," an apex predator who, in the Bitterroot Valley, is a matter of adoration, loathing, and anxiety.

For starters, a mountain lion's vertical leap has been measured at 18 feet, meaning it could easily spring from the ground to alight on your roof and rip out shingles. Also, mountain lions eat like college freshmen.

As I walked on McIntosh Lane in Darby last week, I noticed the corpse of a white-tailed deer whose head was resting 40 feet from its agreed-upon attachment point. The lions, which can easily weigh 150 pounds, attack from astern, landing on their prey's back and neck, then either crimping the windpipe or sinking three-inch fangs into the topmost vertebra, all this amid a lot of slashing and frothing and bad cat language.

They will often eat the heart, the liver, and a smattering of palatable guts, then slink off. Further dismemberment is left to the ravens, vultures, foxes, coyotes, wolves, bobcats, and flies, until the whole disposal is complete—I'm not kidding here—in as little as 36 hours. Nothing left but a few strings of pink gristle and tufts of fur fluttering about as if the deer had exploded.

Some Montanans then use this as evidence that the lions "kill for sport." The same is said of wolves. In fact, a tourist-lodge owner on Rye Creek Road pointed to a fresh mound of dirt where a wolf had cached a mule deer. "See, they don't even want to eat it," he told me. "They do it for fun."

"When you go to the grocery," I replied, "do you buy merely one entrée for that particular day? Well, the wolves don't, either." He didn't grasp my meaning, which is fine, because I've become leery of engaging Bitterrooters in any wildlife tête-à-tête. You can use the logic "We invaded their home and stole their land, so maybe they're a little pissed." So far, that has elicited not a hiccup of empathy, or it leads to the topic of Native Americans' victimization, or is thrown back to accuse me as the specific invader of sovereign Montana territory, with my immediate exit as resolution.

Almost every Bitterrooter covets a mountain lion story, in which the creatures' coats are a mustard color flecked with black, or a shade of brown resembling tanned leather. My gym trainer recalled a lion asleep in her front yard. A neighbor, while walking her dog, came face to face with one, at which point the pet lunged, apparently motivated by pride in a suicidal gesture. The lion hunkered in weeds, clearly intrigued, and waited for the two to pass, memorizing their names and addresses and filing them under, "Meals, Later."

My real-estate agent's motion camera captured a lion in midleap, in monochromatic black and white, looking like ancient cave art. Our neighbor Alice observed a lion frolicking in Tin Cup Creek, after which he padded up to her bird feeder and demolished it as if for a fraternity prank.

My favorite tame household deer, Jamie, showed up October 1 on our porch with two claw marks on the right side of her throat, one on her left, and a two-inch-wide bare strip from between her shoulder blades to her butt cheeks, which I believe are called haunches. Somebody's claws had removed the fur down to salmon-hued skin but no farther. Not a drop of blood. Jamie looked a little wild-eyed for a week, like one of the *Cuckoo's Nest* inmates.

What's more, the gym's receptionist recalled driving to work in the dark and halting for green eyes in the roadway. The orbs belonged to a lion right then clutching the spine of a still-struggling mule deer. Interrupted, Mr. Deer Slayer sat like a dog on the pavement, then released his intended victim, who arrowed into the forest.

"Then he stared at me," she said. "He looked furious, like he was memorizing my license."

Darby's bank manager, Jody Smith, lives only a mile from us and was lunching on her veranda when she noticed motion. Turning, she faced a seven-foot-long lion, its coat the color of orange-blossom honey. This magnificent holdover from the Ice Age clapped eyes on Jody—she was no more than 15 feet distant—then continued padding along silently and indifferently, eventually selecting a shady spot beneath a cottonwood tree, where he flung himself into one of those poses of equatorial torpor you'd expect from a *National Geo* documentary on the veld.

What's surprising is that six white-tailed deer were grazing 100 yards from the lion, yet all affected apathy. If lions kill for sport, why not right then, when the pickin's were easy? Why not take down vulnerable Jody in the process, a tasty twofer? No one knows. Locals claim lions are quick to convey their intentions, either "peace on earth, brother" or "all bets are off, sucker." Attacks are sporadic, brief, unpredictable, often pointlessly harmless.

Biologists discovered that mountain lions loathe human conversation. Who among us could be surprised by this? When the cats approached feeding sites in the Santa Cruz Mountains, they fled 83 percent of the time when encountering yakkity chatters. Meaning that, if you carried a talk-radio host around your neck, you'd never be attacked but would become insane and have no friends.

I've read you're ten times more likely to be slain by a pet dog than a mountain lion, which are also called catamounts. In Montana, I'm able to find published accounts of only two attacks and two fatalities, all four involving children—one riding his tricycle, in fact, which is somehow doubly sad, but not for the cat. What I do know is that every time I leave this house, there is an unseen predator who may or not be sizing me up, who may or may not be aware of my pitiful bipedal top speed, but who is categorizing me by smell and size and who knows more about the woods than Johnny Appleseed.

"You know what else?" a Montana park ranger noted. "The young ones are goofy." His exact words.

This lends life a certain zest. Not fear, really, but a critical, heightened situational awareness, as if swimming off the coast of Durban. I always felt that if dinosaurs still slinked and slithered and salivated, we'd never set out for just a jug of milk. Errands would require courage, and a gun would provide protection but only if you shot the blue-haired lady nearest you for the Velociraptor's convenience.

Julie lashed a motion-detector camera to a tree beside our salt licks, which in truth is technically on U.S. Forest Service land and may earn me a year's worth of community service. A week passed before we downloaded the images, and, sure enough, there were huge moving objects on film. Not *Puma concolor*, however. It was a blue Toyota truck humping the final 150 feet into our warm garage, with me slack-jawed at the wheel. We did locate paw prints, each maybe 20 percent larger than my head. Julie said not.

And then, there he was. The motion detector caught an eerie midnight tableau of a lion in full stretch, front legs locked rigidly around the neck of a white-tailed deer I'd named Ronda, with both predator and prey at max adrenaline in a flee-or-be-feast tableau as ancient as the Bitterroot Mountains. It was a startling depiction of forest hierarchy captured via bluish-black flash. Mother Nature in her backyard confessional.

We later searched for the corpse, but it wasn't at the murder site. Not even a tassel of fur. Just another friendly forest face who will be missing at dawn's roll call. Spreading cracked corn, I had helped fatten Ronda, helped infuse that sheen and whiteness in her tail, now a small roll of fat encircling the hips of a seven-foot-long cat. When we dubbed this place the Double-J

Cat Ranch, it applied to our own plump mousers, one weighing 23 pounds. Multiply that by seven or so and you'll invoke the cat we're now indirectly feeding.

Here's something else about our predators: The grizzly bears that reside in Yellowstone National Park—just east of here—comprise the species' southernmost population in North America. There are 700 of them. As late as 1980, those bears seemed content to roam within the borders of the park, which no one can explain to me, inasmuch as there are no fences. But since then, they've apparently been leasing time-share units, because they've multiplied in a 360-degree bubble, as far north as Livingston and as far west as Dillon, which is not far from where I squeeze strawberry glop on toast every morn. I don't mention this as if it were bad or scary. There are already 13,307 black bears in Montana, who represent no pressing threat to human welfare when left to their own furry affairs.

Turns out, however, that these dirty-blond bruins are easily offended by black bears. A territorial thing, in which deadly dust-ups are likely as the two teams work out a contract for brown-versus-black integration. Frankly, I'd sooner abide grizzlies than the non-inoculated Mormons. As if I had a choice. Montana's state animal is the grizzly, which so far hasn't done them or the U of M footballers a lick of good, although it has enriched untold Chinese T-shirt manufacturers.

What does concern me is that the grizzlies are now delisted, which sounds as if they can't vote or co-star in any movie starring Alec Baldwin. What it means is that they're no longer considered threatened so that, (a) locals may indict them as a menace to their sheep, cats, cows, and tricycle riders, and, (b) my Midwestern Anglo-Saxon guilt about their continued welfare will further itch and throb like poison ivy.

You will have to take my word that there exists a state-sponsored organization called the Interagency Grizzly Bear Committee. The IGBC, before I arrived, suggested introducing these predators into the Bitterroot Valley. A maelstrom ensued. Locals alleged that toddlers would be carried away to root in garbage and learn to hibernate. The IGBC's bold stated response was the kind of silence you'd expect in Grant's tomb, not the Grant you're thinking of but a friend of mine named Grant. You know, in the past 50 years, if I'm reading my statistics correctly, grizzlies have killed 20 humans in the Continental U.S. In the past six months in Montana alone, 20 people expired from versions of influenza. Came close myself.

Grizzlies are certainly on the way. A blocky-headed, 250-pound two-and-a-half-year-old male was recently trapped on a golf course 35 miles north of Darby, where he was breaking flag sticks and digging his own holes on greens and heckling caddies. A second griz scared the Carhartts off an elk hunter in the Big Hole just south of us.

Those two events set off 15 governor-ordered meetings, with the useless words "outreach" and "proactive" monstrously overused, intertwined repeatedly with "as we go forward" (a phrase politicians love because all of us have no choice but to go forward unless suicide is that day's plan), and concluding with a report neither endorsing nor opposing hunting, the kind of political petrified wood that doubles as Mitch McConnell's brain.

John Muir observed, "When we try to pick out anything by itself, we find it hitched to everything else in the universe." What humans are hitched to is that millimeter of brain stem that irrationally fears dark-complected ogres hiding under the Stearns & Foster.

On which topic I'd like to point out that, in all of America's history, there have been but two citizens dispatched by healthy wolves—both recent, strangely, in 2005 and 2010. In both cases, the victims were trekking borderline wilderness, with no witnesses present, and the post-mortems were as vague as a sixth-grader's book report. One investigation, in fact, dragged on for a year, in part because a bear or a mountain lion might have made the kill initially, departed, then consigned the human carcass to the wolves, who rode the rap.

Wolf behavior biologist Dave Mech, in the matter of one of the deaths, came to no conclusion at all, saying he had "suspended judgment." The scientific translation: "Damned if

I know." Wolves don't view us as food. Too large, too much potential trouble, too many calories expended for an uncertain outcome. In numerous studies, including those by lifelong observer Mech, wolves do not pursue 90 percent of the animals they encounter in the woods. For starters, the pack is not always intact, and hunting solo so imperils a loner that his demise the following winter is almost ensured. A fractured leg is a death sentence. Plus, the wolves in my backyard have to attend choir rehearsals.

A century ago, Americans shot nearly all the grizzlies, bison, bobcats, and wolves in America, then encouraged them to return with government assistance, then resumed blasting: a wretched cycle of aggression and undisciplined ferocity interspersed with glints of diffused angst and affected compassion—like high-school dating. If there's anything that lays bare the human psyche, it is our dysfunctional relationship with the mammals we're evidently intended to share the planet. We love our dogs but revile the wolves. We love our neighbors but only if their skin is a Pantone equivalent. Of course, I now hate the house-destroying flickers, so there you go.

A man named David G. Haskell spent two years peering at a single scraggly tree on Manhattan's Upper West Side. During that spell, Mr. Haskell observed starlings, house sparrows, pigeons, a single red-tailed hawk, and one lost warbler. Five species in two years. Whereas in my backyard there are maybe four million. I could be wrong about the number. Three million, if we include the flickers. I guess we have to.

THE VOLUPTUOUSNESS OF TEDIUM

Were you to walk about ten miles west of my valley's sylvan splendiferousness, you would cross the unmarked state line and burst into Spud Country, where there will be no one to greet you. You'd find yourself atop one of Idaho's 7,000-foot granite stacks, some of which even have names. It's the Selway-Bitterroot Wilderness, and most of its 1,347,644 acres hide beneath old-growth cedar, spruce, and fir. Few Americans—almost none—have cast peepers on this much "unimproved" territory. Snaking through the Selway is a 103-mile two-track leading from my Darby home to Elk City, Idaho, a "city" comprising a café and gas station. The end. You will view no human interference along that drive. Didn't bring enough fuel? You and the kids will die. Ask kayakers about the Selway River's schizophrenic indifference. They'll tell you all about dying.

Living in Montana, I realized I needed Forest Service maps, geo-survey maps, and three-dimensional U.S. Army topographic maps fashioned from flexible plastic. The 3-D topo maps represent the finest invention this side of the Egg McMuffin. For one thing, both you and blind people can read them. For another, the location of my house appears on U.S. Forest Service map NL 11-6. Well, not really, but I drew in a little stick-figure house in the corner with me waving up at God and the garbage czar.

Rubbing your fingers on a 3-D topo map, you can feel how screwed you are if you position yourself between, say, Big Fog Mountain and Otter Butte. At that point, your best bet would be to fling yourself into the Selway River and float to Oregon, and here's why: My friend Scott the carpenter who is Jesus launched a raft from the little jumping-off point known as Paradise, where Julie and I sometimes camp. During his week-long float, Scott had but one encounter with a human: At midday, he spied on the river bank a deputy's 4WD truck—this was in off-the-grid Idaho, remember—and as Scott glanced down to ensure his raft was correctly aimed, he noticed a second pickup truck, except this one was below him in about nine feet of water as clear as Pella's finest. Scott worried he'd see a dead man's hand fluttering from a submerged window, so he yelled at the shoreside cop, asking what happened.

Turns out, a fellow in the underwater truck had indeed drowned, but it was a year earlier.

The loitering deputy then explained, in disconnected shouted bursts, "A kid swam across the river here…this morning…presumed drowned."

By this time, Scott's raft was beyond hailing distance—there is no paddling *up* the Selway without a 250-horse MerCruiser—so he gleaned no further details except to be on the lookout for, well, anything drifting with acne.

"That's an evil stretch of water," Scott later told me. "For the rest of the day, I was spooked." I asked if that would spell the end of his solo Selway adventures, and he said, "Oh, no, I love that place."

In a subsequent trip, Scott and his wife, Heidi, floated 135 miles over the course of a week and saw exactly two human units, also rafters. They always include their dog, Zoey, who falls asleep, then falls into the river occasionally, but she wears a customized K9 preserver and evidently enjoys awakening in ice water.

You know what I think this is: "The voluptuousness of tedium," as writer Machado de Assis put it. He had vowed to stop allowing himself to be carried along on the back-and-forth of daily human events. It has become my goal, too.

Julie and I camped at the put-in Scott used, sleeping in a tent erected atop the Tundra's bed. This was in October, and we became so cold that I started pounding my feet at about four a.m., creating a bass-tympanic booming that alerted wildlife for miles and also Julie.

Anyway, it had been a wet week—so wet that the gravel track leading to Paradise had twice suffered 100-yard washouts, one of which trapped a nervous covey of church kids who obtained a firsthand look at God's works in opposition to their parents'. In Darby, the consensus was "Let God save 'em—He started it," but I believe a heavenly helicopter was dispatched.

In any event, the rain had roiled the Selway until it resembled a horizontal Niagara, with surface water whiter than blue. The next morn, after sleeping in the Tundra—I'm not sure why this had earlier sounded so fun—four fishermen were preparing to set sail on their own diminutive drift boat, following in the paddle strokes of Scott. None looked eager to engage that wild watercourse, but all were too prideful to say so. They asked me to grasp a tether as they boarded, their last chance to reassess. Then into the froth they swirled, each passenger a fat little doughnut in a too-tight life preserver, with their raft immediately whirling like a windmill and all four emitting whoops and yelps as if hugely amused, although the looks on their faces said otherwise. Hypothermic terror was more the look.

I yelled, "A world of good luck to you!" then turned to Julie and said, "Dead. They're all dead." She watched for a minute and said, "Should've asked for dental records. Plus their cash."

John Phillips

I'M GONNA BEAT THE SHIT OUT OF IT

Poet Robinson Jeffers wrote: "For the first time I could see people living—amid magnificent unspoiled scenery—essentially as they did in the Idyls or the Sagas, or in Homer's Ithaca."

While I was searching for my own Ithaca, namely, a cabin in the Montana woods, I rented a Toyota 4Runner from Thrifty at the Missoula airport. The franchisee, Owen Kelley, greeted me at the desk, saying, "I know who you are." I struggled to think of any Thrifty rentals I might recently have wrecked. But just as I came up with nothing, Owen added, "I read *Car and Driver*. Plus, I own a bunch of Mustangs, including a '67 Shelby GT500."

"Cool," I replied, fairly certain Owen might be the kind of guy who sold goat glands in high school. Shelby Mustangs are rare and fetch a fortune. "We should go for a ride sometime," I said, assuming we wouldn't.

"Sometime" arrived in October, on one of the brightest fall days of our planet's Tilt-A-Whirl about its coddling star—larch trees like gold ingots and the aspens and cottonwoods sun-shot unto tints of highway workers' vests, plus a whiff of wood smoke in the air.

Needless to say, Owen indeed owned a '67 GT500, hunter green with white stripes, the most flawless Shelby I have ever seen. When I met Owen at Darby's Cenex station, the car's hood was raised and strangers were posing for selfies. Montanans don't give a pinch of kitty litter for Ferraris and Maseratis, but they adore trucks and Mustangs.

Owen bought the car 35 years ago, when he drove to a Mustang club convention in Calgary, Alberta, just north of us. At that point, the car was filthy, faded, and—with 54,000 difficult miles on the clock—already weary. Owen paid $7,800. Since then, he has personally repainted the car in its original colors and has driven it 40,000 miles, including a trip to Las Vegas where it was 105 degrees. "No A/C, of course," he noted. "My wife and I wore bathing suits."

Over the years, Owen has met the car's creator, Carroll Shelby, at club events. Ol' Shel signed the underside of Owen's passenger-side visor—"I couldn't bear having him scrawl all over the dash, which always looks to me like vandalism"—and was surprised that Shelby didn't extend a palm for payment. At the time, Shelby was partly supporting himself, à la Pete Rose, by hawking autographs on everything from mud flaps to 1966 seven-liter Ford Galaxies, one of which Owen also owns.

"The man was a quick draw with a Sharpie," Owen admitted. As he walked away, Shelby said, "I'll never forget the boys from Montana." It might have been a compliment. It might have been a threat. Carroll Shelby was always roughly four minutes from indictment for interstate fraud.

In any event, I drove Owen's Mustang on Highway 93 through Darby, over the mountain pass, and into Idaho. It transported me to the '60s. I felt hormones tingling. The steering was so awful that it would have been rejected on WWII landing craft. That a lot of folks herded these cars around racetracks strikes me now as suicidal, and I was one of them. Plus, there was the familiar waft of unburned fuel; an exhaust boom that overwhelmed conversation; a clutch pedal heavy as a navy destroyer; an amount of wind noise that would have flustered the Wright brothers; and furnace-quality heat flowing unimpeded through the firewall. My Orvis fishing shirt was a mop in 30 minutes.

Moreover, I tried to shift into the nonexistent fifth gear maybe 200 times, which made Owen clear his throat like Richard Nixon. Otherwise, he's a lovely 56-year-old guy. I saw no evidence of goat glands.

Owen doesn't care for pretentious car shows. "If a judge were to say, 'Hey, you got a rock chip over here,' I might try to hurt him," he told me. "I remind people, 'I *drove* the car here. See? No trailer.'"

In fact, on our Sunday drive, I sent plenty of gravel flying and Owen never flinched.

"When I retire," he said, "I'll make a two-year project of repainting the car again. In the meantime, I'm gonna beat the shit out of it"—a sublime mantra for a guy driving a Mustang worth $125,000. In fact, after our drive, I looked up an Arizona '68 Shelby GT500, same color as Owen's. The asking price was $189,900.

I'm pretty sure the point of our drive was no point. We just sloshed around in his car's considerable aura as Owen described, among other wonders, his 1985 drunken dinner in Missoula with Hunter S. Thompson, back when Hunter spoke in sentences. Oddly, I haven't undertaken an aimless drive in years. It's not as if I haven't had access to fabulous cars or enchanting roads. It's just that driving a car has always meant writing about a car, which meant thinking about a car, which meant work.

Not in Montana.

MAYTAGGED AND POSTAGE-STAMPED

I eventually invested $2,800 for a banged-up drift boat, which is basically an inflatable blue rubber Zodiac with an aluminum frame supporting three swiveling seats and more Coors holders than in a Texas roadhouse.

The rower faces forward but pulls the oars backward to counter the current. Steering takes tedious practice—it would be easier to play Chinese pickup sticks upside down. To alter course, you must row with more force on one oar than the other and sometimes row forward with one or both oars and sometimes backward with one or both oars and sometimes you dunk the oars in the water and hold steady, and all the rest of the time you curse the notion of a benevolent God and a boat filled with empty Coors cans. The first time out, I said, "Why is this happening?" about 20 times. It'd be easier to steer Ted Nugent to the repertoire of Édith Piaf.

During my first rowing lesson on the Bitterroot River, my instructor was Orvis guide Dread Pirate Dave. As I sailed through the first riffle—which is whitewater, but they don't call it that in Montana—I panicked, and the boat looped in a 360-degree spin. On the second riffle, I induced a 360-degree whirly plus a head-on collision with the left bank. Amid the third riffle, there was another clockwise twirl, another collision with the bank, and one oar explosively burst free of its oarlock, scaring Dave's dog.

That's how the afternoon progressed: tiring, frustrating, with Dave saying, "It's hard to fish when the boat is spinning," and, "You might wanna choose a bank for collisions—left or right—then stick with it." Under my navigational hand, the boat became a marine pinball. Dave's dog barfed.

Eventually, I accidentally coxswained us into the most dangerous maneuver possible, first try, no problem, you're welcome. Yet again out of my control, the boat dashed into the crotch of a massive fallen pine that formed a giant tuning fork pointing upstream. Boat and occupants were seized. Below, it sounded like all of Butte's toilets swirling at once. "You're fucked, now," said Dave.

Using the oars was impossible because I was hard against the trees. Rowing did nothing but scrape bark. For a long while—well, probably only 30 seconds—Dave allowed me to agonize over the crisis I'd summoned. Then he jumped overboard into fast-moving water almost to his waist and somehow manhandled us back to the "safety" of the main channel, where I promptly rammed the far bank.

If the water had been a foot higher, I don't know what would have happened, but we might well have been Maytagged and postage-stamped, with Allstate making my wife marginally richer. I felt like the captain of a Scud missile in a *Nutty Professor* movie. What's more, rain pelted down in drops the size of kidney beans, blurring my vision; the ambient temp dropped to 40 degrees; and a gale out of the north whipped up whitecaps that slapped over the bow, something Dave had never seen. The river began to look inky, opaque, and poisonous, despite being an oasis of human salvation for centuries. Another outing that concluded at the liquor store.

After I'd slugged some Pendleton while sitting in the back of my own truck next to a dripping dog with vomit breath, I resolved to quit fishing. I felt defeated because I was. There were, however, three smallish upsides: (1) Dave caught a pig of a 19-inch rainbow, (2) I underwent a much-needed upper-torso workout, and (3) we saw a black mink and four harlequin ducks who have white spots on the backs of their black heads so they look like they're staring at you even while retreating. My boat suffered a foot-long scrape resembling a dueling scar. I asked myself if the fish were worth the angst, cash, and sogginess. But I don't even have the experience to answer.

More depressing: Before I took delivery of my boat, I watched its frame being welded by a young man named Dave Norton. He and I kidded that the aluminum latticework resembled a race-car chassis. Not long after, Dave disappeared on his bike. A month passed before he was found hanging from a tree near a den of wolverines being studied by Defenders of Wildlife. Burleigh Curtis and his search-and-rescue crew made the recovery, along with pilot friend Ravi Fry. It's tempting to think Dave took his life after watching me bang up his handiwork. Truth is, no one knows his reasons. Darby went quiet for a week.

I tend to describe nature in bellicose and combative imagery, but it isn't a struggle that Mother Nature even knows she's waging. She doesn't, never has, won't. It's just me worrying about my role as perceived top-dog protagonist trying to follow a script too complicated to comprehend. One of those scripts, apparently, is rowing a boat.

John Phillips

One Man's Homage to Hardware

An annual rite in Montana comprises the late-October winterization of the house, a tedious rigmarole that takes two days. Outdoor spigots must be insulated and turned off, as well as the indoor valves feeding them. There are woodpecker holes to smear with wood-filling goo that resembles Silly Putty and has the advantage of sealing little cuts and scrapes on my hands. There's a pressure tank to drain, a brush cutter to lube, six portable power packs to unplug and store. My puny firefighting hoses must be drained and coiled in the basement. The bikes, flower pots, and summer truck tires find homes under tarps, along with both kayaks and stuff I don't remember buying, such as an electrically heated cathouse, which Julie told me doesn't come inside but stays out for Rennie the fox.

Various power blowers and suckers must be serviced. All three chain saws and the weed whacker spend their winters at Murdoch's for backrubs and sharpening but first must be purged of fuel and oil. The engine hoist must be disassembled—in the living room, as it turns out. Studded tires must be installed on both vehicles by October 15, signaling the final appearance of the hydraulic floor jack, car stands, air wrench, crapitus squared, and 18 mousetraps that I gather up because I cannot abide killing rodents during their most ill-fed and uncomfortable months, a reprieve from the governor of the Double-J Cat Ranch.

In fact, where did all this gizmoggery come from? From Harbor Freight is the answer, where I float a whopper account that right now includes a brass air-inflation chuck that I can't wait to use for purposes opposite its design, such as blow-drying a cat. I hope I acquired all this tackle because I really need it and not because it somehow buttresses my psyche as a cow-roping and fence-riding mountain man who listens every afternoon to a children's program on NPR.

A mile from us lives neighbor Mike Phillips, off the grid. His motto is, "No more mergers and acquisitions." If he owns something he doesn't use for 24 months, he "Goodwills it" or burns it. He's like Bruce Chatwin: "Things filled men with fear: the more things they had, the more they had to fear. Things had a way of riveting themselves on to the soul and then telling the soul what to do."

Mike Phillips eschews the paeon to paraphernalia, the homage to hardware, the joy of junk, the reverence for retail recklessness. He also abhors alliteration because it's a curiously callous collection of consonants.

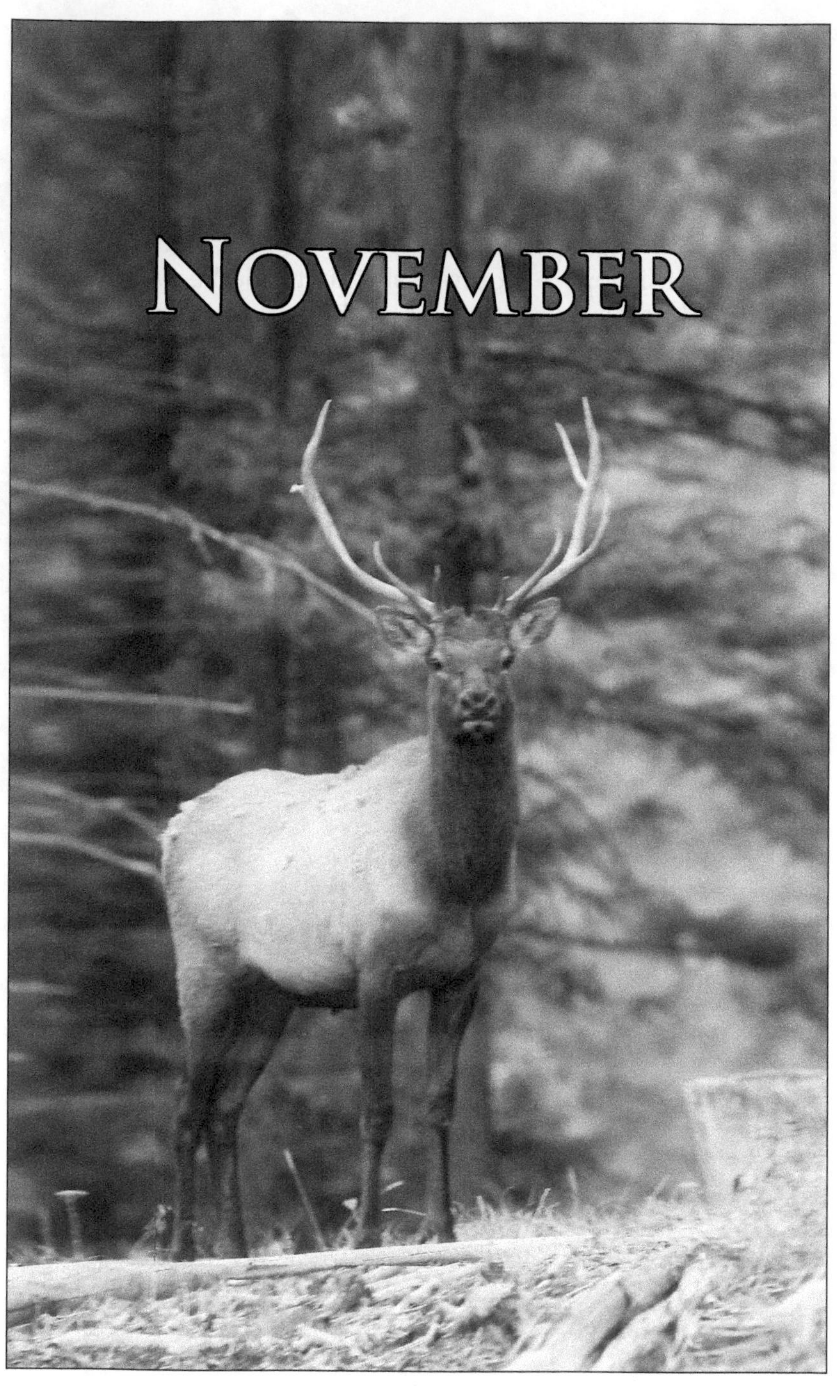
NOVEMBER

YELLOW MAN

Allow me to backpedal to the previous November. Before I moved to these hillocks and spires, I hauled my first load of tatty furniture to Darby via U-Haul truck #1. Julie and I had purchased the Darby house a year before we could inhabit it, summoning 365 agonizing dreamscapes at four a.m., wondering if the place was burning, being gnawed into bite-size pieces by pack rats, or serving as a tactical command center for vaping teens. So this first load was storable stuff from our Michigan basement, the synonym for which is crap.

When I set out for the empty house, the sun was lasering the rye grass until it glowed ochre and amber. I recall being giddy and pounding the rental truck's steering wheel as I approached my yet empty domicile, price tag recently removed. As I herded the laden 20-foot truck up Moose Meadow Lane, I began to notice the two-track was covered in, first, a thin sprinkling of snow, then a skim, then a reasonable facsimile of a glacier. This didn't seem possible, witness the temperate breezes in Darby, 440 feet below. It was the first week of November.

At the peak of the steepest hill, forward progress diminished until there was a motionless tick of static balance.

Then, naturally, the truck initiated a reversal of fortune. Rearward velocity wasn't worrisome—one or two mph—but I was countersteering like a drunk, my arms a blur of inaccurate and acute-angled corrections. But the truck didn't care what angle I selected. It simply skated 100 yards downhill until the left-rear tire slopped into a yard-deep ditch, with the rear bumper flattening a nest of pine saplings on my own property. Euphoric contentment morphed into ValuJet failure. The truck rested cockeyed across the snowy road, one tire buried, preventing access to my home and, more important, to two of my future neighbors' homes.

I climbed down to appraise my predicament, but I was right then wearing $230 Cole-Haan leather-soled loafers, so I couldn't walk without grasping the filthy truck. That's when I heard four-wheelers roaring, headed my direction. This took all of 90 seconds. Eventually, a quartet of ATVs and riders parked in a circle surrounding the truck, each man clutching a walkie-talkie and expressing military commands and strategic authorizations: "Echo foxtrot one-niner. Incident at mile two-point-two, north brink, clearance zulu-zero. Straps, winches, come-alongs required. Mentally ill driver. Over."

These four saviors were neighbors I'd yet to meet—Pete Bonnell, Ted Almgren, Kemp Conn, and Chic Gerlach—with "neighbors" meaning they lived within two miles. Noticing my footwear, they were loath to risk conversation. But when I announced my plan to summon a tow truck, Chic agreed it was, as plans go, among the best.

"I'll call Simple Towing," I suggested. They all howled.

"Simple Towing?" snarked Ted. "They're drunks. They're also simple."

At the time, I didn't even know my new area code. There's only one for all of Montana, yet I had to inquire. The Rescue Quartet was appalled.

"It's 406," Kemp informed as if encouraging an infant during toilet training. "You're retiring here?" An electric bolt of embarrassment zinged down my spine. I tried to look more Montana-ish by spitting on the ground.

An hour later, a tow truck with six chained wheels

arrived. It was the size of a Coast Guard cutter and apparently as powerful, because it free-lifted the front half of the U-Haul, made a three-point turn at the crest of my hill, then dragged the stricken vehicle (with me inside doing nothing) to pavement two miles distant.

I asked the driver, "How much?" and he replied, "Five hundred oughta do it, not including a gratuity, if that's how you roll." I must say I was happy to pay, because I had been transported to a location where no mocking neighbors were assembled.

The following day, I rented a flatland storage unit from Dennis Bush, a Darby fixture, and unloaded my furniture with the help of no one, not that I asked. At day's end, I was so exhausted and filthy that I swallowed four stale doughnuts and collapsed on a motel bed that was rented by the hour. But not before accidentally backing the truck into a light stanchion that caused a chrome attachment ring and the huge bulb to hurtle down onto the vehicle's roof, creating a sound like a church bell bursting through a plate-glass window. I left the whole mess where it landed. I assume it eventually vibrated off the truck, but I neither heard nor saw it go.

The next morning, I drove to Missoula and rented a black Jeep from Owen Kelley, with whom I would eventually become close. Piloting the Jeep, I was indeed able to ascend my own driveway, and once inside I spread my sleeping bag on the living-room carpet, alongside the fireplace.

Because the real-estate agent had uttered terrifying warnings about possible freeze-ups, I'd earlier paid to have the plumbing drained, filled with antifreeze, and the main valve cranked off. Thus, no working sinks, toilets, or showers. I located a discarded bucket in the garage and used that as a urinal for two nights in my not-so-warm home.

On the morning I departed, I carried the chamber pot, if we may so delicately describe it, out the front door, intending to dump it in the forest, an insult to creatures who do not stockpile their sewage. But I slipped while descending the icy steps. I don't expect you to believe this because it sounds like a script for a TV sitcom starring John Ritter, but I cartwheeled with arms and legs flailing, during which I was showered with my own cold urine on my own cold porch on my own cold property in the Montana woods.

You've heard of Burning Man? I was Yellow Man, burning mad. I could hear deer chuckling in their reserved woodland seats. What little urine that missed me splashed on the concrete patio, freezing into a golden skating rink. Back inside, I microwaved a gallon of bottled water, stripped, stood in the shower and anointed myself for the second time in three minutes. I donned dry clothes—using them first as towels—then threw the pee-infused items in the trash, where they remained until we returned a year later, causing Julie to pose a series of difficult questions.

I viewed this as another hazard of the West, a test not conquered but protractedly endured. As warm welcomes go, Montana's wasn't.

A BANK VAULT FILLED WITH KITTY LITTER

My wife is more social than I, which is to say she's more social than J.D. Salinger during lent. But you know what worried us? Would any actual, you know, *people* be involved in our lives?

Julie resolved the matter by volunteering at the library and also fashioning gift cards from her wildlife photographs—official-looking custom stamp on the back, her signature in gold ink, and frilly envelopes that would satisfy a French bureaucrat. She ferried the cards to the mercantile where the owner placed them on display just inside the front door. Here was a chance to earn up to $30 a month but mostly an opportunity for Julie to meet Darby's citizenry.

That's how she met Jody Smith, the manager of our 7-Eleven–size bank, who arranged for Julie to sell candy at our block-long antique store. She succeeded at that for ten days, so Jody hired her at the bank as a teller, a post for which Julie had neither experience nor training nor eager aptitude. She was often assigned to the drive-through, where it was not uncommon to serve a customer on horseback.

When Julie relayed this tidbit to her Michigan relatives, they were thunderstruck.

"Well, it's not quite such a big deal," she explained, "because the rider has to dismount to be served. It's a rule."

At the bank, Julie met half of Darby's residents. She also earned $7.50 an hour, no benefits, no free checking, but did have unlimited access to the old-fashioned vault. I asked what it contained. "Deeds and stuff, not much," she said. "Oh, and also a bag of kitty litter serving as an emergency toilet."

The manager explained it would likely be employees trapped in the vault, having been herded there by a robber or a bear or the Brinks guy with garlic breath. It was not clear whether employees should spread the kitty litter on the floor and relieve themselves thereupon or just urinate into the bag itself, which seemed preferable and more private to me. Except, then, does a single dousing despoil the whole bag? I asked Julie to research further corporate details.

Here's her training in case of a holdup: "First, apologize to the robber," she recounted. "Then grab my own checkbook and write a check for $20 or whatever I feel comfortable with, then apologize a second time." Ha-ha.

The bank has never been robbed, which surprised me because escape routes are legion. Simply driving south, for instance, leads to near-zero civilization for 75 five miles until Salmon, Idaho. Or trot any direction east or west for half a mile to be engulfed by wilderness where an exploding dye pack will stain only piss fur.

Darby's Marshal Larry polices the bank occasionally, once to roust a teen in the parking lot who was copping the bank's Wi-Fi to watch porn, and a couple times to enforce the "no guns within the bank" regulation, which is locally considered a reckless infringement of human rights and the dress code alike. Here's their argument: A man must carry a gun inside the bank because what if there's a man inside the bank carrying a gun?

As a teller, Julie had access to everyone's statements. She was forbidden to recount specifics, although she stared with her most earnest face and said, "There is a lot of money in this valley, almost none of it held by people born here." Which added sand to my psychic barrel of guilt.

One of the tellers became locally notorious for robust excavations of her nostrils, which so distressed even the gun toters that they would stand in any line but hers, an arrangement that allocated bonus time for booger selection. You won't believe this, but the nose molester quit the bank to draw blood at a nearby clinic. During my last physical, she drilled for mine. When she donned surgical gloves, I requested a pair myself.

Then the bank decided it didn't require part-timers, so Julie was shown the door, conveniently only four feet away. It was a blow, because I had enjoyed telling people, "My wife is in banking."

Julie fidgeted about the Double-J Cat Ranch for five days, then secured a job as a clerk in a touristy arts-and-crafts shop. I noticed she was hauling books to work. "Yesterday, we had one customer in six hours," she explained. Then the business folded, big surprise, with its contents slated for auction, including several of our hardcovers.

She next volunteered at a llama-rescue farm north of Darby. At first, her job was to shovel manure into bags for sale, llama shit apparently being highly regarded for use in poultices and political campaigns. Julie was quickly promoted to feeding the beasts, in which service she noted, "You *will* be slimed by random gobbets of llama spit launched at the speed of sound."

On one llama-servicing day alone, Julie took four llama loogies to the chest and neck. This was the only job in her life for which, before setting out for work, she donned her filthiest clothing. Then she was promoted to exercising the llamas, as well as a couple of minority alpacas with chips on all four shoulders. Llama slime makes your black sweatshirt look as if you've sneezed and drooled during a seizure.

Julie next volunteered at Hamilton's animal shelter—a no-kill facility, bless their liberal hearts—where she landed the position of "cat whisperer." She sat queenlike on the floor in the cat gallery and gently interviewed all troubled felines.

"They'd walk up one at a time," she told me, "as if for an appointment, then unload their emotional burdens." When one cat would linger overlong, she'd whisper, "Well, I see our time is up, so, same time next week, and remember what I said about your mother."

Then the school district asked Julie to act as a substitute teacher. We have the full muddle in Darby, grades K through 12, but, again, Julie had zero experience in teaching unless the kids needed to learn the ins and outs of ophthalmic surgery, including her ability to extricate "vegetable matter" from the eyes of boys who have been firing compressed-air potato guns. But the school didn't seem to care about blindness. All they wanted was Julie's fingerprints and skill at shouting.

After her prints cleared the FBI or Marshal Larry or the library's overdue-book department, Julie found herself shepherding a class of third-graders, most of whom had yellow eyes and pink horns. One kid warned, "You're really in for it now. You know that, right?" At noon she emailed this: "These kids are fucking insane," typed more or less phonetically.

Back at home, her hair was wild and one sock was wadded up in her shoe. I offered a glass of cabernet, which she downed in one pull. I tried to plumb details. She recounted—not necessarily in this order—a desk toppling with inhabitant therein; a surprise visit from the principal who uttered a threat that scared even Julie; a staged fistfight; a box of colored pencils and other airborne missiles too numerous to count or collect; uniform refusal to perform any assigned work; the smell of something burning; snot deployed as an instrument of mass destruction; and the son of Wendy, one of Julie's bank buddies, trying to comfort her by saying, "You'll get through this, I know you will. You should have seen what we did to the last lady."

I asked Julie if she'd cried. "Shown weakness?" she asked. "Crying would have summoned at least three of the Four Horses of the Apocalypse." I asked if the third-graders might do her physical harm. "I don't think so," she reckoned. "Fifth-graders, maybe." She thereafter was reassigned to high-school students. After an eight-hour shift, she netted $55.

Julie forgave all trespassers when actor Jeff Bridges arrived to praise the school's breakfast program. No, we do not know why. Teachers said to the students, "Hey, kids, it's the Dude," as in Lebowski, but the nippers knew the Dude only as Ricky's fat alcoholic uncle somewhere down on Water Street, so a celebration of celebrity failed. Bridges seemed relieved. Afterward, the school ceased calling Julie for any service whatsoever. I believe she was judged too likely to be permanently traumatized.

That seemed like plenty of employment, but no. Julie next volunteered at Darby's Bread Box, a one-room house converted into a depot for surplus food earmarked for the needy. They'll even feed pets. Darby's own People's Market regularly contributes a pile of not-so-stale staples. But it wasn't until Julie started writing thank-you notes to donors that she discovered a couple contributions of five figures, every quarter. Checks for $2,500 were common.

That so much cash poured in was stunning because no one had solicited it. All word of mouth. My sister in Ohio even donated $150, because she is a superior person who is a docent at an art museum and is fluent in French. I only mention this because whenever she visits, she becomes Montana's only authority on Seurat and Proust while talking Gallic-lipped smack to a Parisian chef she met in Hamilton. Which sounds like the first half of a joke.

Allow me here to tip my noncamouflaged hat to the Bread Box as the gold standard for perfect trickle-down egalitarianism. No one is paid. When postage is purchased for thank-you notes, Julie sometimes coughs it up herself. Donations alone maintain the building and pay for collecting food. Every soul in the valley is welcome, no questions asked, no condescending attitudes, even if you roll up on a horse or in Charlie Scripps's Bentley. The Bread Box is an example of people doing good for the sake of it, expecting and receiving no recognition. Some of them are even Republicans. (Well, one.)

I shouldn't have been shocked that the valley's conservative majority derides the Bread Box for "encouraging welfare." Okay, fine. But here's a true tale the critics will find useless but I do not: We hold dear a neighbor named Mark, who retired to the Bitterroots after succeeding as a mail-order wine merchant on the West Coast. Upon arrival, Mark built a miniature farm—goats, chickens, and one sheep the size of a donkey. Then his wife contracted early-onset Alzheimer's that became a hasty death sentence. After which, Mark's savings had been blown on overpriced prescriptions, Shylock doctors, gouging hospitals, failed health plans, and corrupt insurance schemes.

Local conservatives blamed Mark for not purchasing better health insurance, but the reason he didn't is the reason we didn't: absolutely unaffordable. Let me merely note that what saved Mark was the Bread Box and Obamacare. When he regained his balance, he accepted the night-manager's position at nearby celebrity-laden Triple Creek Ranch (Bill Gates, Sandra Day O'Connor, K. Costner, The Dude, Richard Gere, Dread Pirate Dave). "While tending to a sick wife," Mark remarked, "I developed skills at wandering the halls at four in the morning. So they hired me."

When I interviewed Joe Biden, he said, "The world respects America because we do big things." If so, how come our health care's efficacy ranks 27th worldwide even as our per-capita spending for same is twice any other nation's? I can't even *name* 27 first-world nations. If America's Olympic basketball team finished 27th, citizens would torch the White House, and *Sports Illustrated* would cancel the swimsuit issue. Hell, if Americans were healthier, we could invade more countries. Pardon me, but we pay *twice* per capita what France pays, and that's comparing us to people who intentionally combine raw milk and mold to create a spreadable appetizer flecked with sparkly blue boogers.

In any event, when I awake each morn, Julie is usually gone. If she comes home stinking, well, that was the llamas. If she comes home with rotten apples for the deer, that was the Bread Box. If she comes home with one eye glued shut, a bruised larynx, and two broken fingers, that was the third-graders.

I am so proud of her.

Wade Cox as Dishwater Boggett

There's an active gold mine not far from my home. Shocked me, too, like finding a weasel in my sweatpants. It's up the West Fork Road. Before running out of pavement, you turn left for 12 miles along ludicrously lumpy Hughes Creek Road, all of it nasty, irregular stone that bounces my truck until the receipts above the sun visor rain down. Eventually, the road plunges into gloomy wilderness but not until you've passed the abandoned one-room Alta Ranger Station, where, by local legend, one ranger murdered another during a notably strenuous winter. I believe a deck of cards was involved. When Hughes Creek Road concludes—if feels like the chapped lip of creation—you'll notice a blink of a turnoff to the left, marked with enough "No Trespassing" signs to lend visitors a second thought and third.

Here's how I know about the mine: Long before purchasing our Darby ranchette, we became fixated on 20 acres of bare land on the aforementioned Hughes Creek. In fact, we made an offer, which I'm delighted was refused, because Hughes Creek is off the grid and off its rocker. The few residents back there have garage-size pantries, and they deploy 55-gallon barrels set out at the road 12 miles from their front doors, to act as emergency-ration drops.

Our real-estate agent, Sherry Wildey, raised in Darby, drove us to Hughes Creek to inspect the parcel. She insisted we first obtain a septic perc test, because if you can't create an adequate turd dissipator, then the so-called sanitarians will deny a building permit, although it's unclear how many Bitterrooters abide by legal phrases printed on paper. I asked who might dig a test pit. Sherry replied, "Wade Cox."

Mr. Cox, it turns out, is a professional digger. It is he who operates the gold mine. His name, in my opinion, is almost too perfect for a scrappy western prospector. Almost as good as Rooster Cogburn, Dishwater Boggett, or Turkey Lawless (a Darby citizen Julie knows). Wade's place is so far back in piney nowhere-ville that the ferrets carry Forest Service maps.

Sherry drove us down Wade's driveway, which was more like Wade's reality TV show called *Knobby Ruts of Death*. Along his driveway, Wade has erected sign after sign detailing what will happen to your carcass should you continue an inch farther. Being shot is one option, stabbed another. Wade has fashioned a full-size human effigy with a hangman's noose cinched tight around its neck, an apparition that dangles from a tree beside his two-track driveway. There's a sign on that, too, but I can't recall the message because the effigy had paralyzed me. I may later have seen a sign warning of insane mountain men who haven't contacted actual women in 46 years, although I later learned that Wade is happily married. Well, I have no idea how happy he is, but he's married and his wife has been observed smiling.

I repeatedly told Sherry we could terminate the trek at any time, thank you, but she assured that Mr. Cox might be somewhat gnarled and eccentric but was otherwise often harmless. Julie likewise recommended retreat, then saw a yellow-belly marmot (also known as a "whistle pig") the size of our last Siberian husky and agreed to proceed on the premise that she might see another. "There you go," encouraged Sherry.

At Mr. Cox's placer mine we found outbuildings galore, but I couldn't tell which was his abode or housed excavation equipment or toilet seats. Poised over what I assumed was Hughes Creek proper, there drooped an aging power shovel with a dragline dredge the size of a minivan. I say "assumed" because the creek resembled an air force bombing range.

The water was the color of Guinness, flanked by gravel-strewn banks piled with hummocks of tailings stretching beyond the waterline for 50 yards. I will not climb atop my tallish horse to bitch about the ruin wrought upon Hughes Creek, because it has been a gold-mining site since a guy named Barney Hughes discovered it in the mid-19th century. Back then, environmental thoughtfulness meant crapping *next* to the waterway instead of in it. Wade Cox didn't initiate this mess. But I feel compelled to report that it recollected a miniature Fort McMurray tar-sands project, a place I wrote about in the '80s.

During our visit—we were cowering in Sherry's gray GMC Yukon—we determined that Wade wasn't home. Or wasn't reacting to Sherry's honking. I still can't fathom how a man could subsist out there, picking at a trickle of a stream, clawing at the earth sometimes with a shovel alone. There is no electricity, just diesel generators to help dig and separate gravel, so maybe those engines occasionally illuminate a lightbulb or two. The site is at some altitude, so coldness is a presence, as in minus 35F the previous winter.

Wade owns an ancient dump truck with plow—a "blade" in Montana—and he'll sometimes emerge midwinter, ursinelike, to plow Hughes Creek Road, even continuing for a distance if he feels frisky. It is a blessing for other all-season residents whose "heavy equipment" has been purchased from Sears. Of course, starting a diesel engine when it's minus 35 is its own adventure in arson, in which you hope not to set the garage alight because the volunteer firemen serving Hughes Creek stress the word volunteer.

Various prospectors have been picking at the scabby creek in this locus since the Civil War. After Barney Hughes trekked over the mountains to Idaho, searching for more gold—and naming a second creek Hughes Creek, having apparently run out of imagination—a group of Chinese prospectors took up residence. They managed to extract $4 to $5 in gold per day, which I guess was ambitious money back then, because the Chinese continued to fuss at the site until 1877. After they vamoosed, reasons unknown, the succeeding occupant erected a flume several hundred feet long, carrying water to the site, exiting through a six-inch pipe.

By 1898, a weekly stagecoach was servicing the mine, which soon boasted a general store, a sawmill, and two saloons. Why a dozen guys would require two saloons is a mystery that stinks of Old Crow, but I'm told it was necessary to obviate internecine riots of race and lineage. Now that I think of it, downtown Darby likewise harbors two saloons facing each other. Someday I plan to revisit Hughes Creek to poke around Wade's woodsy perimeter in search of traces of the old town, if it ever really amounted to a town.

Not a few of the gold prospectors in Montana arrived here as penniless homesteaders known as "Hunyrockers" and "Scissorbills." No one can tell me why. From 1904 to 1952, the mine coughed up $254,412 additional ore via dragline dredge. Geologists have since surmised that the gravel contains gold "in quartz veins in quartzite," if that clarifies matters for you, and the source may not be the creek at all. That is, there might be a billion-dollar glowing loaf hidden beneath a porcupine den mere yards from Wade Cox's outhouse, and if Wade finds it, well, bless his quill-infected fingers. I think of Wade Cox as Grizzly Adams with a degree in hydraulics.

But let us return to my proposed septic pit on Hughes Creek, because I know you're worried about it. When Julie and I undertook our final tour of this wild property, it was midwinter. Sherry and I donned snowshoes to traipse the lot lines, and within ten feet of exiting her Yukon I placed my right snowshoe atop my left and cartwheeled into snow deep enough to foul my comb-over. Sherry was ahead of me and didn't observe this bit of burlesque, and I never mentioned it. In any event, Wade Cox had agreed to haul one of his smaller backhoes to the site, feeling confident he'd hit pay dirt or whatever dirt would best dissolve human dirt.

The man appeared wraithlike out of a snowstorm. Stocky, round face, walking like a Hollywood gunslinger, he wore a snowmobile suit with his head blanketed in scarves and goggles and those red rags that mechanics use in repair shops. I backed up a little. Wade arrived with a shotgun stashed in a PVC pipe mounted on the fender of his ATV, barrel jutting skyward. I don't know why I was so intimidated, but Wade's legend stipulated an untamed mountain man who ate the raw livers of cougars while the rest of us watched *Jeopardy.*

Wade slid off his ATV and set about the fussy task of unwrapping his head. I remember a beautifully striped skunk—also known as a wood pussy—slogging atop the snow 20 yards behind him. As soon as Wade's mouth and eyes materialized, I said hello as you'd say hello to a beloved dog. Wade was silent and unwrapped more rags and scarves, like a mummy disrobing.

Finally, he extended a hand and said, "How-de-do, young fella."

He turned out to be as kindly as my Uncle Seth except he didn't play the flute. He pointed to a likely spot to excavate, then bent to his work, sinking a white plastic pipe whose purpose went unexplained. I offered him $500, whereupon he allowed as how half that sum would suffice, thanks, and then he rode off toward his hanging human effigy. I never saw him again. But according to Darbrarians, he's still out there, excavating as ferociously as a prairie dog. I don't know if that's wonderful or horrifying.

All my life, I've jotted down various unique sentences uttered in my presence, the sort of sentences you're certain never to hear again. "You live next to a gold mine" qualified as one. It made me recall another: Back in Michigan, I was extorted into hosting a stag party, so I hired two strippers, a sister act, as it turned out. There came a moment when Stripper #1, wearing only high heels, sidled up to me in my own kitchen, looked left and right as if sharing a Pentagon secret, then whispered: "John, do you want me to put my clothes back on so I can strip again?"

Children of the Lake Go Feral

You may recall my forced familiarity with the valley's industriall-size tow trucks. Well, it was one of those behemoths that starred in what we now call "Incident at Lake Como," a rusticatingly comely body of water a mile north of town. It is hunkered below the "Three Sisters," snow-capped crags whose official names no one seems to know. As it happens, my Orvis guide, Dread Pirate Dave, had driven to the lake to investigate ice-fishing possibilities. That's when he observed a monster tow truck's arrival, along with a cadre of youngsters whose purpose at the lake was unknown. Dave described them as "maybe the cast of *Cats*." The driver and his assistants exited the tow truck to study an abandoned car on the shore.

Here's what Dave learned: About 48 hours earlier, two tourists from the Pacific Northwest had driven to Lake Como to absorb its wintry splendor. The lake was snow-covered, so it was difficult to discern where rocky shoreline concluded and crusty lake ice began. In this instance, the couple overestimated by five feet. The nose of their sedan, which I believe was a Dodge K-car, burst through the ice, and water flowed over the hood and up to the base of the windshield before the driver hit the brakes and sought assistance.

The tow truck should have arrived right then, and that's because the temperature had plunged overnight, such that icy tentacles enveloped the car's engine block, radiator, front suspension, grille, and bumper. There no longer existed open water around the hood. Just ice, and it was fast thickening. Locked in Lake Como's frigid leg trap, the car resembled a dart stuck in a white duvet.

The tow-truck's driver and co-pilot huddled. Plan A was to affix chains to the rear bumper and pull the car out slowly. In this undertaking, the car never budged, but the bumper did, popping off with a ping and then a pong as it landed. The kids and Dave sat on a driftwood log as spectators. They clapped and tossed snowballs.

Dave told the tow-truck operators, "You need to break the ice first," but was ignored. So Dave remained on the log with the animated cast of *Cats*.

Next came Plan B: Attach nylon straps to rear suspension members and nudge the tow truck forward at three or maybe four mph, allowing the straps to cinch firmly. "Come on, *faster*," the kids and Dave urged as the truck initiated its forward roll. This time, the truck visibly shivered, then nearly stopped in its tracks. But not for long, because the K-car's suspension struts ripped off and were dragged up the shoreline, banging and snapping as they made their way inland. The car itself moved not a tick.

The kids cheered. Dave whistled.

"I could have helped," Dave told me. "They needed a chain saw to cut the ice. But when they ignored me like that, I sorta took a 'fuck you' attitude." He packed his fishing gear.

Plan C: Affix all the tow truck's chains, a steel cable, and stronger straps and ropes and fasteners not only around the rear beam axle but also to the rear door hinges and the C-pillars and B-pillars and to any metal protuberance at all, then accelerate the truck to serious velocity in order to yank the car out of the ice in one astounding and decisive whiplash snatch.

Here, finally, was drama. The frenzied kids worked themselves into a frothy fit, dancing and pumping fists, then drew nearer. The tow-truck operator told them to back off.

"Why?" asked one child. The operator responded, "Well, just because," when he should have said, "Just because we don't know what we're doing."

The driver revved the monster diesel engine, and the truck vaulted forward. Straps and cables stretched and strained. The kids screamed for more speed and the driver concurred.

That's how the Dodge sedan was torn in half.

The chains pulled sheetmetal into jagged shapes, the remainder of the suspension burst free, as did the gas tank and a score of vital automotive pieces, some briefly but remarkably airborne. The tow truck took a moment or two to stop, leaving behind a trail of taillights, glass, ribbons of rusty steel, two tires and wheels, one beam axle, pieces of carpet and upholstery, a bent trunk lid, jagged pieces of rear window, an empty pizza box, and a couple dozen items of debris that no one could identify.

"I think I saw a condom," said Dave.

The car had halved behind the front seats. That's all you could see, just the driver and passenger seatbacks, both absent headrests. The car was no longer a Dodge or even a sedan. More like a two-wheel, open-air carriage, a lump of scrap and broken plastic, although, in fairness, the leftovers would have availed its driver a panoramic view of Big Sky.

The kids went feral, knocking each other down, and then set upon the debris like bottle flies, rooting around for the finest mechanical mementos.

Dave sat stunned for a spell, then stood and said, "Tourists ain't driving *that* home."

One of the kids responded, "Fuckin' A."

On his cell phone the tow-truck driver ordered a flatbed truck, because the car had pretty much morphed into less an automobile than a commercial aircraft crash.

"Uh, no, *definitely* not towable," said the driver into the phone.

Why would an automobile's destruction supply as much pleasure as its creation? Why would this American symbol of freedom be as riveting torn asunder as it was a shining whole in the showroom? No one cared.

The next day, Hope the barber cut my hair. I asked if she'd heard about "Incident at Lake Como."

"Oh, God, yes," she replied, her eyes brightening. "It made everyone happy." Then she told me about Darby's annual grade-school winter pageant the night before. "Seven kids vomited on stage," she reported. "A chain reaction thing, looked like."

That made everyone even happier.

DECEMBER

HALLUCINATING BJÖRK

Our first winter in Montana could have served as training for Inuits. I've never known snow to fall 90 consecutive hours. It pelted down in what I can only describe as thickets, with flakes the size of quarters and nearly as heavy. Julie and I didn't need to leave the house—at first—so we lolled about enjoying the hoary spectacle.

The sky went opaque. Then glacier-quality slabs of snow began whoofing off the roof, landing with *1812 Overture* cannon shots, scaring the cats into formation and then into the fire room. The snow eventually blocked all exterior doors, so we had to exit and enter via the garage. Drifts were so deep just outside the garage that they lifted Julie's truck a foot skyward, leaving only an inch of clearance. The view from our front windows was snow and, beyond that, inestimable whiteness that represented a mobility dilemma even for the elk. Neighbor Chic Gerlach said, "Blizzards like this'll hang balls on a heifer."

If you live in the wilderness, you own the biggest propane tank possible. Ours is 12 feet long and five feet tall. It resembles something the Cousteau family might have owned. But the snow rendered it invisible. It didn't seem possible. It was like misplacing a submarine. The tonnage of snow on the roof threatened a wholesale implosion, perhaps squishing me laterally out of bed, probably at four a.m. amid a dream about a pint of French vanilla and a paintbrush.

Shovel in hand, I climbed onto the roof, which was easy because no ladder was required. I just walked up there. Well, waded up. I began shoveling, wondering if this finally would induce an aneurysm the size of a Wiffle ball. Then Julie demanded I tie myself off with a rope. I was hoping I could use the word "belay" for the first time but, in truth, falling off the roof would involve a tumble of about 36 inches into a nine-foot-deep powdery drift where I might briefly disappear in a poof of humiliation but without injury.

Still, she insisted. So I affixed a rope around my waist, Alpine-style, then flung the loose end over the far side of the steel roof, where it hung limp, attached to nothing but my imagination. Julie couldn't see the loose end whipping in the wind and was satisfied. If the rope inadvertently hanged me, I tried to imagine the story in our local paper, with the subhead, "City Boy Hangs Self Against All Odds and Common Sense."

On about Day Five of this whiteout, I noticed the alcohol supplies dwindling. Julie noticed a shortage, too, although her concern was more along the line of entrées. We coaxed her Toyota, with its transmission in low range, for 1.7 miles to the nearest paved road. But it took 55 minutes, and, at one point, the vehicle became high-centered, which must have twisted something vital because the windshield cracked from side to side. I thought we'd been shot. That was the end of Windshield #1. Many more were to die.

Our Darby grocery, petite but not usually in disarray, right then resembled something between anarchy and the U.S. Electoral College. The meat cooler contained only week-old frozen chickens from, oh, I don't know, possibly Bulgaria, and there was a paucity of paper products. Still, we packed three Glad garbage bags with staples such as red licorice and Clos du Bois pinot, then drove home.

Julie's red Toyota refused to climb even ten feet up our ridiculous driveway, so it was abandoned at the bottom like a muddy dog. Then came the business of lugging the plastic bags up our mountain through snow that in some places tugged at our hips. I feared wine bottles shattering into shards on which I might fall and bleed to death 40 feet from my own door.

When one of your legs plunges into snow until only your crotch holds you upright, the next step pitches you into circus acrobatics. It took us a minor epoch to reach the warm house, where I decimated some Pendleton, which did not raise the cats' spirits.

In the midst of this tempest, our juvenile bull moose appeared, wandering to within 20 feet of our porch, wading awkwardly through drifts and reenacting Monty Python's repertoire of Silly Walks. Walter would days later leap out from alder bushes at the far side of Tin Cup Creek as I drove over the bridge. I jammed on the brakes. The moose stood six feet tall and stared through the Toyota's windshield. He was reluctant to move, his huge upper lip quivering as he sniffed his way through the standoff. I wondered if he recognized me from our mutual hike in the spring. His antlers were still twin nubs—my favorite alien—but it occurred to me that his rack would have no trouble collapsing the already-cracked windshield. Alas, Walter is a peaceful soul and galumphed off with both ass cheeks jiggling, refusing to abandon the center of the road for 250 yards as I idled behind. I couldn't blame him. The road was plowed. The forest was not.

The snow continued to fall, nay, bombard "like twelve mad bastards," as Hunter Thompson once said. At the time, I possessed a *Car and Driver* BMW, and the magazine asked me to accept an emergency writing assignment in Monterey. So I piloted the all-wheel-drive BMW—equipped with Arctic-rated studded tires—for multiple hours through shadowless ruts. It felt like driving over curbs and dead cows. After four hours, I was 80 miles from home. Even without chemicals, Lance Armstrong could have done better.

Snow clogged the rear wiper, which ceased its duties, then the grille became glacially blocked. Bingo: an overheated engine in an ambient temp of 12 degrees. I deployed a ballpoint pen and a 99-cent plastic scraper to gouge out maybe five pounds of crystallized crud the consistency of gum beneath a school desk. Mine was the only vehicle on the road.

I lived most of my life in Michigan, so you might grasp my sacrificial readiness to drive into the teeth of gales that have about them a whiff of mortality. After two and a half days, I did indeed reach sunny California, where Julie and I swallowed a $32 pitcher of dirty martinis and fell into bed. But the drive home, of course, carried us back through the same frosty netherworld, past the site of the Donner Party's party and along a 100-mile stretch of near whiteout conditions that eventually closed part of the Salmon River Scenic Byway. Toward the end, I began hallucinating all-white objects—Tom Wolfe, Björk, the NRA. Along that road, by the way, there was no fuel to be had, not that it's important or anything.

Eventually, I began having trouble closing one eye, and one butt cheek had gone numb. That's when the BMW surrendered to a snowdrift ten feet from my garage, as if it had been relieved of its duties and had permission to die. The car was, right then, the filthiest object since Bigfoot landed in the snow-cone stand. *Car and Driver* published a photo of me attaching straps and cables to the car, trying to coax it the last few feet into my garage. The caption read, "Phillips always wanted to be a big strapping man."

Digging out of our driveway involved hiring a 30-foot-long commercial Caterpillar grader sporting six sets of chains. Price: $300. When owner/driver Brad departed, he failed to notice one of my 55-gallon steel drums containing gravel and salt. It was buried under snow, naturally. The grader's blade cut the barrel neatly in half, as if it were meatloaf. Two equal pieces. Talk about fun.

Brad called the next day to say, "I'm never coming back."

THEY'LL EAT STALE ÉCLAIRS

During a lull in the blizzard, I drove 70 miles to Missoula, pants afire and seething, feeling defeated, with Mother Nature evidently singling me out for castigation and freeze-dried earlobes. At the Toyota dealership, in the space of about 40 minutes, I purchased a $39,000 Toyota Tundra TRD truck with an extra inch of suspension lift and $2,500 worth of the most aggressive Goodyears on record. On the front bumper I installed a 9,000-pound electric winch, like something off a Panamanian freighter. The winch can also be transferred to the rear trailer-hitch receiver, as long as I can lift 90 pounds. I've never known why no one installs rear-mounted winches. It's the moving-forward part that deposits you in danger; the obvious route to safety is always backward. My new truck resembles one of those commercial rigs for servicing high-tension power lines.

Then I assembled 75 pounds of survival equipment in three duffels resting under the back seat: tire chains, freeze-dried food, pup tents, space blankets, flares, whitening toothpaste, headlamps, a plank to steady a jack, and bear spray with a 40-foot range to afford extra contemplation of mauling.

I bought a camping tent that fits atop the truck's bed, plus an air mattress and pump. Also knives and compasses and water purifiers. Also tow straps and snatch straps, pulley blocks, a pair of 8,000-pound come-alongs, a farm jack, a socket set made in Taiwan, an emergency jump-start battery, an ax, a hatchet, a SvenSaw, and an explosive fire-starting chemical that the post office refused to ship. I tossed in three flashlights, two-dozen batteries, four gallons of fresh water, a copy of *True Adventure*, and four pairs of gloves in two sizes and two thicknesses with rose motifs. I mailed this checklist to Tom Collins, my off-road guru and instructor for the Borneo trip. Tom emailed back, "*Jesus*, John."

That was Step #1 to vehicular independence.

Step #2 was the purchase of a $30,000 Toyota FJ Cruiser for Julie, marking the cessation of our disposable income. It resembles a 1960s Jeep Wrangler designed by a puffer fish but with a massive bull bar on the snout and the same $2,500 death-march tires as on the Tundra. It took Julie a month to master the FJ's dual-stick 4WD system. She named her homely trucklet Frida, after the tarantula-unibrow artist Frida Kahlo, and when Julie walks through the door after defeating that day's icy battlements, she says, "Frida is a climber. Frida is a beaut." You might like to know that the FJ's registration says, "Vehicle Type: Rugged Terrain." Where else but Montana will the state officially validate your manhood for $369?

A month before we bought the FJ, Julie had test-driven a variety of Subaru Outbacks. During one drive, she asked, "Is our driveway gonna break this little thing?"

"Not in the first week," I replied.

The driveway leading to our Double-J Cat Ranch is a two-mile festival of filth: mud that sucks off boots, ice of the Greenland bergy type, ruts that sometimes flip ATVs, razors of granitic outcroppings, and a senile madman named Patrick behind the wheel of a deathtrap Mitsubishi Montero. The road is navigable sometimes at walking pace only. Along the way, you might encounter a pair of mountain lions—Sid and Nancy—who recently tried to eat neighbor Red Schields's dogs at two in the morning. Red's dogs fought back. One dog latched onto Sid's snout and wouldn't let go. There ensued a horrifying, bloody tug of war, with Red circling, hoping for a rifle shot that wouldn't kill a pet. Minutes passed before some sort of détente descended, whereupon Red flopped back in bed, assuming his dogs' various lion-inflicted wounds could wait until daylight. He was right.

Anyway, I assembled a bug-out bag for the FJ as well. It contains a handsaw, foil bivouac bags, army MREs (weighing as much as skin-diving weights with the same density and flavor), solid-fuel tablets (a largish explosion might alert rescuers), a forest-green gallon canteen the color of the FJ, a buck knife that would scare O.J., and 42 other items. Seriously. I counted.

The bug-out bag is so dense that beams of light bend around it. Just for assurance, I tossed in some Percocet. I'm pretty sure all I'll ever need is the Percocet. Now, when we travel someplace risky, which is everywhere in southwest Montana, we carry the Tundra's bag and the FJ's, comprising enough survival gear for Sherpas ascending Annapurna.

Montanans assemble bug-out bags for three reasons: first, to prepare for nuclear winter or climate change's perpetual summer; second, to prepare for catastrophe-prone liberals who spawned Hillary Clinton ("She runs the largest crime syndicate the world has ever known," insists a former Darby town councilman); third, to prepare for rudimentary setbacks such as holed radiators while bumping along the Magruder Corridor (103 miles, no humans, no structures, no services, just trees).

Mine is perhaps the sole Montana bug-out bag containing no firearms. "I stuffed three Glock nines in mine," declared the aforementioned Hillary hater. I told him he should sell his guns and buy a membership to the gym, his massive jiggling paunch representing a greater impediment to survival than firepower. "Ha!" he said as he turned his back and huffed off. I later paid to have him smothered.

Of so-called preppers—right-wingers preparing to flee all government oversight and CNN—there are plenty here. But they aren't fleeing. They're already in the place where preppers most want to flee.

John Phillips

The bull bar on the nose of Julie's FJ is not her favorite accessory, but we are knee-deep in bulls here. Not just bull elk and moose and bighorn sheep but escaped bull bulls of the Texas variety, all snorting and pawing and power-defecating mere feet from our kitchen. The previous summer, the cattle had escaped from the Chief Joseph Ranch 440 feet below us, where Paramount's *Yellowstone* is being filmed. At large in the Bitterroot Forest, they look relieved, as if the specter of Burger King no longer loomed. One day I fed them a box of stale éclairs.

We'd complain about the at-large livestock and their Samsonite-size turds, but the rancher sometimes purchases permission from the Forest Service to graze his herd on public lands, and the beasts kindly mow some of the flammable undergrowth. The cattle seem to stop by my place first, enjoying a two-day hiatus of salt licking and Olympic power shitting, then they filter into the woods behind our home, never again to be seen. Why aren't they eaten by wolves, lions, and bears? All three carnivores are assuredly back there. My other question: Once the cattle have dissipated within 22 miles of uninhabited outbackery, how in the name of beef-free Hinduism do you locate them for a roundup? I've asked a dozen times. No one knows. If the cows sport little GPS transmitters welded to their cowbells, I've never noticed them. You know what naturalist John Muir called cows? "Hoofed locusts."

Julie and I drove 20 miles south, along the East Fork Road, to a miniature eatery in the woods called the Broad Axe Lodge, which valley residents of course call the "Broad Ass Lodge" in deference to roast-beef servings accounting for a quarter of the animal. On the way, we were surrounded by 20 bighorn sheep licking minerals off the road. One backed into Julie's FJ and shook the whole rig. (In Montana, it's a rig, not a truck.) A fat ram who was protecting his harem sized up the Toyota's nose, as if preparing to kick tires and make an offer. Julie rolled down her window and said, "Don't even *think* about it," which consumed enough time that he lost focus. Julie's mother, Agnes, was in the truck, too. The notion of being intimidated by wild ungulates with sharp curlicue horns, while en route to beef *au jus*, gave her a story for the ladies back home. Meanwhile, I could have peddled the bighorn photos to Toyota for a sales brochure.

Before the arrival of white men in this country, there were something like 1.5 million bighorns. After being extirpated by unregulated hunting and diseases contracted from domestic sheep, there are now 80,000 to 90,000. They are calm and curious creatures, not particularly alarmed by metal boxes hurtling along tarmac trails. To their peril, of course.

Back home, Julie somehow spun her FJ trucklet 180 degrees on ice covering our driveway's "Climbing Turn," 100 yards below our house. I nosed the Tundra to her rescue, fashioning a fantastic web of cables and straps and D-rings that could have maimed all of the Flying Wallendas. I fired up my new winch, which made three grinding revolutions, then the FJ popped out of the ditch like a champagne cork. A miracle. I felt as if I'd nudged another inch toward native Montana-ism. To reward myself, I drove to the feed store and bought a leather Carhartt vest insulated with a half inch of merino wool. No cowboy hat. I'd told Julie before moving west, "If I ever even look at a hat—or boots—I want you to shoot me in the face and bury me under the garage." Real cowboys in Montana are relatively rare. And my definition of a cowboy is generous: stepping in cow shit. Even once. I have. Five feet from my front door.

Our driveway is so steep that I often study the inclinometer on the FJ's dashboard. If you sink a wheel into a ditch during the climb, the FJ will be tricked into believing it is rolling. In response, fuel ceases to squirt, a safety feature that unfortunately means you cannot restart the engine until you tow the rig to level ground and shake it on its suspension a couple times, as if slapping a man who has just fainted. Then you depress a hidden switch—a screwdriver is needed to twirl the thing—and turn the ignition key simultaneously, articulation that would have defeated Gerald Ford. It's a maneuver I've never performed pre-Montana, I might add.

Speaking of drugstore cowboys, I've recently observed

a Montana bumper sticker bearing the legend, "If you take my guns, *this* is my weapon." The decal is invariably on pickup trucks. Does it mean that, during bank holdups, the driver will brandish his Chevy Silverado? Does it mean that, when liberals invade, the driver will flatten them with his deeply lugged IROC Super Swampers? Does it mean that, as he hunts white-tailed deer, he'll do so from within his heated F-150? Hold on. Hunters already do that.

If you'll allow me to trot out further arcane automobilia, I will: Goodyear's tires did not hack it during our first winter. Tire Rack advised I switch to a set of General Grabber Arctics with scores of tungsten studs as sharp as Ginsu blades. To make God laugh, tell him that your future depends on spiky pieces of rare metal.

You know what else? Montana is our galaxy's epicenter for broken windshields, to which I earlier alluded. Julie and I would eventually see two shatter pronto, then have to repair two more with Permatex crack-repair kits that require four hands and 90 minutes of tedious fussing, sticky fingers, and discolored hood paint. I'm not complaining. I chose to live here, but I've had to befriend Dave at Bitterroot Glass, who will, conditions permitting, appear at your house to replace a windshield in 90 minutes. Nothing to it, as long as you don't mind writing $650 checks. When I traded in Julie's previous SUV at the dealership in Missoula, the salesman noticed the fissured windshield and said, "At least I know you've lived in Montana for a week."

I so adore Julie's funky FJ Cruiser that I'd like to own one of the '60s-era originals. I've already espied a restoration-worthy candidate in a Bitterroot Valley junkyard, and I will bid on it as soon as I calculate how much rust costs per pound. I may soon be flat-towing an FJ behind an FJ. Symmetry lowers your blood pressure.

So do stale éclairs.

A GOAT CHARGED WITH MANSLAUGHTER

When I'm ferrying guests in the car and we're enjoying one of those 30-to-60-minute spells of encountering no other vehicles, I'll suddenly pound the steering wheel and shout, "*Goddamn*, what's with all these dipshit drivers?" It isn't funny, but it encourages me to share a secret about traffic in the "wide-open West."

I've yet to encounter a Darbrarian who has visited Glacier National Park or Yellowstone more than once. Know why? Traffic. When I lived in California, I had no choice but to suffer the 405 Freeway daily, a study in manic vehicular overflow and human perseverance in the face of fatuous futility. Well, it's nearly the same nowadays with Glacier's Going-to-the-Sun Road, where a ranger halts vehicles until he receives some sort of telemetric "all clear" from above, awaiting cars to exit before allowing yours to proceed with children dipping deeply into digital slavery in the back seat.

In Yellowstone, traffic jams manifest for marauding carnivores wandering anywhere remotely close to the road: bears, wolves, Gérard Depardieu, coyotes. (By the way, that last is pronounced "KYE-otes," two syllables in Montana, never three, even though you'd never pronounce Wile E.'s name that way.) Onlookers park not on the berm but in their lane of traffic, exit their cars, and wave cameras erratically at anything that moves, including their offspring urinating on the berm. How's that for celebrating nature? Billowing car exhaust and park rangers in Crown Vic cruisers with blue and red lights strobing, sirens wailing.

On my first visit to Yellowstone I thrummed my fingers in sweaty agitation throughout a colossal bear jam, cruel because the park is close enough that I would otherwise visit weekly. The bear in question was a taffy-honey grizzly—"Clearly a female," I was informed by a New Jersey tourist whose last animal sighting had been a Norwegian brown rat in his foyer. The bear was overturning fallen timber, examining bugs. Yet 70 feet distant stood a lone elk mowing grass. Here again were predator and prey within hailing distance, with no animus in one or fear in the other. Why?

Even as our parks overflow, former Secretary of the Interior Ryan Zinke—a Montana resident, sadly—pursued a *decrease* in wilderness acreage, claiming the land must revert to corporations so that people stalled in bear jams can enjoy 7-Eleven, Pizza Hut, and instant reverse mortgages amid a hydrocarbon *Hee Haw*. Zinke rides horseback while wearing an inapposite cowboy ensemble, possibly with assless chaps, hoping to conjure Teddy Roosevelt. I saved a PR photo of him at his D.C. desk across from a Native American. Mr. Secretary was wearing a suit, beaded moccasins, and stars-and-stripes socks—a starter kit for a rodeo clown.

Zinke was interviewed in Glacier Park during a photo op in which he was fly-fishing from a paved parking lot. A reporter noticed that Mr. Z.'s fishing line was tangling, and that's because the reel had been installed upside down, a Class One Felony in Montana.

I am proud that Montana offers 55 state-managed parks, compared with 40 in Wyoming and 44 in Colorado, and I'm confident my federal representative in this matter despises every single one.

Parks draw tourists, and tourists, in general, are not to

be left idle with cigarette lighters, Leatherman tools, or their own pointy-headed newborns. Ask any park ranger. I did, and that's how I acquired a four-year study of tourist deaths in our national parks, a nonpareil twinkie of a statistical gem.

Consider: Drowning is the most common way to expire in a national park—350 fatal dunkings in one year, in fact. The second-most-common killer? Traffic accidents. Yes, indeedy. Vehicular mayhem massacred 250 asphalt aces. Suicide was also a leading killer, and I imagine the deed was undertaken in reaction to stalled traffic. "Preexisting medical conditions" was next on the list, with spitting rage and furious pounding of the steering wheel no doubt inducing clots the size of prunes.

But here was the preeminent stat: The *least* likely way to perish in a national park—apart from not visiting in the first place—was via contact with wild animals. Surpassingly rare. As in, four deaths due to bears, one via snakebite, and one by mountain goat. That last casualty, by the by, involved a 63-year-old hiker who tried to shoo away an endearingly cute billy in Glacier Park because the animal had "stared him down." That's what it said in the police report.

What happened next is somewhat fuzzy, although medical assistance did not materialize for 50 minutes, at which point the hiker had no pulse and showed "blood on his leg," which isn't a rare occurrence when I hike or even in my own house. If the goat had been charged with manslaughter and hauled to court, I'm not sure a jury of his peers—other goats, a few bighorn sheep, plus a lone Bukharan markhor—would have convicted him. (Defense counsel: "Your honor, might you kindly inform jurors that Mister Markhor does not speak English?")

But, of course, in this real-life drama, the mountain goat was convicted before his victim had even expired and was thus "put down" by park rangers. It's always the animal's fault and always a euphemism: "put down," "taken," "euthanized," "collected for necropsy," "harvested." That last is especially pernicious. Who would consider saying that jihadists, on 9/11, "harvested" New Yorkers? Hunters here boast, "I took two pronghorn yesterday." Sounds like theft. So easy to subvert language to soften our unmanageably lethal urges.

Now, one final statistic: Biologists estimate that there were 50,000 to 90,000 grizzlies in the contiguous U.S. before Europeans arrived bearing gunpowder. In 100 years, we assassinated—with minor help from Native Americans—all but 1,000. I mean, holy turds on a toasted taco, you'd have to inflict something like laser-guided Ford Pintos to slaughter as many as 89,000 mammals as large as Civil War statues. Certainly, Lewis and Clark had ceased provoking grizzlies by the time they reached my valley, having been chased by the beasts across rivers and right into their own campsites. Their solution was to stop fucking with the bears. And you know what? It worked.

That there are too many of us is obvious. Well, I guess it isn't, because no one talks anymore about the population explosion, yet explode it does. Upon my birth, there were 2.5 billion of us jumping up and down on sidewalks. Now we are approaching eight billion, and if we all jumped at once we'd knock the planet off its axis and into a Venusian alley. In my lifetime, the population has more than tripled. Although I wish the parks weren't so clogged with humankind, I dare to wonder if that same glut of gawkers, having witnessed native glory in all its miraculous majesty, might thereafter vote to sustain it. Here I lay bare my naïveté for your enjoyment.

Up to this point in Montana, I'd been trying to focus on nothing more complicated than the wondrousness of the forest and on creatures not of my species. And yet my mind, chattering gibbon that it is, stubbornly returned to the specific and tangible, the most common complaint of rookie Buddhist meditators. (That and falling asleep.) The thing is, in another 28 years, a bonus two billion humans will have joined us, and our daily lives will resemble a Manhattan elevator filled chest-to-armpit with voluble, vaguely violent commuters with hemorrhoids, hoping to commandeer another million dollars that day by rearranging financial digits for investors right then identically crammed into overloaded elevators. We, us, have become a bloom of red algae that depletes the ocean of oxygen.

Like most poisonous blooms, it happened fast—in our case not in thousands of years but dozens.

In any event, fewer than one person per decade dies of a bear attack in the Northern Continental Divide Ecosystem—even though our species can afford to give up many more—which is fairly astonishing because the NCDE includes Glacier National Park, where tourists backpack with honey-glazed donuts and pickled Vienna sausages.

I hasten to add, by the way, that Glacier Park once contained 150 glaciers but now displays fewer than 25, most the size of Ping-Pong tables, so hurry if you care to look. (Possible new park name: Rolling Meadows Estates.)

According to Montana Fish, Wildlife & Parks, the last grizzly-inflicted fatality in the NCDE was in 2015, when a mountain biker tore around a blind corner and collided head-on with a bear whose noggin was the size of an Igloo cooler. The bear was sufficiently irked that he did something to prevent it from happening again. A task force was assembled to kill the bear for having occupied a game trail that he and his forebears, ha-ha, had used for millennia. That's like a Texas Ranger shooting you for walking through your kitchen.

It's now nigh on established that we have embarked on the sixth mass extinction in Earth's history. When we found out about it, we swallowed two Ambien and continued microwaving our Hot Pockets. This time, it's not the threat posed by Comet Kohoutek. This time *we're* the comet. And I'll bet four car payments we won't do anything about it. To halt CO_2 emissions as they stand right now, global emissions would have to be reduced by almost 75 percent. No nation on Earth has made such plans, least of all us.

Charles Bowden wrote: "Our civilization destroys the foundations that support it by devouring the earth…But we don't have the courage to back away, to stop, to restrain ourselves. I know I don't."

John Phillips

Over Niagara Falls in a Frigidaire

Yesterday, Ed the raven flapped past on his scheduled four p.m. recon, one whoosh per flap, which I find soothing, even though he acts a little like a guard in a prison tower. As Ed peered into our living room, he delivered his best eagle impersonation. Eagles are imposing killers, regal and ostentatious psychopaths, but they make a sissy chirp, a derisible presentation. Ed mocks them.

I'm right now too old to be cute, too young to be hearse freight. On most days, I don't awaken until 10:00 a.m., an overreaction to having arisen for 50 years of dawn commutes, slopping tepid coffee on my thighs while cursing at fellow drivers slopping tepid coffee on their thighs. As I age, experts say I'll need less sleep. But right now, I'm content with 12 hours nightly. In the book *Stranger in the Woods,* author Michael Finkel interviewed a certified recluse who had subsisted alone in the forest for 27 years. Finkel asked if, during the man's resounding solitude, he had unearthed any of life's big lessons. "Get enough sleep," he replied.

For breakfast, I drink a smoothie, then clomp down to the walkout basement to write. I do not Tweet or install my face on Facebook because I don't know what they are. I have never owned a BlackBerry or a "personal digital assistant" or laptop or tablet. I own no phone other than a flip-up edition that won't play back messages and apparently must be strapped to a cell tower to obtain signals. Texting? Isn't that what I'm doing now? In Montana, I've managed 65 days without touching a phone. If I'm needed for an emergency—hasn't yet happened in my lifetime—it will be routed to Julie's phone, which operates at up to three locations in Darby, and she can relay the tragic details after we've enjoyed drinks and dinner and another drink.

Montana is 550 miles wide, yet the entirety of Big Sky comprises the same area code—406—so you can make a 400-mile phone call that is local, which won't mean anything to today's Zuckerbergian tele-addicts but would have caused my parents to faint in astonished appreciation. Back in the day, we made long-distance calls sparingly. At college in England, I called home exactly once to beg money and might have called twice except I knew my mother would solicit my profs' home phone numbers.

In my home in the Bitterroot National Forest, I eat lunch for breakfast, then drive to Darby's tiny gym three times weekly. On non-gym days, I set out for McIntosh Lane and walk 30 minutes, feeding fallen apples to roadside horses and llamas. Sometimes a cute border collie joins me at the halfway mark. She pees whenever I praise her. I had a girlfriend who did that.

By then it's four p.m., or close enough to activate my inner Morse code summoning happy hour. On the Missoula NPR station my preferred show is *The Pea Green Boat*, hosted by Annie Garde. It is a children's program that infuses me with chocolate-coated kindliness as Annie spins songs about bears eating peanut butter in the woods. It's practically the show's anthem. I know all the words. Then it's off to bed for more reading and another period of hibernation that would satisfy a bear eating peanut butter in the woods. I frequently forget what day it is and feel no shame asking.

When I first started at our local gym, I pondered the Darby dress code, a protocol that does not exist. It was of interest, because when I was young my mother insisted that if

I didn't wear clean formal clothes, onlookers would label me a "jit." Not a "git," which is a British pejorative, but a "jit" which rhymes with snit.

I had a troubled in-law who had been near fatally struck by a train and was once evicted from a motel by a SWAT team. He was a jit. So I wore pressed slacks, a starched long-sleeved shirt, and a tie for 45 years of office work. The skin around my neck yet bears third-degree chafing. When I moved to Montana, I discarded my ties but continued wearing dress shirts and slacks with creases as straight as handrails.

At the gym, Heidi set me straight: "First, buy sweat pants, any color. Second, sweat socks, any color. Third, a T-shirt you received for free and has someone's logo on the chest. Fourth, any baseball cap, preferably camo. *Voilà*! Darby is your oyster." Or my tainted whelk. I dress now like I've given up on life.

Last Tuesday, I'd been wrestling with tire chains, removing them near our mailbox where a salad of snow, salt, sand, and mud had tossed itself into an espresso of festering filth. I rolled around in that for a spell, then drove to Darby Distribution, our hardware store, wearing the same sodden sweat shirt and sweat pants I'd purchased at the grocery for $6.99, as well as Barbour high-top rubber boots that looked as though a dysentery-plagued cow had targeted them for relief. Not one single person stared or asked how I'd attained such vile grubbiness, even as globulations of mud and wet sand were being deposited like signposts in my wake.

On the way home, sans chains, the Tundra performed an involuntary pirouette on Rushing's Hill—a two-track roller coaster of ice—then slid ass-first into the inside "gutter," as we call it, where shame awaits. Still skidding in 4WD low-range, my truck bounced and wove until it punched into an eight-inch diameter pine that absolutely put an end to motion, as if in freeze-frame.

I climbed out to inspect: a smashed taillight, a concave fender, a missing wheel-arch flare, and an assortment of gouges and slashes you'd expect on a goalie's mask. I had not been wearing my seatbelt. I didn't exactly fly out of the driver's seat, but a bottle of cherry Gatorade levitated out of its nook and spun in a 270-degree arc, dousing me, the dashboard, the passenger-side window, and both seats with splatter that, when dry, hardened unto pink library paste.

What came next (as if right then I sought further excitement) was a dirty blue Toyota 4Runner on studded tires, driven by neighbor Robin LoMonaco. She had swerved to avoid both me and a troupe of wild turkeys crossing the iciest portion above. As if bowling for dollars, Robin likewise slopped into the gutter until her truck high-centered upon a boulder that wedged under the oil pan. Result: two Toyotas 20 feet apart, front wheels off the ground, rear wheels in deep snow, traction co-efficient of about 00.1—a measurement I just made up.

A half dozen well-meaning neighbors materialized like hyenas out of the gloaming, all with complicated extraction theories, although each first attempted to excavate the boulder from beneath Robin's 4Runner. That created a mud pit. Then Gene Honey and his tow truck magically arrived, as would a magical invoice for $220, although that came two hours later. Gene's truck could lift the 4Runner's nose only four inches—don't ask why, but his rig appears to be of Laurel and Hardy vintage and hilarity, a tub of rust with a sideshow of leaky hydraulics.

So I hoicked up the left side of Robin's truck with my own hydraulic floor jack, and Gene raised the right with his, suspending her vehicle at three shaky attachment points, swaying a little in the breeze. What we did next was crawl underneath, which on anyone's scale of stupid was up there with running Niagara Falls in a Frigidaire.

Nevertheless, Gene and I managed to drag out the boulder, inch by inch. It surely weighed 150 pounds, and its forcible removal was being performed by two 65-year-old overweight men with mild dementia. On the other hand, Gene brought his insanely happy dog, Socks, who thought we were trying to root out a malicious marmot and had his own strategies in mind.

Sans boulder, vehicle extraction was a piece of cake, if

the cake had been frosted in mud, ice, and tiny slices of granite. The mud covered my bloody fingertips, so I couldn't even wheedle sympathy.

Just as we all left in search of alcohol, I asked Socks his opinion of the federal trade deficit.

NOT YOUR AVERAGE KMART TIPI

I tend to perseverate on winter's deadly assaults, "perseverate" being a word that I appropriated from Michele Rivette, a psychologist I dated in the 1990s, and, yes, her interest in me seemed professional. She invited me to meet her on New Year's Eve at one of Ann Arbor's ERs—in a hospital the size of the Pentagon—where she was on suicide detail. The surrounding trauma docs had converted a medical gurney into a mobile bar: a dozen liquors, mixes, proper glasses, maybe eight wines. They were imbibing this cornucopia between various car-crash gore-a-thons and a psych patient who locked himself in the ER's toilet for two hours.

"You wanna come out now, Mr. Carver?" Michele intoned every 15 minutes after handing me an excellent gin and tonic. He did not. My point here being: On New Year's Eve, eschew all bodily risk.

Which I did not.

I was contemplating that night with kind Michele when friend Corinne Anderson and Dread Pirate Dave invited us to their New Year's bash to celebrate the arrival of flu season. I had to be told what day it was.

Dave's house is on the far side of what Darbrarians call the "Rye Creek hills," which, at 7300 feet or so, are hills in the sense that the *U.S.S. Iowa* is a yacht. Technically, Dave and Corinne live in the Sapphire Mountains, a landscape of juniper and sagebrush amid the stumpy remnants of devastating recent fires.

Alongside Dave's house is a tipi. It isn't your average Kmart tipi, either. It's the real thing, I believe, having never seen the real thing: 16 feet at the base, weathered canvas wrap, held erect by lodgepole pines, and no pictographs of wolves or Kevin Costner. With the ambient temp at minus eight degrees that night, five of us crawled inside with five dogs, then lit a fire in the central pit. Each occupant had a warm canine sprawled across his feet. I wanted to sit there until June.

It was so cozy that we shot right past midnight and almost to one a.m. before anyone realized we'd missed the annual—and always clinically depressing—toast to the new year, a holiday devised to pick at the scabs of the previous year's personal failures. So we all coughed up phlegm and recited New Year's resolutions. Mine was never to use the word "very" again, which Corrinne said was very wise.

I won't try to justify this, but I drank two bottles of wine, two glasses of champagne, two beers, and two overflowing shots of Jack Daniel's. Drinking for two, apparently. I was able to make that computation only on the following day, which, I assure you, was a botanical garden of wretchedness. I remained bed-bound until two p.m., followed closely by a three-hour nap, at which point my day, productivity-wise, was torpedoed. There wasn't any throwing up, but there was a lot of throwing down, such as "I will *never* crawl into a fucking tipi again," which seems a resolution I might easily uphold.

Julie was no arbiter of sobriety, either. As we departed Dave's alcoholic bacchanalia, I noticed she was on the ground wrestling our friend Carin Kiphart. *Wrestling,* I say. When I opened the truck's door for her, she became a live Slinky, with some sort of instinctive go-to-ground circuitry that gin had activated. So Dave and I took turns correcting her sliding and slumping, attempting to fold her into the seat when her true target was the floor.

We departed the tipi-o-rama at 2:30 a.m., both making about as much sense as Rick Perry when he lost his glasses. There was some drunk driving involved on gravel mountain roads. It's shameful, I know. But we imperiled only ourselves—and one huge cow elk who had to be honked out of the way—because during that 45-minute return trip, we saw not a single automobile. The sole light we observed, in fact, was shining in Darby proper, and it was attached, I believe, to one of Marshal Larry's video cameras. So I waved while tightening the muscles in my face to look less piss-abled in case I later campaign for town council and damning photos are unearthed.

Reaching our garage, I said, "You okay to walk?" Julie assured she was independently mobile, so I idled the truck the last 30 feet to safety. Unbeknownst to me, she had placed one mitten on the right side of the vehicle to steady herself and kept it in place as the truck inched forward. Her hand thus described a perfect mud-free trail o' tears starting at the passenger door and ending at the taillight, which is where—finally free of vehicular support—my wife investigated a snowdrift with her face. She did not recall these acrobatics the next morn and was baffled that one of her mittens was a sopping mud pie.

If there exists a universal creator, I'll bet burritos to bubblegum that He looks down upon these sorry soirées and wonders why the creatures on whom He spent the most creational effort seem daily to anesthetize themselves against life on a planet that might be more gratifying than any other. "What the fuck," He must sometimes mutter, turning, perhaps, to the ghost of Will Rogers to apologize for the language, with Mr. R replying, "I was thinking the same, Chief."

Sorry. That might be the Jack talking.

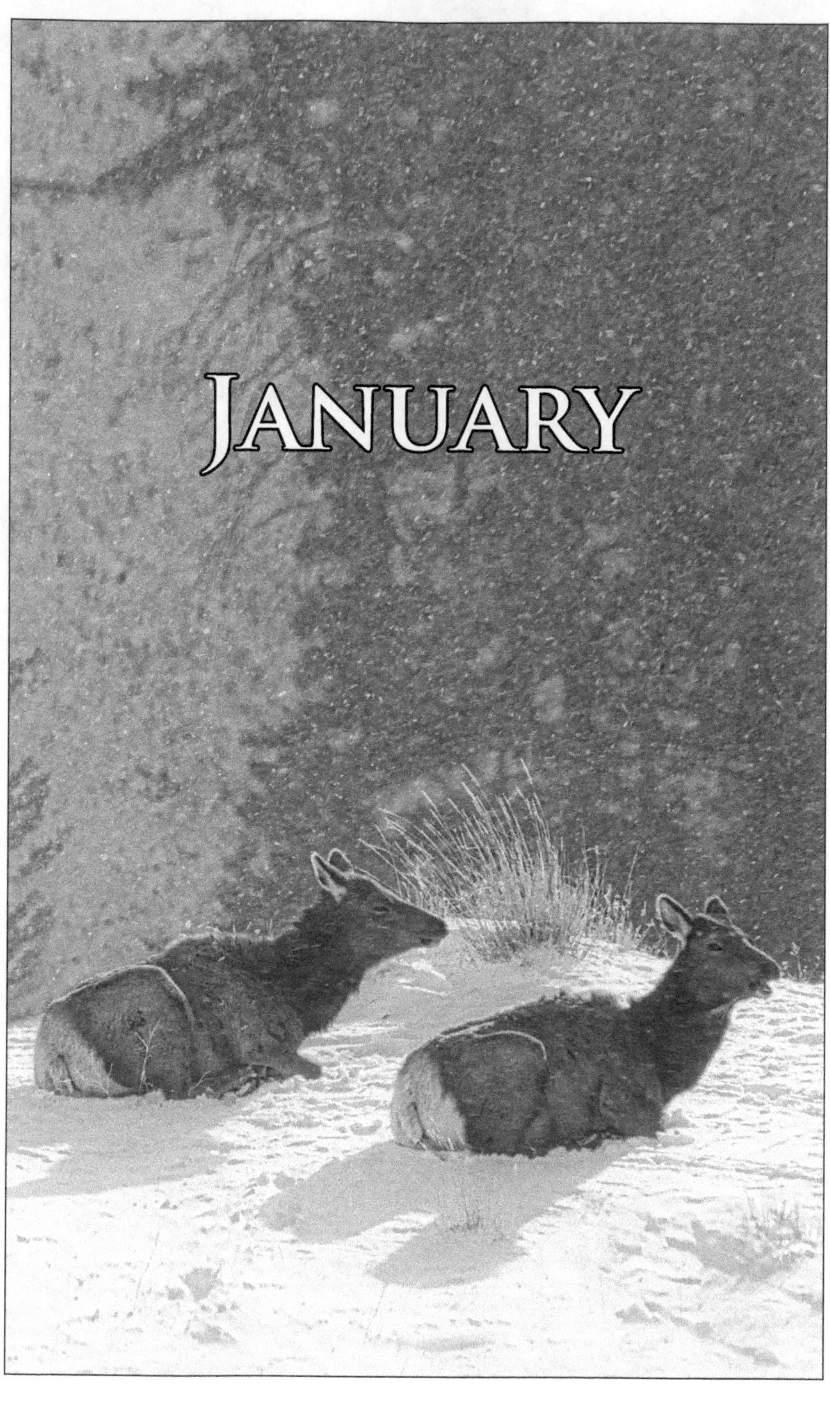

JANUARY

I THOUGHT THEY WERE ALL DEAD

When I moved to Montana, I bid *adios* to exotic cars. Or so I thought. Somehow, the car enthusiasts in the Bitterroot Valley located me, and that's how I wound up attending "Thursday Nights in Lolo," a weekly get-together in Gary Meuchel's car-renovation shop, Cherry Lane Motors. It rests tentatively upon the side of a mountain, between the villages of Florence and Lolo, north of me about 65 miles—a stone's throw from Lewis and Clark's Travelers' Rest, where the Corps peed liquid mercury before their Big Climb.

At Gary's place, I envisioned balding fat men encircling a sticky VFW table, discussing tedious rules of order and the names of members with unpaid dues. But no. At my first meeting, I found Gary sipping a bottle of Dr. McGillicuddy's, his preferred tipple. The road to his shop ascends a gravel drive interrupted by a hundred yards of pavement where club members perform burnouts. "It's how people knock on my door," Gary explained. Nowadays, 15 to 20 guys and three women filter through Gary's shop every Thursday. They've been doing it for 22 years.

At one time, Gary owned 200 cars in various stages of decrepitude. "Then the locals jumped on my ass," he says, "so I pared it down to sixty." Gary is 57 and looks like Kenny Rogers after Kenny's chicken empire collapsed.

One of his early resurrections was a Ford cop car, previously used by the police in his home town of Hamilton, 25 miles north of Darby. Gary drove the faux cruiser on Halloween, and that's how he landed in jail at age 17. He had long hair at the time and used his coif as evidence that he could not possibly have been impersonating anything cop-like. His friends surrounded the lockup and shouted, "Free hairy Gary, free hairy Gary!"

In Gary's shop, engines and body parts adorn the walls and ceilings as if flung there by a geothermal event. Surfaces of desirable cars serve as shelves for shop manuals, porcelain signs, ashtrays, and drag-racing slicks. Gary further owns 12 vintage bank vaults and an art deco scooter. Using angle iron, he fashioned a contraption that holds an engine separately from the car in which it belongs. By way of demonstration, he started a Ford Mustang 289 V-8 in this "engine dyno" and the blast from the left bank of exhaust headers blew down a nudie-girl calendar from 1996.

As soon as Gary concludes the renovation of a 1970 Dodge Charger that belongs to a Montana wheat farmer, he's building a 200-mph Lincoln Mark VIII for the Bonneville Salt Flats. Also a '28 Model A "as a mobile platform to shoot gophers." That particular car's passenger seat, as I examined it, was home to the largest wasp nest this side of the Amazon basin. It should be noted that Gary is Gary's only employee.

There are no membership fees apart from beer, an unspoken obligation. The weekly gathering might consume one hour or six. Sometimes, target shooting becomes the night's focus, although in the blackness behind his garage it is difficult to discern anything like a target. "We blast away at shapes," Gary explained.

Of course, it occasionally attracts the law. "Some kinda war goin' on up here?" the first cop asked.

"Want a beer?" Gary offered.

"I'd love a beer," he replied.

Gary told me he'll never retire, and I can't imagine why he would, neck deep as he is in a blissful mosh pit of gray-at-the-temples car enthusiasts and a dozen cases of beer fast approaching skunkitude.

I thought those guys were all dead. Which is ridiculous, because I'm not.

Lassoing a Naked Haunch of Beef

I purchased a pitchfork to break up sand and salt in our 55-gallon steel barrels. One of the tines snapped off, and I was contemplating a fix.

"Take it to the blacksmith," instructed Hope the barber.

Sure enough, Darby possesses a blacksmith housed in three conjoined buildings sharing a whimsical but credible façade right out of Artemus Gordon's *Wild, Wild West*. The reclaimed wood has been fashioned to resemble a hotel, livery, and mercantile store. The three doors fronting the faux livery are 15-feet tall, hung on iron hinges that are 20-inches long and were fashioned by the smithy within. He calls this operation "Ulcerville."

As blacksmithing shops go, his seems large, possibly 3000 square feet, although I've never set foot in a blacksmith's lair and don't know anyone who has. Dave Harper, 57, has toiled alone here for 23 years. He has lived in Darby since he was nine, having left his Ohio home to cross America with his single mom.

"Don't have a clue why she picked Darby," he told me.

In front of Ulcerville rests Dave's red-and-white 1956 Willys 4WD pickup truck. Its hood was warped in a forest fire, so he repainted the vehicle outside in an unhappy experiment.

"I'd watered the driveway to tamp down dust," he recalls. "But as soon as I began painting, my neighbor lit a bonfire. Wind blew the ashes my way." He owned a second '56 Willys—a green one—but a customer driving a Ferrari bought it for his wife. I don't imagine a lot of blacksmiths do business with Ferrari owners.

Dave's teen years were lively. He fled his mother's household at age 14, hoping to survive with an alcoholic father-figure. When that sadly fetched upon the rocks, he secured an apartment over Darby's liquor store, an alley's width from the Sawmill Saloon.

"Big action below my window almost every night," he remembers. "A guy was stabbed down there—some sort of dispute over a baseball game. I also watched two guys haul a table and chairs from the saloon into the middle of the street. They sat down with their beers, then halted motorists. Charged 'em a fee to enter town."

Inside his shop, which is on Longstory Lane (with the long story never divulged) Dave covets all manner of inexplicable devices harking to the 1800s. Need a wagon wheel replaced? Dave's your man. He owns a cast-iron tool that measures wooden spokes, then shapes them to length. When wagon wheels become "sloppy," Dave subjects them to "wheel shrinkers" that grasp the metal band surrounding the spokes. He heats that band—it's technically called a "fellows"—until it's malleable, hoping not to set spokes on fire. Once the band cools, it shrinks so tightly that no other mechanisms—nails, clamps, duct tape—are needed to affix it for another thousand miles of the Chisholm Trail.

And how would you know when you had traveled a thousand miles?

"You'd use this 1870 Roadometer," Dave explained while grasping a bronze device constructed in Philadelphia and tucked within a baseball-size leather pouch. "You strap it on the wagon wheel, and every time the wheel turns upside down, the Roadometer records it. Multiply that by the wheel's circumference, and you've got distance traveled. It was far more accurate than the traditional method, which was to attach a handkerchief to a spoke and ask your kid to count the revolutions. What kid would stay focused for eight hours?"

Dave owns a covey of ancient anvils, one almost four feet long resembling an iron weasel. Then there's his 5000-pound power hammer, although he doesn't lend it much credence. "That there's a recent machine," he complains. "Made in 1950."

Dave's abiding devotion to metal began with a 1932 Chevrolet. "It's how I learned to weld," he recalls, "in Darby High's industrial arts. Our class had three students."

From there he taught himself to shape metal in any of the three 2000-degree forges he built himself. "Propane-heated," he confesses with a frown, "because coal of the proper purity costs $75 per bag, and I was burning a bag a day." When one of the forges is huffing, the temp in the shop can exceed 100 degrees, so Dave's extended forgery manifests mostly in frosty months.

Today, blacksmithing is barely a business. The money isn't in horseshoes. It's in architectural iron, such as decorative pine trees made from chain-saw loops. Also life-size steel grizzly sculptures—one currently selling for $25,000—and trivets formed from iron casts of bear, wolf, and mountain-lion paw prints. Real prints.

"It's better than working in taxidermy," he says, which was his previous profession for 18 years, when he toiled under the tutelage of Darby's own Marshal Larry—not only Dave's boss but later his father-in-law.

There are perils aplenty in having a controversial town marshal as a relative, but they don't exceed the perils of blacksmithing. Dave's arms are a patchwork of pink welts, white scars, and purple pockmarks inflicted by errant gobbets of molten metal. His crotch and the inside of his thighs are similarly scarred from smelted scraps falling off the workbench. I didn't look. Took his word for it.

"One thing about working for Larry," recollects Dave, "is the guy was a freakin' mad scientist. He'd get all worked up, then rush off to buy bolts at the hardware store, but in his wake he'd scatter all manner of nuts and bolts he'd forgotten were already in his truck. And when he'd climb on a snowmobile, holy God in heaven, watch out. Larry once launched himself over a hummock at 50 mph and broke his nose on the windshield. Blood spurting everywhere. I took a photo. I told him, 'Selling these for dartboard targets.'"

Darby today isn't the Darby that Dave knew as a boy.

"The sawmills used to employ just about everybody," he remembers. "One mill alone stretched from the railroad tracks north of town all the way to the high school. Sitting in class, I remember the whistle blowing for shift changes. But I never wanted to work there because I never met a rich logger. Just injured loggers, like two guys I knew named Wally and Porkrind. One had broken his neck, so he stared at the floor all day. A tree fell on the other, so his thinking wasn't exactly right. When Darby's fire siren would howl, he'd run outside and wave a stick to direct traffic, except there wasn't any traffic. Then when he saw girls on Main Street, he'd moon them, which was hilarious until he passed out, which was a minute later.

"I also remember a guy who owned a '67 Corvette who did burnouts in front of the saloon. He spun the car over a 16-inch concrete post. Tore the whole bottom off. Remember streakers in the '70s? The cowboys would carry their lariats into the saloons, and when a streaker dashed past, they'd lasso the guy and rope him up like a naked haunch of beef."

Dave's smithery abuts his house, so the commute comprises a 30-second walk in the woods.

"Feels like I'm in art class every day," he remarked. "When the time comes, I'll be happy to lay my hammer on the anvil and just fizz out."

Human Ashes Mixed With Oatmeal

Once folks appreciated that Julie and I owned an acceptable little ranchette and had on occasion come to grips with Montana's chiseled ruggedosity—no wolves in the foyer, yet—they began arriving in droves. Well, half a drove.

I don't care for people, as I've mentioned too often, but I can't say no to relatives, to various in-laws of immaculate character, and to Julie's lifelong lady pals and their husbands. You know why Einstein's Theory of Relativity is so hard to live with? Because it's about relatives.

I try to limit guests to three days, that being the max before the fish achieves the city limits of Funkyville, but we live so far from civilization that most guests decide the trip was too arduous to warrant 72 hours only, so they stay a week.

That doesn't work for me. For starters, I awake at about 10 a.m., having no real job except moose observation, but my guests often ramp up their social agendas at dawn. I tell them the night before, "Tomorrow, just proceed without me," but they're leery of solo treks after noticing the canisters of bear spray and the photo of the mountain lion eating Ronda on our doorstep. So what happens when I awake is that I comb my eyebrows, then step outside the bedroom—in my boxers, hair askew, and one eye gooped shut by 12 hours of coma-quality sleep—and there stand before me fully dressed houseguests, impatient and somewhat judgmental about an amount of snoozing they associate with critical brain bleeds.

Julie and I drive guests 30 miles along the West Fork Road to the source of the Bitterroot River, where it is five feet wide. Then we tour the Scripps compound. The braver guests we'll haul over the mountain to Shoup, Idaho, but only in the truck carrying the bug-out bags.

Next, we drive them down the East Fork Road, stopping for a meal at the Broad Ass Lodge, open only when the cook feels like it, where every table offers binoculars to view the antics of bighorn sheep. Then we hit the bright lights of Hamilton, population one resident short of 4000, where the gaudiest attraction is an ancient Kmart featuring the men's Gusset Collection with reinforced crotch and industrial seams.

Finally, we'll drive home on the gravel east-side road flanking the Bitterroot River so we can cross the rickety one-lane bridge and shout at fly-fishermen. "All is lost," is my usual advice.

One reason guests keep reappearing, says Julie, is that we possess one bear-proof room—apart from the basement fire room—and it happens to be our guest room. It offers one window about 20 feet above ground and a solid-cherry door as hard as concrete and four inches thick, as if that might stop a bear with saber-saw paws.

Also, we have wolverines in our front yard—there are two to three hundred in Montana, boasts the Forest Service—who eat not only bones of dead creatures but also their teeth. Wolverines spray a foul musky concoction as a territorial marker, sometimes letting loose in hunting cabins, rendering them uninhabitable for a couple years. Which is why Montanans call them "skunk bears." Didn't know that, did you? Julie just signed up for a Defenders of Wildlife skunk-bear study two miles from here. I may buy her a Tyvek suit.

Guests also visit because we treat them to beef and bison from Hamilton Packing, which is a butcher. I know because entire cows hang from hooks near the display cases. Cows saunter up a ramp to the rear door and exit the front door in white paper packages under my arm.

Only once did I spy bison T-bones, eleven dollars per. I bought four. The butcher's apron is not just dappled in blood but dripping with 3-D gore, a chainsaw massacre, Leonardo DiCaprio post-maul. The man is a werewolf with blades. I always count his fingers.

Guests have sometimes departed unhappy. It is as quiet as an anechoic chamber here, with few signs of human occupancy. We have no landline, just cell service operating in synch with sun-spot emanations and that's not even our sun. If you've just arrived from, say, New York City, I guess that's unnerving.

What's more, our electricity is as reliable as Gary Busey on a long weekend in Tijuana. We once had midwinter guests when the current ceased, and I had to ignite three mobile propane heaters to stave off digital frostbite. In the end, we all dozed beside the fireplace, and I worried we'd perish from carbon-monoxide poisoning, although it would have ensured pink-faced corpses.

We've had guests who were boggled by the unalloyed inconvenience of the place: the miniature airport with limited flights, the two-hour drive therefrom, the dearth of Broadway plays, the threat of Marshal Larry's handcuffing skateboarders.

I attached a camper's lantern as well as twin strap-on headlamps to our bedpost. I was similarly equipping the guests' bedposts when Julie said it looked too much like coal-mining equipment. We once had a four-foot-long snake sunning on the porch. Lodgers didn't care for that either.

We bought a guestbook. After a winter outing here, my sister wrote: "Let's see. All-day rain, followed by a seven-hour blizzard, not one but *two* lengthy power outages, and no wildlife. I'm never coming back." Then this from Ridlon and Carin Kiphart: "How come everything smells like smoke?"

We had one guest who, before arriving, purchased stick-on gold stars—the kind awarded to grade schoolers for not disemboweling Mrs. Fletcher—and she affixed five of them atop a logo she drew for the Double-J Cat Ranch. It features animal ears and whiskers, in contrast with the "Y" brand that Kevin Costner sears upon *Yellowstone* cowboys' chests just below us.

My mother-in-law Agnes brought the ashes of her husband—in what resembled an oatmeal carton—and asked us to spread the cremains in the Bitterroot River, possibly a felony. Unfortunately, the river right then had risen to Johnstown ferocity. So, Julie, her sister, and I lined up in a kind of Three Stooges set piece, each of us holding the belt of the person in front—we nominated Julie for the dangerous waterline work—and in this perilous posture we spread ashes as best we could, although I noticed they basically pooled in a milky-colored eddy six inches from shore. The idea was for Julie's dad to float to the Columbia River, thence to the Pacific, but I think he's stranded on a rock near Conner, Montana. I'd like to apologize to the trout for that.

Other guests have become huffy that their smart phones achieved no bars here, and whenever I can't achieve bars, I am offended, too. The cell service and internet connections are leanest on hot days. No one knows why. A magazine editor once emailed: "Could you swap graf 2 with graf 4 and configure a conclusion that makes a point?" But then our internet vanished, so I had to snail-mail a reply in which the entire text was, "Okay."

Our internet serviceman, Ernie, has visited so many times he knows the names of our cats. In turn, we know the name of his neighbor who, like us, was frustrated by day-on/day-off internet connectivity, so he erected his own microwave tower by lashing cables to the top of a 92-foot-tall pine tree. It worked so well that he sold "bleed-off" service to neighbors. Stuff like that never happened back in Michigan, where our proudest invention was car-jackings.

We've also had guests who weren't all that much into nature, which always makes me wonder why they came in the first place. Did you not consult a map, Sir Thunderturd? Then there were guests whose cars couldn't climb our driveway. One brought a camping trailer that had to be dropped in the valley.

The other, car-journalist Michael Jordan, showed up in

a baby-blue Porsche 911. That didn't work to benefit of man or machine, either, but Michael is not a complainer. After he partook the rough-hewn grandiosity visible from our guestroom, he stayed a second night. It allowed us to drag him to one of our neighborhood mammal roasts, where he likewise wondered if a standard convection oven would not have been the superior option.

Among my retired neighbors who interested him: a physicist who helped develop nuclear weapons carried by fighter jets; a songwriter/lyricist for several country-music celebs in Nashville; a Tacoma detective specializing in gang warfare; a former Toyota exec whose retirement gift was not a gold watch but an $80,000 Land Cruiser; and a retired M.D. plus her husband who own a Cessna 170 tail-dragger but not a TV.

We also have a former GE turbine engineer who rebuilds antique engines in his cottage, 300 yards from my house. His name is Wally Karr, and he famously visited the Fukushima nuclear plant to explain the importance of lifting backup generators "the hell out of those pits," which he predicted might fill with sea water. Famous last words from Wally.

If you need an intake valve for a 1949 Explodamobile, Wally is your man, not because he has any in stock but because he will *make* one. He adores flathead Fords, whose engines rely on babbitt material instead of premade bearings. Wally fashions babbitts in an H.O.-scale foundry from which he pours molten metal in scary gulps—a first for me, the know-it-all car guy.

MIT contacted Wally to construct a simple one-off engine that would allow students to study fuel-consumption rates. All of this out of a cabin in the Bitterroot woods, just two German shepherds and ol' Wally alongside a potbelly stove, listening to Schumann while singeing his eyebrows and uttering Teutonic obscenities whenever he scalds an extremity.

Guests sometimes surprise me. We were hosting Julie's mother, who is hard of hearing in the sense that hearing aids act as beans in her ears, as well as Aunt Irene, who can't climb steps and proved it by nose-diving in our new Dollar Store. Anyway, the ladies arise before bats have headed for bed. Three or four hours later, when I had achieved sentience, Agnes said, "We saw a moose. Two, in fact."

"I don't think so," I said. "Walter and friends are rare. You saw two bull elk with coat racks. They come in pairs because they're excommunicated when their mothers begin to calve. Kicked out. That's why they look so sad. Betrayed by Mother."

"Pretty sure it was a moose," insisted Agnes.

I fixed breakfast and while later busing egg-smeared plates I glanced out the dining room window to see, of course, two bull moose at our salt lick. For a moment, I thought of sticking with my original argument, which was petty of me. So, I summoned Agnes and Irene to the window and said, "Now, *those* are moose, unlike what you saw earlier." As I say, petty.

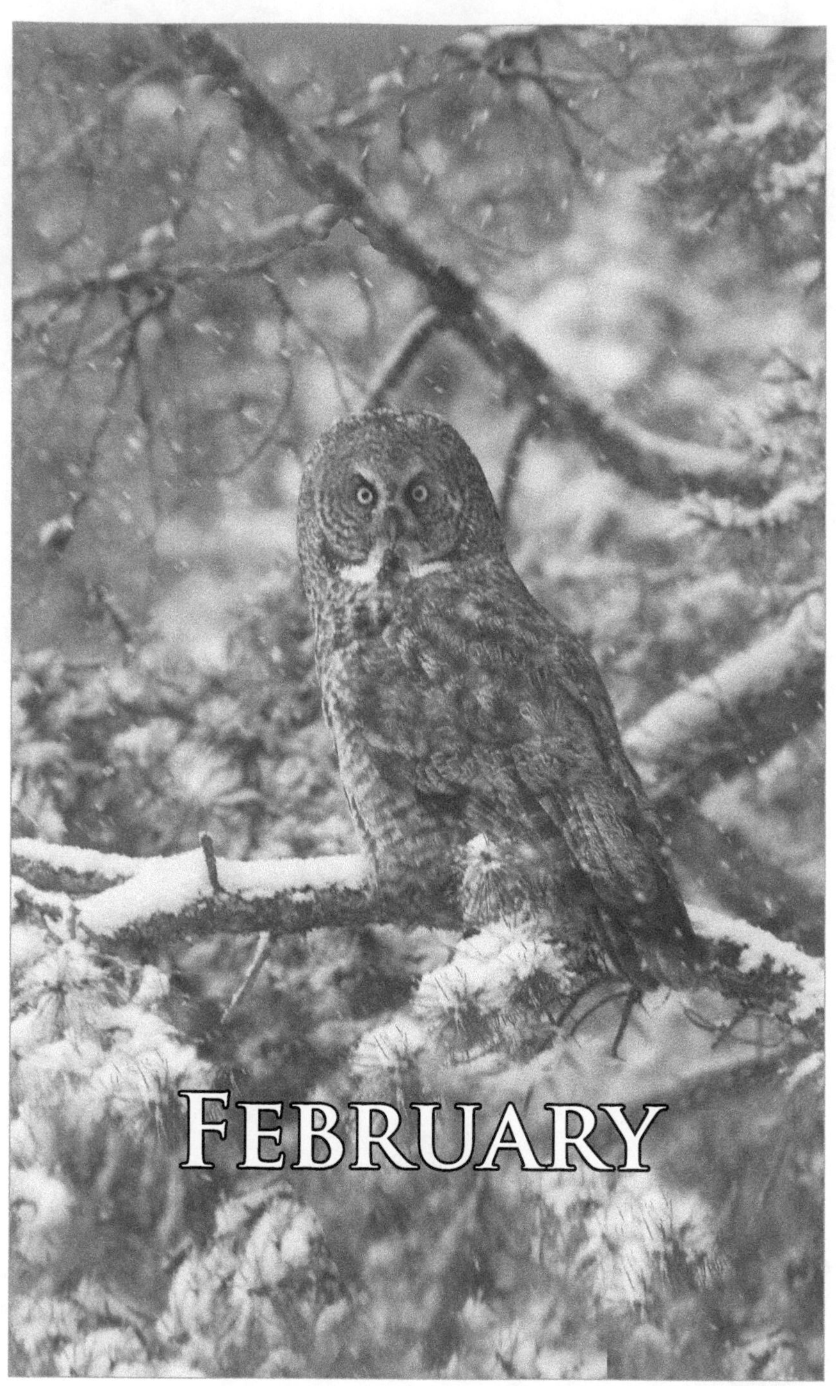
FEBRUARY

COWBOY POETRY

Darby is favored by a handsome library whose exposed wooden posts and beams refer to bygone logging days. We sometimes haul visitors there as a winter tourist attraction to corroborate local literacy. I enjoy the place not so much for books, which are few, but for a fly-tying station where the necessary pliers and forceps and hackles are supplied for free, as long as you promise to use a barbless hook. How could this be better? Only if they offered a metal Sanka can on the floor, into which I could expectorate Mail Pouch loogies.

Like many libraries, ours occasionally invites guest speakers. Julie and I had already attended one such event, focused on, of all things, an African American family struggling in Montana in the early 1900s. Pretty much a tale of jealousies, egos, hatreds, and racist mosh pits, which is what I expected. Darby, as I've noted before, is as white as papal underwear. In any event, the speaker earned a standing ovulation, as they say here.

Buoyed by that limited success, the library next invited a Missoula college professor, Samir Bitar, whose lecture was to be "Perspectives on Islam." Mr. Bitar is an expert on Arabic languages and cultures, subjects he has taught since 1999.

What happened next you can guess. It was like stepping on a wolverine's tail. The library began receiving florid calls suggesting that Mr. Bitar's purpose in the backwaters of Montana was to recruit school kids to radical Islam, teaching them to craft suicide vests from $2.56 worth of goods available at the Dollar Store.

The backlash seemed to be led by one Rocky Lanier, a chap I do not know, who said: "I've been overseas, and I've seen how these people are. I've seen how they promote what they do in other countries. So to have someone come here and tell us they are just here to be peaceful—no, they won't. Once they come over, they'll take over." Take over what? Darby? Anyone could capture Darby with two Boy Scouts and a roll of Scotch tape.

I was gratified that our mayor, J.C. McDowell, replied, "If the topic of Islam is not of interest to the community, there will be an empty room." *Yes.* Good dog, mayor.

Rocky Lanier's comeback was, "I don't care what people think about me," but, of course, that declaration would never have occurred to Rocky if he didn't care what people think of him. Like all of us.

In the event, the room was not empty. In fact, the library legally holds 123 people and, on the night of Mr. Bitar's talk, had overflowed such that the fire marshal asked standees to establish themselves elsewhere, such as the Valley Bar. The library's director, Wendy Campbell, said, "No presentation at our library has drawn this much interest. At our cowboy poetry event, we're getting close to a hundred. We've not seen anything like this."

The crowd embraced Mr. Bitar, some literally, and the clapping almost knocked books off shelves. I wrote him a note expressing thanks for risking his neck to prove he was slightly more interesting than cowboy poetry.

DAVE DEDMON DEAD

I noted earlier what an unlikely cross-section of folks dwell within this green-and-umber valley. Included in that list are Carin and Ridlon Kiphart. Unusual names, yes, and Ridlon has heard every Ritalin joke ever devised. Funny thing is, he's, uh, an *energetic* gent. His family hails from the Orkney Islands. He told me his forebears were Vikings who became so seasick that they begged to be dumped on the nearest shore. That he's half Scandinavian, says Ridlon, explains why he is prone to fidgeting in the face of all the gamboling that Americans get up to.

Ridlon and Carin, in their early 50s, live in a log house on the opposite side of our valley, in the Rye Creek Hills. Specifically on a mountainside facing west toward Trapper Peak, whose serrated shoulders are the handiwork of glaciation. One of his neighbors said to me, "Well, I guess that's if you *believe* in glaciers." Fronting that massif are ice-gouged gutters a quarter-mile wide. At sunset, their run-off refracts light within internal luminescent pools that turn blue and pulse disconcertingly. Landing strips for aliens.

Ridlon and Carin are travel gurus servicing the filthy rich, who, as luck would have it, are rarely filthy. They first started with far-flung scuba-diving sprees in Fiji and Tahiti and other islands whose names end in vowels and not long ago ran amok with 200-pound lizards and cannibals.

Then they leased a Boeing 757 for around-the-world trips for the plump and gout-bedeviled swells, stopping at foreign cities for a day or week in whimsical spurts. Their clients are California heart surgeons, New York hedge-fund bilkers, the inventors of Viagra, senators on parole, and dictators' sons. Not surprisingly, the clients indulge in unruly eruptions of entitlement.

During Ridlon's last arduous round-the-world jag, one passenger demanded to disembark at an Asian airport where the jet was stopping merely for fuel. As she stomped down the gangway, she fired up a Marlboro 30 feet from two tankers pumping jet juice. A largish cadre of Asian cops descended, applied choke holds, and marched her to the terminal for a corrective interview, with Carin and Ridlon trotting anxiously behind. Much shouting and negotiating ensued, and some money passed hands. The smoker was eventually marched back onboard in the understanding she would quickly self-deport, having already cost everyone a two-hour delay and a conflagration that might have been visible from my porch.

"The worst part is I have to smile at these people," Ridlon told me, "when what I really want to do is stab them in the eye."

Ridlon is a master snorkeler and one day decided to view the bottom of the Bitterroot River, even though the water is so clear that the bottom has nowhere to hide. Ridlon knows his geology and explained that the river drops astounding quantities of sediment atop a dropping fault block, and this is desirable because the valley would otherwise be a lake. Via snorkeling, he reckoned he could view this sedimentary shapeshifting in a kind of latter-day aquatic Robert Ballard expedition.

In fact, water filled the Bitterroot Valley 15,000 years ago—so-called Lake Missoula. Even today, the river annually re-arranges so many mega-tons of gravel that its channels alter drastically, often catching kayakers and drifters off guard every spring. "Go left. Go, right. Who's carrying the defibrillator?"

Anyway, our man Ridlon strapped on fins and mask and waded in, hoping not to die of frozen nipples. At the end of his swim, he told me, "I found four pairs of sunglasses."

Somewhat later, Ridlon and Dread Pirate Dave tubed down the river, which I've never seen even a tourist attempt. Their little floating party initially worked satisfactorily, with Dave shouting directions until Ridlon ignored him and collided with a downed tree. His inner tube burst like a fat water balloon, slapping him firmly against the log, barely above water, spitting and coughing. Dave raced to the scene, if there's such a thing as racing while one's ass is wrapped in inflated rubber. He climbed onto the offending log, reached down, and yanked Ridlon skyward by the elastic waistband of his trunks.

"Nuclear wedgie," Dave reported. Ridlon emerged slightly blue.

"Water and log," joked Dave, *"Waterlogged!"*

Ridlon did not smile. His life was intact but not so much his ego. Anyway, today everyone has forgotten this near-extinction event. Except me. I talk about it constantly.

The Bitterroot River is a swirling hooligan, a sorcerer of watercourse illusions. Which is odd because it's mostly as shallow as a three-man hot tub. We had a local fishing guide—a veteran who had also been a county deputy—who intentionally set out on the narrow swirlicues of the East Fork of the Bitterroot to report where channels had been blocked by fallen trees. He wasn't even fishing, just scouting as a public service and, one might assume, paying attention in a boat free of beer. Yet he and his wife steered into what rescuers called "a weird eddy," weird enough to flip his boat.

This was more or less directly across from the Rocky Knob, a popular roadhouse for evening DUIs, although none of the customers realized a life-and-death scenario was playing out 120 yards from their Bud Lights. The scout's wife escaped intact although hypothermic, but the fishing-guide-cum-cop whose name—and I am not making this up—was Dave Dedmon, was a dead man despite numerous resuscitation attempts.

Following that bit of unpleasantness, another fishing guide, Chuck Stranahan, said: "This river tends to claim a life every year. The river is sneaky dangerous. You can be in water that looks placid and idyllic, which all of a sudden gains momentum and brings you into sections that are dangerous."

I was hoping he would say the river "harvests" a life every year, that agricultural terminology being so popular here.

There further was a 74-year-old Darbrarian who, with two other friends, navigated into a submerged log. He was tossed from the boat, abruptly concluding his peaceful retirement, kaput, *adios*. A life jacket will keep you afloat only long enough to topple you upside-down and into underwater limbs that act as spears. Grab on—maybe poke out an eye—and see how long you last, with seven minutes being about the max before numb hands refuse to clutch.

Our Bitterroot search-and-rescue team is fast, but it would take them at least an hour to achieve, say, the Rocky Knob. At which point, your body would be its own little unguided raft, floating downstream at a jaunty clip, with the cutthroats staring upward and remarking, "Oh, for Christ's sake, there goes another."

Dread Pirate Dave says he'll teach me to navigate the river in a drift boat, but it will take multiple trips, starting below Painted Rocks Lake and concluding at the Darby Bridge, a forty-mile float that takes more hours than you will want to spend on water. There will be no fishing along the way, either, just oar etiquette and marine protocol. What's more, Dave is a professional and does not float even in his bathtub unless cash is proffered. Which is fair.

So, learning the river will be a $2000 investment, I'll bet, and a used boat is another $2800, not to mention the requisite $2500 for frame, oars, anchor, seats, tie-down straps, coolers, and trips to the liquor store. Then the Whole Shebang, which is a good name for a boat, requires a $1500 trailer with electric winch so you're not herniated yanking the rig out of raging water. Plus, as I've mentioned, you'll need about $2000 worth of Orvis-branded folderol so the fish respect you. (No, I'm not going to add up the total.)

But allow me to return to the charming Kipharts.

When Cuba opened to Americans, Carin discovered a demographic "eager to visit before we trash it." She devised a multi-day tour that hit Latin hot spots, boned up on her Castro Brothers gossip, handed out Che T-shirts, and made a killing. Last time we spoke, she'd completed her 53rd trip. How can anyone tour Hemingway's *Finca Vigia* 53 times? It had become such a mundane affair that, after each excursion, Carin was spending a few days hiking the length of the island piecemeal. For a book.

In one Cuban village, cops scooped her up, demanding she explain trekking solo in "bandit territory." She flashed her passport, which was plastered with 53 Cuban entry/exit stamps, and the officials figured she was recruiting sex slaves for Hillary. Then some money exchanged hands.

I advised Mrs. Kiphart against continuing. She said, "Oh, I'm fine. It takes me away from the tour group." She did, however, face half of all extant Cuban Romeos, who flirted and groped and woofed and pumped pelvises at her until she told me, "I shouldn't have taken along my boobs."

I believe that Carin and Ridlon have boarded more aircraft than your average Air Force Colonel. They claim to enter suspended animation while flying and afterward can't remember details, even delays. Their advice: Noise-canceling headphones and silk eye masks. Then they slide into somnolent torpor, which, from my own 60 years of flying, I can report is impossible for a person psychotically averse to enclosed spaces filled elbow-to-elbow with belching peanut-farting human whoopee cushions amped up on Red Bull. Have you noticed that the rush to board a commercial flight is equal in intensity to the rush to disembark? One of those can't be right.

The Kipharts have explored corners of the planet that Captain Cook intentionally avoided. I thought I was well-traveled and began naming remote destinations they hadn't noticed. "Kathmandu," I said, and they immediately listed all their Nepalese friends. "Plains of Tibet," I offered. Ridlon whipped out his phone and played a ten-minute homemade video entitled, "The Toilets of Tibet," with Carin as on-screen talent. Finally, I conjured a corker: "Kota Kinabalu." Carin sighed, then said, "We used to scuba-dive there, but now it's too crowded."

John Phillips

I had to move to an uninhabited expanse of the Bitterroot National Forest to meet neighbors who consider the northern tip of Sabah a teeming madhouse.

BIG BALLS LLC

You may recall that I was asked to join a car club—well, I wasn't, actually, but nobody keeps track of joining or unjoining. The club has no name apart from "Thursday Nights in Lolo," and here is its Constitution: "Article 1, Section 1: Drink beer and talk about cars on Thursday nights."

There is no Article 2.

There exists one amendment, though: "Bring beer that is not Old Milwaukee." Our putative president, Gary Meuchel, somehow discovered that a wealthy nearby collector owned more than 100 exotics, so he begged for a viewing on behalf of the club and all that we hold dear in fine pale ales. In his quest for reclusiveness, unfortunately, the owner proved a tad more unavailable than Howard Hughes' hamster. Or, as Gary put it, "Harder to locate than a nun's tit on Easter."

Gary had actually been angling for an invitation for two years. *Two years*, I say. Then, suddenly, one of the collector's full-time mechanics phoned to say, "Tomorrow, 9:00 a.m., don't be late," then hung up.

I live two hours from the cars and promised to collect Gary on the way, which meant—for the first time since retiring to Montana—I would learn what the territory looks like at 6:00 a.m. Same as 6:00 p.m., it turns out.

Eight club members assembled Saturday morn, all evincing various degrees of night-before damage and creeping sorrow. Our guide for the collection—claiming his name was "Steve," though I think he was fibbing—fished around in his pocket for a ball of keys the size of a small porcupine, opened an unmarked steel door, then led us down two flights of stairs to a black pit. When Steve hit the lights, there before us shimmered a panoply of glamorous, scarce, and matchless automobiles that would not, in nature, have ever been parked next to each other.

The first was a 1947 Gordon Diamond, powered by a flathead Ford. It looked like a slice of aluminum pie. "Its turning circle is infinite," said Steve. "Pull up next to a telephone pole, stick your hand out, and you can drive 360 degrees around the pole without ever lifting your fingers." I asked if many people had asked for that particular feature, but Steve had disappeared into the underground garage's dank recesses and fallen silent.

Next to the Gordon rested a late-model sports car that was five shades of mirrored coal-mine black so sullen that it reflected Satan's fingernails, a car I'd never seen before. Turned out to be a Ferrari 550GTZ Zagato with no badges except the designer's stylized "Z." The aluminum body was custom-made: a nose like an original Testa Rossa's; a tail like, oh, a squashed Alfa 8C's; and a pea-green quilted leather interior. A Ziggy Stardust Zagato.

I opened the glove box—no one seemed alarmed by this—and the registration simply stated, 2004 Ferrari M57. No such car exists, although it perhaps refers to the 5.7-liter V-12. Steve claimed the car had sold for $1.6 million and that only five exist in any universe known even by Neil deGrasse Tyson.

Alongside the Zagato sat a turquoise 1948 Tucker valued at €1.34 million. Why in Euros? No one knew. In front of the Tucker posed another Tucker but in pieces. Not far from a neon-green 1981 Lamborghini Countach S was a 1925 Voisin Torpedo, and scattered hither and yon were a '72 Ferrari Dino, a '90 Ferrari Testarossa (that I would later drive into the Lolo Forest), and a '61 Corvette convertible.

That's when Steve asked, "You ready to see Building #2?"

I may have swooned.

I'll spare you the entire repertoire but should mention that Building #2 housed what might be the world's finest collection of '50s and '60s top-line Chryslers, including a '56 De Soto that had been an Indy pace car. Next to that I found a handmade, fully functioning miniature steam locomotive that carried two people. Why? Steve couldn't explain that, either.

"So, let's tour Building #3," Steve said, whereupon the needle on the Weirdness Factor snapped right off. Consider: seven original Buick Rivieras; a B-17 radial engine that had survived a crash; a Borgward station wagon; and—well, here's where my train of thought derailed—four Lockheed 18-cylinder P2V airplanes equipped with magnetic anomaly detectors to locate submarines. Your average car collection rarely includes that.

I asked curator Steve what the reclusive owner drove daily. He pointed to a banal 1990 Cadillac Sedan de Ville with 15,000 miles, the collector's mother's car, then to a 1994 red Dodge Viper with 3100 miles. "When he bought this Viper," Steve mentioned, "he also bought all the service tools from Chrysler and attended Chrysler's mechanics' course."

"I need to meet this guy," I informed Steve.

"No can do," he replied. "He'd ship me off to live with Ed Snowden."

Turns out, Montana is lousy with multi-millionaires' vehicular galleries. The state collects no sales tax, so it is a relatively joyful experience to indulge motorized baubles. At car shows around the country, I've begun noticing rows of Maseratis and Alfas with Montana plates. Here's how it works: Rich guy contacts Montana lawyer, lawyer sets up (for about $2500) an LLC registered in Montana. The LLC then buys your Ferrari as a "company car," registered and insured in Montana, but no individual's name appears on the title, only the company's. Owners have become imaginative: Big Balls LLC, Boys Club Chrome Inc., and Jimmy's Spaghetti Bowl of Headers.

This legal jiggery-pokery evidently does minimal harm to the state's coffers, because it has morphed into a cottage industry among local solicitors. Of course, it *does* prevent other states from collecting whopper sales taxes—as much as $25,000 on a single Ferrari, for instance. That's why California and Colorado now urge residents to snitch on neighbors driving Winnebagos and Porsches bearing Big Sky plates.

To do all this legally, of course, you'd want to conduct business out of your Montana-registered "company car." What business? Invent one, I guess, although there won't be much room for fax machines or suitcases full of Swiss francs. Or you can set up residence in Montana, all legal-like, staying for a handful of months or pretending to. Is this all perfectly vague?

When Julie and I arrived here, we drove 55 miles to obtain our drivers' licenses, for which we were asked to show proof of residence, perhaps Montana's nominal effort to cut down on fresh-minted tax evaders. A utility bill might suffice, I was told. To be safe, I brought my passport, the deed to my house, and six photos of me floating the Bitterroot River.

"I won't be needing that," the clerk said, abandoning me to deal instead with a red-cheeked Hungarian-accented gent who had arrived in a Bentley Continental GTC.

I sometimes fear Big Sky will squash me flat.

MARANELLO MEETS THE LOLO FOREST

So, I befriended John Bennett, a Missoula barrister whose entire practice focuses on registering tax-free supercars. John owns a 2008 Ferrari F430 Spyder and two classic Fiats more fun than a pail of frogs, which not many people have ever said about Fiats. John stashes his cars in a warehouse adjacent to the airport, as do 20 other collectors.

When I first walked in, I faced an aromatic funk that encompassed about 50 years of my enthusiasm: lacquer, leather, Castrol, fresh rubber, cleaning fluid, wax, and rotten cork gaskets. I'd pay $500 for an air freshener that smelled like that. Inside I found three Bugatti Veyrons, one with $100,000 worth of Gulf Oil orange-and-teal paint; a maroon Ferrari La Ferrari sucking on its custom $5000 prancing-horse trickle charger; and a matching pair of Porsche 911GT2 RSs.

Then there was some moldy crap no one cared about: a '57 Mercedes 330SL, supposedly the first shipped to America; two De Tomaso Panteras, one an ex-Jackie Stewart car; a '57 Ferrari 250GT California Spyder prototype reportedly worth $10 million; a 1970 Dodge Charger Daytona owned by David Spade; a '64 Porsche 904 Carrera GTS, into which I tried to fold my jiggling ass but failed; a purple '70 Monteverdi 450SS

Hai (yep, it's a Hemi); and a RENNtech Benz E60 that I drove for *Car and Driver* decades ago from Florida to Myrtle Beach, whereupon it shucked a belt so rare I had to fly home after learning to despise boiled peanuts.

As I mentioned, new pal John also owns a '67 Fiat Dino, the one with the Ferrari V-6, as well as a '58 Fiat 1200 Turismo Veloce, both of which I will swindle out of him shortly, a stratagem he has yet to surmise.

But the car in the warehouse with which I was friendliest was a 1990 Ferrari Testarossa with only 4000 miles. I harbor inestimable sentimental attachment to the TR after driving one on a 1992 assignment from Newport Beach to New Jersey, then the home of Ferrari North America. The company attached no deadline, so I whooshed along blue highways for a fortnight and was once halted by border guards near Nogales. The subsequent cargo inspection took four seconds. The Testarossa rode on Pirelli P Zeros, the first 18-inch tires we'd ever seen, and there was no spare. Instead, the owner's manual suggested: "It is imperative that the tires are kept in *excellinition*."

Twenty-seven years later, here I was again wheeling an identical TR, this one from Bennett's collection, all scarlet strakes and whale-fin turning vanes, in Montana's Lolo Forest. Of the car's quirks, I'd forgotten the motorized-mouse seatbelts; the unassisted steering; the absence of anti-lock brakes; the view forward revealing not one cubic centimeter of the car's prodigious snout; the hand brake as intractable as the Plague of Justinian; and a plastic eight-ball shifter resisting gate number two. What I thought was the fuel gauge was instead the temp gauge—a half tank of gas no matter how far I drove!

On my original adventure, I was interviewed by a reporter in Olney, Illinois, simply for nosing the Testarossa into his town's civic park, looking for albino squirrels. Too many hacks have extolled the resonant wonder of 12-cylinder Ferraris, including me, but the boxer is an aural indulgence Dave Grohl could fashion into a teen anthem. It's a raspy, gruff-but-resonant smoker's cough, morphed into three-part harmony by the whir of gears and accessory belts that shouldn't soothe but do.

Accompanying me was not John but one of his Montana-born mechanics, age 21, already possessing one of the best jobs ever, the little prick. On his upper-left thigh is a tattoo of the Nürburgring racetrack, and on his right buttock is another that reads "Enzo" in Ferrari's font—his payment for a lost bet over a Formula 1 race. I told him someday a lover will ask, "So, uh, how long did you date this Enzo fellow?"

Driving the Ferrari, the metallic jingle-jangle of each gearshift reminded me of liquor bottles tumbling inside the mini bar I accidentally overturned at the Hotel Maranello Palace outside Ferrari's main gate. You know what isn't upside down all these decades later? The Testarossa. In fact, it's *excellinition.*

But that's enough about cars. They were no longer affording the exquisite pleasure they'd infused back in Michigan. I had come to view automobiles with near indifference. Far indifference, too.

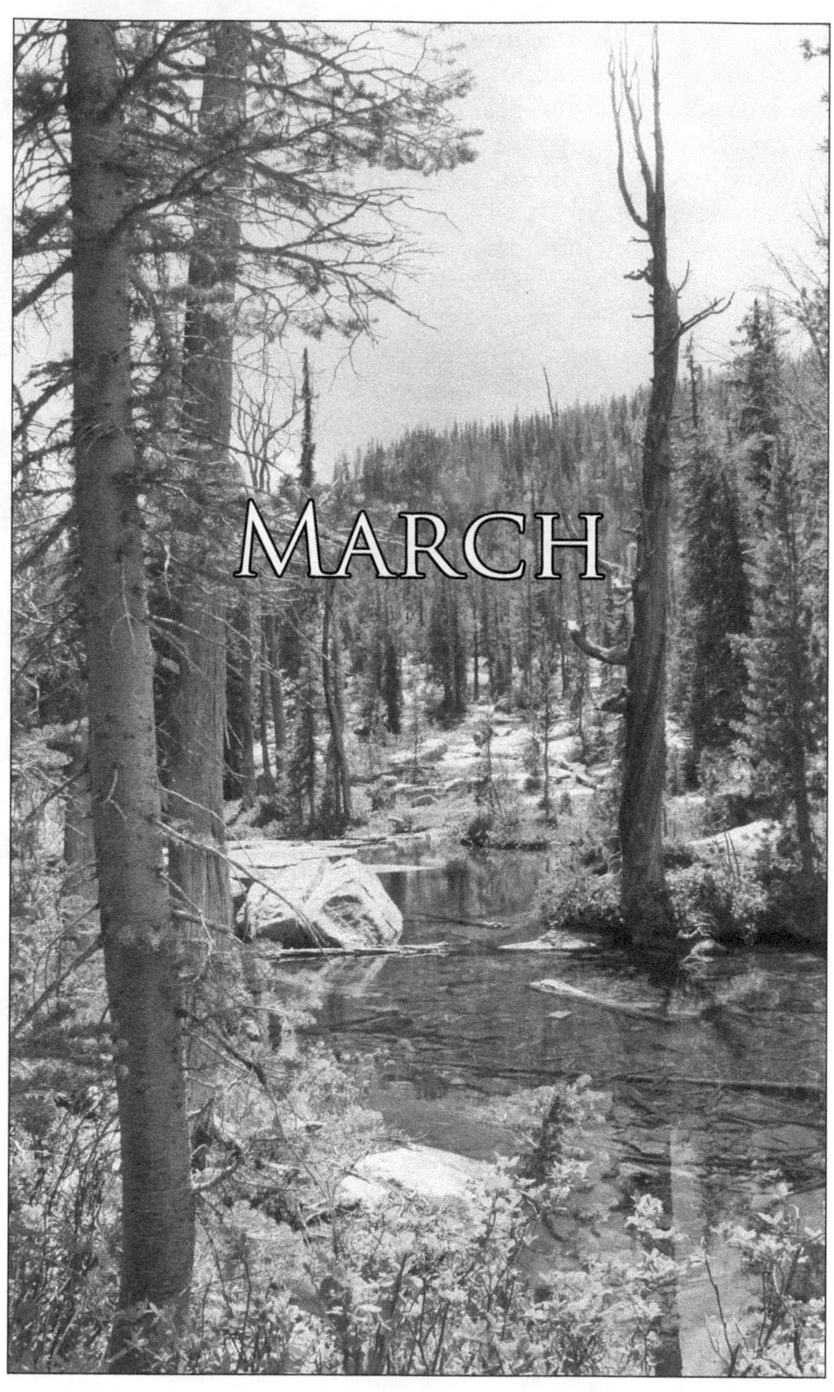
MARCH

BAND-AIDS FOR SNAKES

Our house offers a pantry roughly the size of an urban bowling alley. I considered installing a basketball hoop in there or one of those commercial glass refrigerators, the kind that hold 1000 bottles of beer. A large pantry's purpose is to ride out the valley's wintry cataclysms while inmates are hugging the four-burner stove. It's a subsistence regimen familiar to Montanans. The Costco in Missoula stocks five-day survival bags, and they always sell out.

Missoula is at the top of the Bitterroot Valley, 75 miles north. The drive from Darby is mostly clear and fast yet requires two hours each direction when snow is afoot and especially when it's a foot. Missoula is our best bet for anything more complicated than Listerine. In Missoula we can buy computers, hardware from Lowe's, shirts with actual buttons, and Tex-Mex that isn't contagious. But it's an all-day excursion from which we rarely return before dinner, which itself is forestalled by the tedious unloading.

Compared with our woodsy seclusion, Missoula feels like Chicago during the summer riots. The traffic is fierce. That's actually a lie, but once you're accustomed to encountering five cars per day, a couple hundred make you feel as if you're in the mother of all Macy parades. Understand, we don't even have a traffic light in Darby, and if you accidentally cut someone off, a maneuver that would require some sort of flow chart, the victim will gently yield and offer a little salute that says, "Jeez, did I cause that?"

Unfortunately for our psyches, Costco is the cheapest route to a full pantry, and we shop there once every six weeks, racking up a $1700 bill, with our record pegged at $2734. Right now, I live in a Hermit Kingdom, so Costco represents bedlam, as in the original U.K. asylum with inmates shrieking at the zenith of their feces-flinging.

Did you know that the marketing strategists at Costco are savants? Items are arranged so as to confound, complicate, and confuse, to stop you in your tracks for spells of bewilderment.

Last spring, I toured an aisle featuring bed linens and 9000-pound truck winches offered at a discount serious enough to demand my attention. Yesterday, I spied a nine-foot inflatable fishing dinghy beached upon a reef of double-A batteries. Such product juxtapositions are baffling—something you'll only experience at garage sales in Nebraska—and in older folks the result is spontaneous paroxysms. This is not an accident. It is Costco's considered stratagem.

At Costco we overfill our truck, both the six-foot bed and cockpit alike. The purchases are unnerving: one pound of Saigon oregano, 488 Q-Tips, and eight quarts of Kirkland spaghetti sauce that require Rolaids just to stockpile. I once drove home blind astern because of a new cat bed that our cats refused to touch even though it would have slept four Syrian refugees. I recall driving home on a minus-20-degree day and the alcoholic-size bottles of pinot grigio froze, with two of them pushing out their corks. Wine slushy.

When I enter Costco, my fundamental essence sags and screams for intravenous sedation and an adjustable hospital bed. Once after Julie and I emerged from the store, we sat in the truck and drank merlot from the bottle. Otherwise, my hands were shaking too much to drive.

I sometimes seek solace by asking Costco clerks for items I know they don't have. "Which aisle offers Occam's razors?" "Do you have Band-Aids for snakes?" "Any transsexual underwear with pockets?" "Is everyone in this store on a diet of lead paint?" It's my only pleasure.

Costco resembles a dreary airport terminal someone converted into a rat's maze that must be navigated prior to a prize of sharp Kirkland cheddar. Plus, Costco only intermittently sells tea. You can buy a brand-new Chevrolet at Costco, but Lipton bags? Nope. So here are some new rules to improve the Costco experience. I may use some profanity, so feel free to skip ahead.

First: No more cell phones in the store. Leave your phone in a cardboard box at the entrance, where it will join 500 others and you will have to search for the little bastard before departing. Phones left overnight will be detonated by SWAT teams in the parking lot, just because it's fun.

Second: You may not shop at Costco for 12 or fewer items. Doing so demonstrates a twisting injury from the brain stem up, landing you in the continuum known as "minimally exceptional." Customers must purchase 36 or more items or serve two weeks as salad fluffers at Applebee's.

Third: No more food samples at the end of every aisle. Costco is not a tapas bar. If, while shopping, you must consume six Vaseline-glazed Dijonnaise pimiento pickles glued to poppyseed sweater buttons, it's because you missed lunch. Return to your automobile to locate a restaurant that serves food. People do it all the time. Your relatives can help with the tricky details.

I recently witnessed a man gobbling samples of what looked like diced coconut on chocolate langoustines. He was so fat that if he ever went skydiving, he'd kill four ducks on the way down. He had nothing in his cart. He was there for the samples.

Fourth: If you come to a standstill—showing neither locomotion nor movement of appendages—there is a Navy Seal sniper in the rafters who will shoot you dead. Seriously. His name is Dan, and he has been angry since the third grade when he first noticed his shriveled leg. After you've been fatally perforated by Dan, your ass-scratching offspring may proceed to Aisle 16, Section C, to inspect caskets at deep discounts. There will be a Costco rep offering free samples of vulcanized eel with Philly cream cheese on rabbit intestines.

Fifth: Let us dispense with the employee at the door who won't let you exit until you wave a receipt. Other grocery stores don't do that. Shawna (said her name tag) is the equivalent of the European Union Finance Minister dictating fiscal covenants to kids running a lemonade stand. Yesterday, Julie and I were wheeling three carts filled with $1795 worth of God knows what—and God didn't know, either—whereupon Shawna glanced at one overstuffed cart and announced, "You're good to go." It took two seconds. Shawna didn't verify shit. And I'll tell you something, there was some shit in our carts. Who has ever shoplifted three carts jammed with hand sanitizer and four baked hams? It has never happened. Plus, if it ever *did* happen, I want to congratulate the thief. Let him join me in the truck for a swig of shiraz.

Sixth: If you're not strong enough to propel your own cart at a speed surpassing Cambodian striped newts, you must abandon the enterprise and walk home, thereby achieving practice at walking. Costco's public-address announcer will declare your left-behind items up for grabs, and shoppers crazier than a bucket of greased worms will be loosed to swarm. First-aid kits are on Aisle 6, Section P, alongside the sacramental wafers and oversize brassieres.

When the exit-door warden deigns to emancipate us, we then push our 300-pound carts a quarter mile through a parking lot filled with glassy-eyed motorists, all the while traversing giant yellow speed bumps that cause our carts to pull sideways wheelies. The receipt lady at the door should say, "Well, thanks for shopping with us today, and good luck getting to your car, you dumb fuck."

Such an abundance of choice reliably feels perplexing, befuddling, and dissatisfying. It obscures what's important in the moment. Americans crave more and more of everything until it's an insatiable demand. We fawn over merchandise endlessly—like watching TV—hoping to locate one object shinier than all others, which allows a choice to be made. If it were up to me to sell Kellogg Special-K, I'd recommend chrome boxes.

One more thing, which I guess would be Rule #7: No more children in Costco. If you don't personally hold cash to buy your own 9000-pound truck winch, sit in the car. Maybe take it for a little spin, check out the top speed. I don't care.

There. Now I'm done.

Muddier Waters

No, I'm not.

I'm pretty sure I can cause a sliver of your brain to shoot right out your ear canal and stick to your sleeve. And I can do it with one sentence: Last year, Costco sold 543,000 new cars. Costco did *what*? Maybe they sold 543,000 bags of teriyaki tater tots, but entire automobiles? You know, one of the largest dealership groups in America belongs to Rick Hendrick, and last time I checked, ol' NASCAR Rick was selling "only" 111,845 new cars per year. Maybe he should offer tater tots.

During my previous visit to Missoula's Costco, a Chevrolet Impala was parked outside. On some level I inferred it was for sale. But it had to be the only automobile in Costco's possession, right? A one-car sales lot, no test drives, no showroom. Who, exactly, on a day of shopping, says, "Oh, I need Pampers, 22 pounds of kitty litter, and a Chevrolet Impala with five-spoke alloys and a sunroof?" See, I don't think that could happen.

Costco claims that buying a car from them "cancels the fear of negotiating" with an actual car salesman. Their words. So, I inquired about buying an Alfa-Romeo 4C Spider and was informed it could be purchased at Costco for $64,407 plus $1595 for delivery, a total of $66,002. Of course, the car wouldn't be delivered to Costco. It would be delivered to an Alfa dealer. Costco nonetheless insisted I'd save $2493 over a dealer's price, although how could Costco possibly know what deal a desperate Alfa salesman might strike with me at 5:00 p.m. on Saturday?

What's more, Costco won't actually tell you the exact cost of the vehicle. Only the dealership can do that. Here's their disclaimer: "Costco...does not sell vehicles or negotiate individual transactions." Say what? Isn't that what they just promised? If I made a deal to buy Costco's Alfa, their next instruction was, "Go to the participating dealership and talk to the designated commodity salesperson." *Commodity?* An Italian-made Alfa? If Costco's position is that Americans are afraid of car salesmen, how helpful is it for the buyer to now deal with *two* salesmen instead of one? How efficient is it to buy a car first from Costco then again from the dealership?

If there's a starving molecule of efficiency in any of this, it surpasseth human understanding. It reminds me of that faux commercial for "Mr. Tea" on *Saturday Night Live*. You boil water in your own kettle, then pour it through the Mr. Tea funnel into your own cup holding your own teabag.

Now I'm really done.

Over-Skidding a Skid-steer

March was much upon us. Two feet of snow chucked down, flavoring the forest air with a clean acid tang. "It has to do with the ozone," a neighbor claimed, although he was of an age that a trip to the mailbox marked a peril-packed safari.

He was also the man who told me snowflakes "scream" when they land in water. "It's something like capillary action," he offered, "as the oxygen molecules are squeezed out of the ice crystals from the bottom up. Makes 'em squeak." After recommending he commit himself to Broadmoor, I trotted to the Bitterroot River and cocked an ear to the surface as fat flakes dove to their deaths. All I heard was my own cursing as a wavelet evidently from Greenland anesthetized my cheek.

The clearest mystery is water. "So blue yon winding river flows, it seems an outlet from the sky." Longfellow said that. Not me. I was not in that kind of mood.

It was snowing so hard I could not see beyond the first fleet of ponderosas, whose boughs were sufficiently bent that they occasionally snapped with the sound of mortar blasts. One of the smaller limbs splatted laterally across the driveway, barring passage, although the driveway wasn't useful anyhow because I couldn't locate its hairpin turns.

In the Bitterroots, when a tourist asks, "Where does this road go?" the locals reply, "I've never seen it go anywhere. Stays put."

I own two Husqvarna chain saws, but they won't start at temps below 20 degrees, and right then it was 13. My snowmobile suit has holes in the knees. So, no lumberjackery today. I backed the Tundra out of the garage after shoveling the initial two feet so the truck wouldn't be leveraged into the garage-door track. Then the door opener broke, and at about the 30-foot mark, the Tundra was pretty much high-centered, wheels churning more icy Treasure State atmosphere than snow. I could have installed chains but didn't have the Nyquil necessary to deal with the unpleasantness.

So, I won't be exiting the house today. Or tomorrow. I have a jam-packed pantry, a dual-cone propane heater, 27 magazines, maybe 1900 books, and, for now, electricity. The latter will fail shortly, of course, given the weight of the snow and innumerable limbs hurling themselves at power lines. Every room in the house is littered with flashlights. I stepped on one, rolled the slipper off my foot, and fell like a walloped harp seal.

Whenever you read about alpinists climbing Denali or Everest, they mention that snowstorms on mountains don't resemble snowstorms anywhere else. It is so. Mountain winds here blow in three compass directions in as many minutes. A "confused sea" barely describes it. I experienced the effect the previous summer with pal Ravi Fry, in his 50-year-old Cessna that we hoped to nurse over 11,000-foot Trapper Peak. An unlikely headwind materialized, lowering our indicated ground speed to 38 mph. We couldn't gain altitude. Instead we flew south to Wisdom, in the Big Hole—whose watershed contains the last remaining fluvial graylings in the Lower 48, one of which almost drowned me—and landed on the town's grass strip, narrowly missing a badger the size of a bowling bag.

"Ground-traffic controller," informed Ravi. "Big Wisconsin fan." The next day I saw two more.

We now have almost five feet of snow on the ground.

"Walking" in it entails a series of gymnastic dismounts with no judges displaying scores. We purchased steel cleats to strap onto our boots. They make the damnedest clicking sounds on concrete, like Tiger Woods in the men's room just before crashing another SUV. Of course, the spikes are irrelevant in five feet of snow. It's disappointing that humans are evolutionarily equipped for one season and winter is not it.

Winter also bedevils our downstairs bathroom, located in an outer corner of the foundation. It could serve as a meat locker. I wrapped the outer wall with tacky yellow insulation and layers of particle board, which created a 1970s trailer-park effect, although I finally own a home that no humans can see, so no one is disparaging my trashiness. There's still some slush in the pipes, and the toilet flushes as if saying, "I'll work on this later." So, I lit a space heater in that bathroom, aimed at the feet of whoever might be athwart the throne, toes ablaze as his spine seizes from frostbite.

More pressing is the driveway. I've filled four 55-gallon steel barrels with salt, gravel, and sand and placed them at the climbing turns. Unfortunately, inserting the working end of a shovel into barrels is like shooting pool with a rake and also a feat that threatens to snap the coils in my back. What's more, the lids regularly freeze to the barrels, at which point they're so like vaults that you might as well stash stock certificates in there.

So, what I did was cut down a metal wheelbarrow—remove its namesake wheel and metal understructure. Then I installed a pair of sled runners fashioned from hardwood baseboards. I attached a nylon strap to the nose, enabling me to tow it behind the truck. Into this "sledbarrow" I now load sand and salt in the relative warmth of my own garage, with the truck dragging the mixture to where it's needed, which is everywhere.

Unfortunately, the towed sledbarrow achieved more speed than my truck. Body damage ensued (the truck's, not mine.) I've already crunched the Tundra's tailgate three times and imploded the FJ's driver's door on an icy hill. So, there will be a third trip to J&D Auto Body at the north end of town. I owed them $1500 for the last job, and when I whipped out a credit card, the "J' said, "Just pay me when you have the cash." I returned with hundred-dollar bills four days later. The owner had to be reminded of what I owed and why. Business isn't transacted like that in, say, Newark.

Filling my barrels with gravel is as complicated as disarmament talks. My half-mile-distant neighbor, Pete Bonnell, son of singer/actress Gale Storm, maintains a whole hump of pea gravel behind his home, free to neighbors in distress. But how to transfer that gravel from his pile to my barrels? Pete has been diligent about delivering loads in his tractor's bucket at $20 per, a losing proposition for Pete. But I can't further expect him to fill the barrels at the top of the drive, because the steepness causes his tractor to pull terrifying reverse wheelies.

"So, drive your own truck to Pete's and fill it yourself," suggests everyone. Okay, sure, but have you ever used a garden shovel to pack 1000 pounds of loose rocks into the bed of a pickup and then, an hour later, unload every stone shovel-by-shovel into steel barrels? That's actually a war crime. Short of buying my own tractor and bucket, which I can't afford, I remain stymied. In the Bitterroots, impassable doesn't mean impossible, but it does suggest you bone up on your *TV Guide*.

My pilot pal Ravi has a driveway steeper and more cruelly twirly-isted than my own. It is just over a mile long, ascends 900 feet, and demands 4WD low-range all year 'round. When I asked how he plowed it, he smirked while leading me to a remote garage. Inside reposed a yellow Caterpillar skid-steer on crawler tracks, about 10,000 pounds' worth of unstoppable iron and diesel puissance, the sort of thing you'd use to build a Burmese runway. It is the Lagrangian Point of snow removal, a battle wagon whose operation requires a week of schooling.

Ravi and spouse, Dr. Jen Clothier, haven't watched television for 18 years. They spend their time driving the Cat and an enclosed-cockpit "Danger Ranger" ATV that can climb walls. Now I have skid-steer envy, and as a tease the two of them mailed me a toy Caterpillar made by Tonka.

I must tell you that Ravi stopped smirking when he rolled the entire five-ton rig four times down the cliff he refers to as "our hill." All six-and-a-half-feet of him emerged bruised and bleeding but with limbs attached. Twin black eyes. Damaged right foot. Multiple lacerations. The Caterpillar's previously inviting glassed-in and heated cockpit was smashed flatter than its operating manual. It took four days, two tow trucks, and a grid of dangerous chains and cables to extricate. A tree was flattened. I didn't ask the cost. Afterward, when Ravi started the skidder's engine, two quarts of oil exploded out of the muffler, polluting his paradise as surely as the *Exxon Valdez*.

Then I became emotionally frazzled when our freezer and clothes dryer committed suicide within days of each other. A team effort. I phoned Lowe's in Missoula, speaking for 45 minutes to a Lowe's "assistant sales marketer," who right then seemed busy studying for Monday's Spanish exam.

He declared my order beyond human contemplation. "Too much," he blurted, recommending we contact Amazon. Amazon eagerly accepted our money, but then, within 24 hours, called to say, "We don't deliver appliances anywhere near your part of the planet, if, indeed, it *is* part of our planet." Their representative could not locate the Bitterroot Valley on a map even with my helpful geographic pointers, such as, "See that big state up on the Canadian border?"

"There are a bunch of 'em," was his reply, and I could hear him making coffee and, I believe, later unzipping before a urinal.

So now we're having a freezer and dryer shipped to Missoula, where we will collect them in my much-abused Tundra. What about the hoisting? Well, I've undertaken this rigmarole several times now, and here's how it works: Julie and I will rendezvous with a filthy 18-wheeler at a truck stop somewhere near an exit from I-90. We'll back up the Tundra until we're tailgate to tailgate. Then, after exchanging pleasantries, the beard-stubbled and beer-breathed driver and I will manhandle boxed appliances from his truck to mine, rolling them atop six PVC pipes that I've cut for the purpose, much in the fashion of the Druids hauling sarsens to Stonehenge. I will then hand the driver a twenty-dollar bill as a false token of my esteem and drive home with new freezer/

dryer covered in a windborne crust of snow. That's the way it works here.

Of course, the appliances being replaced must be shunted outside, an insult to Mother Nature and rust alike. At some point, Julie and I will lift them via engine-hoist into the Tundra for another 60-mile run to our nearest landfill. This particular dump is roughly the size of a dentist's parking lot, and the loads of refuse are deposited directly upon a paved turn-around for reasons unclear. But I tell you, pushing an aberrant appliance out of a truck and watching it smash—with the dryer window exploding in pieces ricocheting five feet—is one of life's unlikely pleasures. Unfortunately, a Refuse Official driving a crud-encrusted Bobcat witnessed this breakage, so we guiltily brushed glass shards into a tote bag we received for subscribing to *The New Yorker*. Then another hurdle: The dump demands $24 for each appliance that you "gift" them. Why not an even $25? No one knows.

It reminded me of a stat I'd just read. One minute of automobile manufacturing in the U.S. costs $460,706. I love when monster statistics like that are parsed to the last dollar. Were those final six bucks invoiced for, say, some chubby worker's ham-on-rye in Hamtramck?

Effecting a Crisper Crown

Three things I've learned: First, tire chains are dear, as in $170 for the rear duo alone. Second: Each chain weighs as much as the Lusitania's anchor. Third: One of the instructions warns, "Try to keep your chains dry," which is like telling a Federal District judge to avoid legal jargon.

Even buying chains is fiddly. The NAPA clerk wouldn't sell me anything until she'd personally examined my truck. She scanned the wheel wells, her forehead all scrunched in concentration as if she were probing for deer ticks.

Then she said, "No chains on front. Rear chains, okay, but install them tight, or shit is gonna tear shit up." I asked for specifics about the shit, and she said, "Well, how fond are you of your brake lines?"

If you've never installed snow chains, it's about as much fun as wire-brush dentistry. All labor is performed on hands and knees or on your ribs so that rocks lacerate kidneys. It's like high-school wrestling except the opponents are snow, mud, rusted-together links, and frozen steel. You'll need a snowmobile suit or Carhartt overalls, which you'll have to strip off or risk filthening your vehicle's upholstery, which you unfortunately must do in the middle of this routine in order to drive 18 inches onto the outstretched chains.

While chaining up, I regularly despoil three sets of gloves as each becomes soaked. Touch the chains barehanded, as I did on a minus-12-degree day, and you won't have to worry about FBI identification. Moreover, the Tundra's exhaust is aimed at my face as I attach the right-side chain, so afterward it is wise to avoid operating heavy machinery, such as the Tundra.

Once the chains are attached, the riotous vibration threatens to collapse the truck's headliner. Right about now you're wondering why a man enmeshed in a lifetime of auto enthusiasm hasn't installed chains before. All I can tell you is that the owner's manual for a $1,373,700 Bugatti Veyron never mentions the topic.

One 20-degree afternoon, I drove the truck through that day's accumulation of snow, traveling 100 yards on my driveway before bogging in an icy drift that reached the right-side door handles. I attached the winch cable to a tree. The winch turned two revolutions, stopped, and began to smoke. The truck's severe angle meant the farm jack wouldn't stay upright. So, the truck sat where it was, blocking the driveway for *seven days*, with the would-be occupants digging and fussing over it daily between 1:00 and 4:00 p.m.

The frustration of being housebound caused me to rev the engine, which tore the rear chains into metal confetti, a $170 tantrum. On the eighth day, we displaced snow in front of the truck to allow a downhill run, and the Tundra popped out of its snowy grave like a blue torpedo, careening down the drive with almost zero steering and the anti-lock brakes pulsing madly during a 20-second uncontrolled descent of terror. I bounced off three or four snowbanks, each saving me from 15-foot drop-offs on the right. It so unnerved me that I climbed out of the cockpit and sat on a snowbank for five minutes.

Our private road extends 1.76 miles. We share it with a half-dozen other souls exhibiting similar social-adjustment issues. So, this is *our* road, by which I mean we pay for and perform 100-percent of its mucky maintenance. There are annual dues and exciting new expenses, such as an $83,000 bridge.

Our biannual road meetings are fraught affairs, with agendas dictated by our three elected Road Czars, one of whom quit in the middle of last week's soirée, demanding to be replaced. (Eyes focused on me as I continued to study my grubby Barbour boots.) We discuss topics that few folks cover: issuing clearer instructions to Wes who drives our commercial Cat grader to effect a crisper crown; avoiding windrows (look it up); driving under 10 mph so one's tires don't fling costly surface gravel into the adjoining ditches, a regulation we'd enforce but the potholes do it for us; filling our 55-gallon barrels with pea gravel and salt and spreading dust-avoidance chemicals and arguing about nonexistent guardrails, which will remain nonexistent because the plow driver would then have nowhere to shove snow. We also erect signs. One says, "SLOWER" in four colors.

Then there's the business of size, grade, and texture of replacement gravel. This alone has been known to tear Bitterroot families apart. I mean, you've got your #10, known as "screenings," which is like kitty litter, and your #3 or #4, effective in soft ice because their sharp edges point upward to grab rubber. Our favorite is "3/4-minus," although it's heavy to shovel out of the barrels. We thus purchased metal feed scoops, which go missing every spring. That's because, as you fling a scoop filled with gravel, it sometimes departs your hand to take up residence in a powdery drift behind a bush, pulling a full Jimmy Hoffa.

We recently replaced our sad little bridge over 35-foot-wide Tin Cup Creek. The first bridge was a rusty railroad flatbed covered by two-by-eights. Like Mister Ed, it was swaybacked and groaned, with pieces falling into the creek. (*Crick*, sorry.) We were shamed into action when a neighbor died and willed $50,000 for a replacement. Not quite enough, of course, so we each kicked in $1500 or so, whereupon a massive crane arrived and plopped a DOT-approved prefabricated concrete bridge into place at a cost of eighty-three Large. It doesn't possess the old bridge's character, which is to say it will withstand the weight of a Darby firetruck.

During the installation, our sole access to civilization was via our emergency fire-escape route, which wends along a two-mile rut through privately owned Chief Joseph Ranch, where you might collide with Kevin Costner portraying John Dutton in *Yellowstone*. At the unveiling—of our bridge, not *Yellowstone*—I hoped to smash a growler of Bandit Brewery's ale on the southern piling, a fine christening, although Julie feared it would require ten minutes to pick up all the glass. Another neighbor christened it for us. It required ten minutes to pick up all the glass.

We then conned the local high-school metalworking class into fashioning a sign that reads: "Julie Grauer Memorial Bridge," with Mrs. G. depicted on horseback, because it was she who willed the fifty grand upon her demise (which wasn't on horseback). When she was alive, she was known as "Grouchy Julie." We don't call her that anymore.

The American Society of Engineers recently calculated that America's roadway infrastructure now requires $3.6 trillion for repairs. For at least two miles of that infrastructure, I believe I have done my part.

Be Like Mike

You may recall my off-the-grid neighbor Mike Phillips, a splendid surname but no relation, who has willingly subsisted with neither electricity nor running water for 32 years. That's a fact, Jack. He dwells alone in a cabin of his own manufacture, set so far back in the forest that birds leave trails of bread crumbs. His house has red siding and a green metal roof and is the size of a one-car garage. It contains a living room, kitchen, and bed—all petitely packaged for a lone occupant weighing 150 pounds. Fall over in the kitchen and you'll land in Mikey's bed. An outhouse, sans door but with requisite half-moon cutout, stands 60 feet from Mike's entranceway. You could easily plop his house on a trailer and haul it to Missoula for servicing.

Mike, now 72, exits his cabin every morn carrying a five-gallon bucket and two one-gallon buckets and fills all three with Tin Cup Creek's frigid water for drinking, bathing, and cooking. It has never made him sick. In fact, it has turned him into the healthiest 72-year-old American since Bartholdi bequeathed Miss Liberty.

The walk down to the creek is treacherous, and Mike occasionally falls in. At his water hole, he has fashioned a seat between two trees, and the view of Tin Cup Creek and the overarching woods is something that would launch any naturalist into hallucinatory palpitations. John Muir would drop dead with envy except he already has.

Mike doesn't resemble a hermit. His hair is regal silver, he's slim and tall, with legs as thin and bendable as Twizzlers. He exudes a whiff of hippieness and proudly admits to Haight-Ashbury predilections. In fact, he looks a bit like John Phillips of the Mamas and the Papas, but that presents one too many Phillips's interfering in the business before us.

Mike was raised on a Minnesota farm and occasionally rode his pony to school. Then he rode a nuclear-powered aircraft carrier for two tours in Vietnam—I love that the military refers to them as "tours," as if they're led by a Brit offering tea and scones under a red brolly. Mike barely survived his final tour, not from malice waged by Charlie but from a warrant officer who despised his nonregulation haircut and was further inflamed by Mike's disapproval of immolating noncombatants with napalm stored on their own ship.

When Mike made it back to the farm, he studied astrophysics at the University of Minnesota, then found himself an itinerant carpenter in Santa Barbara, where contemplation of stars was limited to the black holes that were Ronald Reagan's Secret Service agents, whom Mike befriended.

Then something odd: "My friend Bobby asked if I'd like to cruise on his 65-foot tuna boat," Mike recalls. "Bobby said, 'Well, this trip, you know, we aren't fishing. This trip, we'll rendezvous with a Thai cargo ship. This trip, we'll bring back three-and-a-half tons of weed. Want in?'" At the time, Mike was crewing on a potential America's Cup contender, twirling winches to raise and lower sails. So risky life at sea suited him.

Mike and Bobby converged on the 110-foot Thai freighter 300 miles south of Hawaii, having traveled about 1500 miles farther than intended. The foreign crew launched Avon inflatables overflowing with two-kilo bricks.

"I stashed everything in the hold," Mike remembers. "Bobby was messed up on Wild Turkey and cocaine. In fact, when the Thai freighter edged too close, it was me who steered us to safety. I stacked 7000 pounds of dope that day, alone. At one point, our boombox was playing the Eagles' *Smuggler's Blues.* I wondered if I was the first smuggler to listen to that song while smuggling."

The Thai crew donated the diesel fuel necessary for the return leg, but it was contaminated, and Bobby's tuna boat's fuel injectors fouled every 24 hours.

"I became a world record holder at replacing filters," Mike recalls. "It was horrible, in seas so rough I got tossed out of my bunk. I eventually moved below, sleeping on the marijuana, along with a stowaway cat. I fed her tuna from cans. She gained weight. I lost 15 pounds."

Nearing the California coast, Mike and Bobby were met by a pre-arranged armada of private sailing craft, each accepting a small load of inbound dope.

"They were day sailors and never sailed in international waters," Mike explained, "so the coast guard never hassled them. In the end, I was paid in stacks of twenty-dollar bills in brown paper bags. A *lot* of bags. My plan, afterward, was to move away from people forever. So, I paid $2000 an acre for 20 acres in the Bitterroots—right up against Forest Service land—and I excavated the little gravel path leading to it." That gravel path today leads to my driveway, too.

I asked what Darby looked like 30 years ago.

"The only major changes have been the new library, gym, and brewery," Mike said.

That's our six-year-old Bandit Brewery, operated by the town's mayor and a former HQ for Darby's dogs, united and untied. Mike Phillips plays his guitar at the brewery on Saturday nights, close enough to the vats to suffer sloshing events. He isn't paid but earns tips. Otherwise, if Mike has an income stream, its headwaters are murky. He is nevertheless incalculably content, meeting me at the gym where his half-membership affords no access to exercise equipment but to the showers.

"Sometimes I sneak into the sauna," he says, as if he's stealing silverware.

For a spell, Mike was employed in Darby by Christopher Lloyd, Doctor *Back to the Future.*

"His wife once asked me to cut some cattails from a swampy area," Mike told me. "I figured they were cleaning up the yard, but, no, she wanted them for a salad."

Mike's main vexation is excretion. "I'm on my seventh shitter," he explains. "They're like geese and pigeons. You gotta let 'em fly to spread out the crap."

He's also become sanguine about blizzards. He doesn't leave the house, is how he deals with them. He once laid out 30 days in his cabin simply reading, awaiting Red Schields to plow his drive, which is two degrees superior to an abandoned logging road.

"When I can't make it through the snow, I feel like I'm not supposed to," Mike told me. It's just as well because Red's vintage 4WD truck's transmission blows its gears to birdshot every February, leaving all of us snowbound and drinking Kirkland spaghetti sauce while trying not to feel like inmates.

Mike has a vivid history of face-to-face encounters with wildlife.

"There's a window beside my pillow," he says, "and it once filled up with a black bear's face." Later, when chipmunks were partying on his roof and interrupting his slumber, Mike unsheathed his .22 at dawn, ready to splatter guts. "Walked out the door, turned sideways, and there was a bear sow with a cub. She immediately charged. I only had time to lift the gun a little—shot into the dirt between us, and, incredibly, she stopped. I was almost her breakfast."

I envy Mike's self-reliant philosophical subsistence, but my cabin-fever limit is a week. After that, I feel compelled to perform a statistically futile gesture.

Mike owns no pets, no computer, no spouse. "Truth is, I don't get lonely," he told me, although I noticed him staring greedily at my books, to which I issued him an imaginary platinum library card.

Because of Mike, I felt a cosmic finger jabbing my chest. Here was a Phillips who'd planted himself so profoundly in the woods that he had attained placid equilibrium almost as a side effect. Distancing himself from other humans had alone done the trick. Meanwhile, the other Phillips was searching for assurance in abstractions, still trembling on the cliff. I was seeking wisdom by looking within, which felt too much like a chore that ought to be rewarded afterward by pointless diversions—buying something expensive, gambling on the Superbowl, worrying about the Dow. It was starting to feel as if too much self-awareness might simply be distracting. Like preparing a tax return while playing baseball.

Mike and I first met when the post office juxtaposed our magazine subscriptions. As he hand-delivered my copy of *The Week*, he eagerly related his latest project: a four-square-foot solar panel to supply enough wattage to illuminate a breadloaf-size black-and-white TV from the '70s, a lash-up for which he'd amassed $200 of brewery tips. Affixing the antenna to a tripod of lodgepole pines, Mike's goal was to receive—atmospherics permitting—any PBS station featuring David Attenborough narrating the love songs of humpback whales. Mike asked if the three-tree antenna was sound. I had no clue but did express concern about a 72-year-old scaling a pine towering above a newly dug outhouse pit.

The first TV signal he captured made him giddy. "When did they start running that many commercials?" he asked. I wanted to tell him, "Thirty years ago," but didn't have the heart.

Mike is a much beloved fixture in Darby, unexpected considering the bottomless anti-hippie sentiment that has festered here since before any resident met one. Mike steadfastly lives the life so many malcontents theoretically crave—that platitudinous impulse to retreat, relying on nothing more tangible than self-discipline, three plastic buckets, and Mother Nature turning a softer cheek.

Truth is, Mike's life diverts dramatically from the romantic when the nightly jog to the outhouse is in sub-zero weather. Romance fetches upon the outer banks when fresh pits must be dug to accommodate excrement. Ditto for outdoor trips to wash dishes or his crotch in a tub of iron-hard water mixed with splinters of ice and the occasional brook trout, knowing that tomorrow and the next will offer two entertainments alone: used books and a jumpy black-and-white TV. Well, that and chopping firewood, always a treat for two minutes or until the first splinter connects with retina. Mike drives an ancient Subaru Outback that he expects never to replace.

When Mike joined us for dinner—braised ribs and Brussels sprouts—he confessed he'd been fasting for 24 hours to rev up his tastebuds. He is infectiously optimistic and has never expressed the slightest desire for brushed-steel appliances or granite countertops. He is in sync with a beaver's work ethic, yet is capable of a guilt-free day in bed if his energy is off or the weather is on.

"I try to engage life while making the smallest mess possible," he says. "You know that Forest Service motto, 'Pack it in, pack it out'? I try to do that. I'm no longer in 'Acquisitions and Mergers,' if you know what I mean. And I live where I live for the same reason you do. It's just a matter of degree."

Be like Mike.

John Phillips

Eating a Bowl of Muscle Relaxants

I've endured an ulcerous gutfull of worrying about snow clogging the driveway. It's the worry that worries, of course, not the reality. Usually. There's just a blemish of leftover Midwestern WASPish guilt about allowing snow to accumulate. It's unclean. Sign of a sloppy mind, like the chauffeur's fingerprints on the limo's door handle.

So, I'm studying the vocabulary of snowplows that attach to the front of pickup trucks. You've got your "shoes," on which the plow skids across things that shouldn't be plowed, your power-angling versus self-angling blade, your hydraulic versus electric screw-type rams, your flexi and rigid deflectors, your locking casters, and, of course, the plow itself, except it's not a plow, it's a blade. Not even that. The curved dish is technically a moldboard. You could ask a farmer.

In winter, my driveway morphs into an Olympic luge run, a galaxy of crags, heaps, and stacks that would dispirit Sir Hillary. I've been forestalling the plow purchase because the mountain-suitable versions start at $4000. But, now, I either buy one or rely on outsiders—Brad, Kent, Red, Pete, Cowboy Mike—whose equipment first plows their own drives and whose enthusiasm waxes or wanes with exploding transmissions.

So, on a sloppy day of slush—the sky looking like it was filtered through newspapers, and me sick in bed—it was left to my saintly wife, first, to intercept the truck driver carrying my new plow and, second, to scour our village to locate a forklift that would hoist it into our truck. Our NAPA store obliged. Price? A dozen doughnuts for the clerk who previously helped me buy snow chains. Turns out my new plow weighs as much as the Raiders' old stadium. In the Tundra's bed, the plow sank my truck to lowrider status.

Unloading it was equally enchanting: hydraulic floor jack, farm jack, ropes, blocks, and tackles sufficient to outfit Manhattan window washers. Next came the intermezzo known as "some assembly required," with my butt angled toward a twin-burner propane heater that I hoped right then wasn't filling the garage with CO_2

Surprisingly, I actually managed to wrench the plow into looking similar, but by no means identical, to the photo in the instruction manual. Well, apart from the pump-o-lator thingy cross-edgewise with the Johnson bar. The thing you should know about assembling a snowplow is that the blade forever threatens to slam down in response to any provocation at all, easily guillotining feet and chipping concrete. After that, you'll be fitted for a motorized wheelchair and won't care about snow, meaning the plow has served its purpose.

Next came tangled electrical connections, not one of my strengths. I couldn't locate a hole in the truck's firewall through which the wiring might poke. But I did briefly insert my right arm until it was trapped amid A/C conduits and a warren of plastic radiator shrouds. Disengagement drew blood, a sentence you'll hear only at the Pentagon or in divorce court. I should have drilled a dedicated wiring hole, but its inner circumference would have been jagged, a short circuit waiting to happen and another entranceway for mice. So, I simply drooped the loom over the radiator without regard to even one of the manual's 19 "Warning" notices, two "Danger" admonitions, and nine "Caution" citations. (Really. I counted.)

But, hey, plowing is a frigid endeavor, so how could the radiator become hot enough to melt wires? Tempting fate like that makes me feel like a rebel. The rebel nonetheless installed a fire extinguisher, because the top of the Tundra's battery is now a colorful entanglement of cables, lines, leads, and flex ties resembling a Portuguese gill net.

Then I spent three hours adjusting the blade to rest at its specified 0.75-inch height. It's suspended by a chain, and each link accounts for 1.5 inches of travel—twice what I desired. Plus, the $200 adjustable shoes aft of the blade add to the calculus. More shims? Fewer? I've seen IndyCar engineers dial in ride height more rapidly. And now my truck's headlights illuminate the back of the blade, so it's possible I'll drop a wheel off the north edge of my driveway, over the precipice and through the woods to grandmother's house we go. Will skinny pines halt the rollover of what now feels like a four-ton Toyota? Doubts are what I have.

The final instruction was to mount the lift/lower controller in the cabin, but I was low on energy, so I "mounted" it by tossing it into the center console. So now I'm awaiting an electrical malfunction smelling like scalded coffee. Smelling more like scalded bourbon, to be honest, because that's what Montanans drink while plowing. Red built a plywood bar between the seats of his truck.

On the topic of actually moving snow, here's what I learned right off: Everything happens at the speed of wood glue. Whenever I lift or lower the blade, the truck rises or squats like a hobbled buffalo. You've heard of a world of hurt? I'm in a world of oversteer. Plus, the whole works juts proud of the grille maybe four feet. It's like sitting down with elk antlers attached to your ass—doable but requiring tedious arrangement. There's a worrisome measure of squirmy-jumpy slack in the plow's trellis of steel braces, too, and under operation it sounds like a Renault falling down a coal chute. It's what I imagine a fatal roller-coaster accident sounds like.

During my second plowing adventure, I guess I forgot to insert the main cotter pin, or linchpin, or the brooch that attaches the plow to the truck. Well, I shouldn't say I *guess* I forgot. I *did,* is what. I thus shoved a wall of snow onto the lip of a steep drop-off—where I'd dumped tons of pine slash the previous summer—and when I backed away from this impressive monument, I noticed that the truck felt oddly lively and unburdened. That's because it was. The entire plow had escaped my personal orbit and buried itself implacably in the snowbank I'd just created, where it stayed. A $4000 sculpture.

Julie and I searched for the missing yellow linchpin for 20 minutes, a ridiculous mission given the ten inches of fluffy new snow, plus the pin was not in the snow at all but in the garage on my workbench, although I learned that vital piece of news the following spring.

We had to carry a hydraulic jack to the scene, yanking the jammed plow a few inches rearward, whereupon I rudely drove the truck into the receiver sleeve—Julie issued a "calm down" directive—and even though plow and truck had mated with a tentative half inch of connectivity, I drove the goddamn thing to the top of the hill, parked, and stomped inside to eat a bowl of salted peanuts and muscle relaxants.

My plow already bears war-like scars and dents and warped hinges after only a dozen outings. Moreover, this whole undertaking represents more abuse heaped on my poor 13,000-mile Tundra: freshly gashed flanks (I sideswiped our discarded oven); missing chin spoiler (severed twice by hidden granitic outcrops); two new windshield pings (call Dave at Bitterroot Glass); and a cargo bed that appears to have hosted bazooka testing.

If I ever trade in the Tundra, I'm just gonna tell the salesman, "Hurricane Katrina. Son of a bitch."

Massive Clogs in Montana

In the final hours of March, my homestead was again imperiled by glacial slabs of plasticky snow—36 inches on the roof, maybe more, curling like surf off the gables in glorious ice-blue breakers. I like to watch them creep inch by inch, until they tumble with a jet-like whoosh. It won't be long before I can walk onto the roof again, which I have minimal interest in doing without massive insurance upgrades.

The satellite dish is so clogged that the TV signal is not much more than dancing phantasms, and our true-crime dramas after dinner reveal parts of the plot but often neither the murder nor murderer. Right now, what's showing looks like a green jellyfish in a Watson/Crick double-helix, and maybe that's because it's Fox News.

I yet clutch to my bosom malevolence for Rupert Murdoch, even though he attended my wedding reception at an A&W Root Beer stand in Dexter, Michigan. His gift was a case of Foster's beer, which he almost demolished singlehandedly. I cherish a photo of the Rupe, as we called him, shotgunning brew like a frat boy. Someone from the magazine drove him to the Detroit airport, only to return to the A&W to fetch his forgotten crocodile briefcase, which was then scooped up and transported to the first-class lounge where the man sat with face on chest, insentient. I always felt it was an error on my part not to have opened his briefcase to sign a few contracts he had pending with Satan.

Rupert reminded me of Donald Sutherland playing the role of a deranged Down Under despot dismantling democracies worldwide. In our editorial offices he once asked, "How do you come up with a lead sentence?" It was a harmless query but sounded to me like, "Did you sleep with my wife and kill my goldfish?"

In any event, thanks to the snow here, it appears Thursday will be another in-house day. That's three in a row, just us and the cats, who flee hysterically to the fire room every time the roof sheds a glacial tongue that lands like a poufy sectional sofa. I still have a pantry full of Krazy Glue, no-brand saccharin, and fake salt. But if the electricity fails, and it will, the motor in our well ceases to pump, meaning zero water except what I've bottled beforehand or what I can salvage from the toilet tanks. In my bug-out bags I've stashed military K rations, although they taste like jerked bamboo sautéed in chemical gravy. I don't think I could eat a cat. Our fat feline Teddy Roosevelt's default state is contentment, a four-legged example for the rest of us —as opposed to Freud's assertion, that humans' default state is diffuse misery. Maybe in Alabama but not Montana.

In the basement, as a precaution, I've filled dozens of five-gallon jugs with well water, jugs previously containing cat litter. The water immediately turned fetid and sour; it's nigh on impossible to remove every particle of litter. I doused them with boiling water, but the gravel yet adheres like grape seeds that will break your teeth. So each jug has some "body" to it, and the water is not opaque but twenty shades of gray. I could supplement our supply by dipping into the cistern, although its lid is buried beneath so much snow that locating it would require a bathysphere.

The emergency jugs occasionally break the flimsy shelving and fall to the concrete floor, where they burst in five-second, five-gallon floods that pool around the furnace. I'm not much of a survivalist, and what I haven't yet hoarded is kitty litter. Toilet-wise, the cats are on their own, though I've seen photos of felines sitting on a commode while reading Elmore Leonard's *Cat Chaser*.

I have always put too much emphasis on planning, conscientiously worrywarting over future hardships in order to lubricate my life but not simplify it. It provokes disquietude, I think. So, I decided to emulate my cat: When the future comes, I'll deal with it. Plus, who knows whether I'll even be here for Madame Fate's arrival, meaning all my preparation will have been wasted. The day should be sufficient, right? God knows I've already dealt with 23,725 of them. How bad can another be? Yes, I know that tempts fate, but morning comes whether you set the alarm or not.

Encouraging that relaxed resolution was our calico fox, Rennie, son of Silver Streak, who braved the icescape via a deer trail to trot across our porch. He surveyed the property as if he owned it, and maybe he does, inasmuch as my mouse problem in the past month has been 99-percent resolved. Rennie is a philosophical fox, prone to introspection and thoughtful grooming of his fleecy tail, which is as large as his body. When he notices me watching, he turns his back and settles his skinny arse, snubbing me with foxy indifference. I think he's courageous because I'd earlier witnessed him eyeing a wild turkey his own size. I wanted to explain the inherent dangers of turkey-lifting, detailing their demonic talons as long as Cher's fingernails.

I eventually coaxed the chained-up truck to the post office. On the wall I noticed the FBI's most-wanted mugs, bookended by a local version that offered "A thousand-dollar reward for the arrest and conviction of whoever shot my cat on Robbins Gulch." Meanwhile, the clerk was reading a copy of our valley newspaper, prominently featuring this:

Bar Owner Sues
By Eve Byron

The owner of the Plum Loco Saloon and Casino is suing the owners of a former neighboring

> *restaurant after they allegedly caused $20,000 in damages that included pouring kitchen grease down a drain, which caused a massive clog.*

In the Bitterroots, that's what we fear. Massive clogs.

Deadly Dishwasher Regurgitation

Speaking of clogs. You will grasp the vapory indolence of my life when you hear what considerably raised my blood pressure: a dishwasher that perished in steamy exhaustion, leaving behind a small Salton Sea of semi-opaque liquid on the pine floor. Obtaining a replacement in March—with Pleistocene drifts yet suffocating our driveway—would be touch-and-go, with way more going than touching. Of course, to the extent that appliances don't actually sustain us, the dishwasher's loss was less a tragedy than an inconvenience, because I believe dishes can yet be scrubbed manually.

I held my breath and purchased a dishwasher shipped from somewhere northwest of Ulaan Baatar—two weeks of logistical snafus—whereupon Julie and I loaded it into my truck. That took all day. Then, miraculously, I installed the device myself, no help at all, not that any was offered and also none from an instruction manual that would have been superfluous even as ticker tape for Pete Rose.

Here is something to remember if you ever install a dishwasher: There is a rubber tube that dumps putrid water from the bottom of the appliance, funneling it to your sink's drain. It's about an inch in diameter and holds maybe a quart of warm liquid mixed with the detritus you should have scraped off plates: corn, chicken tendons, your sister's earring. Those items have been fermenting in hot water for, oh, I don't know, let's say a week. If you happen to be under the sink to dislodge this tube, with your face angled upward as you unscrew the worm-gear clamp—and there's no other way to unfasten it—a tidal wave of vomit will express itself into your eyes, ears, nose, and throat.

It's a cliché from a Lucy episode, I know. Experiencing this cinematically colorful event, you will bolt upright, smash your head on steel pipes, then dash to the toilet to empty your own pipes of vomit, because what comes out of the dishwasher's drain pipe is vomit, as I may have mentioned. Think about it: food fermented in warm goo for a spell and emerging from the wrong conduit. Vomit.

I was pretty sure you'd want to hear about that.

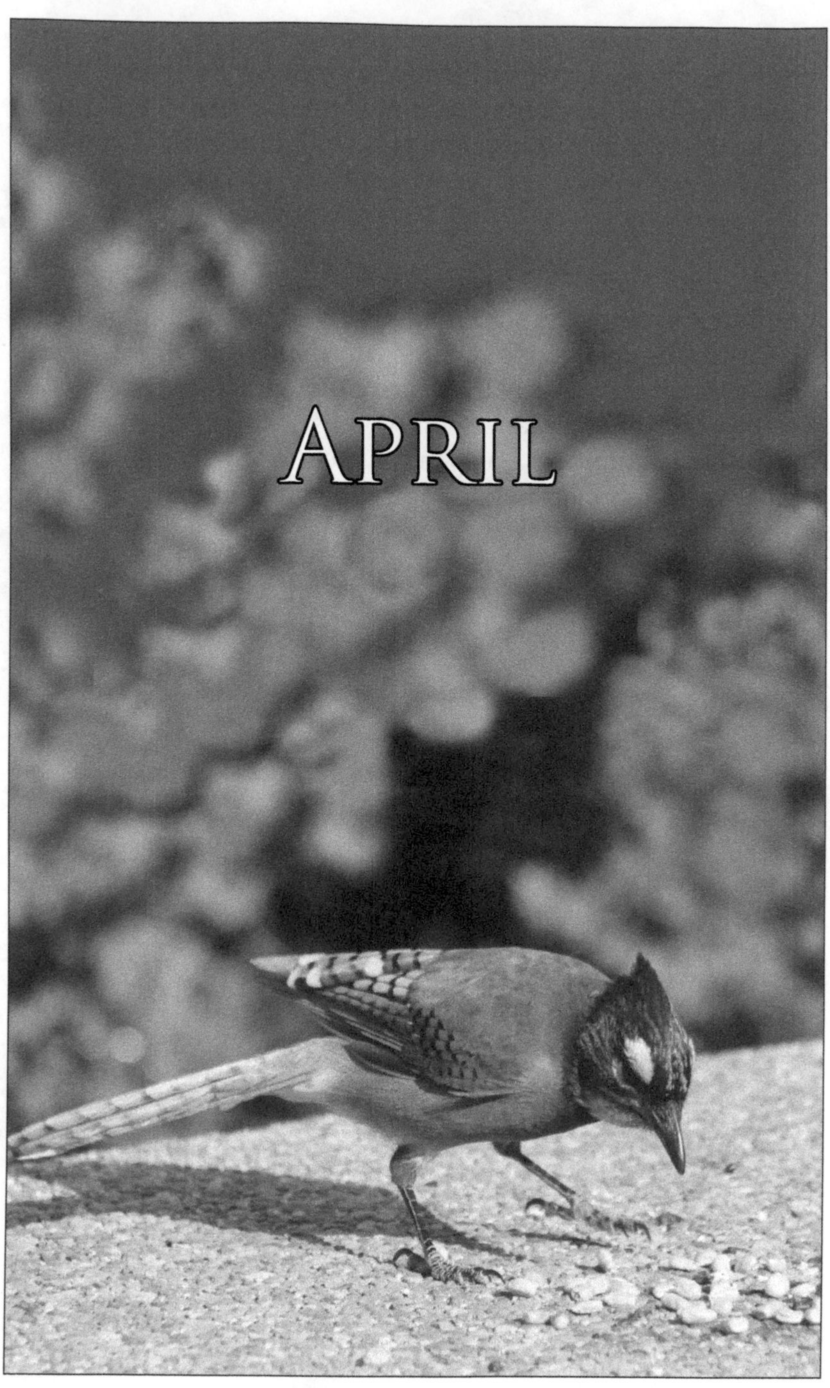
APRIL

A LEAKY SACK OF IMPERILED ORGANS

I fret for my forest and its occupants.

"We have spent our history shitting in the sandbox and giving ourselves rewards for it," said novelist Jim Harrison not long before he died in a sandbox in the southwest. As far back as the 1990s, Richard Leakey warned that human activity had initiated a "sixth extinction."

Statements like that should have been communally dissected at Cracker Barrel's all-you-can-ladle Gravy Lake but were not.

The level of carbon dioxide in Earth's atmosphere is now at its highest in 800,000 years—small taters compared with melting permafrost, which will expel twice the carbon currently stuffing our atmospheric baked potato with a triple order of Velveeta. Another food theme: Since humans established a daily appetite for meat, we have wiped out 83 percent of all wild mammals. Just in the past 40 years, the number of earthly beasts has decreased 50 percent. At the zoo these days, we should all demand a refund.

To be fair, thousands of animals and plants went extinct long before we applied our opposed-thumb ingenuity to the enterprise. At this point, though, we might as well wave the white flag. We're past our own sell-by date. Trying to undo the damage feels like shoveling hot lava back into Krakatoa.

Americans currently consume 68 percent of this planet's synthesized energy. What happens when the other eight billion bipeds demand a swinish equal—air-conditioned saunas, bottled water shipped from Fiji, and 6000-pound Hummer H1s with lane-change assistance?

I once drove a V-12 Ferrari from L.A. to New York City on what was broadly a capricious sightseeing lark, although I was paid to write about it. The Ferrari drank a gallon of boosted-octane fuel every 11 or so miles, so I don't pretend to be innocent in this ruinous romp. You know what Americans first did in reaction to icebergs cleaving alarmingly from Alaskan glaciers? We launched surfboards to ride the concussion waves. Naturalist John Muir nailed it when he said, "Nothing dollarable is safe."

Not far from my Montana home rests a geologic feature called the Burgess Shale, formed 500-million years ago. Fossilized in that shale are the earliest creatures believed to have scuttled, wobbled, and oscillated upon our planet, among them a gelatinous splotch with five eyes and a claw-tipped tube on its head. (I did not make that up.) What geologists posit is that if that miniature ogre and its primordially soupy colleagues had genetically mutated in any fashion other than they had, humans wouldn't look the way we look today. Nor would we think the way we think today, and that's only if we'd evolved into something beyond a leaky sack of imperiled organs. Maybe we'd have failed to invent guns, leaving Ollie North at loose ends.

If you rewind history 500 million years and let it run its course again, the odds of humans turning out as humans fall between zero and fly speckage. On the order of universal health care. My point being, we are about to become extinct. Our replacement might be amoebic glitter with fruit-fly legs vaping e-cigs. But it won't be us.

When we bring down upon our sorry eminences a planet so sweltering that residents of coastal cities have fled to, oh, let's say Ellesmere Island in the High Arctic, where no agriculture is possible, Mother Nature will cast us aside as unfit to pay dues to Mr. Darwin's posh club. Our cards to operate the front door will be demagnetized and we'll pull a species-wide Wicked Witch meltdown, adios to the bully brainiacs who fouled their nests, then denied it, then resisted a fix, then fainted from the rigors of adjusting their Sleep Number mattresses.

Said Konrad Lorenz, "The capacity of an animal to cause damage is proportional to its intelligence."

I figured the global urgency would weigh worryingly when behaviorists reported that chimpanzees in the wild will become extinct in our lifetimes, chimps being our closest genetic kin and also more skilled at predicting the weather and electing leaders. If a glitch in the chimps' environment dooms them—the glitch being us—how are we not at equal risk? We've adapted a fluid ability to alter the environment to our own convenience, and we won't stop. How do I know? Because Americans are content having not experienced a colder-than-average month since 1984. One of my doctors wasn't even born then. (The one with the potty mouth.) Siberians above the Arctic Circle have already sweated through an afternoon that reached 100.4 degrees.

There's nothing unnatural about extinction. Thousands of creatures failed to stay current with the genetic homework assigned to them by predators or unchecked populations or faltering food chains. And what happened is that they existed, then didn't, becoming fossils to entertain us at the Field Museum. We're next. Why shouldn't we be replaced by, oh, let's say dolphins, whose brains are larger than ours, or redwood trees that live hundreds of years longer, or bacteria that outnumber us?

I'm a pessimistic reactionary, I admit, but my various crackpot theories were recently bolstered by historian Yuval Noah Harari, who counts Zuckerberg and Gates as adherents. "In 200 years, I can pretty much assure you that there will not be any more Homo Sapiens," Harari said. If he's correct, American kids right now may be the great grandparents of the last man standing. And I'm sure Harari knows what he's talking about, because he drives a Porsche SUV that averages about 15 miles per gallon.

In the midst of my doomsday prophecies, I must say I'm sometimes heartened. *Sometimes.* Right now in Montana, for instance, there's an initiative to create the American Prairie Reserve (APR), using private money to interconnect 3.2-million acres, or 5000 square miles of grasslands along the Missouri River. The idea is to stock it with 10,000 Big Sky bison, native vegetation, and no fences. See what happens.

What more immediately happened, of course, was ranchers launching a "Save the Cowboys" campaign to defend their colleague cowpokes rounding up cattle via helicopters, leather-cockpit Chevy Silverados, and $25,000 Polaris ATVs.

One of the APR ecologists noted, "The constraint on wildlife populations is not what the habitat will support but what *humans* will support."

"Evolution loves death more than it loves you or me," said Annie Dillard. "The universe that suckled us is a monster that does not care whether we live or die—does not care if it itself grinds to a halt."

That right there, folks, is the ambivalence of infinity, which is not a luxury sedan. Or, as *Harper's* Lauran Groff gruffly put it: "We have fucked ourselves into a massive die-off…I am goddamn ready for the guillotines."

There is no Plan B because there is no Planet B.

It's thoughts like these that have kept me from getting ahead in life.

ON NOT HAVING A FUTURE

I've merrily plunged into a rough-and-tumble utopia interspersed with the occasional mountain lion, rubber boa, fat coyote, fight-club turkey, and camo-hatted bloviating councilman—paradise with a slow leak. So, the idea of taking a vacation from this valley seemed incongruous. Nevertheless, my wife adores Livingston, a berg east of Bozeman and two valleys to the right of our own.

I had reason to visit, too. We'd be sharing quail and French wine with novelist-gourmand-raconteur Jim Harrison. Jim lives south of Livingston in the aptly named Paradise Valley, through which tourists funnel to Yellowstone. I first met him through meals shared with publisher David E. Davis, where Jim's attire comprised a terry-cloth bathrobe, undies optional. I remember Jim saying, "The notion that there's a light at the end of the tunnel has mostly been a boon to pharmaceutical companies." Jim was a little dark, by pigment and temperament both.

Jim's Montana neighbors include Tom McGuane, Margot Kidder, Michael Keaton, Dennis Quaid, John Mayer, Russell Chatham, Tom Brokaw, Jeff Bridges, Peter Fonda, Tim

Cahill, and neon-speckled trout in the Yellowstone River, which Jim has always preferred to humans. I think of that valley as a kind of bohemian retreat if bohemians wore bandoliers. Michael Keaton recently delivered a commencement address whose conclusion was, "So just remember two words, kids: I'm Batman."

In Livingston, Julie and I always stay at the Murray Hotel, circa 1904. Its motto: "Fireproof and strictly modern." It was originally a four-story "skyscraper"—their word—with the town's only elevator, an Otis hand-cranked contraption that has surely maimed a handful of guests.

In the late '70s and early '80s, Hollywood director Sam Peckinpah rented the Murray's top floor, in the shadow of the Absaroka and Crazy Mountains, true purple mountain majesties. On the subject of crazy, Sam attached a sign to his door that read, "The old iguana sleeps, and the answer is still no." What that meant was open for debate, but it scared off the maids. When Peckinpah was overserved, he'd blast holes in the ceiling. He tried to transform his cats into a modified Manx breed by shooting off their tails. No cats were harmed, thanks to enraged hotel personnel and Peckinpah's alcohol-addled aim.

Attached to the hotel is the Murray Bar—live music, dogs, trout fishermen galore, among them occasionally Anthony Bourdain and Jim, of course, who once told his waitress, "I was a dog with a short chain, and now there's no chain." Stricken by ill health the past few years, Jim said, "At my age, you don't think about the future because you don't have one."

He had that right. Between the day we established our drinking date at the tail end of March and the day I nudged up to the Murray Bar, Jim ceased to be. Official cause of death? Livingstonians asserted he was "plumb wore out." Toward the end, Jim resembled Ernest Hemingway if Papa had been dragged two miles behind a freight train. I say that knowing it would make Jim smile, although I think he hated Hemingway. Anyway, this was the first time I've kept an appointment with a dead man.

Julie and I covet Livingston's musty bookstore, where the elderly manager occasionally rushes outside to curse at skateboarders. I bought Jim's final book, and the store lady said, "He'd have signed that for you, but he got cranky at the end." She further claimed that when Jim died, he dropped his writing pen. I insisted it was more likely he dropped the Spirit cigarette in his left hand and the jelly jar of Domaine Tempier Bandol in his right. "He had three hands?" she asked.

In the dwindling days of Jim's general animation, he was a spectacle of used-up skin, a caricature of life lived at its spiritual zenith. His face was craggier and more wrinkled than Keith Richards's; his nose was both flat and bent; three upper teeth had separated themselves from Jim's enterprises; his hair hadn't been combed in months; and his bad eye was gooped shut all day.

I'm told that Jim had abandoned the Murray after no-smoking regs were imposed. He'd located a downscale saloon where smoking was apparently mandatory and the customers were, in Montana-speak, "a bunch of numpties and scrotes." You knew when Jim was tippling if his dream car—a Toyota Land Cruiser that he'd sometimes let Bourdain drive—was parked at an absurd angle and half atop the curb. In his failing years, Jim's driver's license was revoked and he was furious about it. He had no reason to be, having already conducted several hundred crash-free midnight runs from bar to bed, a miracle worthy of apostolic pronouncement.

Last I spoke to Jim, he asked about my own dream car. "A 1967 Bizzarrini 5300 GT Strada," I told him. Jim pondered that, then blew a small cloud of smoke in my face. I recall two Subarus Jim borrowed from the magazine to effect deep dives in the Cowboy West. Both returned looking as if a 50-pound ashtray had exploded inside a Burger King dumpster.

The morning after our failed meeting, my own car's right-rear tire went flat—well, not completely, but the bottom was rumpled like scrambled eggs. I'll bet 90 percent of all my flats have been discovered in the morn, after a tiny leak performed its work in darkness. The tire was in the gutter, hard against the curb. Behind me—at a distance of maybe four feet—were breakfast diners at sidewalk tables, offering the amount of advice you'd sling at a five-year-old golfer. The onlookers were appalled when I loosened the lug nuts before raising the car.

Then a diner shouted, "Wait, *there's* your problem," pointing to the car's California license plate. I earned a small round of applause when the spare was affixed. What I never earned was a small round of assistance.

I first met Jim Harrison, as well as Elmore Leonard, on the same glorious day, in Ann Arbor, Michigan. Leonard autographed a book for me thus: "John: No more dick jokes." Our brunch featured pheasant that Harrison had shot 24 hours earlier. At the table was also a priest from the University of Michigan, for reasons unclear.

The priest set sail on a prayer that included heaven and hell and 78 points between. Before the prayer concluded, Jim had crammed a gravy-dripping gobbet of bird into his mouth. We all stared. He continued chewing, then said, "I thought that prayer was *never* gonna fucking end."

Jim always owned up to his faults and was quick to detect—and announce—false notes in acquaintances. Both a heroic and childlike figure, he espoused this lifelong mantra: "My mom and dad preferred the straight and narrow, where I, for nongenetic reasons, have favored the wide and crooked."

A SHOUT-OUT FOR TINNITUS

I live in a place that *Lonely Planet* might describe as lonely and maybe not on the planet. When the wind dwindles, I can hear Wes's caterpillar grading our road a mile away. It makes a hiccupping grumble, like popcorn in the microwave. Of course, I'm not alone. I recently read that 670-million other Earthlings live in high-mountain regions, from Nepal to the Andes. I wonder if, like me, they've all become irritably sensitive to the clamor below. Because nowadays, it greets me with a smack in the earhole.

On a recent trip to Missoula, I refueled at a Flying J truck stop, where activating the gas pump set off about 120 decibels of synthesized AM radio, studded with admonishments to eat what sounded like blow-dried Alpo for $3.99. The voice within the pump squawked about the VW Beetle being discontinued, a car the deejay implied was made famous by Herbie in *The Love Bug*, knowing nothing about the Kafer's late-'30s roots in fascism. Layered atop her scripted claptrap was the hydraulic exhalation of a garbage truck; the thick rattle of a jake brake from a passing 18-wheeler; the Flying J's own piped-in Muzak blasting *It's a*

Miracle by Culture Club; the echoed orders from a conjoined drive-thru window; a distant police siren; and an unmuffled dune buggy with unmistakable Herbie-sourced power. I about popped the threads on the few rust-free bolts constraining my psyche.

Then, as I climbed back into my truck, there came a BBC broadcast called, *Sounds of Tinnitus*. To my recalibrated ear, it was locusts singing Mariachi music, a boat anchor dragged through a jungle gym. Radio off.

I had the same experience returning to Ann Arbor to write about two cars, arriving there still discombobulated from the onslaught of cross-country noise. So, I recombobulated inside a motionless Tesla 3, parked under a tree, where I learned 1) that you must consult the Tesla's towering LCD screen to open the glovebox, and, 2) that the adjacent diesel generator juicing the Tesla right then had snapped to life with a thunderclap I'd been expecting all day but from the firmament.

By then my brain was mottled with prickly fungus, so I drove alone to the Hell Creek Saloon, not far from my previous Michigan home, and sipped salty chili alongside a troupe of leathered-up orthodontists masquerading as Hell's Angels. Why do Harleyhoggers present themselves as loners yet travel exclusively in packs? I'd mention lemmings here, but lemmings don't spend $17.50 on iron-cross key chains.

Let me catalog, briefly, the noises I daily do not perceive in my Montana home: church bells, trains, pumps, jackhammers, stereos, ventilators, compressors, street sweepers, dirt bikes, lawnmowers, jet skis, rap booming, motorcycles, and televangelists. What I do hear, I admit, is chain saws, including my own, although the neighbors have tacitly agreed to lay off limbing on weekends. I also endure random shotgun and rifle blasts, which cause our cats to jump. "Target shooting," said a clerk at Mr. T's mercantile store. "Not actual hunting—well, hunting for runaway spouses, maybe."

THE LONE JUSTIFICATION FOR COWBOY BOOTS

As Julie and I were bumping along Moose Meadow Lane, we spied a yearling white-tailed deer who had somehow wedged herself between two parallel fences. She was trapped in a space 18 inches wide, wild-eyed and flailing. Her mother was nearby, bolting in crazy circles as we drew alongside. Julie and I approached from opposite ends and floundered about, lifting and bending barbed wire and yanking out rusted steel staples, managing only to tear fingernails. The imperiled deer commenced bawling like a sheep or newborn calf. I didn't know they cried like that. It added to the angst. As Julie and I traded possible solutions, a real cowboy arrived—well, real inasmuch as he wore hand-tooled boots and a Stetson and resembled Sam Elliot at a Cheyenne dogie-punch.

In fact, he was our newest neighbor, "Cowboy Mike," who immediately leapt from his truck and foot-stomped the lowest wooden fence rail into three pieces. An impressive bout of kick boxing. He then grabbed the deer around the neck, rodeo-style, and lifted her up and forward, nearly squeezing out her eyeballs.

It's hard to imagine what she thought of all this. But as soon as she caught a glimpse of open space, she bolted across the road, kicking up dust, then dissolved into the adjacent woods, all in two seconds.

I clapped and whistled, then announced, "We've earned a few karmic points." But the cowboy, who still hadn't uttered one word, climbed back into his truck and drove off in what closely resembled a real-life Lone Ranger tableau.

Months later, we all convened at a summer-solstice soirée, where Cowboy Mike showed up. We rehashed the deer-saving incident over Rolling Rocks, and he said, "You know, I broke my ankle doing that."

In the room the women come and go,
Talking of Michael and the doe.

YOU'RE OUT OF YOUR ELEMENT

In April, we welcomed an unannounced guest named Robert "Shortcut" Spong (rhymes with "gong") and nowadays I use his surname as a verb. As in, "Sadly, we had to *spong* Bernie after he used three wads of toilet paper and clogged the plumbing." Seriously, the plumbing here is dodgy, so we affixed little handmade signs alongside the toilets: "Flush as many times as you want, but two wads of TP per."

We met Shortcut Spong at the Blue Joint Café, the only establishment in Darby then offering evening victuals. This was after Deb, who owned Deb's Café, retired in fuming wrath when her employees' scattershot performance matched their scattershot attendance.

"I notice our choices are limited," Mr. Spong observed. Shortcut seemed weary and was. He'd just hiked solo from the Mexican border, 2079 miles south of Darby. He'd been on the trail 97 days and had already demolished three sets of shoes and six toenails. His purpose was to march the entire 2608-mile Continental Divide Trail—it passes not far from my house—having already completed the Appalachian Trail. Robert was vague about motives. Eccentricity played a role. He suggested that I should not judge, having morphed into a crypto recluse myself.

At the restaurant, Shortcut gulped a sausage/bacon/pepperoni pizza, a burrito, and three beers, accomplishing the task with efficiency and speed. He inverted one slice of pizza atop another, then inserted both while winking at fellow diners. The entire pie was MIA in ten minutes. While on the trail, Robert explained that his finest dinner, usually reserved for Saturday nights, was three strips of beef jerky dunked in a bowl of ramen noodles. That's why the pizza looked like *chateaubriand* prepared on the Left Bank, although in this case it was the left bank of the Bitterroot River. I must tell you that Robert never explained his nickname, mentioning only that everyone on the trail had to have one, which alone seemed reason to avoid it.

For Shortcut, this was a rare day of relaxation, a "zero day," as he and fellow hikers called it, which now describes every day of my existence. To my ear, Robert's forest travails sounded like something pirates endured in the Sargasso Sea, so I shepherded him back to our home for bonus food and drink. He sat with us on the deck, drank three more beers and ate a bowl of pistachios, flinging the shells over the railing. We watched the sun set. A juvenile cow moose sauntered by, almost directly below us, which we were thrilled to point out. But Robert had met so many moose on the trail—almost ramming one face-to-two-foot-long face—that he'd lost count.

Twenty-three days after his visit, Shortcut attained mile 2608 in Waterton, Canada, at which point he'd been hiking four months, not all of which sounded like fun. He now expects to tackle the Pacific Rim Trail, the third of the Big Three, but only after he regains weight, which *does* sound like fun. At the conclusion of the CDT, Shortcut had taken on the physique of Barney Fife with stage-six intestinal blow-through.

I told Robert that when I first moved here, I harbored anxiety about occupying space that humans maybe weren't intended to annex. It left me out of phase, uneasy, off-balance. Like wearing hideous sweat pants to the Metropolitan Opera. The natural world here buzzed not with animus but jangling apathy—nature engaged in business in which my fiddling was grating and incompatible and also ignored.

For the first week, I'd awaken every few hours and turn on the lights to see if some sort of fang-toothed malefactor was scratching to enter. Robert said he felt the same while pitching his tent on wild parcels where it was possible no man had ever slept. The night noises from the Bitterroot Forest—any forest—are legion, an alien language whose subtle subtext was acutely reiterated in *The Big Lebowski*: "Donny, you're out of your element."

Eight months passed, then Robert mailed us a coffee-table book of CDT photos and detailed narration, self-published. My favorite chapter was "Zero Day in Darby," in which he described only us and our home, citing it as "beautiful," by which he meant what surrounds it is beautiful. Still, if he elects to visit again, he must make a reservation like everyone else. We'll bequeath him the bear-proof room for three days max. After that, Mr. Spong will be sponged.

Underground Vampire Vines

You are probably waiting for me to talk about beargrass. Okay, I will. Because all things in Montana must apparently by law be both large and contradictory, beargrass is not grass at all but an indigenous flower from, well, Jupiter, is my guess. Its stalk climbs skyward five feet, as if overnight. From that stalk emerges a green phallus doohickey that causes Mormons to blush.

"Looks like a Jovian johnson," I told Julie. Around the johnson grows a soft sphere of tiny white flowers, forming what appears to be a golf ball used by Fred Flintstone. I named it "Fred's Dick." (Just bear with me. I expect to attain maturity momentarily.) The Indians apparently made all manner of crafts from Fred's Dick, affixing the blooms to buckskin dresses and jewelry, for instance. They couldn't get enough of the stuff.

Having discovered bear dens littered with beargrass, the Salish assumed the animals consumed the plants as a laxative after hibernation, during which inactive period ursine guts become bunged. Not true. Bears use Ex-Lax like the rest of us. The Indians believed that beargrass bloomed once every seven years. Wrong again, Big Chief Biomass. It blooms whenever moisture levels allow. Beargrass is also known as turkeybeard, although my guests think I made that up.

All this lore came from a Bitterroot Forest ranger wearing khaki shorts—he was more like a tourist-herder, a border collie with a badge—who became the first ranger in my experience to inform that Indians didn't always understand nature, same as the rest of us. By the way, here's another fun Indian fact: When Lewis and Clark marched through Montana, they learned that the Crow used the same word—*shua*—for the colors blue and green. That's how Lewis one day wound up at the Missouri River instead of the country club.

Montana hosts another eerie flower. It's called Indian paintbrush and is otherworldly, like something carnivorous you'd find poking out of a rotten log in Borneo—red, yellow, and orange, with a densely hairy galea (which apparently is amazing if you know what a galea is). Flower experts describe Indian paintbrush as "spidery," as if it might climb your chin to insert tangled roots in your nostrils. It is a plant in the broomrape family and grows to about 12 inches in height.

The Indians sometimes nibbled paintbrush to induce a druglike high, but the plant can often contain toxic levels of selenium that will tie a fatal clove hitch in your colon. How's this all sounding so far? Well, it gets better. Ranger Dan informed that paintbrush roots poke around like underground body snatchers, looking for nearby healthy roots. The plant then stabs its neighbor's leg, as it were, sucking vital nutrients vampire-style.

Back in Ohio, we didn't have such plants. Nothing with sexual organs jutting into the sky, nothing with vampire fingers. We had dandelions. There are a few dandelions in Montana but in spring the bears eat them. Julie and I picked some for a salad. They taste a little like wilted lettuce sprinkled with isopropyl alcohol. It made me admire the bears even more.

Pork Chops Nailed to the Garage

The Bitterroot Valley is a birder's utopia. What we mostly have is Steller's jays, which are oversize, aggressive blue jays that bark and bellow a guttural prehistoric screech and occasionally steal car keys. We call them the Big Blue Bastards.

When William Clark first spied the BBBs in 1806, he believed they were "of the vulture family." Jay or not, they poke at hanging blocks of suet with ferocity sufficient to sever the metal hanging chains. We also enjoy a more docile variety known as gray jays, which are a tasteful amalgam of hues you'd find in the Royals' polo closet, and they are receptive to being hand-fed—Triscuits being a favorite—although they occasionally glance at your eyeballs with ravenous looks. Montanans call them "Camp Robbers." We call them "Camp Cleaners."

We are further visited by majestic Great Gray owls that stand 20-inches tall and have X-ray vision that allows them to see into your soul, attaching all manner of blame to your misdeeds. The Grays study you as if you owe them money. On a drive near the Big Hole battlefield, Julie photographed one perched on a branch—a dusting of snow on his head—an image so startling that it was published in *Montana Magazine.*

Just as a side note, Julie's owl was photographed at the site of an exploratory oil well drilled to a depth of 16,047 feet in 1980. For 14,000 feet of that distance, the bit penetrated nothing but Bitterroot Valley gravel. Whatever was at the bottom was not noted, but the geologists stood in awe of the 2.65-mile stratum of loose sediment. Even things you can't see in Montana are bigger than anyone else's things you can't see.

The owls in this valley leave me speechless, which is sure to please them. As most folks know, owls can turn their heads 270 degrees, a useful if disquieting talent if you're on the witness stand. Their feathers have evolved to allow almost silent flight. They have binocular vision and, despite what you probably were told, can see just dandy in daylight. Owls' hearing is so discriminating that they hunt in total darkness, and some owls have one ear larger than the other so they can locate prey by aural triangulation.

The owl that Julie photographed is capable of poking its stiletto-like talons into mice hiding beneath two feet of snow. As killing machines go, they are not perfect but close. Eagles fear owls. In fact, our Darby candy store once sold a device that plays back bird calls so you can confirm a species as you stroll through the woods. But when the manufacturer recorded an owl's call on the tape—the "tu-whit and tu-whoo" as celebrated by Shakespeare—it caused the whole forest to fall as silent as a felon in church. If you're a forest bird, an owl is a spy and a sniper and the whole SWAT team combined.

Dana, who owns Darby's gym, has great horned owls nesting in a pine tree in her yard. So far, three owlets have poked out their white faces to determine who's responsible for the racket below. I don't want to belabor this staring thing, but when an owl gazes upon your countenance, it is *you* who will first break the gaze and walk away saying, "Sorry, didn't know you were here."

Then Julie photographed a western tanager, a photo published in *Birds & Blooms*. They sent money but I'm not sure Julie reported it to the IRS because she's a good woman but not a perfect woman.

Here's Clark's list of Bitterroot birds from July 1, 1806:

"The dove, the black woodpecker, the lark woodpecker, the logcock, the prairie lark, sandhill crain [sic], prairie hen with the short and pointed tail, the robin, a species of brown plover, a few curloos, small black birds [probably American dippers], raven hawks, and a variety of sparrows, as well as the bee martin and several species of Corvus genus are found in this valley."

Lewis and Clark were universally praised for their biological discoveries here, but when they first encountered prairie dogs, they named them "barking squirrels." Take that, Carl Linnaeus.

My trial-lawyer father occasionally said, "We are judged by the size of our complaints." Well, I have a complaint. More like a dwarf grudge. And when I harbor a grudge, I carry it all the way to dry dock.

Worse than barking squirrels are the Bitterroot Valley's woodpeckers, a bias they don't deserve, of course, because they preceded my arrival by some 12,000 years. The most prevalent peckers are downy, hairy, Lewis, and pileated—the latter standing 18-inches tall with a fluorescent-crimson head, the bird we know as cartoon Woody. I have a gym friend who fears pileateds. She dashes inside at the mere mention. "Those tiny necks and huge heads—not normal," she claims, which is true.

In front of my house, I watched a pileated excavate a billiard-ball-size hole in a stump in 20 seconds. Upside-down, an adult pileated latched onto one of our deck's support beams and commenced freelance demolition. Had this vandalism been inflicted by, say, a neighbor, I'd have called Marshal Larry. But this feathery clown so amused us—despite having a bill like a swordfish's—that we allowed him to excavate the post unto a pile of splinters. I later nailed up a supportive hardwood plank and stained it to match, on the theory that the deck will at least look good as it collapses.

Which brings us to the flickers, a species previously unknown to me. You wouldn't think there'd be a riot of ill will engendered by a cute little flicker, but you'd be wrong. We have northern yellow shafted flickers, and what surprised me is that these cute criminals are tree-clinger/climbers—about ten inches long—which is to say, woodpeckers. We are knee deep in the NYS flickers (a good name for a '70s punk band). Before I slander them further, I must say they possess exquisite plumage: orange, gray, yellow, brown stripes, and a kind of X-pattern on their heads that looks like spray-paint graffiti. "So beautiful, so what?" as Paul Simon asks.

Your basic NYS flicker is a prick. Or as I rudely render it, "Flickers are fuckers." I'm sorry to say that, because it means I'm not accepting diversity in the domain of our feathered friends. But what the flickers do in the spring is jab holes in the far side of my house, where there are no windows—the safest wall to destroy because I can't observe their work. I think of them as roustabout oil riggers, excavating divots the size of silver dollars right through the wood and all the way to yellow insulation, which for them is the equivalent of a gusher.

I am told that the incessant pecking has nothing to do with locating edible insects. It's intended to impress nearby girl peckers. Why not perforate the trees surrounding us? Because trees don't make the resonating "bonk" that my siding radiates. Like the flickers, I've pulled some ill-advised feats of derring-do in the pursuit of females, so I'm trying to let it go.

Not really. The flickers are still pricks.

What I'm talking about is 75, maybe 100 holes chiseled into my homestead in one month, all the way through plywood until the little vandals can see me reading *The London Review of Books*. And I need not mention what all this jackhammering sounds like in bed at 6:00 a.m., but I will say this: Have you ever heard Tito Puente go insane on the timbales? And that's how I came to hate NYS flickers, in which NYS now stands for "Not Your Siding."

Julie and I purchased a gallon of goopy and stupidly expensive wood filler in a beige hue that must have been difficult to produce, inasmuch as it matches no known wood on earth. Then I backed up the Tundra so the tailgate was flush with the damaged wall, where I could erect my tallest aluminum ladder in the truck's bed, made level by a pile of flat river rocks I'd collected at Tin Cup Creek, all of this as shaky as a hog on ice. Julie refused to let me climb to the top of this swaying scaffold unless she could clutch my butt. Which meant that if I fell, she would, too.

She asked, "Does calling 911 accomplish anything in this valley?" I didn't know. So, I grabbed a 12-foot aluminum extension pole intended to clean windows. I lowered the business end to Julie, who loaded it with a blob of beige putty about the size of a golf ball. Then I'd raise the "loaded" pole, which always threatened to topple both of us, until I could swing it like a slow-moving cricket bat, and the putty—occasionally—would splat into a pecker hole and camouflage the yellow insulation at the bottom. At least the wind doesn't blow through the bedroom anymore.

This took all day. I'll say that again. All fuckaroony day.

At one point, neighbor Kemp Conn arrived. "You gotta shoot 'em," he said. "You know that, right?"

Julie cringed. We loathe guns, have never owned one, and are proud to say so. But I didn't mention it to Kemp because our neighbors fret that we are insufficiently armed. So, I did what the NRA suggested America's teachers do while under ballistic attack: I stockpiled a bucket of rocks to chuck at the evil-doer flickers. Turned out the rocks further dented and scarred the wood and distracted the birds not at all in their dedication to denting and scarring.

We pondered this dilemma for a month, then unfurled 20-foot-long sheets of aluminum foil that we reinforced with twin stripes of duct tape. We taped paint stirrers to the ends, for heft, as you'd tie a tail to a kite. We nailed the foil, fluttering in the breeze, to the flickers' favorite walls. Sunlight made it flash like a disco strobe, certain to frighten the lice off birds everywhere, apart from Ed the raven who seemed entertained by it.

I now wonder whether neighbors observing an entire wall of swaying aluminum foil will conclude we are shielding ourselves from alien rays. They're correct insofar as the assault is coming from the sky. Anyway, yesterday I continued filling woodpecker holes. When hole #87 was smooth and drying, I climbed down the tipsy ladder and asked Julie, "What do you think?"

"Hard to say," she said. "Would you be upset if I said, 'We'll never sell this house?' "

So, I might buy a BB gun to deter the most frail and delicate of Mother Nature's creatures, this side of butterflies. In Montana, gun-owning isn't difficult. In fact, I just heard an electronics store offering "a free .22 handgun with every satellite-dish purchase." Americans own almost half the guns in the world—far more guns than we have citizens. When I purchased home insurance, the agent asked, "How many firearms do you own?" Not "*Do* you own one?"

Speaking of firearms, the man who laid our basement floor, John Hammack, recently called to inform he couldn't continue work because he'd shot off his toe. Weeks later, I noticed him standing at the side of Moose Meadow Lane, and I was all set to ask about his decapitated digit. But I shied away when I realized he was urinating on a larch tree.

One of our neighbors places a loaded .45 on his night stand, with its twin on his wife's night stand, and has two shotguns in the kitchen. Then he inserts a different handgun into his butt crack, and that's the weapon he carries while hiking to the mailbox. In Darby's grocery, I once encountered a fellow packing two revolvers, one per hip, I guess in case the cabbages started talking smack to the lettuce.

Red Schields, my rust-bearded neighbor who operates our community plow, owns just as many firearms, but when the twin mountain lions tangled with his dogs, Red realized he could not shoot one without holing the other. There's a lesson about firearms there, which I plan to mention to no one.

One more thing about lovable Red: For Christmas, his gift to us was two pork chops, still wrapped in the store's plastic with price yet attached. He delivered this gift when we were absent. Worried that bears or lions or Ed would consume the chops if left on our doorstep, Red nailed them—*nailed*, I tell you—above our garage door, where we couldn't possibly miss them upon returning. No written note attended this gift, so I figured it was some sort of Montana mafia recrimination, like a severed horse's head, or maybe a Christian pork crucifixion. I might add that Red has amazing eyebrows. I believe each holds an individual power station.

I have one last complaint. Before we moved here, no one explained the Bitterroot Valley work ethic, but it laid itself bare when I towed my drift boat to a man in Darby who sells and services such craft. I know, because a monster sign on his storefront says BOATS & BOAT SERVICE in red paint. I asked if he'd repair a small hole in my boat's rubber. "Well, I don't like to dick around with boats," he said, staring directly at Julie behind me. The immense BOAT SERVICE sign hung three feet over his right shoulder.

Then we tried to hire a rugged Irishman whose ad in the yellow pages stated, "TREE REMOVAL!" I offered him $150 per hour—his advertised fee—to fell 12 trees that were a fire hazard. "Well, I'm not sure," he said in a voice that told me he'd rather study tax forms than be standing before me. He promised to return in October. We never saw him again.

Then this: When I first called a dentist in Hamilton, the receptionist's only question was, "You don't have anything wrong with your teeth, do you?" I told her I was calling merely to see if they fixed boats.

SPASTIC GLIMMERS AND GLINTS

Here's what I intended to say before I worked myself into the sniveling whorls: In Montana's Bitterroot Valley, I have never been more content. Not even close. It's partly because my job has shuffled into past tense, although I still suffer vestigial Sunday-night trepidation preceding the work week. But never in the course of a day have I stopped so often and said out loud, "Well, spank my ass and call me Suzy, look at *that*." And it will be Ed the raven or Walter the moose or a fire on a mountaintop or a cougar eating Ronda or the soothing white noise of Tin Cup Creek rushing under our $83,000 bridge, or a ripped-to-pieces lenticular cloud resembling six spaceships, or a storm shucking snowflakes as big as cows' eyes, or a neighbor who legally named herself Queenee B. Honey. Nature blooms, glints, enthuses, kills, reprieves, whispers, and threatens to self-immolate every moment.

At night we examine Carl Sagan's "billions and billions" sans light pollution, air pollution, and noise pollution. The Milky Way, as observed from 440 feet above Darby, looks like a bomb detonated in a Baskin-Robbins truck carrying ice-cream sprinkles, like kitsch you'd buy at a Texaco station. The stars are so bright they stare back, like owls questioning your intentions.

National Geo says that 99 percent of the continental U.S. now suffers light pollution, and it increases two percent per year because of LED bulbs that are allowed to burn all night. Not in my backyard.

These days, I'm nudging the city limits of decrepitude, but also, I hope, a modest run of Montana immersion therapy. Living in the woods has engendered a warm cessation of affected attitude, although it's not my place to say so. It makes my soul clap its hands.

How intergalactically lucky can one man be? I was born in America as a Caucasian male to white-collar parents who handed me a costly education that coughed up a gratifying career—a triple on the first pitch and I wasn't even the batter. When Tibetan Buddhists observe such luck, they say it's like being dropped into the center of an ocean and miraculously surfacing with your head poking through a life-ring that fell off a yacht 60 years before. That's how unlikely it seems to have dog-paddled into this providential backwater of ponderosas as tall as the Washington Monument. Right now, my life is unstructured, uncontrolled, unregimented. I'm a three-toed sloth in a fecund fig tree, operating freely in low range.

The man who built this house lived in the basement, his wife on the upper floor, and I'm told they communicated grudgingly by phone. The isolation of this place, he said, kept them picking at each other's faults. He told me I'd fast attain a bellyful of the dirt-road trek in and out. That hasn't happened.

From our rough road, you should see, for instance, the full moon reflecting off Tin Cup Creek. It's a shrieking kaleidoscope of mirrored sparks and electric tremors, a riot of refraction, the firefly Olympics, a carnival of spastic glimmers and glints. (I believe I outdid myself there, I feel a little faint.) Of course, the instant you try to describe the ethereal is the instant you demean it.

Vlad Nabokov said, "Solitude is the playfield of Satan." Bullshit. Solitude, here, is my permeable skin osmotically absorbing Bitterroot self-fulfillment, and Satan doesn't know the first thing about it.

When Julie and I are housebound for days, our little

ranchette adopts the mien of a miniature castle, a soothing bulwark against the buffeting storm, even if it isn't buffeting. The snow is our moat. If the electricity is alive and propane yet hisses, we loll in deep puddles of gooey serenity.

What's more, I've enjoyed a year in Montana without glimpsing Twitter, Instagram, Snapchat, Reddit, Tinder, Pinterest, or Facebook. In the last 12 months, I've answered the phone perhaps six times. We don't have a land line, and Julie carries a phone so complicated that it comes with two physicists from Battelle. I've never looked at it.

Never have I been so acutely aware of Mother Nature's handiwork so lavishly varnished and with such painstaking brushstrokes. So few sloppy parts. The Bitterroot Valley not only dazzles but is elementally flawless in its natural grace. It's an ecosystem that contains nothing except itself: no human footprints, no mapped paths, no litter, no edifice contrived. It manages its affairs without my help or interference or observation, and does so as if following a complex musical score. "One light is left us," said poet Robinson Jeffers, "the beauty of things not men."

Our forest had me paying attention deliberately and non-judgmentally. No moment dwelling on past or future. Mental puzzles and agitations discarded. What a relief. But what mechanism was responsible?

Before I headed to Montana, I remember telling Jim Harrison that the people there must be nobler because of the splendor of their environs. He said, "That's not the way it works at all. Maybe *less* likely."

I plan to die here, if I may solemnize this discourse. The opaque veil will soon prevail. I'd like my ashes fluttered about the Double-J Cat Ranch or dumped in the Bitterroot River to be eaten by firm-flanked trout with fluorescent stripes and orange lips. "John has passed away and now expresses himself as fish shit." I'm fine with that.

In Montana, it turned out, I didn't have to focus on the natural world to salvage a psyche-saving infusion of serenity. For one thing, the natural world isn't serene. It's often monstrous. Five feet of snow, six-foot bull snakes, and seven-foot mountain lions knock the corners off your ego. The planet is forever upsetting even itself—incomprehensible, chaotic, supervised by laws we cannot decipher that nonetheless steer our every wakeful moment. We still don't know how gravity works. Watching all this, my ego had become a round and soft Gummy Bear. Which, in turn, helped me cultivate an attitude of indifference, too. Not to my immediate surroundings, particularly, but to human events, diversions, illusions, hubris, even altruism.

Is this the consolation I sought when I first arrived in Montana? I don't know. I'm indifferent to that, too.

So, the answer is yes.

HOW LONG?

Last night, as more glacial trains of ice chugged off the roof, with no caboose in sight, I was re-rereading *The Worst Journey in the World,* Apsley Cherry-Garrard's grotesquely painful description of Capt. R.F. Scott's ill-advised trek to and from the South Pole. You may recall Scott's partner in frostbitten purgatory, Titus Oates, who awoke in the tent and realized he could not continue. Oates turned to Scott and said, "I am just going outside and may be some time." And he did take some time. Eternity is what he took.

As a kid, I was moved by Oates's bravery. In school I'd flash a pained look and say, "I am just going outside and may be some time," but my teachers were familiar with this ruse and an inevitable skyhook ensued.

Anyway, right after I read that passage, the power lines succumbed to crumbly ice. I strapped on my camping headlamp and fell asleep listening to the roar of two emergency propane heaters, somehow as tranquilizing as the cats dozing on my legs. In the morning, I knew I'd have to wrestle with the plow and my goddamn 200-pound, 20-horsepower snowblower, which has the same effect on snow as cursing at it.

So, I studied yawnography until 10 a.m., then turned to the smarter of the cats, Teddy Roosevelt, and said, "Ted, my man, I am just going outside and may be some time." He was content for me to take all the time I needed.

Before moving to Montana, I had separated myself from the natural order. So had our whole species, actually, 12,000 years prior when mankind learned to convert swaths of the earth to neat rows of grain, then 2000 years later mastered the domestication of goats, followed by sheep, followed by, among other breeds, our own kind as slaves. What's left for me is an impulse attributed to everyone from Philip Roth to Oscar Wilde to Spiro Agnew on the day he claimed to have invented socks: "The point of life is that it ends."

In Montana, I'm therefore sampling life's flavors as fervently as a dotty marten, 10,000 woodland courses preceded by photosynthetic hors d'oeuvres. Frankly, I'm amazed Mother Nature is still talking to our species. We are the default stewards of this basilica, yet our only contributions have been blood and excrement. When I survey the forest behind my house, I wonder, "How long? Fifty years? Ten?"

If money doesn't buy happiness, then a place shouldn't either. But it has. Does.

Will?

ACKNOWLEDGMENTS

Julie Renee Gothrup is the brightest asteroid in my cosmos. She and my sister Angela Ann Phillips are unstinting supporters, editors, and soft-hearted critics upon whom I've disbursed too little celebratory payback. Gratitude to Annette Chaudet for her Wyoming-keen eye and ear; to Patti Maki, the Michigan Wolverine of copy-editing; to Susanne Vandenbosch and Ravi Fry for photo assistance; and to Scott Manning for his marketing savvy.

Thanks moreover to the citizens of Darby, Montana, especially: Jen & Ravi, Scott & Heidi, Theo & Ashley, Dave & Corinne, John & Robin, Ridlon & Carin.

All errors are mine. If any assertion offends, I beg forgiveness and offer free pale ale at Darby's Bandit Brewery. Mind the wrecked car on the way in.

About the Author

John Phillips has written for magazines for 45 years and is the former Executive Editor of *Car and Driver.* He has contributed to *Harper's, the Toronto Globe & Mail, Elle, The Cleveland Plain Dealer, Condé Nast Traveler, Smithsonian Air & Space,* and *Sports Illustrated.* He was the recipient of the Ken Purdy Award for journalism in 2007; enjoyed a one-on-one interview with Joe Biden; and is the author of the novel *Slippery* as well as the true-crime saga *God Wants You to Roll.* He lives with wife, Julie Gothrup, in Montana's Bitterroot Mountains.

CPSIA information can be obtained
at www.ICGtesting.com
Printed in the USA
LVHW050103101221
705796LV00004B/20/J

9 781941 052556